# THE EVERYDAY NATIONALISM OF WORKERS

# THE EVERYDAY NATIONALISM OF WORKERS

*a* SOCIAL HISTORY *of* MODERN BELGIUM

Maarten Van Ginderachter

STANFORD UNIVERSITY PRESS
*Stanford, California*

STANFORD UNIVERSITY PRESS
Stanford, California

© 2019 by the Board of Trustees of the Leland Stanford Junior University. All rights reserved.

No part of this book may be reproduced or transmitted in any form or by any means, electronic or mechanical, including photocopying and recording, or in any information storage or retrieval system without the prior written permission of Stanford University Press.

Printed in the United States of America on acid-free, archival-quality paper

Library of Congress Cataloging-in-Publication Data

Names: Van Ginderachter, Maarten, author.

Title: The everyday nationalism of workers : a social history of modern Belgium / Maarten Van Ginderachter.

Description: Stanford, California : Stanford University Press, 2019. | Includes bibliographical references and index.

Identifiers: LCCN 2018050185 | ISBN 9781503609051 (cloth : alk. paper) | ISBN 9781503609693 (pbk. : alk. paper) | ISBN 9781503609709 (epub)

Subjects: LCSH: Nationalism—Belgium—History. | Parti ouvrier belge—History. | Working class—Political activity—Belgium—History. | Ethnicity—Political aspects—Belgium—History. | Belgium—Languages—Political aspects—History. | Belgium—Politics and government—1830-1914.

Classification: LCC DH491 .G56 2019 | DDC 320.5409493—dc23 LC record available at https://lccn.loc.gov/2018050185

Cover design by Kevin Barrett Kane

Cover image: Amsab-Institute of Social History. Universal suffrage manifestation, Lokeren, 1912.

Text design by Kevin Barrett Kane

Typeset at Stanford University Press in 9.5/14 Sabon

# CONTENTS

|  |  |  |
|---|---|---|
|   | Preface | vii |
|   | Introduction: Workers into Belgians, Flemings, and Walloons | 1 |
| 1 | A Socialist Pillar of a Hyperliberal State | 11 |

## PART I
*Trickle-Down Nationalism: The Institutional Forces of Nation-Building*

| | | |
|---|---|---|
| 2 | Voting the Nation | 33 |
| 3 | Nationalist Celebrations and Mass Entertainment | 43 |
| 4 | An Anti-Militaristic State in Militaristic Times | 55 |
| 5 | The Royal and Colonial Paradox | 71 |
| 6 | Schooling the Nation | 87 |

## PART II
*Everyday Nationalism: Performing the Nation in Daily Life*

| | | |
|---|---|---|
| 7 | Encounters with the Belgian Flag and the National Anthem | 105 |
| 8 | Proletarian Tweets | 125 |
| 9 | Language, the Flemish Movement, and the Nation | 145 |
|   | Epilogue: The First World War | 163 |
|   | Notes | 175 |
|   | Bibliography | 229 |
|   | Index | 257 |

# PREFACE

This book was a long time in the making. It is the culmination of the postdoc project I started way back in 2006—reader, take note: slow science works and books matter. In the course of writing this book I have incurred numerous debts. A warm thank you goes out to my colleagues in the Department of History of Antwerp University for providing such a stimulating and congenial work environment. *Merci* Houssine Alloul, Michael Auwers, Marnix Beyen, Bruno Blondé, Chiara Candaele, Noel Clycq, Greet De Block, Nel de Mûelenaere, Bert De Munck, Dominiek Dendooven, Henk De Smaele, Malika Dekkiche, Pierre Delsaerdt, Luc Duerloo, Wannes Dupont, Dagmar Germonprez, Hilde Greefs, Christian Laes, Karen Lauwers, Guido Marnef, Jeroen Puttevils, Vincent Scheltiens, Roschanack Shaery, Peter Stabel, Steven Thiry, Ilja Van Damme, Herman Van Goethem, Karen Vannieuwenhuyze, Gerrit Verhoeven, and Reinoud Vermoesen. At Ghent University I would like to thank Koen Aerts, Jan Art, Berber Bevernage, Thomas Buerman, Julie Carlier, Hendrik Defoort, Gita Deneckere, Barbara Deruytter, Bruno De Wever, Eric Vanhaute, Christophe Verbruggen, and Antoon Vrints; at the Catholic University of Leuven, Tom Verschaffel and Lode Wils; and at Amsab-ISG in Ghent, Herman Balthazar, Luc Lievyns, Geert Van Goethem, and the indomitable Paule Verbruggen.

This book has further benefited from informal talks and email conversations with John Breuilly, James M. Brophy, Martyn Conway, Jon Fox, James Kennedy, Jeremy King, Janet Polasky, the participants at the History Research

Cluster symposium "Critiquing the National" in September 2016 at the University of New South Wales (a warm thank you to Mina Roces, Martyn Lyons, Grace Karskens, and Richard Waterhouse for their boundless hospitality), the members of the Department of History at UNC-Chapel Hill, which hosted my sabbatical in the final stretch of writing the manuscript (and particularly Karen Hagemann, Don Reed, Lloyd Kramer, Fitz Brundage, and Konrad Jarausch), and the Triangle French Politics and Culture group at UNC-Chapel Hill, Duke, and NCSU (and especially its convenors Ellen Welch and Jim Winders). Thank you also to the FWO-Research Foundation Flanders for providing the original postdoc funding in 2006, which lies at the basis of this book,[1] and for providing the funding for the final write-up in 2017, and to the Faculty of Arts and Humanities and the Department of History at Antwerp University for granting me a sabbatical. At Stanford University Press acquisitions editor Margo Irvin was supportive of my project from the very start. Her and assistant editor Nora Spiegel's feedback were the most useful I ever received from a publisher. I would also like to express my thanks to production editor Jessica Ling and copy editor Richard Gunde; and to the two anonymous peer reviewers for their incisive critique.

Finally, a big shout-out to Maureen, Andy, Will, Max, Yvette and Leo Berner, our mirror family in Carrboro, NC, for exchanging homes, schools, and offices in the fall of 2017; to my parents, Bea and Bert[†]; my in-laws Rita and Robert; and to my wife, Griet, and our kids Winne, Nina, and Otto: thanks for bearing with me, especially when I dragged y'all to Chapel Hill, NC, to finish this book.

# THE EVERYDAY
# NATIONALISM
# OF WORKERS

*Introduction*

# WORKERS INTO BELGIANS, FLEMINGS, AND WALLOONS

In September 2007 *The Independent* asked tongue in cheek: "Is Belgium on the brink of breaking apart, and would it matter if it did?"[1] The British newspaper was reacting to the drawn-out institutional crisis the country was experiencing at the time. Belgium even went without a national government for over a year and half because of a political stand-off between Flemish-speakers and French-speakers. These events played to the clichéd image of Belgium as an artificial invention of international diplomacy. Merely held together by the monarchy, the national football team, waffles, chocolate, and beer, Belgium is a supposedly superficial and unnatural juxtaposition of Flanders and Wallonia. This view goes all the way back to the country's foundation as an independent state in 1830. In his *Histoire de la révolution française* (1847–1853), the great French historian Jules Michelet wrote that Belgium was "an English invention. There has never been and there will never be a Belgium."[2] Even Leopold von Sachsen-Coburg-Saalfeld, the German prince who became the first king of the Belgians, was pessimistic: "Belgium does not have a nationality and given the character of its inhabitants it will never have one."[3] Many contemporaries cast doubt on the viability of the country. Rather than a reflection of the weakness of the young nation-state or the inevitability of ethnolinguistic discord, their nay-saying was a response to the geopolitical uncertainties Belgian independence had created. Because of its central

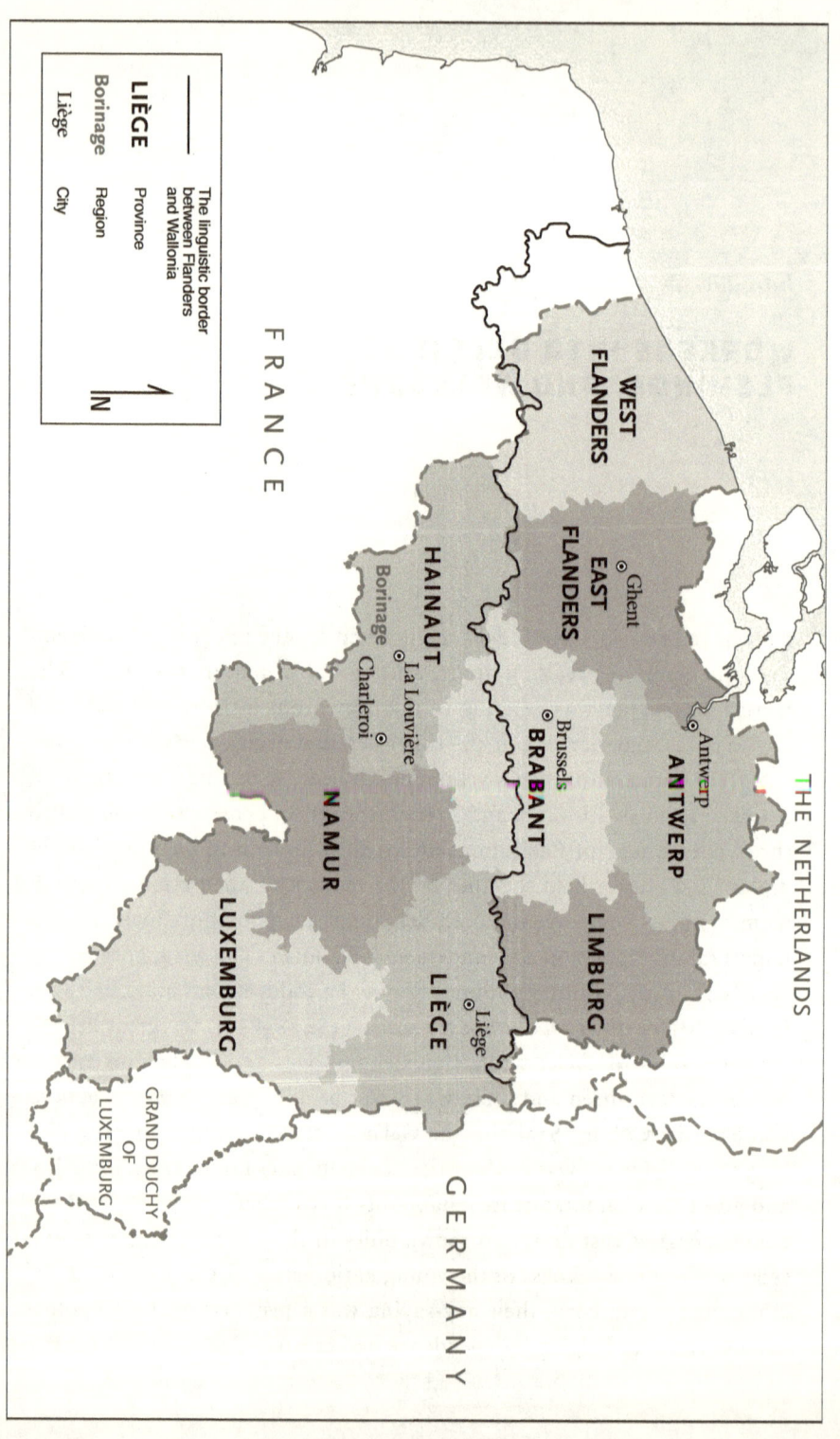

MAP 1 Nineteenth-century Belgium. Adapted from Paul Fredericq, *Vlaamsch België sedert 1830*, vol. 1 (Ghent: Vuylsteke, 1905), iii.

location in Western Europe—the "keystone of the European order" in the words of the French king Louis-Philippe[4]—the Belgian territory was coveted by France, Britain, Prussia, and the Netherlands. But it was easier to deny the country's viability than to annex it.

The image of Belgium as an accident waiting to happen or as a lost cause from the start has been refuted by academic research. Flanders and Wallonia are by no means more natural or more ancient than the so-called artificial Belgian nation-state. The linguistic divide only became a separatist wedge issue after the First World War.[5] As the paragon of European modernity, nineteenth-century Belgium was even a frontrunner in nation-building. Densely populated and urbanized, covered by a network of busy railroads, canals, and highways, it was the first industrialized country on the continent. Its liberal constitution protected the freedoms of religion, press, and association, and supported a thriving civil society in which conservatives interacted with progressives, Catholics with anticlericals, and Flemish-speakers ("Flemings" from Flanders, the north of Belgium) with French-speakers ("Walloons" from Wallonia and educated Flemings).[6] In short, a framework to mass-produce citizens was in place. Some historians have even argued that "the transformation of 'peasants into Belgians' [. . .] happened certainly as one of the earliest on the continent."[7] But did it really?

The viability of Belgium and the draw of nationalism in general have been debated from any number of angles, but one has been conspicuously overlooked: the perspective of ordinary people. What if scholars shifted their attention from the explicit purveyors of nationalism in government agencies and bourgeois associations to the audiences they targeted? A different picture would arise. A close examination of the experience of ordinary Belgians disproves both the academic and popular narrative. Belgium's industrial precociousness did not translate into an early nationalization of its population, but neither were Flemish and Walloon ethnicities more natural categories of belonging.

## EVERYDAY NATIONALISM

At the heart of this book lies a simple question: How did ordinary people experience nationhood in everyday life? The role of the masses in the rise of modern nationhood remains one of the great unresolved issues in nationalism research. Historians have generally examined processes of national identification through the lens of elites and institutions, neglecting the perspective of "ordinary men and women."[8] These people have remained elusive to historians for two reasons. Obviously, they have left fewer sources than the higher social classes, but, more crucially, they have been the victim of a scholarly bias. The classic constructivist paradigm in nationalism research, as developed by the likes of Ernest Gellner, Eugen Weber, and Benedict Anderson, views nation-building as the logical outcome of an inescapable modernization process that pounded *peasants into Frenchmen*, to use Weber's famed phrase.[9] As a result, we still know little, as Eric Hobsbawm once remarked, about how ordinary people experienced nationhood.[10]

This study aims to fill this gap. It probes the grassroots supporters of the socialist Belgian Workers Party (BWP)[11] during the fin de siècle. In this period, between ca. 1880 and the First World War, Belgium and Europe experienced the concurrent rise of nationalism and socialism as mass movements. Drawing on often underexploited source materials from the major urban and working-class centers of Belgium,[12] I set out to uncover the everyday nationalism of the rank and file. Per Fox and Miller-Idriss's definition of everyday nationalism, I "examin[e] the actual practices through which ordinary people engage and enact (and ignore and deflect) nationhood and nationalism in the varied contexts of their everyday lives."[13] In a word, this book seeks to bridge the gap between nationalism studies and social history, linking discourse to daily life and micro-level analysis to macro-level explanation.

At the turn of the nineteenth century the BWP was arguably the strongest socialist party in Europe after the German Social Democratic Party (SPD), both in terms of membership and of representation in legislative bodies.[14] Presiding over a parliamentary, nonrevolutionary movement spearheaded by consumer cooperatives, the BWP's socialism was of the social-democratic, reformist variety. It was focused on reforming society through participation in the political process and elections, not on a violent overthrow of capitalist society. Scholars have interpreted the party's reformist streak as one of the main causes of its integration into the Belgian nation.[15] In the words of the American historian Val R. Lorwin, "the socialists became, for all their lip service to Marxism and internationalism, the most national of Belgian parties."[16] Like other Western European social democrats, the Belgians gradually embraced a so-called *oppositional* or *radical patriotism*. This was a supposedly benign working-class form of patriotism as opposed to a malicious bourgeois chauvinism.[17]

The international scholarship on the link between socialism and nationalism has focused on party institutions, cadres, and leaders.[18] In-depth studies of the rank and file are scarce.[19] For the Belgian case, the grassroots perspective is virtually nonexistent, but this has not stopped several scholars from advancing a range of contradictory and empirically unfounded opinions.[20] Most famously, Eric Hobsbawm claimed that by the turn of the nineteenth century the Belgian proletariat in general, and the social-democratic rank and file in particular, saw themselves "primarily" as Belgians. To Hobsbawm they were unaffected by Belgium's linguistic divide.[21] In a similar argument Miroslav Hroch contended that by the First World War the Belgian proletariat was firmly integrated into the Belgian nation.[22] My analysis, however, demonstrates that the impact of official, top-down nation-building was very uneven in pre–World War I Belgium. Socialist workers exhibited a low degree of nationalist loyalty across linguistic lines. Many Flemish-speaking BWP supporters felt a weakly developed civic allegiance to Belgium, while they did share a sense of Flemish ethnicity that at times had anti-Belgian undertones. Various French-speaking workers, by contrast, espoused a Latin, exclusively francophone interpretation of Belgian nationhood.

## THE BELGIAN EXPERIENCE IN EUROPEAN PERSPECTIVE

The disparate sense of belonging Flemish- and French-speaking socialist workers felt exposes the limits of the classic constructivist paradigm. It particularly challenges the link Ernest Gellner posited between industrialization and national homogenization (see the last section of Chapter 1).[23] Neither were the diverging identification patterns a natural or inevitable reflection of ethnic-linguistic difference. Rather, they resulted from clearly identifiable social and political processes within the specific historic context of the fin de siècle. The new system of plural voting of 1893 and proportional representation of 1899, in particular, induced socialists to interpret democratization trends and divergent electoral outcomes in ethnic terms (see Chapter 2). This finding punctures a central assumption associated with Anthony D. Smith's ethnosymbolist approach to the study of nationalism,[24] namely that ethnic cleavages are the hard core undergirding national conflict. This book shows that nationalism is not a direct translation of ethnic-linguistic difference.

My analysis particularly questions teleological accounts that describe the "awakening" of "oppressed peoples" after the Great War as the structural result of a slow maturation of nineteenth-century ethnic sensibilities. By comparing the Belgian experience to imperial Austria, I argue that the postwar breakthrough of small nations, the so-called Wilsonian moment, was the contingent outcome of a sudden shift. The unprecedented disruption of the First World War transformed ethnicity from a social category among many others to the preeminent basis for collective identification and action. In Rogers Brubaker's terms, the war turned ethnicity into a definitive marker of "groupness."[25] As such, this book helps explain how Europe's pre–World War I patchwork of crisscrossing identifications gave way to a twentieth-century landscape dominated by language and ethnicity.

I have not only built on a well-established tradition of regionalism research that nuances the top-down transmission of nationalism, but also on a recent string of pioneering monographs that investigate the construction of nationhood at the local level.[26] The work on "national indifference" in East and Central Europe, in particular, has been an important influence.[27] This revisionist literature, inspired by Brubaker, has inverted the correlation between the strength of nationalist discourse and its impact in society.[28] The intense propaganda of German and Czech nationalists in late imperial Austria, these scholars argue, was more an admission of impotence than an accurate reflection of their success. Ordinary people were not in thrall to nationalism. On the contrary, they were agnostic, ambivalent, or opportunistic vis-à-vis nationalist propaganda.[29] In short, they reacted with national indifference.

By extending this innovative approach to Western Europe, this book offers an unexpected bridge between "Eastern" and "Western" studies of European nationalism. At the same time it adds two important new dimensions to the national indifference perspective. First, it moves beyond the materialist interpretation of ordinary people's daily lives as determined by primary needs.[30] At times, the literature on national indifference contains a binary subtext of "the *normal* dynamics of village life" versus the artificial loyalty of nationhood.[31] Undoubtedly, nationalist behavior is a construct that needs to be problematized, but so are the so-called self-evident categories of local, ordinary, or everyday interests. These are constructs in their own right, mediated through different languages of class, nation, religion, gender, and so on, that coalesce in different ways in different situations. The second new dimension this book brings to the literature on national indifference is its sustained focus on sources *from*, and not merely *about*, ordinary people.

The critical methodological innovation is the use of a database of over twenty-seven thousand so-called propaganda pence. This unique source has never before been used in international research.

## ORDINARY PEOPLE TALK BACK: THE PROPAGANDA PENCE

> Crooked Charles is bonkers, 0.10. Instead of a seat in the town council he's got a seat reserved in the nuthouse, 0.10.
>
> Friends, what about it? Shall we give that blue dunce who sends his children to the brethren's school a concert with tin pipes, 0.10.
>
> I am glad to have received *The Little Whip*, 0.16. I read it at the gents', 0.10. And then I sent it to its destination, 0.10.[32]

These are the wry, humorous words socialist workers from Ghent leveled against the establishment and their ideological opponents more than a hundred years ago. "Crooked Charles" (*Kromme Karel*) was Charles de Hemptinne, the Catholic owner of one of the largest textile mills in Ghent and—as witnessed by the above quote—the butt of at least one disgruntled worker's ridicule. The "blue dunce," an unidentified liberal free-thinking bourgeois, was threatened with a charivari, a performance of rough music, because he sent his children to a Catholic school affiliated with the Congregation of the Brothers of Charity. And finally the Catholic workers' movement's journal *The Little Whip* (*Het Zweepken*) would go the way of all excreta: down the drain, used as toilet paper.

These curiously direct workers' voices have been preserved in an exceptional working-class source: the "propaganda pence," or *denier de la propaganda/denier de la lutte* in French and *strijdpenning* in Dutch.[33] The name is probably derived from the Saint Peter's pence, *Denier de Saint-Pierre* or *Peterspfennig*, an international Catholic initiative to collect money for the Holy See during the late nineteenth-century *Kulturkampf*.[34]

The propaganda pence were basically a subscription list. Supporters gave money to the BWP—see the numbers in Belgian francs at the end of each statement—and at the same time contributed a short written statement in colloquial language, usually no longer than a few short lines. All messages were subsequently published in a dedicated section of the party paper. Because of their succinctness, mundaneness, and expressiveness, the propaganda pence can be usefully compared to today's tweets. Workers used them to speak their mind and to communicate.

These proletarian tweets are a unique window into workers' values and loyalties. They offer two important methodological advantages.[35] First of all, they help us to overcome methodological nationalism.[36] Unlike the sources nationalism scholars typically rely on, the tweets are not skewed toward the institutional and the national(ist). Originating in a milieu outside the government and organized nationalism, they are reflective of daily life and provide a view on unsuspecting or implicit (non-)manifestations of nationhood. Through the tweets we can capture everyday nationalism "in the act" without nationalist militants or middle-class bureaucrats intervening. Second, one of the classic difficulties in analyzing identity discourses is assessing the relative importance of different loyalties vis-à-vis each other. The tweets allow us to draw up an identification matrix. We can classify the different social categories available to workers in their everyday lives and gauge the importance of nationhood and ethnicity in relation to class, religion, nation, gender, etc. In a word, this source brings out the voices of ordinary people.

**NAVIGATING THIS BOOK**

The first chapter sets the stage with a condensed history of Belgium and its nation-building project in the long nineteenth century. The remainder of the book is divided into two parts that focus on the socialist rank and file during the fin de siècle. Chapters 2 to 6 critically engage with the "resonance" question. Obviously, nationalism was out there in the public arena, enshrined in institutions such as the school, the army, and the monarchy, performed in commemorations and celebrations, and communicated through political discourse and the act of voting. But did it resonate? In what way did socialist workers engage with such classic, institutional vehicles of nation-building as the act of voting, public celebrations, the army, the monarchy, the colony, and the schools?[37]

Part I opens with a chapter on suffrage rights and political participation. In 1893 plural male suffrage replaced the elitist, tax-based census vote but there was no official agenda ingraining the vote as a patriotic duty. Nevertheless, fighting for their political and social rights within the Belgian arena and shouldering the responsibility for local government gave socialists a taste for oppositional patriotism. They did not experience this civic identification uniformly, however. Due to the diverging electoral outcomes of the plural voting system in the urbanized and industrial parts of the country as opposed to the rural and small-town regions, socialists increasingly interpreted ideological divergences within an ethnic framework of Flemings versus Walloons. The introduction of proportional representation in 1899, though meant to assuage such tensions, in fact aggravated them within the BWP.

The most conspicuous occasion to bring the nation to the public were Independence Day festivities, the subject of Chapter 3. The BWP urged workers to keep their distance to avoid being contaminated with bourgeois chauvinism, but to the despair of the party, its supporters often joined in. Mere exposure to nationalist entertainment did not simply turn workers into Belgians. The actual outcome was dependent on the strength of nationalism in other realms of their public lives. That is why the next chapters turn to three central cogs in the state's nation-building machinery.

Chapter 4 examines why the Belgian army did not realize its full potential as a nation-builder before the Great War. First and foremost was the obsolete recruitment system. In 1909 Belgium became the last country in Europe to abolish military recruitment through drawing lots and to introduce personal military conscription. Up to that moment public opinion remained firmly opposed to army service and did not view it as a civic duty.

As the cornerstone of bourgeois nationalism, the king was the ultimate icon of the nation. Chapter 5 relates the lengths the royal entourage went to to popularize the king and to propagate Leopold II's gruesome exploits in the Congo. The court's propaganda was unable to change the deep-seated enmity toward the person of Leopold II, but it was successful in convincing people that the monarchy was a natural part of public life. Leopold II's colonial agenda in the Congo was caught up in a similar paradox. While pro-colonial initiatives did not turn socialist workers into eager imperialists, they normalized the idea of European dominance over the purportedly inferior black race.

Public elementary education is the subject of Chapter 6. Teachers and pedagogues often complained in private about the gap between the (successful) theory and the (ineffective) practice of nationalist education. Many pupils left school with blatantly mistaken notions about Belgium and its history. Yet proletarian children reassembled these faulty building blocks into an idiosyncratic working-class form of nationalism.

The second part of the book turns to the workers themselves and to the mundane experiences that make up the nation in everyday life. These chapters are meant as a complement to the mainstream literature, which tends to focus on those moments, organizations, and protagonists that wear their nationalism on their sleeve.

Chapter 7 explores the accidental encounters of the socialist rank and file with the most visible tokens of the nation: the national flag and anthem. A string of incidents in the Walloon mining province of Hainaut in the late 1880s shows that many French-speaking workers vilified the Belgian tricolor and the national anthem as symbols of bourgeois and clerical oppression, but still they identified as ethnic Belgians. By 1905, the party cadres and the rank and file seemed to have come to a grudging acceptance of the flag and the anthem. Yet, in Ghent—the most proletarian city of Belgium and the undisputed spearhead of socialism in Flanders—wariness remained. The flag and the anthem were not only rejected as bourgeois symbols, but also as signifiers of Belgianness.

To examine this further, Chapter 8 turns to Ghent and the unique source of the propaganda pence. An in-depth investigation of these proletarian tweets demonstrates that social categories such as class, profession, and anti-Catholicism were central to the everyday experience of socialist workers. Nation, ethnicity, and language were only marginally present in the propaganda pence, as were some of the supposed core values of socialism, including internationalism and republicanism. This raises the question of whether the low frequency of a particular social category is proof of its limited appeal as a source of identification. Or, conversely, whether that category was so self-evident that it did not have to be made explicit. More crucially for our purposes: Are we dealing with national indifference or rather with a mundane form of nationalism that has retreated into the background—something akin to Michael Billig's banal nationalism?[38] Chapter 9 looks for an answer.

At the turn of the nineteenth century, Ghent, like all other major cities in Flanders, had a significant French-speaking community. Scholars have generally assumed that workers were exposed to a daily routine of bilingualism. Surprisingly, though, an analysis of the propaganda pence shows that Ghent workers lived in a practically monolingual environment where Flemish ethnicity, though hardly relevant in everyday contexts, held more potential appeal than Belgian nationhood. The Epilogue, finally, ties in the book's findings to Belgian and European history at large.

Chapter 1

# A SOCIALIST PILLAR OF A HYPERLIBERAL STATE

After declaring Belgium's independence in 1830 its elites engaged in a modern and optimistic nation-building project catered toward the country's bourgeois voters. These enfranchised male citizens, 46,000 in total, only accounted for 1 percent of the entire population, the rest of which was duly ignored. This indifference toward the vote-less majority was at that time a common characteristic of European liberal democracies. However, in contrast to neighboring France, Britain, the Netherlands, and Germany, the lack of engagement with the populace at large remained a defining characteristic of Belgium's governing system deep into the nineteenth century. This chapter tells the story of the government's hands-off approach to nationalizing its citizens. Building on the contradiction between the central state's relative weakness and the interventionist nature of Belgian civil society it argues that Belgium, despite its industrial precociousness, its lively public opinion, and its liberal democracy, did not mass-produce Belgians.

## A UNITARY, NONCENTRALIZING STATE

Before gaining independence in 1830 the Belgian territory had been known for centuries as the Southern Netherlands or Southern Low Countries, a series of distinct principalities governed by the same crown, the most important of which were the county of Flanders and the Duchy of Brabant. While the Northern Netherlands gained independence with the Dutch Revolt

(1566–1648), the Southern Netherlands remained a part of the Spanish and later the Austrian Habsburg empire.

In 1789–1790 a revolt in the Duchy of Brabant against the Austrian emperor Joseph II marked the beginning of the end for the Ancien Régime. Because modern Belgian nationhood took shape during this Brabantine rising, it has also been dubbed the first Belgian revolution.[1] For the first time in history the Belgian vocabulary began to refer to what we today call Belgium. Previously, the Latin *Belgium* or French *Belgique* did not exclusively apply to the Southern Netherlands, but also referred to the whole of the Low Countries as they had existed before the Dutch Revolt. The Flemish term *België* did not even become common until after 1830.[2]

In 1795 the French republic annexed what was then called *les ci-devant provinces Belgiques* (the former Belgian provinces). With the defeat of Napoleon, the European powers joined Belgium to the Dutch republic, creating the United Kingdom of the Netherlands, a new monarchy under the house of Orange. This attempt to reestablish the Low Countries failed when Belgium seceded in 1830.

Belgium's bourgeois revolution surprised contemporaries and has sometimes been described as a Brussels charivari gone awry due to King William I's ham-fisted reaction. The more structural reason behind the secession was the monstrous alliance between Catholics and liberals. They only agreed on one thing: ousting William I because he was too Protestant for the former and too despotic for the latter. Independence was founded on a compromise between ideological opposites. The constitution consecrated the relative withdrawal of the state from the public domain in the name of freedom. That way liberals obtained a separation between state and church, but, in exchange, Catholics did not have to fear a strong, pervasive laic state. Thanks to the freedoms of association, religion, and education, Catholics could retain their grip on society through their extensive network of social institutions.

The new liberal state resembled the British model more than the French.[3] The constitution boasted British elements such as a bicameral system, a constitutional monarchy, checks and balances, ministerial responsibility, and suffrage for the propertied classes.[4] A majority of Belgian revolutionaries abhorred Rousseau's interpretation of liberalism with its emphasis on the *volonté générale* and its implied need for centralization of state power. Navigating between centralism and local autonomy, the founding fathers laid the groundwork for a unitary, but noncentralizing state.

This might seem a counterintuitive combination, but from a broader perspective it is not. Through comparative research of the Italian and German unifications the American historical sociologist Daniel Ziblatt has shown that the founding of a unitary as opposed to a federal state is not necessarily the outcome of a high centralizing tendency, but rather the opposite.[5] Both in preunification Germany and Italy federalist ideology and heritage were strong. Bismarck and Cavour both favored federalism. Yet Italy established a unitary state, although Piedmont was a far less dominant and militarily impressive state than Prussia. Ziblatt argues that Piedmont had to choose a second-best solution because the other possible subunits of an Italian federal state lacked constitutions, parliaments, and effective administrations to govern themselves in a federal system. Piedmont simply had to take responsibility for the weaker parts of the country, partly in order to safeguard the international security of Italy and to avoid foreign intervention. In sum, the crucial element in Ziblatt's explanation is the preexisting infrastructural capacity of national subunits.

In Belgium, federalist thinking, in the sense of an acute historical awareness of the autonomy of the ancien régime principalities, was strongly developed around 1830. The idea of unity in diversity was baked into Belgian bourgeois nationalism. What imposed continuity and uniformity on the fragmented past of the Southern Low Countries was the Belgians' eternal love of freedom. Their history was a dramatic succession of peaceful periods under just princes and violent risings against foreign oppressors.[6] Accordingly, the Belgian revolution of 1830 was both modern, being a democratic rising for political and social rights, and ancient, as a "natural" revolt of the old, freedom-loving Belgian "race" against tyranny.[7]

Despite the autonomist and localist tradition, Belgium's founders opted for a unitary and not a federal state. Following Ziblatt's logic it is clear that at the time of the Belgian secession the subnational units necessary for a federal system were weak or even lacking. The ancien régime principalities had been completely abolished almost half a century earlier and the Flemish-Walloon division was still in the distant future. Given the insecure international position of Belgium, any other solution than a unitary state was off the table, but for historical reasons this unitary state would not have a heavy centralizing footprint. The lasting mark of Counter-Reformation Catholicism and the peripheral position of the Southern Netherlands within larger states such as Spain, Austria, and France, determined this choice.

Because the Southern Netherlands was the historical seat of the Spanish Counter-Reformation, the Belgian church had gained a monopolistic position in the administration of basic social services, especially in education and welfare. At the end of the sixteenth century there had been about three hundred thousand Protestants, but by 1830 Belgium had become monolithically Catholic with barely 7,568 Protestants (0.17 percent of the total population) and 1,900 Jews. In the absence of a tradition of religious cohabitation, neither the state nor any other secular authority developed into an autonomous overarching arbiter, as happened in the Dutch republic. The Belgian constitution confirmed this state of affairs and respected the church's social monopoly.[8] Moreover, the negative memories of the recent centralization attempts of Emperor Joseph II, the last Austrian ruler of the Southern Netherlands, and those during the period of French annexation and in the United Kingdom of the Netherlands, disposed a majority of both Catholics and liberals against a strongly centralizing state.

As a result, nineteenth-century Belgium had "the most laissez-faire of all European governments."[9] Outside the economic and the industrial realm, where it directly intervened to create a unified economic space, the Belgian state acted as a night watchman, that is, a classic liberal state with minimal functions and little centralizing zeal.[10] Article 41 of the constitution consecrated the principle of local autonomy. Unlike in the Netherlands and France, the municipalities retained a significant number of responsibilities, including local taxation, subsidies to schools, churches, and charitable groups, and control over the local police.[11] The central state was in charge of national defense, diplomacy, law and order, and security, but all other state functions were left to the municipalities "as long as—in the spirit of the time—private initiative did not take care of them."[12] In Belgium's first half century there were many private, Catholic organizations—hospitals, welfare agencies, and schools—that fulfilled tasks of public interest. As collective needs expanded beyond the reach of private organizations, however, so did municipal responsibilities. During the latter third of the nineteenth century, it was progressive liberal and socialist municipalities that tackled urgent social needs, fought the rising cost of living, established minimum wages in public works, and founded unemployment funds. These issues were all the more pressing given the breakneck pace of industrialization and urbanization the country was experiencing.

## INDUSTRIALIZATION, URBANIZATION, AND THE DIVIDES OF RELIGION AND CLASS

At the end of the eighteenth century the first industrial revolution swept over Belgium. Cotton mills in Ghent, extractive industries, and metal workshops in the four Walloon coal basins mechanized swiftly.[13] Between 1840 and

1910 the country's per capita steam-driven horsepower figures were only surpassed by Britain's. Rapid industrialization was fed by an abundance of easily exploitable raw materials (mainly coal and iron ore) and a highly productive agriculture that was able to sustain a growing population despite its falling share in the total workforce. Agricultural employment went from 32 percent in 1846 to 17 percent in 1910. Lower percentages only obtained in Britain. Industrial development, however, was uneven. The two Walloon provinces of Hainaut and Liège accounted for 84.4 percent of all steam-driven horsepower in 1846 and this figure was still at 57.5 percent in 1910.[14] In Flanders industrialization only took off in the textile city of Ghent. Two other cities in the Flemish-speaking part of the country were of high economic value: the port of Antwerp and the administrative and financial center of Brussels. Outside of these areas, artisanal and cottage industries remained important up to the First World War.[15]

Industrialization went hand in hand with urbanization. Historically, the Southern Netherlands was among the most densely populated and most urbanized regions of Europe. In 1550, 22.7 percent of the population lived in cities with at least ten thousand residents, the highest urbanization rate in Europe at that time. In the ensuing centuries the Southern Netherlands lost its lead, but in 1850 Belgium's urban population of 20.5 percent was still third in Europe after Britain and the Netherlands.[16]

Throughout the nineteenth century Belgium's population almost doubled, from 4.3 million in 1846 to 7.4 million in 1910. The percentage of people living in cities with five thousand or more residents increased from 33.5 to 56.6 in the same period.[17] The mostly rural provinces of East Flanders and West Flanders, Limburg, Namur, and Luxemburg were areas of out-migration, while the main recipients of internal migration were the Walloon coal and steel provinces of Liège and Hainaut, Brabant with the capital Brussels, the province of Antwerp with the eponymous port city, and the industrial island of Ghent in East Flanders. Between 1831 and 1900 Antwerp's population grew by a factor of 3.5, Liège's by 2.5, Ghent's and Brussels' by 2.[18]

Belgium boasted no large metropolises like Paris, London, or Berlin. Brussels had about 100,000 residents in 1830 and 175,000 in 1890. The capital's growth was especially concentrated in its suburbs, collectively known as the Brussels *agglomération*, which grew from 140,000 residents in 1830 to 520,000 in 1890.[19] This points to one of Belgium's idiosyncrasies: urbanization was in essence the suburbanization of the countryside. The growth of the urban population was concentrated in smaller cities dotted across the land.

In 1910 half of the urban population lived in towns with fewer than 25,000 inhabitants. Only one in eight urban-dwellers resided in cities with more than 100,000 inhabitants.[20]

Suburbanization was driven by a spectacular growth in labor commuting, assisted by the extension of Belgium's railroad network from 20 kilometers of railway in 1835 to 4,600 kilometers in 1900.[21] This was the second densest network in the world, with 13.2 kilometers of railroad per 100 km$^2$ in 1900, only surpassed by Britain's 13.4 km/100 km$^2$ and well ahead of Europe's number three, the Netherlands, with 7.8 km/100 km$^2$.[22] In the last quarter of the nineteenth century this infrastructure was further refined by the construction of a light rail system (3,900 kilometers long by 1913) and of local tramways (382 kilometers in the same year).[23] The Catholic government actively promoted commuting to work by train, light rail, or tram and introduced cheap tickets for the working classes.[24] By 1910 a third of the industrial labor force commuted daily, most of them over short distances to the next town.[25] This arrangement allowed people to continue living outside the large urban centers, much to the satisfaction of the Catholic government, which wanted to keep workers away from the cities' bad, anticlerical influences. Yet, in actual fact these policies suburbanized the countryside and had secularizing effects.

The changes brought on by industrialization and urbanization introduced the divides of religion and class into Belgian politics. Up to 1857 Belgium was governed by joint Catholic-liberal governments. These were called "unionist" in the spirit of the concerted resistance against the Dutch king William I. In 1857, however, the unionist era ended and the confessional divide between Catholics and anticlerical liberals began to dominate politics. Up to that point the Belgian church, being one of the main beneficiaries of the new constitution, had been fully committed to the success of the young state, lending its personnel, its gathering spaces, and its church bells to mark national celebrations and royal visits to the smallest of villages.[26] From 1857 onward the Belgian church and Catholic society became increasingly wary of the state.[27]

The Catholic–anticlerical conflict culminated in the so-called School War of 1878–1884, which heralded the beginning of mass politics in Belgium. Catholics mobilized massively and successfully against the liberal Education Act of 1879. The act, aimed at centralizing and declericalizing the Belgian school system, was immediately revoked on the Catholics' return to power in 1884. The stage was set for a thirty-year period of Catholic rule in parliament and government.

The School War marked the onset of "consociationalism." Also called "pillar formation" or "pillarization" (*verzuiling* in Dutch), this phenomenon is typical of Belgium, the Netherlands, and a number of other smaller Western European countries. It refers to the compartmentalization or segmentation of society into strong confessional or ideological communities.[28] These so-called pillars comprised a host of social organizations from political parties and trade unions to mutual-aid societies and consumer cooperatives as well as sports and leisure clubs. In a word, they catered to the social needs of their members from the cradle to the grave.

Being a tool of conflict regulation in plural, highly segmented societies, pillarization made Belgium into a unique European testing ground.[29] Arend Lijphart even called Belgium "the most perfect, most convincing, and most impressive example of a consociation."[30] Pillarization is a local variant of a broader European phenomenon. It is an offshoot of the transnational conflict between church(es) and state during the second half of the nineteenth century. The wave of secularization that swept over Europe threatened the power of the church(es). Where tensions between secular and religious authorities ran high, the so-called *Kulturkampf,* or culture wars, politicized religious elites and stimulated their creating a separate sphere.[31] An international movement of Catholic counter-secularization initiatives was created, partly made possible by the new mass media.[32] Among liberal anticlericals an analogous process was in full swing and the young socialist movement also contributed to the hectic climate of the culture wars.[33]

In Belgium, ultramontane Catholics, who did not accept the primacy of the secular state over the papacy, had displayed much organizational fervor since the end of the unionist era in 1857. Their activity did not yet amount to pillarization because it was aimed at the restoration of a Catholic Belgian state and the reversal of secularization rather than the creation of a Catholic sphere within a plural, secularizing society. During the papacy of Leo XIII (1878–1903), who encouraged accommodation with liberal regimes, the ultramontane ideal of a complete restoration of the Catholic state was relinquished and a more activist intervention of the secular state in social affairs was accepted.[34] In Belgium the move away from ultramontanism starting with Leo XIII was eased by the thirty years of absolute Catholic majorities in parliament starting in 1884. The Catholic acceptance of pluralism, of the existence of two separate spheres, one secular and one religious, made the formation of "a state within a state," or pillarization, possible.[35] During the fin de siècle three pillars gradually took shape: a Catholic, a socialist, and a smaller liberal community. Importantly, nationalism, ethnicity, and language did *not* drive the pillarization process. Its engine was ideological dissension over religion and class.

The onset of pillarization in the 1880s coincided with the rise of class in Belgian politics. The social-economic divide between the haves and the have-nots began to rival the Catholic–anticlerical cleavage as the major fault line in society. The foundation of the Belgian Workers' Party in 1885 and the bloody Spring Revolt of 1886, the largest wave of labor unrest ever to hit the country, leaving twenty-four workers dead in clashes with police forces, epitomized this evolution.

## SOCIALIST PILLARIZATION

Ever since the 1830s followers of French socialist thinkers had been active in Belgium, attracted by the freedom of press and association the young state offered. The first wave of Belgian socialism was bourgeois in character and did not succeed in attracting working-class support. After the repression of the European revolutions of 1848 a new generation of labor leaders and free-thinker societies rose from the artisanal milieu. Immediately a rift appeared between anarchist and political strands of socialism. In the Walloon industrial centers a revolutionary, apolitical, and anarchic socialism inspired by French theorists was dominant, while in Ghent and Brussels political action and organization in the vein of German social democracy prevailed.

The establishment of the Belgian Workers' Party in 1885 marked the breakthrough of social democracy in Belgium. Because of the artisanal and middle-class sensibilities of the Brussels' labor movement, any reference to socialism was dropped from the new party's name. Nor was there any common ideological manifesto. The local chapters of the BWP, which were called "federations," had a large measure of autonomy. Their unity was underpinned by a very concrete program of reform hinged on general suffrage, a revision of military conscription laws, better labor conditions, and higher wages.

The driving forces behind the foundation of a united, social-democratic party were Ghent and Brussels. Ghent was Belgium's most proletarian city, with the highest ratio of factory workers to the total population. Because of the relatively slow growth of its textile industry, Ghent had a comparatively low immigration rate. Between 1880 and 1910 the ratio of Ghent-born city dwellers to the total population hardly changed: from 66.9 percent to 64.8 percent, as compared to, respectively, 61 percent and 56 percent in Liège, 53 percent and 45 percent in Brussels, and 63 percent and 55 percent in Antwerp.[36] Workers tended to live in the same neighborhood from generation to generation. The result was a close-knit, monolingual Flemish neighborhood sociability which formed the basis for an exceptionally strong *Organisationspatriotismus*, or organizational devotion,[37] to *Moeder Vooruit* (Mother Forward). This was the affectionate name, borrowed from the SPD's paper *Vorwärts*, by which the Ghent socialist movement came to be known.

Working-class support for Vooruit was massive. In the municipal elections of 1907 two-thirds of all male workers in Ghent voted socialist. With a circulation of 20,000 to 25,000 copies around 1900,[38] the daily *Vooruit* was the most widely read newspaper of Ghent, which had about 160,000 inhabitants at the time. Shortly before the First World War, about 30,000 people were affiliated personally or through a family member to one of the many societies under the umbrella of the Ghent socialist federation.[39]

The tight *Organisationspatriotismus* of Ghent socialists was also a function of their political and social ostracism. The extent of police surveillance and brutality the BWP was subjected to, was closer to the autocratic experience of the German socialists than to that of their comrades in the more liberal French or British political systems.[40] As a result, Belgian socialists and particularly those from Ghent diverted all their negative, anti-system energy into the development of a socialist universe of their own, away from the revolution. This is a prime example of what the German historian Dieter Groh has termed "negative integration."[41]

Not surprisingly, Ghent became the preeminent battleground of the Catholic counteroffensive for the soul of the masses. From the 1890s on, the Ghent BWP branch increasingly had to compete with a vigorous Catholic working-class movement that copied the socialist model and explicitly named itself "anti-socialist."[42] This was the crucial breakthrough for pillarization.[43] Up to that point the Catholic paternalist initiatives had been similar to those in other countries. The pillarized reaction against the Ghent socialists was different because it implied a declericalization of the Catholic labor movement. Lay people from working-class backgrounds began to play an active and leading role. This completed the separation of the religious and the secular spheres, which the concept of pillarization presupposes.[44] Gradually, the Ghent socialist template of consumer cooperatives funding all other movement activities, the press, the unions, the political groups, the mutual aid societies, and the leisure clubs, was copied throughout the entire country, eventually creating distinct socialist and Catholic pillars.[45] Struggling for relevance in the escalating class conflict, the liberal community never succeeded in constructing a truly competitive pillar.

While the labor movement in Ghent had a clear proletarian character, the capital's was more middle-class. The industrialization that had reshaped Ghent and the Walloon coal and steel districts had passed Brussels by. Small-scale, artisanal workshops that mainly produced luxury items for the local market dominated. In 1896 they still accounted for three-quarters of all industrial companies active in the city of Brussels. The average number of employees per enterprise was a meager 3.1. Innovative, mechanized, and large-scale factories could be found outside the narrow confines of Brussels, in the neighboring towns of Anderlecht (textile production) and Molenbeek (metalworking).[46] The capital's labor movement was sustained by highly skilled and well-paid workers and artisans: typesetters, bronze workers, hatmakers, and so on. As French-speakers, they tended to ignore the Flemish-speaking proletariat in the Brussels *agglomération*.

The Brussels federation built a very successful movement on its artisanal and middle-class support. The circulation of its paper, *Le Peuple*, which was also the national French-speaking organ of the party, reflects this success. In its early years it had a daily print run of 12,000, which rose to 25,000 in the early 1890s and peaked after the introduction of plural suffrage at 70,000. This number remained stable until the general strike of 1902 increased its readership by another 10,000.[47]

Compared to Ghent and Brussels, the other Belgian centers of socialism—the Borinage, Liège, Charleroi, and La Louvière in Wallonia, and the Flemish city of Antwerp—lagged behind for a variety of reasons. Liège had a very high concentration of workers in mining, metalworking, and arms manufacturing, but these were dispersed along the 12-mile-long Meuse valley with its steep drops and climbs.[48] Partly because of this geographic fragmentation, the Liège section of the BWP had trouble founding long-lived associations and institutions.[49] There was, for instance, no authoritative local party paper. All the energy of the Liège socialist federation was directed toward electoral propaganda. At the ballot box the BWP was the largest party of the city, but only after 1905 did it succeed in establishing a mass movement commensurate with its political clout.

The Black Country around Charleroi and the Centre region around La Louvière boomed during the nineteenth century, quadrupling in population between 1831 and 1910, thanks to their production of iron, coal, and glass. The last industry relied on highly skilled and well-paid workers, who were the nucleus of the local labor unions organized by the Chevaliers du Travail.[50] Between Charleroi and La Louvière, the strongest European branch of the American Knights of Labor developed. Unlike the British and French affiliates, the Belgian division had a mass following and unlike the revolutionary French Chevaliers, the Belgian Knights skirted ideology. Initially founded among the labor aristocracy of glassblowers, they began to recruit miners and turned into a full-fledged miners' organization after 1884. Among the colliers of Charleroi, the Knights had a larger following than the BWP's unions. The local BWP branch functioned as a loose umbrella organization uniting progressive liberals, socialists, and Knights of Labor. Despite the sometimes contentious relations between the three groups, the BWP held a near political monopoly in the Black Country and the Centre area, supplying the overall majority of the municipal councilors and MPs.

Socialism also dominated local politics in the Borinage, the region (south) west of Mons. Unlike the other industrial centers of Wallonia, the Borinage was a semirural mining district characterized by mono-industry. Reformist influences from Brussels and Ghent hardly reached this remote, peripheral region where French revolutionary thinking continued to reverberate. In other federations one center was dominant: the Vooruit in Ghent, the Maison du Peuple in Brussels, Le Progrès in the Centre. In the Borinage, every village had its own small cooperative surrounded by its own mutual aid society, union, fanfare band, etc. Symptomatically, the national party paper *Le Peuple* did not have one but ten local correspondents for the Borinage. The strong sense of localism in the Borinage was enhanced by the absence of outside immigration. Compared to Liège, where around 1902 only a fifth of the miners were living in the municipality where they had been born, in the Borinage villages this was a stunning 97 percent.[51] Labor immigration of Flemish-speakers was almost inexistent. In 1880 barely 0.463 percent of the local population spoke Flemish; in 1900 this figure was still a paltry 0.651 percent.[52] In the other Walloon mining areas Flemish-speaking migrants accounted for 5 to 12 percent of the local population.[53]

In Flanders, the only city with a sizable socialist presence besides Ghent was Antwerp. Although it was the single largest city of Belgium, with 302,058 residents in 1900, and the country's leading commercial center, the port city had a poorly developed industrial sector. Large-scale industrial growth only began after 1895 with the advent of chemical, nonferrous, and metal industries, and building and paper factories. The local socialist movement insufficiently capitalized on these developments and remained weak until the First World War. Symptomatically, Antwerp's socialist daily *De Werker* (The Worker) was a local edition of Ghent's *Vooruit* rather than an independent paper in its own right. In 1902 its circulation was only 1,600,[54] meager compared to *Vooruit*'s 25,000. Politically, the Antwerp socialists were marginalized. Only after the First World War did they take over Ghent's role as the capital of Flemish socialism. What set them apart from their Ghent colleagues was their openness toward the Flemish movement (see Chapter 9).[55]

## A NONISSUE: LANGUAGE

At the time of its independence Belgium harbored two relatively distinct language groups.[56] The authors of the first population census in 1846 wrote that "the demarcation line between the French and Flemish populations of Belgium has remained more or less the same, despite the efforts of several governments to erase it."[57] The north of Belgium—the provinces of East Flanders and West Flanders, Antwerp, Limburg, and the north of Brabant—was predominantly Flemish-speaking. In the southern provinces—Hainaut, Namur, Liège, Luxembourg, and southern Brabant—dialects of Walloon (a Romance language distinct from, but close to, French) were spoken. French was the standard language in Wallonia and of elites across the country. Ever since the Middle Ages the aristocracy and the higher clergy in the Flemish-speaking provinces had been using French, which in due time had become the language of all civilized conversation, preferred by the aspiring middle classes.

During the nineteenth century the use of French spread in the larger Flemish cities.[58] In Antwerp and Ghent respectively 1.9 and 5 percent of the residents used French in 1846. In both cities these numbers had risen to 8 percent in the 1910 census.[59] In Ghent the majority of these French-speakers were native Flemings, not Walloon migrants. The only Flemish towns with a structural influx of the latter, mostly from middle-class backgrounds, were Brussels and Antwerp. In Wallonia there was large-scale immigration of Flemish-speaking, mainly lower-class migrants into the industrial centers during the second half of the nineteenth century. This explains the presence of Flemish-speakers and bilinguals in and around Liège, Charleroi, and La Louvière. Between 1880 and 1910 their numbers ranged from 5 to 12 percent of the total population, with peaks in certain neighborhoods of 32 percent.[60]

Overall, Flemish-French bilingualism gradually rose throughout the nineteenth century. In 1866, 6.4 percent of all Belgians declared themselves bilingual to census-takers. The number had doubled to 12.3 percent in 1910, 61 percent of whom mostly used Flemish. At that time Belgium's population was made up of 45.4 percent exclusive speakers of Flemish and 40 percent French monolinguals.[61]

The Belgian case differed from the situation in Bohemia and Moravia. The geographic and social language border between Czech and German was much more fragmented. In Belgium linguistic and administrative boundaries coincided to a higher degree than in Central Europe,[62] but the exception was Brussels. Situated in the Flemish-speaking north, it had been the capital of the Southern Netherlands since the end of the fourteenth century, when the dukes of Burgundy had introduced French at their court. This had attracted a French-speaking elite to the capital. At the turn of the eighteenth and nineteenth centuries, the number of French-speakers began to rise, from 5–10 percent of the total Brussels population in 1760, to 15 percent in 1780, and 25 percent in 1821.[63] This shift was occasioned by the centralization efforts of the Austrian emperor Joseph II, the rising prestige of French, and the annexation of the Southern Netherlands by France. After Belgian independence, the share of French-speakers kept growing in the capital and its neighboring communes. In 1866, 39.1 percent of the inhabitants of the capital spoke Flemish exclusively against 20 percent monolingual French-speakers and 38.3 percent bilinguals. Half a century later, in 1910, these figures had changed to 16.4 percent, 26.7 percent, and 48.2 percent respectively.[64] Throughout the twentieth century the Flemish-speaking and bilingual share kept falling in the capital. To explain this shift, which is known as the "gallicization" (*verfransing* or *francisation*) of Brussels, Flemish historians have usually stressed the top-down "incredible social pressure of French,"[65] while their French-speaking colleagues have called it a bottom-up "self-generated shift" of upwardly mobile people choosing French over Flemish.[66] As usual, the truth lies somewhere in between.

Throughout the nineteenth century language was a relatively minor political question. It was overshadowed by issues of religion and class. The revolutionary bourgeoisie that took power in 1830 was French-speaking regardless of its provenance or ideology. In a nod to the linguistic diversity of the country and to their liberal inspiration, the writers of the constitution proclaimed the principle of language freedom. In practice, French became the language of state—at the national level that is, because in Flanders (excluding Brussels) administrative procedures were in Flemish or bilingual at the local, municipal level. Other, more "refined" segments of public life, such as secondary and higher education, however, used French exclusively.

Against this background the Flemish movement arose. From 1835 onward societies were founded in all major towns in Flanders with the aim of cultivating the Flemish vernacular and its history. These associations were reminiscent of contemporary regionalist initiatives like the Association bretonne (1843) and the Jocs Florals of Barcelona (1859). The supporters of the Flemish movement, *flamingants* as they were called, hailed from the socially ambitious, but not yet franchised urban (lower-)middle classes. In the newly founded state, their social position was threatened because it had been closely linked to their command of Flemish/Dutch in the United Kingdom of the Netherlands. They channeled their dissatisfaction with their lack of social power and prestige in their campaign for the recognition of Flemish culture and language.[67]

Possibly, the Flemish movement would have been relegated to the status of a minority regionalism, on a par with Frisian in the Netherlands or Breton in France, if the Belgian government had developed a comprehensive nationalization and language policy. In the absence of such an agenda (see the next section), a sense of Flemish ethnicity developed in tandem with a Belgian civic patriotism. Flamingants considered the Flemish people to be the ultimate safeguard of Belgium's independence. As the epitome of the country's bicultural and bilingual nature, Flemish-speakers were the surest firewall against French annexation.

Thanks to the Belgian patriotic inspiration of the Flemish movement, the government and the establishment were benevolently disposed toward the Flamingant cultural agenda, but well into the twentieth century social elites rejected mandated bilingualism of state services as antithetical to the constitutional freedom of language. In the 1870s parliament passed the first language acts establishing minimal thresholds for the use of Flemish in the courts, public secondary schools, and state bureaucracies in the Flemish-speaking provinces. In the first years of the twentieth century, partly driven by the poor enforcement of existing language acts, the Flemish movement started to campaign for parity with Wallonia. Whether this meant generalized bilingualism throughout the country or the recognition of two unilingual regions remained an open question. The ethnoterritorial link between one language, one people, and one territory was not yet solidified. Nor was Flemish ethnicity sufficiently politicized prior to 1914 to spawn a separatist form of Flemish nationalism.

Symptomatically, against the backdrop of pillarization it proved impossible to found a Flamingant political party independent of the three major ideologies. Flemish militants had to campaign within the existing parties, but after the School War of 1878–1884 there was an ever stronger association of Flemishness and Catholicism, marginalizing Flamingants in the liberal and socialist parties. To Catholic Flamingants, the Flemish language and culture were a rampart against anticlerical incursions from republican France.[68]

In the 1880s a Walloon counterpart to the Flemish movement arose.[69] The epithet "Walloon movement" can be misleading to a twenty-first-century observer, because until the Great War "Walloon" could also refer to all speakers of French in Belgium regardless of their origin or residence. The Walloon movement's main aim was to defend the exclusively French nature of the Belgian nation-state.[70] It was a radicalized francophone and secularist offshoot of Belgian nationalism. *Wallingants*, as its supporters were called, viewed the Flemish movement as a German fifth column or as a Catholic conspiracy to deny Flanders the ideals of the Enlightenment.

Ironically, the cradle of the Walloon movement stood in Flanders and Brussels, where French-speaking officials organized themselves to fight the first language acts. At the end of the 1880s the Walloon movement began to draw support in Wallonia as fear spread that language laws would be applied to the Flemish-speaking working-class minorities in the Walloon mine and steel districts. Wallingants dreaded the creation of so-called Flemish language islets that would vote Catholic, an unpalatable prospect for a movement that was an anticlerical preserve of liberals and to a lesser extent socialists until shortly before the First World War.[71]

The competition between the Flemish and Walloon movements played out against the background of uneven industrialization. While the Walloon coal and steel centers became an industrial power house, the once thriving protoindustrial textile industry in the Flemish-speaking provinces went into a steep decline. The Flemish dialects became associated with poverty and backwardness. The uneven economic development did not immediately translate into a political split. Well into the nineteenth century the Flemish and Walloon provinces voted alike. Across Belgium, irrespective of language, rural districts elected Catholics while cities and small towns voted liberal. This changed gradually during the second half of the nineteenth century. By 1880 small-town Flanders had shifted its political allegiance to the Catholic party, thus ensuring a Catholic majority in parliament. The Belgian historian Henk De Smaele has termed this the "ruralization of urban Flanders."[72] He argues that small-town elites became disaffected with the liberals in the larger Flemish towns of Ghent, Antwerp, and Brussels due to the latter's championing of the new, mainly Walloon industries. The small-town elites began to imagine their world as eminently rural, Catholic, *and* Flemish—a paradoxical development for a region that for centuries had been more densely urbanized than Wallonia. One could facetiously call this the transformation of Belgians into peasants.

## PEASANTS INTO BELGIANS?

Some historians have argued that there were plenty of obstacles to national integration before the First World War. They point to the hyperliberal character of the Belgian state, its lack of centralizing fervor, the tradition of municipal autonomy, the highly developed sense of localism, and the extent of linguistic diversity.[73] The majority view, however, holds that, in spite of these hurdles, the young Belgian state was a frontrunner when it came to turning peasants into Belgians.[74] There were plenty of elements that compensated for weak centralization, including Belgium's advanced industrial development, its active civil society, its precociously dense transport and communication networks, the firm grip of the Brussels high finance on the country's financial activity, and the presence of a looming national enemy, the Dutch.

From 1830 onward, the Belgian elites set out on an enthusiastic nation-building project. Presenting Belgium as a democratic and industrial vanguard nation, they developed a forward-looking civic nationalism and established a cult of Freedom and Constitution. At the same time they projected the ethnic roots of the country back into the mists of time, to the Celtic tribes of northern Gaul, the mythical Belgae. Julius Caesar's quote in *De bello Gallico* about the Belgae as the bravest of all the Gauls became a staple of Belgian nationalism.

Commissioning national monuments, harnessing the national history genre in painting, sculpture, and writing, and stimulating pageants and plays, the country's elites sought to spread the Belgian gospel.[75] Their agenda was successful in the upper reaches of society. This was most evident in the marginalization and eventual disappearance of the so-called Orangists. These loyalists to the Dutch royal house of Orange were a small but influential faction within the liberal bourgeoisie that had profited from the Dutch king's commercial policies. The Orangists wanted to undo the secession, but suffered a debilitating defeat in 1839 when the Dutch king finally accepted Belgian independence and concluded a peace treaty with his southern neighbors.

Most scholars, I argue, have overestimated the reach of the nationalist agenda beyond the elites and the upper middle classes, neglecting or taking for granted its impact on ordinary people. For one, the state did not put its full weight behind the nation-building program. Exhibit number 1 is the poor condition of the army and elementary education, institutions that were instrumental to the making of the nation elsewhere in Europe.

The Belgian army did not function as an effective school of the nation (see Chapter 4). Unlike in France and Germany,[76] the military was generally disdained in Belgium because of the draft lottery and the practice of substitute buy-outs. Between 1830 and 1885, 22 to 37 percent of all draftees opted out by paying a substitute to take their place.[77] This system was not abolished until 1909—Belgium was the last Western European country to do so.[78] Only in 1913 was general military conscription for every young man introduced. As a result, through the first decade of the twentieth century the Belgian army was a collection of poor, undereducated, lower-class men. In 1901 Emile Vandervelde, the unofficial president of the BWP, claimed that 120 out of every thousand Belgian recruits were unable to read and write, against only 49 in France, 6 in the Netherlands, and 0.7 in Germany.[79] The official statistical yearbook corroborated Vandervelde's numbers: in 1900, 10.10 percent of recruits were illiterate.[80] This was due to the low quality of elementary schooling.

There is a tight link between education, nationalism, and industrialization. Ernest Gellner famously posited that nationalism arises when agrarian societies transition to industrialism.[81] The modern industrial world needs multifunctional citizens and these "modular men," to use Gellner's phrase, were molded in the schools. Belgium, however, is a bad fit for Gellner's model despite the country's industrial precociousness. What was missing in Belgium and what is crucial to Gellner, was "cultural homogenization based on literacy in a standardized vernacular language conveyed by means of state-supported mass education."[82] Belgium never had a unified language of elementary education. Although French was the de facto language of state, it was never introduced in Flanders' elementary schools, the only exception being Brussels. The country's literacy rates were relatively low and the state largely withdrew from the field of education. The dismal condition of schooling was the result of a deliberate choice by a hyperliberal political elite. The Belgian case suggests that the state, politics, and ideology play a larger role in the concomitant rise of nationalism and industrialism than Gellner envisaged. He overestimated the importance of cultural homogenization in successful industrialization scenarios.[83]

Throughout the nineteenth and early twentieth centuries Belgium was consistently at the bottom of Western European educational statistics. Around 1880 there were 126 elementary pupils for every thousand Belgians, as opposed to 157 in Switzerland and 159 in Prussia.[84] The Belgian parliament only adopted compulsory elementary education in 1914. At that time it had already been introduced in Germany in 1871 (Prussia had it since Frederick the Great), in Scotland in 1872, in France in 1882, in England and Wales in 1889, and in the Netherlands in 1900. Of course, a late introduction date does not necessarily reflect a sorry state of schooling or of literacy. The Netherlands, for instance, was among the most literate European societies of the time, having an efficient, noncompulsory mass education system since at least 1800.[85] Belgium, however, was not the Netherlands. The Dutch king William I had tried to set up a system of state schools when Belgium was joined to the Netherlands from 1815 through 1830, but his educational policies had been one of the causes of the Belgian secession. The Belgian church had rejected the interference of a Protestant king in what was in effect a Catholic monopoly on education. The newly independent Belgian state did not take educational matters into its hands. The constitution prohibited any restriction on the Catholic initiative to found schools.[86] Using the constitutionally guaranteed freedom of education, the Catholic Church could build its own network of confessional schools, and through the principle of local autonomy, it succeeded in gaining control over public municipal schools in the countryside and in small towns.[87] As a result, Catholics ran more than half of all elementary schools in the nineteenth century. At the end of the 1880s, in the wake of the School War, about 60 percent of all elementary pupils were enrolled in a Catholic school.[88] Rather than teaching literacy and transferable skills crucial to a modern, industrial nation, the Catholic project for the popular classes centered on rote learning the catechism.

As a result, Belgium's literacy rates were low for such a highly industrialized and urbanized nation. Around 1850 the country had an adult illiteracy rate of 48 percent, as opposed to 43 percent in France, 32 percent in the United Kingdom, 20 percent in Prussia, and 20 percent in the United States.[89] Because of large disparities between rural and industrial regions, Flemish-speaking males were four times more likely to be illiterate than French-speaking men in the 1860s. Among women the odds were almost five times as high. Overall, literacy levels in Flanders were ten to fifteen percentage points lower than in Wallonia.[90] As late as 1911 the British scholar Benjamin Seebohm Rowntree estimated the illiteracy rates among Belgian workers of both sexes ten years and older at 21.4 percent overall, 34.69 percent in Flemish-speaking municipalities and 17.34 percent in French-speaking municipalities.[91]

Obviously these discrepancies show a correlation between literacy, industrialization, and urbanization, but they do not confirm the Gellnerian link between state-driven schooling, "modular men," and nationalism. From an international point of view, Belgium's literacy levels were low, even in booming Wallonia. At the end of the nineteenth century average male illiteracy (including backward rural areas) was down to 10 percent or below in France, Prussia, the Netherlands, and England, while Belgium's hovered around 25 percent, near the Irish level.[92] Once again, this was the result of a political choice inspired by a hyperliberal ideology. In the middle of the nineteenth century there was a consensus—even among forward-looking factory owners—that the country did not need "modular men." Liberals and industrialists tolerated the low schooling level of the general population because the success of the Belgian export industry was based on the massive input of unschooled and low-paid workers, including women and children.[93] There was simply no need for better-schooled workers.

Around 1850 average daily wages in the four key industries of mining, engineering, cotton, and glass were comparable to those in Germany, but they were 75 percent of those in France and a mere 33 percent of those in Great Britain. Around 1896 Belgium's wages were still among the lowest of Europe.[94] To keep wages down the Belgian state followed a hyperliberal labor policy. A form of labor inspection was only introduced in 1888 compared to 1844 in England, and the first legislation restricting child labor in 1889 compared to 1839 in Prussia, 1841 in France, and 1842 in England.[95] It is no coincidence that during the first three decades of Belgian independence liberals focused their legislative attention on secondary and higher education, both tailored to the propertied classes.[96] Only from the 1860s onward did progressive liberal pedagogues begin to champion better elementary education and compulsory schooling.[97]

The fin de siècle saw a decisive shift in public attitudes toward the edification of the working classes. The engine was the rise of mass politics in the wake of the School War. In 1893 census suffrage was abolished and the vote was extended to all male citizens aged twenty-five years and older. At the same time an emergent penny press reached larger reading audiences. The ever denser railway network transported more and more commuters all over the country. After 1895 an economic boom drove up industrial wages and almost simultaneously a vocal Belgian nationalist movement around Edmond Picard and Léon Hennebicq began to stir up patriotic fervor and whip up imperialist zeal for Leopold II's infamous adventure in the Congo.

All these developments seemed to call for a more active state, but in actuality the Catholic government outsourced many of its new tasks to private and local initiative. Social policy, for instance, was mainly handled by the pillars. In 1900 the so-called Ghent system took off.[98] Socialist and Christian labor representatives succeeded in having their unions recognized by the Ghent city council. From that moment on union unemployment payments were subsidized by the municipality. This proved to be a crucial step in the development of the principle of *liberté subsidiée* at the national level. The system of "subsidized freedom" involved parliament creating social and educational legislation but leaving the practical realization to the private sector, providing government funding for private initiatives that were state responsibilities elsewhere in Europe.[99] "This policy led to a unique Belgian situation," one historian concluded. "Services, which in most other countries were undertaken by the state, were carried out by private organizations with community funds."[100]

The government's hands-off attitude carried over into its nation-building policies, or rather the lack thereof. In the last quarter of the nineteenth century, local administrations and private organizations started to fill the void that the central state had left. Coinciding with the rise of consociationalism, Catholic and liberal civil society started a nationalist campaign to shield workers from the supposedly violent and nation-less ideology of socialism.[101] During elections, at school, in theaters, at public meetings, during royal visits, at nearly every juncture of their public lives, socialist workers were at some point—and despite the noninvolvement of the central government—confronted with nationalist images and messages. These are the subject of Part I.

PART I

# TRICKLE-DOWN NATIONALISM

*The Institutional Forces of Nation-Building*

*Chapter 2*

# VOTING THE NATION

October 14, 1894, saw the first mass elections for parliament in Belgian history: 1,370,687 men exercised their right to vote, most of them for the very first time. The system of plural male suffrage was stacked against the BWP: family heads over thirty-five years old, homeowners, and the high-school educated received one or two extra votes. All the same, the party beat the expectations of contemporary observers and conquered 28 House seats (out of a total of 152), all of them from electoral districts in Wallonia. The only Flemish-speaking socialist MP was the Ghent party leader Edouard Anseele, who was elected in the Walloon city of Liège. In the party's propaganda he was presented as proof that language and ethnicity did not matter to socialists. Jules Destrée, lawyer, man of letters, and leader of red Charleroi, predicted that before long Walloon socialists would be elected in Flanders "and then the fusion will be complete, the Belgian *patrie* will never have been stronger."[1] Later chroniclers and scholars have also interpreted Anseele's election as evidence of the draw of Belgian nationhood on socialists.[2]

Almost twenty years later, in 1912, Destrée's high hopes for more Belgian unity through elections had been dashed. After the umpteenth failure to break the Catholic parliamentary majority and to introduce one man, one vote, Destrée addressed a notorious and often-quoted open letter to King Albert I: "On the Separation of Flanders and Wallonia." One verbal whiplash of Destrée has become proverbial: "There are in Belgium Walloons and Flemings, there are no Belgians." Destrée believed that "the Walloons have been vanquished for the foreseeable future. They now put their faith in universal suffrage. It is not at all certain that universal suffrage will reward them. It is not at all certain that a leftist government would dare to free itself from the *flamingant* yoke."[3]

What had happened in the twenty years between the first mass elections and Destrée's letter to the king? This chapter tells the story of how universal suffrage, with its potential for civic nation-building, turned into a catalyst for ethnic discord in the BWP.

## A CIVIC OPPOSITIONAL PATRIOTISM

The Belgian constitution of 1831 had introduced census suffrage, granting the vote to about forty-six thousand well-heeled men in the highest direct tax bracket.[4] The replacement of this voting system by universal suffrage was the BWP's ultimate goal. From the outset a true cult of voting took hold of the party. On August 10, 1890, a national suffrage rally convened in the Brussels suburb of Sint-Gillis/Saint-Gilles. Thirty thousand supporters gathered in the local park and collectively took what became known as the Oath of Sint-Gillis/Saint-Gilles, vowing "to battle without rest or repose to the day when, by the establishment of general suffrage, the Belgian *peuple* will have really conquered a *patrie*."[5] An illustrated pamphlet distributed in the wake of the demonstration showed a long column of workers marching behind a red banner toward a man casting his ballot. The man was standing on an anvil, the symbol of industry, at the foot of which a lion, the symbol of Belgium, lay. The ballot would reconcile class and nation.

In anticipation of a suffrage extension and to pressure parliament, local party branches in Ghent, Antwerp, the Borinage region, and Brussels organized mock referenda in 1892 and 1893 with all the trimmings of actual elections. Not coincidentally the Ghent referendum was held on Sunday June 12, 1892, two days before the real elections for the Constituante, a parliament that was to rewrite the constitution and particularly its Article 47 regarding census suffrage.

According to reports in the Ghent party paper *Vooruit*, Ghent was aswarm with voters, galvanized by the party's trumpeters, clarion blowers, and drummers traversing the city. From eight o'clock in the morning people were singing socialist battle songs such as the "Suffrage March,"[6] a seven-stanza long repetition of rhetorical questions: "What can assuage the people's fate? Suffrage! When will the wage slave be honored? With Suffrage!"[7] As a reflection of workers' respect for the ritual of voting, they all wore "their Sunday's

**FIGURE 1** Pamphlet distributed by the BWP after the Oath of Sint-Gillis/Saint-Gilles on August 10, 1890. Institut Emile Vandervelde, Brussels.

best, calm, conscious of the momentous duty they were fulfilling."[8] Barbers were working overtime and women were fidgeting with their brothers', husbands', or fathers' collars and shirts. This, by the way, was the only reference to women in *Vooruit*'s extensive reporting. The apparently self-evident exclusion of women from the ballot box was a clear reflection of gender bias in the male-dominated BWP—even though the official party platform supported female suffrage.

At nine o'clock voting began at the forty-three polling stations set up across town in an array of party premises and socialist cafés.[9] The voting procedure closely mimicked the official process. In 1877 Belgium had been the first European country to introduce the secret vote in private polling booths.[10] Not only did the Ghent socialists strictly adhere to the secrecy of the vote, they were also very serious about other procedural requirements. The party had sent out individual notifications to all its members, which they had to present at the polling station to prevent voter fraud. People who showed up late, even by mere minutes, were turned away. "'We are strict about voting hours,' the president of [the] polling station answered. The latecomers complained, but it was too late."[11]

The grassroots turnout for this referendum was exceptionally high. As many as 21,446 adult men voted in favor of general suffrage, against 188 no votes and 85 invalid ones. The yes-votes represented about half of all would-be voters under a system of general suffrage for men aged twenty-one and older.[12] Similar socialist referenda, sometimes in cooperation with progressive liberal city councils, attracted equally large audiences across the country in 1893, demonstrating real grassroots enthusiasm for the vote. These mock referenda were in a sense better reflections of the rank and file's devotion to suffrage than the actual elections because voting was made compulsory after the abolition of the census system. People simply had to turn up regardless of their commitment or their party's prodding.

In April 1893 the BWP held the first of its three nationwide mass strikes for general suffrage—the others occurred in 1902 and 1913. The Belgians were the only European socialists, except for the Russians in 1905–1906, "to deploy the general strike to achieve a political goal."[13] This strategy came to define the unique revolutionary-reformist path of Belgian social-democracy: an eminently revolutionary tool, the mass strike, stood in the service of the ultimate reformist goal, general suffrage. The underlying idea was that "reforms [...] could be revolutionary" and lead to "substantial, far-reaching social change."[14]

During the general strike of 1893 police forces killed eleven workers in violent clashes with demonstrators. Under pressure of these insurrectionary events, a two-thirds parliamentary majority of Catholics and liberals changed the constitution and introduced general suffrage for all men aged twenty-five and older. With the support of progressive liberals, who—unnerved by the violence—turned their back on their previous commitment to universal suffrage, conservatives on both sides of the aisle succeeded in watering down the principle of one man, one vote.

The first elections based on plural male suffrage, in 1894, were a huge victory for the BWP. Reformist socialists across Europe looked admiringly at the party. Among Austrian social democrats "phrases like 'long live Belgium!' and 'speak Belgian' swiftly became socialist catchwords."[15] To leftwing socialists, however, the BWP's revolutionary-reformist strategy became a lightning rod for criticism. Rosa Luxemburg's initial enthusiasm for political mass strikes quickly subsided. She came to the conclusion that they diluted workers' revolutionary spirit and were a betrayal of Marx. Yet, unlike French and German reformists, Belgian socialists never severed their formal allegiance to the founding father.[16]

As for the government, it had no agenda of democratic nation-building backing the introduction of plural male suffrage. The state failed to use the unifying potential of national elections to promote an impartial sense of nationhood beyond the political divisions of the time. Nor did it infuse the ritual surrounding elections with an explicitly patriotic message. The extensive instructions to local administrations about the practical set-up of polling stations and voting booths remained silent about the symbolic staging of voting procedures. There were no directives about flying the national flag, exhibiting portraits of the royal family, wearing cockades in the national colors, or taking patriotic oaths. In short, the government abandoned the electoral process to the parties and their partisan interpretation of the nation.[17]

Of course, this need not have prevented the elections from providing a platform for nation-building. Just like reading the same national morning papers is a bonding mechanism in imagined communities,[18] voting is a symbolic enactment of the nation too: strangers collectively wait in line, enter the polling station, and cast their ballot knowing full well that the whole (adult male) nation is doing the exact same thing at the exact same time.[19] Even if socialists were hostile to the bourgeois regime and the other parties, competing in elections, participating in the political process, and gaining a stake in the country's administration made them susceptible to the call of civic nationalism.[20]

At the local elections of November 1895 the BWP gained governing majorities in the provincial executive councils of Hainaut and Liège and in seventy-nine Walloon municipalities, which basically represented the entirety of industrialized Wallonia.[21] The integrative pull of participating in local government quickly became apparent. In January 1896, for example, the newly elected socialist executive council of the industrial town of Monceau-sur-Sambre near Charleroi was inaugurated. Four thousand people in a town of barely eight thousand residents accompanied the socialist councilors on their way to their first session. The town hall was decorated with banners celebrating the socialist triumph and emblazoned with the French revolutionary motto and the Belgian national device: "Triomphe 17 novembre 1895; Liberté, Égalité, Fraternité; L'Union fait la force."[22] "United we stand strong" was also a socialist, syndicalist motto, but in this context it clearly carried a patriotic subtext meant to reassure the general public of the BWP's good intentions. To the local party paper, the acting mayor,[23] the socialist Joseph Robat, unequivocally expressed his reformist objectives: "The time of rioting and disturbances is over. From now on workers have legal weapons to pursue the realization of their hopes, [ . . . ] The socialist party [ . . . ] can only have at its head men dedicated to order and organization."[24] Such explicit reassurances were in part a response to the increasingly nationalist electoral propaganda of liberals and Catholics, who discredited the socialists as "Vaterlandsloze Gesellen," comrades without a homeland.[25]

The conciliatory, reformist currents in the party were further reinforced by the improvement of living conditions thanks to the economic growth of the Second Industrial Revolution. Increasingly after 1895, the upper party echelons became proponents of radical or oppositional patriotism. They began to profess a benevolent and civic form of socialist patriotism that stood in contrast to the pernicious bourgeois ethnic chauvinism. Concomitantly, they replaced the cosmopolitan ideal of One World Republic by a belief in strong nations as the prerequisite for true "inter-nationalism."[26] In the same breath, working-class pacifism gave way to an advocacy of general conscription as the safeguard of the nation (see Chapter 4), a virulent anti-imperialism to a "reformist colonialism," and republicanism to a growing affection for

Crown Prince Albert, the popular heir to the throne (see Chapter 5). Yet, the rise of this civic oppositional patriotism did not necessarily diminish the importance of ethnicity.

## ETHNICIZING THE VOTE

Plural suffrage had a polarizing effect on Belgian politics. It increasingly pitted industrial and large urban centers, which voted socialist or liberal, against rural and small-town regions, which elected Catholics. Within the BWP the lack of MPs from Flemish-speaking districts was increasingly interpreted as a sign of ethnic difference between Flemings and Walloons, even though large parts of the rural Walloon provinces of Luxembourg and Namur went for the Catholics and the industrialized enclaves in Flanders, most notably Ghent, voted socialist.

To de-escalate the electoral tensions and to regain their position in the larger cities, the Catholic government—in a global first—replaced the majority system by proportional representation in 1899. Instead of neutralizing ethnic tensions, this actually made ethnicity more relevant in the BWP. First, it turned "poor, poor Flanders" into a core element of the electoral propaganda of the Ghent federation.[27] To maximize the effect of proportional representation in socialist- or liberal-dominated cities, the Catholic government took to gerrymandering. The rural electoral district of Eeklo was added to Ghent. As a result, the Ghent socialists began an intensive outreach campaign in the countryside around the city, addressing the rural population as their "Brothers of poor Flanders."[28] *Vooruit* repeatedly summoned its supporters to save Flanders, often in semi-religious language: "The Ghent apostles have to follow the banks of the [rivers] Leie and Schelde to make the gospel of Progress heard everywhere. [...] Aye, men, a huge task is at hand and laurels are to be reaped. Flanders is in danger! Flanders will be saved!"[29] The assimilation of Christian images of redemption and salvation into a secular worldview was an important factor in attracting socialist support elsewhere in Europe as well.[30]

Besides the stress on "Poor Flanders," there was a second way proportional representation ethnicized relations within the BWP. The parliamentary elections of 1900 brought the grumbling dissatisfaction of Walloon socialists to a head. Although for the first time three socialists from Flemish-speaking districts were elected to the House of Representatives,[31] there was frustration in several Walloon federations. Proportional representation had resuscitated the liberal party. The intense Catholic-socialist polarization since the introduction of plural male suffrage had eaten away at the liberal representation in parliament. By 1899 there had been barely 12 liberals left against 112 Catholic and 28 socialist MPs. Proportional representation reshuffled the balance of power within the anticlerical opposition. By 1904 there were 93 Catholic, 42 liberal, and 29 socialist MPs. Both Catholic and socialist seats had shifted to the liberal party.

The modest socialist success in Flanders had not compensated for the BWP's losses in Wallonia. Proportional representation came at the expense of the absolute socialist majorities of Charleroi and the Borinage. After losing three of its six MPs, *Le Suffrage universel*, the Borinage party paper, complained that "the most enlightened part of Belgium is subjected to the domination of the fanatical and most ignorant part."[32] Behind the closed doors of the Ghent Central Committee, Anseele admitted that a "row between Walloons and Flemings" was brewing.[33] An important catalyst was the legislative attempts to expand the system of language laws. Until 1906 the existing linguistic legislation only applied to the Flemish-speaking provinces. From 1907 onward there were a number of unsuccessful attempts to promote individual bilingualism and to mandate the use of Flemish in Wallonia for mine engineers and labor judges. These bills exposed the language rift in the BWP. Most Walloon MPs voted against while the Flemish MPs were in favor, believing this would safeguard the rights of the 120,000 Flemish-speaking miners in Wallonia.[34]

After the introduction of proportional representation, every national election brought the same hope of ousting the Catholic government, the same frustration of falling short and the same recriminations against Flemish backwardness. Suffrage did not nationalize, but ethnicize socialists. The ballot of 1912 was the high point of this evolution. Although widely expected to break the Catholic majority, a socialist-liberal cartel failed. Three days after the election, on June 5, 1912, Emile Rousseau, former iron worker and director of the cooperative Le Progrès in La Louvière, warned the National Party Council. Across Wallonia, he declared, some twenty demonstrations had been held "against the fraud of the plural vote and also against the Flemings." He voiced what was on many Walloon delegates' minds: "Wallonia went to battle with enthusiasm; we had hoped that the Flemish part of the country would have done the same; we are disheartened." According to Rousseau, all workers knew full well that the Catholic government had survived "thanks to the votes of the Flemings. That is why they have had it with this domination; that is what explains the demonstrations with the French flag, calling for the annexation of the Walloon provinces to France."[35] These expressions of Francophilia were coupled to a surge of Walloon militancy. Two days after

Rousseau's diatribe, Arthur Bastien, the president of the Borinage federation, addressed seven thousand striking miners in the town of Jemappes. "You do not deserve," Bastien intoned, "to be deceived and cheated by the Flemings. There are two distinct races in Belgium, the Flemings and the Walloons. The fanatical Flemings who obey the pastoral staff of priests, and the generous and enthusiastic Walloons. Is it not sad that we, we Walloons, are the eternal victims of the ignorance of the Flemings?"[36]

Perturbed by the increasing language demands of the Flamingants, several Walloon socialists had been veering toward the Walloon movement since 1907. In July 1910, the socialists of the province of Hainaut decided to found an overarching provincial federation "to defend the Walloon interests and resist the Flamingant pretentions," as read the fourth article of their charter.[37] In the Borinage, the local party paper systematically disdained the Flemish language, "this overrated jargon." There was "only one language for all the Belgians: French."[38] Following the catastrophic national elections of 1912, the Borinage socialists even began to campaign for home rule, the so-called administrative separation, to free Wallonia from Flemish tutelage.

Although Wallingant socialists emphasized the incompatibility of the Flemish and Walloon "races," they were not anti-Belgian separatists. On the contrary, they were disappointed Belgian nationalists. Their view of Belgium as an essentially Gallic nation was challenged by the Flemish movement and by the democratization of suffrage which had empowered a mass of monolingual Flemish-speakers. They symbolically retreated to that part of the nation that still corresponded to their Latin image of Belgium, namely Wallonia, willfully ignoring the presence of tens of thousands of Flemish-speaking miners. The result was a sometimes paradoxical juxtaposition of a radically Walloon rhetoric centered on home rule and a Belgian patriotic discourse that presented Wallonia as the last resort against the Flamingant dividers of the country.

This confluence of ethnic Belgian nationalism, Francophilia, and Walloon militancy was superbly illustrated by the Borinage socialists in 1911. On the third Sunday of September—not coincidentally the original Independence Day of Belgium (see Chapter 3)—they inaugurated a monument to commemorate the Battle of Jemappes. In this Borinage village the revolutionary troops of France had defeated the Austrians on November 6, 1792. The memorial was a twenty-meter high obelisk, crowned by a crowing rooster that faced east toward Austria. All over Jemappes, French, Belgian, and red flags flew in honor of "liberty, for which so much Walloon blood and so much French blood has been spilled over the ages." At the foot of the monument, with eight thousand people in attendance despite the rain, two original, bullet-riddled Belgian flags of 1830 were unfurled. Five hundred pupils from the municipal school sang the Belgian national hymn the "Brabançonne" and the "Marseillaise," symbolically reconciling a Francophile "inter-nationalism" with Belgian patriotism.[39]

The climax of the Wallingant evolution of the Borinage socialists was the Walloon Day (*journée wallonne*) of 1913. On the occasion of a royal visit to Mons on September 7, representatives of the Walloon movement intended to present King Albert I with an extensive list of Walloon grievances. Local BWP members were urged to fly the Walloon flag (a red rooster on a yellow background), wear a *fleur de wallonie* in their buttonhole, and buy stamps with the Walloon rooster and the motto *Wallon toujours* (Walloon forever).[40] These trappings of Walloon nationhood were very recent creations that had been adopted earlier in the same year by a "Walloon Assembly" (*Assemblée wallonne*). In addition to a flag and a motto, they included a heraldic badge: the Gallic rooster, because the Latin homonym Gallus means both Gaul and rooster. As the national holiday, the third Sunday of September, Belgian Independence Day, was chosen. Although language had only played a subordinate role to the economic and religious causes of the Belgian revolution,[41] socialist Wallingants believed that "the Belgians rebelled in 1830 in French to combat flamingantism."[42]

On the day of the *journée wallonne*, the Borinage socialists adorned the Maison du Peuple of Mons with two gigantic red and Walloon flags.[43] They provided their supporters with printed cards to clip onto their caps bearing the slogan "Long live Universal Suffrage! Long live Wallonia!"[44] This symbolic juxtaposition of suffrage and ethnicity deftly encapsulates how voting, generally regarded as an instrument of civic nation-building, had turned into a vehicle of ethnic identification over the course of the fin de siècle.

Through this entire history one question looms large: How could the BWP maintain party unity in spite of the growing sense of ethnic discord? There were still plenty of unifying elements: the internal comradeship strengthened by the general hostility surrounding the party, the presence of an influential and conciliatory center group around Emile Vandervelde, and, ultimately, the centripetal pull of class and anticlericalism over language and ethnicity in a heavily pillarized society. But it is clear that given the right circumstances, language and ethnicity could become highly divisive, even in a social-democratic party.

*Chapter 3*

# NATIONALIST CELEBRATIONS AND MASS ENTERTAINMENT

Belgium has been facetiously called a country born from a second-rate opera. On the evening of August 25, 1830, the performance of *The Mute Girl of Portici* (*La Muette de Portici*) in the Théâtre de la Monnaie in Brussels went completely off the rails. This recent, successful opera by the French composer Daniel Auber told the story of the Naples fisherman Masaniello leading an uprising against the Spanish authorities in 1647. In the second act there is a rousing duet, "Mieux vaut mourir" (It is better to die). Young and bourgeois opera-goers were electrified by the chorus "Amour sacré de la patrie" (Sacred love of the homeland). They stormed out of the theater and vociferously voiced their opposition to the Dutch king William I. Street lamps were smashed, windows broken, and people assaulted. This bourgeois charivari was quickly overtaken by working-class food riots, plunder, and luddite actions.[1] After three days an armed civilian militia restored order. In other cities, concerned burghers also took control. The Belgians were rising.

King William I rejected the rebels' call to negotiate and dispatched his army instead. At the crack of dawn of September 23, some fourteen thousand royal troops marched into the barricaded capital. Four days later William's army had to retreat from its stronghold in the park of Brussels and left the city. On October 4, radicalized by William I's intransigence and the nearly one thousand casualties of the violence that had ensued, the rebels declared Belgium's independence.

In the nationalist commemoration cult that quickly followed, *The Mute Girl of Portici* and the so-called September Days were lionized. In a bizarre twist of history, Independence Day would never be held on October 4. From 1831 onward, it was celebrated on the third Sunday of September (and the following Monday and Tuesday) to commemorate the ousting of William I's troops from the park of Brussels. As fitted a hyperliberal state, only the celebrations in the capital were financed by the central government. The commemorative program in other parts of Belgium was rather limited.[2]

The appeal of the September Days fluctuated throughout the nineteenth century. After the European revolutions of 1848, the Belgian powers that be had a shrinking appetite for commemorating what was in essence a popular uprising. Instead of the September Days, they began to promote a less revolutionary date: July 21, the day Leopold I was sworn in as first king of the Belgians in 1831. The rising socialist menace of the 1870s and 1880s even resulted in an official boycott of the revolutionary September Days. Symptomatically, the jubilee for the fiftieth anniversary of Belgium's independence in 1880 was randomly celebrated in the middle of August. For ten years the completely arbitrary date of the third Sunday of August became Belgium's official Independence Day. When it failed to catch on, in 1890 the government instituted July 21 as the official national holiday, which it remains to this day.[3]

## APPROPRIATING THE BELGIAN REVOLUTION

Although the September Days had lost their official support after 1848, the veterans of 1830 continued to stage a low-key ceremony, a so-called pilgrimage, in Brussels. On the third Sunday of September they traditionally marched to the monument of the Belgian revolution on the Place des Martyrs, the square named after the fallen of 1830. In the 1880s the Brussels socialists began to appropriate this celebration. On September 23, 1888, they organized their own pilgrimage to Martyrs' Square.[4] To involve the rank and file, the party organ *Le Peuple* published a special issue dedicated to the Belgian Revolution. It opened with a full-page image contrasting the past of the barricades with the present of their legacy. An old and feeble veteran was juxtaposed to a well-fed and highly decorated bourgeois: "Those who have made the Revolution!" versus "Those who have profited from the Revolution!"

This image represented the theme of the "stolen revolution": workers had spilled their blood in September 1830 to fight Dutch despotism, but they had been excluded from the Belgian state. The fruits of a proletarian rising had

**FIGURE 2** Front page of *Le Peuple* on the 1888 commemoration of the 1830 Revolution. *Le Peuple*, September 23, 1888, p. 1.

been stolen.⁵ All over Europe socialists had myths of great historical victories that the working classes had been cheated out of by the bourgeoisie.⁶

The rank and file responded enthusiastically to the party's call to participate in the pilgrimage. At eleven in the morning the street in front of the Maison du Peuple, the headquarters of the Brussels socialists, was swarming with eight thousand people. Strikingly, the marchers did not fly their red flags nor did they sing the "Marseillaise." The party leadership had explicitly prohibited the display of overtly socialist symbols in order not to antagonize the general public.⁷ The upper party echelons wanted to shed their negative image as *des sans-patries*, or "revolutionaries without a homeland."⁸

The bourgeois press consistently accused the Brussels socialists of being financed by foreign agitators and acting against the national interest. These allegations jeopardized their outreach to the middle classes. By appropriating the Belgian revolution and the pilgrimage to Martyrs' Square they could claim respectability as the direct heirs of the founders of Belgium. Pointedly, *Le Peuple* called the veterans "*our* September wounded" and "*our* forefathers."⁹ At the same time, the allusions to the country's revolutionary origin kept the conservative bourgeoisie under pressure.

The "revolutionary-reformist" tactic of appealing to 1830 as both a *social* and a *national* revolution was common among French-speaking socialists (see also Chapter 7).¹⁰ On the third Sunday of September 1886, for instance, the Liège section of the BWP organized a suffrage rally that doubled as an 1830 commemoration.¹¹ At the foot of the monument for the Belgian revolution in the Sainte-Walburge cemetery the six thousand workers in attendance were reminded of "the dramatic history of the Belgian provinces."¹² The revolution of 1830 and the socialist struggle for rights and suffrage were seamlessly written into the national narrative as a direct continuation of the ancient Belgian struggle for liberty against foreign rulers. According to a police surveillance report, the last speaker even drew a direct line from the present to "the Eburones, Ambiorix and Caesar, [and] he notes that the masses [*les peuples*] have battled for freedom for centuries."¹³ Ambiorix was the legendary leader of the Gallic Eburones tribe that was vanquished by Caesar.

The late 1880s were the zenith of the socialist September commemorations. Bourgeois circles, alarmed by the rise of the BWP, started to reappropriate the pilgrimage to Martyrs' Square. From 1896 onward the Brussels municipal government, controlled by conservative liberals, made the September Days an integral part of its anti-socialist agenda (see the section on

Brussels' schools in Chapter 6).¹⁴ When the Brussels socialists organized their last pilgrimage in 1899 only fifteen hundred people attended in spite of the party's emphatic call to participate.¹⁵ By the beginning of the twentieth century the September Days had lost their appeal, while the royalist date of July 21 was gaining traction both within society at large and among the socialist rank and file in particular.

## RATIONALIZING THE JULY 21 CELEBRATIONS

Ever since the foundation of the BWP in 1885, the Brussels city authorities and the conservative liberal bourgeoisie that dominated city hall had tried to make the official Independence Day celebrations more inclusive to inoculate the masses against the red menace. For the benefit of the lower classes there were shooting competitions, bicycle and horse races, free performances of music and theater, folk games such as darts and sack races, and for the poorest sections of the public, food distributions. Brussels' numerous societies held processions and pageants with giants and historical floats, while all the houses along the way were instructed to fly the Belgian flag. At night the capital's monuments and central boulevards were illuminated in anticipation of the traditional apotheosis: fireworks. Obviously, many of these activities had an explicitly nationalist message, but there was no guarantee that workers interpreted them that way. When Charles Max, journalist of *Le Peuple*, asked a worker what the July 21 celebrations of 1891 commemorated, the man replied with a fine example of national indifference: "Tuesday we've celebrated the societies, Wednesday the military parade and Thursday evening the fireworks."¹⁶

Unlike the French socialists, who often turned *quatorze juillet* celebrations into a clamorous confrontation with political rivals, the BWP never disrupted the festivities. Because of the massive presence of the police on these occasions, the party, like the German SPD, shrank away from staging disturbances.¹⁷ In its early years, the BWP did denounce the official festivities as royalist, "banal or grotesque, meant to distract or numb the masses" and urged its supporters to stay away.¹⁸ Convinced militants did not need to be persuaded. In a letter to *Le Peuple* an anonymous party member from Liège called the festivities of August 1887 a "custom-made tralala," but he admitted that "the great mass of victims and pariahs" willingly participated.¹⁹

Despite the party's skepticism, huge crowds were usually present, attracted by the same *Theatralitik* that was central to the success of similar festivities in Germany and France.²⁰ In an ironic twist, the Brussels socialists were partly responsible for the huge attendance by consistently advertising the celebratory program in their newspapers.[21] Yet they used a number of strategies to downplay the popular appeal of the official festivities. A first option was to deny that there were any workers among the so-called loafers or bourgeois provincials who came to gape at the festivities.[22] This was a well-tested strategy of the German social democrats as well, who claimed that only *Bummler* (bums), *Nichtstuer* (good-for-nothings) and *Gaffer* (gawkers) turned out to watch the *militärischer Klimbim* (military nonsense).[23] Or, secondly, while conceding the presence of some workers, the party papers emphasized their "icy indifference."[24] If, however, there was no denying that workers had clearly been part of the general revelry, a third strategy consisted of representing them as victims of coercion or as paid spectators.[25] It is likely that these strategies were mere rationalizations. In Germany and France socialist party members knew full well that they were supposed to be hostile, or at least neutral, to militaristic and patriotic festivals, but they attended and participated nonetheless.[26] We can interpret this as an expression of what the German historian Alf Lüdtke calls *Eigen-Sinn*, a kind of obstinate behavior workers exhibited toward top-down norms, including those imposed by their own labor movement (see the introduction to Chapter 7).

In the final years of the nineteenth century it became clear that the electoral successes of the BWP did not diminish the popular appeal of July 21. The calls of the Brussels socialists to ignore the official celebrations became empty rhetoric and *Le Peuple* began to report positively on the festivities.[27] While the party shifted toward *oppositional patriotism*, a new rationalization for working-class participation entered the socialist lexicon. Life, it was argued, was so "monotonous and hard for those who labor" that workers understandably seized upon every opportunity to be entertained.[28] The new goal was to conquer July 21 for the proletariat. In 1904 *Le Peuple* deemed "*our* national celebrations" to be dull and colorless, but it looked forward to the future: "Far from being enemies of the festivities, the socialists want to extend them to everyone" because "we too [...] love the country where we live."[29]

## THE NATIONAL JUBILEE OF 1905

During the national jubilee of 1905, which commemorated the seventy-fifth anniversary of the Belgian Revolution, the BWP's shift toward oppositional patriotism became plainly clear. The government lavished three million Belgian francs on celebrations throughout the country. A tricolored fury took hold of all provincial cities. Aimé Bogaerts, the editor-in-chief of the Ghent party paper *Vooruit*, sighed: "Everywhere [tricolored] flags, pennants, balloons, lighting, wreaths, stakes, triumphal arches, greenery, flowers, drapes, inscriptions, etc. etc."[30] More than ever there were concerted efforts to engage the masses. The Brussels municipal council organized a pigeon racing contest, Belgium's most popular working-class pastime, and awarded 2,000 Belgian francs as the first prize, two times the annual salary of a Borinage miner.[31]

Confronted with this nationalist onslaught, the BWP's initial reaction was to refuse to participate. Ambiguity reigned, however. To prevent its supporters from accepting the social status quo and to maintain the image of the revolutionary masses, it was important to keep some distance from the jubilee. At the same time, the party did not want to endanger the power it had gradually acquired over twenty years. As a result of this difficult balancing act, it hemmed and hawed its way through the jubilee.

On June 22, 1904, the National Party Council met for the first time to debate the issue. The Liège MP Léon Troclet declared that "it will be difficult to go against the flow and that we should take part in the celebrations." Edouard Anseele, by contrast, already considered abstention to be "a very moderate position."[32] The council followed Anseele and published its official position in *Le Peuple* on July 14, 1904: the BWP wanted no part of a commemoration that symbolized the economic and moral subjugation of the workers. There were no republican, anticlerical, or internationalist arguments to be found in the text. It only referred to the absence of social and political rights and to the theme of the stolen revolution.[33] Most likely, this manifesto was a compromise between, on the one hand, the Ghent and Antwerp socialists, who wanted to tone down the anticlerical and republican rhetoric in their quest for the rural vote, but who did not mind a dash of radical internationalism and, on the other hand, a majority of French-speaking socialists, who wanted the opposite.

The Catholic and liberal criticism that erupted after the BWP made its official position public forced the French-speaking socialists on the defensive. In late December 1904 during the parliamentary discussion of the budget for the jubilee celebrations, Emile Vandervelde strongly denied that the socialists "do not love [their] country." "We love it as much as you do," he clarified to the Catholic and liberal MPs. The socialist abstention, Vandervelde added, was not inspired by hostility toward the *patrie*. Once universal suffrage was attained, the socialists would celebrate with abandon: "I wish that by the centenary in 1930 justice will be done. But we will not wait that long to celebrate a just and equal *patrie*."[34]

In early July 1905 the Brussels socialists decided that ordinary members and their children were free to attend the jubilee parade of the capital's municipal schools as a way to express their support of the public school system against the Catholic government.[35] A month later the Catholic journal *Courrier de Bruxelles* expressed its relief over the proletarian enthusiasm for the celebrations. Emile Vandervelde responded that the official party position was still noninvolvement, but individual workers could participate because they rarely had the opportunity to enjoy themselves. According to Vandervelde, the festivities entertained the workers "without diminishing in any way their socialist fervor."[36] *L'Avenir du Borinage* also believed that party members could attend "out of simple curiosity" as long as they did not accept the oppressive institutions behind the national celebrations.[37]

In the Flemish-speaking BWP branches of Ghent and Antwerp, the jubilee experience was different. The theme of the stolen revolution, for instance, was completely lacking. The Ghent socialists even denied that workers had had anything to do with 1830. When the city council voted on the public expenses for the local organization of the jubilee, Ferdinand Hardyns, the second in command after Anseele, declared that 1830 "was not and could not be the work of the laboring classes."[38] *Vooruit* and the Antwerp party paper *De Werker* dismissed "the 'historical stupidity' of 1830" as a useless clerical insurgency.[39] The many longer reflections on the revolution *Vooruit* and *De Werker* published in 1904–1905 were written by editor-in-chief Aimé Bogaerts and Steven Prenau, alias Boersen, an elementary school teacher and prolific *Vooruit* contributor.[40] Both men considered Belgium to be an artificial state created by diplomats and superimposed over "the different ethnic tribes [*volksstammen*] that flourished on Belgium's soil." The Belgian revolutionaries were a "bunch of good-for-nothings" and "foreign beasts."[41] Boersen and Bogaerts even expressed nostalgia about the Dutch rule and William I's policies. The Dutch government had dug canals, enlarged the port of Antwerp, founded the state university of Ghent, and governed the "Flemings" in their own language.[42] These views tapped into an older tradition of Pan-Netherlandic nationalism. The ideal of the Greater Netherlands (*Groot-Nederland* or the *Dietsche* nation) referred to a supposedly millennial cultural unity between Flanders and the Netherlands based on language and ethnicity. Anseele had embraced these notions ever since publishing his 1882 novel *The Revolution of 1830*.[43]

The Ghent socialists' opposition to the jubilee festivities was also steeped in the language of radical cosmopolitanism. At the end of July 1904 the socialist city councilors of Ghent announced their boycott of the jubilee celebrations. They were immediately called out by the conservative Catholic newspaper *Le Bien Public* as nation-less traitors. Ferdinand Hardyns reacted to this accusation, but unlike his French-speaking colleagues, he did not try to reconquer the badge of the good patriot. Instead he justified the socialist position with reference to the ideal of the "United States of Humanity."[44] The same radically internationalist line of argument was central to the official jubilee manifesto the Ghent Central Committee published on May 15, 1905:

> Considering that the fatherland is a narrow and outdated concept, contrary to our view as internationalists, world citizens; [. . .]
>
> Considering that [. . .] there is no reason whatsoever to prefer Belgium to our neighboring countries;
>
> That we as workers have the most backward regime of all industrial countries with a similar level of development [. . .]
>
> Considering that we would enjoy more rights, more education, more pay, more protection as Germans, Frenchmen, Englishmen, etc. than as Belgians;

for all these reasons the Central Committee decided that the workers would ignore the jubilee.[45] At the exact same time that their French-speaking comrades were slowly reneging on their vow not to participate, posters were put up throughout Ghent: "We do not celebrate! Workers, don't do it either."[46] Singularly straightforward and concrete rules were set down for party members: they were not allowed to decorate their houses nor to be present at any patriotic demonstration and that included their children.[47] At the height of the jubilee, in July 1905, the Ghent socialists even declared a large cotton strike. *Vooruit* called on its readers to support the strikers financially: "People from Ghent! Flemings! Honor your glorious past, which inspires support, brotherhood."[48] Clearly, while ignoring the Belgian past, the Ghent socialists did instrumentalize Flemish ethnicity.

## NATIONALISM AND MASS ENTERTAINMENT

The 1905 jubilee marked the apogee of the confluence of nationalism and mass consumption. The country was awash with black-yellow-red souvenirs and mass-produced knickknacks such as commemorative jubilee cups for schoolchildren.[49] A well-known Brussels department store offered all fourteen thousand students of the capital's municipal schools a brochure with the jubilee program, lavishly illustrated with national flags and containing ads for the store on every single page.⁵⁰

The commodification of nationalism reflected the rise of a Belgian mass consumption culture during the fin de siècle. Since 1895 the country's internal market had been expanding due to rising salaries, a precipitous drop in unemployment, the extension of the civil service apparatus, and the ongoing process of (sub)urbanization.⁵¹ Workers adopted a new pattern of spending that translated into better nutrition, more comfortable conveniences, and higher expenditures for leisure and clothing.⁵² In this climate of mass consumption, patriotism became an additional selling point and the Brussels BWP went along. The local party paper *Le Peuple* ran ads featuring the Belgian lion, the national flag, the national motto, and the Belgian coat of arms.⁵³ The most patriotic product it advertised were bikes used by the Belgian army: "Only buy bikes made in Belgium—BELGICA-PATRIA."⁵⁴

Brussels workers were also systematically exposed to nationalist mass entertainment. Historical pageants were "singularly successful" in working-class neighborhoods such as the Marolles in downtown Brussels.⁵⁵ They were meant to familiarize workers with the great moments of Belgian history ever since Julius Caesar.⁵⁶ The plays performed in the capital's folk theaters usually had a patriotic climax.⁵⁷ The play *Cocher! à la Renaissance !!* (Coachman! Take me to The Renaissance [theater]!!), for instance, premiered in April 1889 and enjoyed "enormous success." It ended with "the obligatory patriotic apotheosis: a *tableau vivant* evoking the attack on the Park in 1830 [by the troops of the Dutch king William I]."⁵⁸

In 1913 *Le Peuple* reported that the country was being flooded with patriotic films. One of these reenacted a series of episodes from the Belgian revolution. A journalist had attended a showing and had come away quite impressed by the audience's enthusiastic reactions. When the Dutch king rejected the demands of his Belgian subjects, "an irritated murmur rose from the audience"; when the performance of *La Muette de Portici* culminated in a revolutionary meeting, the moviegoers cheered; when the houses of pro-government journalists were torched, "there was crazy delight"; and then, finally, when the barricades against the Dutch were raised, "delirium took hold."⁵⁹

Possibly, the rank and file were influenced by nationalist advertising and patriotic plays, but some skepticism is warranted about a direct link between the commercialization of nationalism, mass entertainment, and the internalization of nationhood. The vicissitudes of the 1905 jubilee celebrations in the rural Flemish-speaking town of Zaventem, close to Brussels, are instructive. The town council had asked all the residents to participate in a celebratory parade. Many had accepted the invitation, but to the consternation of the town's elders only five of the fifty floats in the historic pageant were actually about the country's history. The rest were advertising vehicles for local craftsmen and shopkeepers who seized this unique opportunity to showcase their business.[60] Clearly, there was no guarantee that top-down attempts to stir up national passion had the intended effect. Merely attending Independence Day celebrations, watching nationalist plays, or consuming patriotic products, was not enough to turn workers into Belgians. But what if this propaganda was continually reinforced by other socializing institutions such as the army, the monarchy, and the schools? These are the subject of the next three chapters.

*Chapter 4*

# AN ANTI-MILITARISTIC STATE IN MILITARISTIC TIMES

"The king is satisfied." These were the apocryphal last words of Leopold II on signing personal conscription into law on his deathbed on December 14, 1909. The pen he used to sign the bill was inducted into the national pantheon of small appliances as it became one of the centerpieces of the newly minted Royal Museum of the Armed Forces and Military History in 1922.[1] Today it is still on display there. Leopold's closing act finally dragged the Belgian army into the twentieth century. At long last Belgium was no longer the only European country that relied on a lottery and on voluntary substitutes to fill its military ranks. It took another four years before general conscription for all men was introduced. In a word, the army was badly equipped to serve as school of the nation for most of the fin de siècle.

### THE POOR PEOPLE'S ARMY

For such a central institution in Belgian public life, there is surprisingly little academic research into the army and its impact on nation-building. This reflects the low status of military history in Belgian historiography. Most research has either painted a rather unproblematic picture of the army as a natural school of the nation or has singularly focused on the language issue in the military.[2] Only in the last few years have a number of younger scholars innovated the field.[3] This section builds on their work.

Any analysis of the Belgian army's social impact has to start with the strong anti-militaristic and civilian tradition of the country, which hinged on three traditions. First of all, there was the internationally mandated neutrality of Belgium underwritten by international treaties. The only aim of its military was to wage a defensive war and to safeguard the internal order.[4] Secondly, as a unitary, but noncentralizing state with a heavy liberal bourgeois imprint (see Chapter 1), the young nation displayed a certain distrust of a centralized military apparatus. This was most evident in the institution of the civic guard (*garde civique* or *burgerwacht*), a parallel, local, civilian and voluntary police force, which had the same constitutional mandate as the army: guarding Belgium's sovereignty and internal order. Finally, up until the First World War Catholic public opinion and the Catholic government were adamantly opposed to the barracks, a place of ungodly and liberal mores that drained the countryside of pious farm labor.

These interlocking traditions explain why the Belgian army did not modernize after the Franco-Prussian War. Before 1870 the Belgian military system was on a relative par with that of other European countries. Between 1870 and 1890, however, investment fell and innovation lagged.[5] In this period Belgium acquired its international image as an anti-militaristic state in militaristic times.[6] While France introduced efficient recruitment and well-trained citizen-soldiers after its trauma of 1870–1871, the Belgian army held on to the French losing formula. It remained in essence an eighteenth-century army: relatively small and manned by long-serving soldiers under an aristocratic officer corps.

During most of the fin de siècle Belgium had a standing army of 45,000 men, divided over forty-four garrison towns, and a wartime army of 120,000. This meant the enlistment of 13,300 men each year. At any given moment about a quarter of the male population between the ages of twenty and twenty-five was serving. In the European arms race the Belgian army was woefully understaffed. In 1909 its ratio of annual recruitment to total population was 1 soldier to 400 residents, as compared to 1 to 170 in France, and 1 to 241 in Germany. The wartime mobilization ratio was 1 to 41, against 1 to 7.8 in France, and 1 to 13 in Germany.[7]

Officially the Belgian military was a volunteer army, with a limited cadre of professional NCOs and officers, but in 1886 only 3 percent of soldiers were volunteers, against 85 percent conscripts and 12 percent substitutes.[8] Because there were obviously never enough volunteers, the French lottery system was used to fill the annual quota of soldiers. Each year, all eligible young men participated in a lottery, commonly referred to as the "blood tax" or the "blood law." Gathered at the local town hall, they came forward one by one to draw a number from a cylindrical box. Those who drew a high number were exempted, those with a low number were drafted. Whatever the outcome, the draw was an important *rite de passage* for young men, involving a whole set of rituals,[9] but strikingly none were tailored toward instilling a sense of nationhood in them. The authorities did not use the ceremony in this sense.

Complicating the draw and adding to a pervasive sense of injustice that belied the "school of the nation" ideal, was the system of substitution. Military service was not personal. Well-off draftees with a low draft number could pay a substitute to join the army in their place. In 1881 a substitute cost 2,700 Belgian gold francs, about 15,000 euros in today's money.[10] As a result, the lower classes were overrepresented among the recruits. They formed a "poor people's army," a proverbial phrase in popular songs, plays, and novels, in the penny press, and in the writings of concerned physicians and other observers.[11]

Army service deepened social inequalities. During the fin de siècle between 230 and 450 cases of desertion were tried every year before the military court of Antwerp, the only court for which we have detailed data.[12] A fifth of the soldiers involved claimed to have run off because their family had become destitute after losing a wage earner to the army.[13] This was hardly surprising given the low pay recruits received. In 1906 an infantryman barely made 0.29 francs a day while a worker in the poorly paying Ghent textile mills received 3.50 francs a day.[14] Add to this the bad housing conditions, the low quality of the food, the dominance of French as the command language, and the high incidence of alcoholism and venereal disease, and one can appreciate why military service was generally not seen as a civic duty, but as coolie labor. People were not proud of having served in the army. In pauper letters conscription was nearly always represented as a burden, hardly ever as source of honor.[15]

Well into the 1880s this bad reputation did not seem to bother the government, the general staff, or the upper classes. The army was merely for training soldiers, not for educating citizens, the consensus went.[16] The Spring Revolt of 1886 changed the mind of conservative liberals and of the officer class. Fearing socialist subversion in the army, they gradually accepted the idea of generalized military service and embraced a broader social mission for the army. In the 1890s a conservative liberal militaristic movement arose. Associations of former officers began to lobby for a stronger army and for the introduction of personal conscription. The movement was headed by Léon Chomé, a former lieutenant, teacher at the Royal Military Academy, and editor in chief of the magazine *La Belgique militaire*, and by Alphonse Legros, a former NCO who ran a café in Brussels named after the Congolese port of Matadi. The pub's name was not a coincidence, because at that time militarism, colonialism, and royalism fused in a rejuvenated form of Belgian bourgeois nationalism, epitomized by the Jeune Barreau, or Young Bar, a hypernationalist organization of lawyers (see Chapter 5).[17]

The new militaristic lobby did not see army service as mere military training. No, an 1892 brochure asserted that every recruit had to become "a useful man to the army *and a good citizen*" to boot.[18] Responding to this social pressure, the army introduced civic and moral education as integral parts of the soldierly experience in the 1890s. It was no longer enough to train *soldiers*; officers also had to educate *citizens* and true *Belgians*. Recruits were to be inspired with vivid accounts of Belgium's heroic military history which spanned over twenty centuries and they had to show respect for the national anthem and the national flag.[19]

By 1902 even the Catholic government adjusted its traditional anti-militaristic position. In order to avert the introduction of personal conscription and especially in response to the socialist campaign to end the "blood tax," it tried to popularize the notion of a volunteer army by improving the living conditions of the soldiers and by reducing the period of active military service, from twenty-eight months to twenty months in the infantry. Symbolically, the new army act of 1902 replaced the term conscript "indemnity" by soldierly "wage."[20]

The 1902 innovations did not attract more volunteers. In the end, it was the structural failure to meet recruitment targets, mounting international tensions, and shifting geopolitical alliances that convinced the government and Catholic public opinion of the need for military reorganization.[21] The draft lottery was finally abolished on December 14, 1909. Personal conscription became the law of the land, meaning that one son per family had to enlist in the army. Service time was reduced from twenty months to fifteen in the infantry and the annual contingent was raised from 13,300 to 20,000 men. Finally, in 1913 general conscription for all young men was introduced in the wake of the Agadir crisis (1911) and the Balkans War (1912–1913).

## THE ARMY'S IMPACT

The reevaluation of the army's social mission in the 1890s resulted in a whole array of prescriptive measures to inculcate recruits with a civic sense and patriotism, but these were often at odds with day-to-day practices. Company commanders and officers regularly complained about the lack of patriotism among the young men entrusted to them. In 1899 Lieutenant Deglimes wrote in his instruction manual that "a substantial number [of recruits] arrive at the barracks without ever having heard the word [patriotism]." Instilling a broader love of country in these young men was a challenge: "For us, Belgian officers, our task is more difficult than for our neighbors to the south and the east. We cannot draw, like the Germans, on the prestige of a recent glorious past, and unlike the French we do not have 'a part of the fatherland to recover.'" Deglimes was acutely aware of the limits of propaganda and compulsion: "One does not love because one is told: You must love!"[22] Captain J. Wodon concurred with Deglimes. In a 1901 brochure he compared the recruit to a caged bird: "He will acquiesce in his situation, eat and even sing, but he will always be ready to take advantage of any small opening to take flight and never to return."[23] To cope with military life many young recruits adopted strategies of *Eigen-Sinn*, a kind of stubborn self-reliance directed against bourgeois norms. In a reader letter to the conservative liberal paper *L'Indépendance belge* an anonymous officer complained in 1897 about soldiers' recalcitrance. Disobedience was hard to penalize, he wrote, because it was silent, passive, and underhanded: "[The recruit] does not refuse to obey outright, but he makes his officers repeat the orders, pretends to misinterpret them, procrastinates to execute them. [. . .] He skirts insubordination, knowing how far he can go without falling under the military penal code."[24] The pessimism among militarists persisted despite the massive PR campaign launched by the Ministry of War in 1910 in favor of military service, including a monthly illustrated glossy magazine, *La Vie militaire*, which was distributed gratis in cafés, hotels, and libraries.[25]

Obviously, the assertions of officers about the sorry state of patriotism among the recruits cannot be taken at face value. They served a clear political rationale, viz., pressuring the government into military reforms and larger expenditures on the army. But they need not have been a mere political ploy. The general public seemed to recognize the futility of bombarding soldiers with military propaganda. Popular comedies regularly derided the swollen patriotic language of officers. In one such play a hot-tempered colonel was soothed with "a small patriotic song." He broke down into whimpering patriotic platitudes: "patriotic, fatherland, always good [. . .] in the hearts of soldiers, good sentiments, bravura, always good, always good [. . .] Good, bravo, good, brravisimo, brrravissimus."[26] To which the audience reacted with howling laughter.

Regardless of its impact on recruits, the army may have been a nation-builder in society at large because of its visible and tangible presence in public life. As mentioned earlier, military units were spread across the country in forty-four garrison towns. They went on exercises, assisted the fire brigade, and participated in parades, musical festivals, shooting competitions, gymnastics exercises, and fencing demonstrations. Once a year they staged the great spectacle of the *grandes manoeuvres*, which was zealously followed by civilians.[27] Around the barracks a mutually beneficial local economy arose. The army and the soldiers were in continuous demand of clothing, foodstuffs, tobacco, alcohol, horses, building materials, fuel, and prostitutes. Bakeries, butchers, and laundries within the barracks employed local civilians. What's interesting about this forced symbiosis of soldiers and citizens is that some smaller cities were so dependent on the military economy that regardless of the political color of their administration they facilitated and embraced the army's presence. In the industrial Walloon city of Charleroi, this military-civilian interdependence seems even to have influenced the socialists (see the last section of this chapter).

The German historian Jakob Vogel has coined the term "folkloric militarism" to describe the lower-class acceptance and even celebration of such military-civilian coexistence.[28] In Britain, France, and Germany local veterans' organizations had sustained this phenomenon ever since the 1870s, but a similar tradition of folkloric militarism was lacking in Belgium prior to 1890. Even after that date the Belgian militaristic movement did not have the same clout as similar extra-parliamentary pressure groups like the Flottenverein in Germany and the National Service League in Britain. In 1901, 228 associations were claimed to be part of the National Federation of Veteran Societies, which had been founded by Chomé in December 1897. The organization boasted a cumulative, heavily inflated membership of 350,000, but its popular appeal seems to have been limited. For instance, none of the candidates the National Federation endorsed were actually elected in the parliamentary elections of 1898.[29] Its lack of broader social support was a function of its narrow, conservative liberal, breeding ground.

Against the background of the pillarization process in which Catholics and socialists had taken a firm lead, the militaristic movement failed to grow deeper social roots. This only changed once the military lottery was abolished at the end of 1909. From that moment on grassroots organizations became heavily invested in the militarization of Belgian society. Suddenly there was a wildfire of Catholic and even socialist shooting societies and gymnastic clubs to provide Belgian youth with pre-military instruction. In their quest to support their members "from the cradle to the grave," the introduction of personal (and later general) conscription gave pillar organizations a clear and vested interest in propping up Belgium's mass army. On March 6, 1910, the Association of Belgian Societies for Physical Exercise as a Preparation for Military Service was founded during a ceremony in the Brussels city hall. All three of the largest gymnastics federations—Catholic, socialist, and liberal—participated. Together these organizations had some 250,000 members.[30] They provided seventeen- to nineteen-year-olds with moral and civic education, and physical and military training, including lessons on personal hygiene, marching, map-reading, and shooting with Mauser rifles. When the young men successfully completed the sessions, they received a certificate that allowed them to choose their own regiment and even to shorten their active duty period. For the latter reason the older militaristic lobby looked warily upon these societies, suspecting them of not appealing to young people's better, patriotic angels, but to their baser, opportunistic instincts.[31] If those opportunists came from a socialist milieu, suspicions ran even higher. From its inception, the militaristic movement had a decidedly anti-socialist streak. In the words of its founder, Chomé, it was directed against "the whole pack of nationless people [sans-patries]."[32]

## FROM THE MILITARY STRIKE TO WILLING WAR PARTICIPATION

The anti-socialism of the militarists was matched by the anti-militarism of the socialists. Article 5 of the BWP's foundational charter of 1885 called for the abolition of the draw, of the substitution system, and eventually of all standing armies. The party also refused to support a defensive war if Belgium was attacked, even calling for a military strike if the war was not authorized by a popular referendum. This pacifist position was watered down in 1889 when the party adopted a unanimous resolution of the Second International and proposed its own alternative for the army: the "nation in arms." This originally French republican ideal had become topical in 1888 following the publication of the bestselling brochure *La Nation armée* by the Belgian progressive liberal Georges Lorand. The notion of the nation in arms implied abolishing the army and the barracks, and arming the people. It was meant to counteract the militarization of society and to reestablish civilian control over the armed forces. According to the Brussels socialist leader Jean Volders, it was an eminently national system that "conformed to the national traditions" "of our small country," namely the burgher militias of medieval Belgium.[33]

Although the principle of the nation in arms was radical, its adoption as official doctrine marked the start of the party's shift from pacifist anti-militarism to a pragmatic acceptance of the army as a central, inescapable pillar of Belgian society. As oppositional patriotism became the norm in the BWP in the late 1890s, attitudes toward the army and war participation shifted accordingly. The idea of the *nation armée* was gradually relinquished and replaced among party cadres by a realist advocacy of general conscription and of the improvement of living conditions in the army. A more equitable recruitment system would spread the military burden evenly across society. Although the party's realist turn mimicked the SPD's evolution,[34] the BWP did not refrain from targeting the army with anti-militaristic propaganda, a practice the German socialists had abandoned in their eagerness to avoid a new *Sozialistengesetz* and fear that it would undermine the army against tsarist Russia and revanchist France.[35]

The BWP's anti-militarism remained the most radical leg of its propaganda, but it was only paraded in very specific circumstances—for example, the Boer War[36]—and ritually relegated to its youth organization, the Socialist Young Guard. The SYG was allowed to rail against the army twice a year, once in February on the occasion of the yearly draw and once in September when the fresh recruits entered the army. The organization had been founded in the wake of the Spring Revolt of 1886. The government had given Lieutenant General Alfred Vandersmissen carte blanche to suppress the labor riots. He went about his task so ruthlessly that a report by the French police, who followed the events in Belgium with great interest, described him with a typical euphemism of the time as "more than energetic": "he is violent and rough; since his arrival the army shoots at the rioters without any hesitation."[37] As a result, twenty-four workers died. The BWP was so shaken by the events that at a national party congress secretly convened at Christmas 1886, but attended by several police informers, it officially resolved to infiltrate the army. When ordered to fire into the crowds, socialist sleeper agents would shoot their superiors instead.[38] This resolution remained a dead letter, but the congress was the start of a massive propaganda campaign against the military lottery, targeted at (potential) soldiers.

In the lead-up to the Christmas congress of 1886 a Draftee Circle, a so-called *Lotelingskring*, had been founded in Ghent, the first of a national network of socialist youth organizations. These would become known as the Socialist Young Guard, the party's anti-militaristic spearhead. The SYG gave its members—prospective and recently discharged recruits, but also their younger and female family members—a basic form of insurance against the draft and provided them with ideological instruction.[39]

The most important and visible activity of the SYG was protest meetings on the day of the draw. At that time the socialist newspapers appeared with a black mourning band across their front page and the red flags flew at half-mast at the local Maison du Peuple. In some towns the socialist city councilors gathered the conscripts to inform them about their working-class duties in the army. In other places SYG members made house calls or went to pubs frequented by conscripts. Singing socialist battle songs and waving the red flag, the SYG accompanied the young men to the public hall where the lottery took place. The highlight of the ceremony was the SYG ritual of declining to draw a number with the words: "I refuse to plunge my hand into this evil urn: down with wars, borders, armies: Long live universal peace."[40] This, in effect, was the symbolic negative of casting a ballot in the ballot box.

With radical anti-militarism safely sequestered in the niche of the SYG, the BWP gradually embraced the notion of a defensive war. This doctrine was crucial to the Belgian security system: the army had to hold off any foreign invasion until the international guarantors of Belgium's neutrality could come to the rescue. Successful resistance relied on the unremitting support of all Belgians, workers included, but initially many party cadres refused to commit to this defense strategy. As the BWP began its shift toward oppositional patriotism in the middle of the 1890s, some began to envisage a form of conditional support: if workers were granted complete political and social equality (one man, one vote) they would take up arms for Belgium. As time went by, the conditions for working-class participation in a defensive war were watered down. In 1903 Emile Vandervelde, the unofficial leader of the BWP, addressed the annual SYG congress with the words: "I reject the idea of leaving our country without defense to an invader: I refuse to substitute German autocracy for our regime of constitutional freedoms."[41] Ironically, Vandervelde justified his position by referring to Prussian militarism, while the German SPD's belief in a just war was grounded in its fear of Russian aggression.[42]

After the abolition of the military lottery at the end of 1909, it became abundantly clear that the party's anti-militaristic rhetoric had become mere verbalism. Symptomatically, the socialist gymnastics clubs joined their Catholic and liberal counterparts in the Association of Belgian Societies for Physical Exercise as a Preparation for Military Service. The national party congress of

1913 sealed the BWP's pro-military shift. With a large majority, the congress not only decreed that workers had to commit to their country's defense, it also deemed it "necessary to teach the duty to defend the national soil to all citizens from childhood on and to create institutions to prepare them from adolescence on."[43] Come 1914 the upper party echelons were completely convinced that Belgium—warts and all—was worth defending. But did the rank and file follow?

## THE GRASSROOTS RESONANCE OF SOCIALIST ANTI-MILITARISM

The Spring Revolt fanned the authorities' paranoia about a socialist fifth column in the military. By late 1886 nervousness about the reliability of recruits had spread across the government and the military's top brass. In November a confidential report of the Ministry of War advised "surveilling the new recruits arriving from Mons, Liège and especially from Charleroi. These young people are imbued with very advanced socialist ideas and have been worked by the leaders of the workers' party."[44] In May 1887 the infamous Lieutenant General Vandersmissen warned the minister of war that "recruits from the 10th line regiment, of the 1st, 2nd and 3rd chasseurs regiment, traveling on the train from Verviers to Brussels, sang the Marseillaise on arriving in Liège."[45] In an extreme case of micromanagement, the army banned its off-duty musicians from performing in bands that played the "Marseillaise," the French national anthem, but also the symbol of socialist internationalism.[46]

Because of the suspected unreliability of army recruits from industrial centers, 1886 was the last time soldiers were brought into direct contact with striking or protesting workers. From that moment on, the civic guard, the police, and the gendarmerie took over the army's frontline position. The eleven protesters killed in clashes with police forces during the general strike of April 1893 fell at the hands of the civic guard and the gendarmerie, not of the army. Nevertheless, the violent incidents renewed anxiety about socialist propaganda among soldiers. A month later Lieutenant General Joseph-Jacques Brassine, who had just become minister of war, wrote in a confidential report that "for the past two years the socialist circles have been trying to corrupt the young recruits before they enter service: they preach disobedience and seek to inculcate contempt for authority." According to Brassine, the effects were clearly visible in the class of 1892.[47]

Most disturbing to the army leadership was the discovery in February 1893 of a socialist circle, led by recruits from Ghent, in the barracks of the

Walloon town of Tournai. Nearly forty soldiers were provisionally held in military lock-up.[48] Eventually nine Ghent socialists were brought before the military court, demoted, and sentenced to eight days in prison and half a year in a correctional regiment. Seven of them received a reduction of sentence in June 1893.[49] The socialist press made so much noise about this incident that it was still publishing brochures about the scandal fifteen years later.[50]

Following the Tournai incident, the red scare increased. In December 1894, after the first elections on the basis of plural suffrage, the army commissioned a report about the infantry recruits from industrial centers. It concluded that out of seventeen regiments only four were not "swayed by the new ideas." The Second Chasseurs Regiment posed the greatest risk, because it had 275 soldiers from the Borinage and 197 from La Louvière, which, the report matter-of-factly stated, "was absolutely too many."[51]

The authorities were so concerned about the anti-militaristic propaganda that they brought the publishers and printers of the SYG periodicals and brochures, which were distributed by the tens of thousands to recruits, before the assize court of Brabant on five different occasions between 1889 and 1896. In each instance the accused were found guilty of "maliciously and publicly attacking the rule of law" and sentenced to two to six months in prison.[52]

Most historians have pointed to the common interests of the BWP and the army leadership in exaggerating the impact of anti-militaristic propaganda within the military. For both sides, emphasizing the red grip on the army was a way to frighten bourgeois audiences and extract concessions from a Catholic government unwilling to abolish the military lottery and the substitution system. In this sense the red scare was more myth than reality.[53] The same confidential report of the Ministry of War that expressed concern about the spread of socialism among recruits in November 1886, identified only four confirmed propagandists in the entire army.[54] In 1887 the sizeable Ghent SYG section had 135 members of whom 14 were actually in the army, while the annual contingent of young men from Ghent who were called up for the draw was 1,500.[55] Following the discovery of the "socialist conspiracy" in the barracks of Tournai in February 1893, the minister of war, Lieutenant General Brassine, ordered a nationwide inquiry to uncover secret socialist societies in the army. During this investigation, overseen by the local corps commanders, the lockers and personal belongings of all soldiers were ransacked in a search for suspect pamphlets and brochures. In the end only two soldiers were found to have attended socialist meetings.[56]

All in all, socialist activity in the army itself seems to have been rather limited. Despite its often fiery rhetoric, the SYG pragmatically recommended young soldiers keep a low profile, avoid punishment, and stay away from personal altercations with NCOs and officers.[57] After the commotion about the socialist conspiracy in the Tournai barracks, the SYG openly advised recruits against forming secret societies in the army because they were ineffective and dangerous.[58]

The socialist anti-militaristic propaganda did not lead to more subversion in the army, or at least there were hardly any convictions for socialist insubordination by the military court of Antwerp. Between 1886 and 1911, 16 percent of the cases initiated before the court involved insubordination.[59] In just three of these cases socialism—specifically republicanism—was the cause: shouting the socialist slogans "Long live the republic" and "Down with the cardboard king"—*Le roi carton* being Leopold II's moniker. The main reason behind insubordination was not political conviction, but rather banal and everyday tensions between officers, NCOs, and soldiers about menial cleaning tasks or violations of sartorial rules.[60] Desertion, a propaganda tool advocated by anarchists, was rejected by the SYG.[61] It was concrete pecuniary problems, homesickness, or bullying, not abstract anti-militarism and socialist propaganda, that made soldiers take flight rather than endure military service.[62]

The SYG tried to steer its active duty members away from directly confronting army norms, an attitude that was mirrored by the military leadership's intention to de-escalate potential conflicts with socialist recruits. There was an important PR dimension to this policy. The army wanted to avoid creating socialist martyrs who could be publically paraded by the BWP. That is why the three cases involving socialist insubordination did not lead to a conviction by the military court of Antwerp. All were sent back to the corps commander for some sort of disciplinary action. The usual punishment was relatively minor: eight days of lock-up in the local barracks.[63] It also explains why the authorities were less inclined to prosecute the SYG before the assize court after 1896. It had become clear by then that each trial gave more notoriety and prestige to the SYG and increased its membership.[64]

At its peak, the SYG probably had about seven thousand paying members, but it inflated the number to thirteen thousand to suggest an equivalence with the yearly contingent of conscripts. After 1910 the organization entered a period of contraction because its core propaganda issue had suddenly disappeared with the abolition of the military lottery.[65] Also depressing its recruitment numbers was the increasing competition with Catholic and liberal youth organizations that offered pre-military training. In 1913 the Brussels SYG section attributed its dire situation to "the attraction of bourgeois gymnastics clubs [...]. The Catholic party draws a large part of the working-class youth who eventually become members of yellow [i.e., Catholic] trade unions."[66]

Regardless of the actual membership numbers, only the SYG cadres seem to have been really invested in anti-militaristic radicalism. Throughout the entire fin de siècle complaints surfaced about the lack of enthusiasm among the SYG's rank and file.[67] The case of the industrial town of La Hestre, near La Louvière, is particularly instructive. As one of the largest SYG groups in the country, with about seven hundred official members in 1913 out of a total population of 4,291, its general meetings were attended by only about fifteen people. A local SYG leader bemoaned the absenteeism: "This evil is widespread, and the remedies that have been tried to this day have not been able to eradicate it."[68] In Haine-Saint-Pierre, near La Hestre, "many members simply pay their dues without ever attending the meetings."[69] Often the only effective working affiliates were the board members, which further qualifies the importance of the SYG's self-reported membership numbers.[70]

Due to this lack of internal cohesion, the SYG mission of providing ideological instruction to young impressionable people, the ultimate specter of the authorities, often turned out to be a futile endeavor. In 1903 the *Sower (De Zaaier)*, the periodical of the Flemish-speaking SYG, organized an essay competition on the question "What is socialism?" to improve the low educational level of "the vast majority of working-class readers."[71] The editorial board not only expressed its regret over the small number of entries it received, but also had to admit that the winning essay, submitted by the SYG secretary of the western border town of Menen/Menin, brimmed with "false ideas and untruths" that were in "so many young minds." The essay did not contain the words "property," "class," or "class struggle" even once.[72]

Unsurprisingly, the SYG's anti-militaristic propaganda did not necessarily sway the BWP's rank and file, especially in the years immediately preceding the First World War. At that moment many socialist organizations felt the increased pressure of militarism within Belgian society. Some drama groups, for instance, resolved the tension between pursuing socialist orthodoxy and staging financially viable, but militaristic plays in favor of the latter. In 1912 a controversy erupted in the *Bulletin of the National Federation of Socialist Drama Societies*. Ferdinand Mercier, a Walloon SYG leader, could no longer bear the fact "that most of our societies continue to stage plays that go completely against our principles and that glorify the bourgeoisie, the nobility, and militarism." "Completely dumbfounded," he had read an enthusiastic review of the play *Devant l'ennemi* (Facing the Enemy) staged by a socialist drama group. "Each line, every word was meant to evoke the nation as the highest ideal." To Mercier's dismay "the audience had wildly applauded the end of this play which ends in an atmosphere of bravery."[73]

Mercier did not identify the drama society in question, but the reactions to his contribution made clear that it was not an isolated case. Florian Wautelet, the secretary of the Regional Federation of Socialist Drama Societies of Charleroi, admitted that such "chauvinist plays" were in the repertoire list that was circulated by the National Library of Socialist Drama Societies.[74] Emile Hénin, a member of the SYG from Trazegnies, a small town in the industrial heartland between Charleroi and La Louvière, seconded Mercier's criticism but he saw three practical objections to programming more political plays. First, they were too abstruse and, as Hénin put it, the audience "not understanding them, pays no attention to the subject, and loses every interest in them." Second, the staging of political plays was relatively expensive, which was reflected in a higher entrance fee. "Now, the audience that has been fooled once, will not be fooled twice. It will completely desert the shows and the drama society will go bankrupt three quarters of the time." Finally, there was great competition between the different local drama societies.

> If the neutral circle plays stupid, silly and ridiculous dramas [. . .] with kidnapped lovers, adultery, etc., as the central theme and a crime or a suicide as the apotheosis, and the other, socialist circle stages a political play, which requires reflection and sustained attention [. . .] it will not take long for the evenings of the socialist circle to be deserted!

Hénin referred to the experience of the socialist drama groups of the deeply red towns of Couillet, Marcinelle, and Mont-sur-Marchienne in the suburbs of Charleroi, which had all been out-competed by liberal or Catholic drama circles—a consequence of intense pillarization. Hénin concluded that these difficulties were no excuse to stage dramas that ran directly counter to the principles of socialism. There were also popular plays that did *not* exalt militarism and capitalism.[75] Apparently, Hénin's was a minority view. In Wallonia political plays were consistently less popular with socialist theater groups than vaudevilles and melodramas. In 1912, for example, the lighter genre was favored two to one.[76]

Emile Hénin's singling out drama societies from the Charleroi region hints at the local variance in the popular appeal of militarism and its spell on the socialist rank and file. Throughout the entire fin de siècle the center of gravity of the SYG was located in the industrial province of Hainaut, and particularly in and around Charleroi, which in 1902 accounted for 56 of the 113 SYG groups. Flanders only accounted for 10 percent of the total SYG membership.[77] Yet there was no one-on-one correlation between high enrollment numbers and anti-militaristic fanaticism, as evidenced at one end of the spectrum by red Charleroi's embrace of local military life, and at the other end the forceful rejection of the army by socialists in Ghent and Antwerp.

The strength of the SYG groups of Charleroi was a reflection of the central place the barracks played in the city's life and their potential pull on a working-class audience. Outside of the SYG the relationship between the local socialists and the resident garrison was snug. At the close of the nineteenth century the local party paper, *Le Journal de Charleroi*, explicitly encouraged its readers to attend military festivals and reported on them in the most glowing terms. In August 1896, for instance, a large military celebration was staged in the Charleroi barracks. In the courtyard an enormous triumphal arch had been erected, decorated in the national colors. B.Y., the reporter of the newspaper, rhapsodized about the *tableaux vivants* representing crucial scenes from the Belgian past: "The 'Defense of the flag' [. . .] is a very successful tableau of soldiers, mounting the bayonet, surrounding the standard and protecting it against the enemy, while heavy artillery thunders."[78] For its praise *Le Journal de Charleroi* received a cordial letter of thanks from the local commander, which it duly published.[79] The paper regularly devoted space to events like this. On May 9, 1897, an enormous headline read: "Sixtieth anniversary of the artillery battalion," followed a day later by a rapturous review of the celebrations.[80]

It was situations such as these that inspired Edouard Anseele in 1900 to dissuade his Walloon comrades in the House of Representatives from their notions of Flemish backwardness. He declared that "Flanders does not love the army, in the Walloon country they respect it."[81] Indeed, in the barracks towns of Ghent and Antwerp socialist anti-militarism remained more critical and radical, steeped in notions of cosmopolitanism and anti-nationalism, even after the turn toward oppositional patriotism.[82] In Antwerp this attitude fed into a local tradition of protest against the central government's defense plans ever since the 1860s. The citadel of Antwerp and the belt of military fortifications around the city were the linchpin of Belgium's defense strategy. Yet they were an obstacle to the development of the city and its suburbs because strict zoning regulations prohibited the erection of civilian structures around the military forts. This precarious situation had given rise to a virulent anti-militaristic and Flamingant movement, called the Meeting Party, that permeated Antwerp's politics and its socialist movement alike.[83] The local BWP pilloried militarism as a curse on Flanders, rather than Belgium. In early February 1896 its paper, *The Worker*, ominously presaged the upcoming military lottery: "Within a few days, an infectious epidemic will again strike. A black plague will stalk *Flanders' flowering meadows*, to strangle with its nasty claws all that is youthful, vigorous, and full of hope, to tear off all those flowers of the future with a single swing of its deadly scythe. Within a few days is the Draw!"[84]

Unlike in Germany and France, the army did not function as a school of the nation in Belgium for most of the fin de siècle, but neither was the BWP's anti-militaristic propaganda effective beyond exploiting the obvious and widely shared resentment of the "blood tax." The speed with which attitudes changed after 1909 demonstrates that Belgian anti-militarism, including its socialist variant, did not oppose the army per se, but rather the inequitable system of the military lottery and the substitution. Socialist anti-militarism clearly instrumentalized the popular hostility to the "blood tax," tapping into young men's indignation about being drafted into the poor people's army. In this sense the BWP's anti-militarism was part of the Belgian mainstream. Consequently, it cannot be automatically interpreted as an obstacle to the spread of nationhood, although there clearly were differences at the local level and between Flemish- and French-speaking socialists. In sum, Laurence Cole's conclusion about the role of the military in imperial Austria also applies to Belgium: despite its integrative potential, "the army can be understood most effectively as a polarizing force, albeit one that worked unevenly across social and ethnic cleavages."[85]

*Chapter 5*

# THE ROYAL AND COLONIAL PARADOX

"If your Majesty would only send me a little money to help buy an elephant." A. M. Clarke, a seventeen-year-old American boy from Youngstown, Ohio, presented this unusual request to the Belgian king Leopold II in March 1903. Clarke made money by letting people ride an elephant he had bought with the inheritance of his parents. Breathlessly Clarke recounted: "I was beginning to become successful when one day a man ignorantly gave the elephant some tobacco the elephant in his rage killed the man." The police shot the animal and now Clarke expected Leopold II, presumably because of his interest in all things African, to help him buy a new one.[1] This is but one of the tens of thousands of citizen letters the royal family received since Belgium became an independent kingdom in 1830. Clarke's letter is exceptional as it is one of the few that came from abroad, but it evokes the two central themes of this chapter: the king and the Congo. And for those left wondering: no, Leopold II did not come up with a new elephant.

## WRITING TO THE ROYAL FAMILY

The monarchy was *the* keystone of bourgeois Belgian nationalism. In schools, in the nonsocialist press, and in other realms of public life ordinary people were taught to respect this venerable institution.[2] This chapter focuses on the interaction of the royal family with working-class people, the BWP and its rank and file, using among other sources citizen letters like A. M. Clarke's.

Personal letters were the most direct channel linking ordinary people to the monarchy. A rough estimate suggests that between 1865 and 1934, spanning Leopold II's and Albert I's reigns, the royal family received tens, if not hundreds, of thousands of citizen letters. Most were so-called *demandes de secours*, or "letters of request," that asked the king for money or help in kind.[3] Only a few dozen of these letters have been preserved, as yet uncatalogued in the Archives of the Royal Palace in Brussels.[4]

When a member of the royal family received a letter of request, the palace administration turned to the local authorities and the police to make sure it was bona fide. A file was compiled containing a detailed social profile of the requester with information on his or her sex, address, age, job, wage, family composition, and so on. Few of these files have survived though.

Based on a sample of sixty *demandes de secours* that have been preserved, we can establish that the authorship of roughly a third is unclear, about half were undoubtedly written by the requesters themselves, and about 15 percent by an intermediary.[5] Doctors, priests, local dignitaries, or public writers could prod people to turn to the royal family for help, even writing on their behalf and in their name.[6]

A content analysis of thirty surviving letters of request addressed to Leopold II from the period 1880 to 1904 sheds light on the resonance of the king's image among his subjects. People who turned to Leopold II hardly ever appealed to the traditional qualities of the good sovereign—justice, wisdom, and power—nor to his kindness and generosity.[7] The image of the king as father of the nation was generally absent from the letters.[8] The idea of Leopold II as a caring, even metaphorical, father probably seemed too far-fetched given his rambunctious lifestyle and the rumors of debauchery, prostitution, and pedophilia swirling around him. It is no coincidence that Leopold II was the favorite target of many caricaturists, while the press published almost no caricatures of his successor Albert, who was seen as a model family man.[9]

Strikingly, only middle-class supplicants embellished their letters with their moral or patriotic credentials. They would write things like "My father fought in the Belgian Revolution," "I have served in the army," or "I have written a patriotic hymn."[10] Such arguments, explicitly playing to bourgeois expectations, were generally absent in lower-class letters. Perhaps ordinary people had insufficient command of what the anthropologist James C. Scott has called the "public transcript" or "the official discourse of deference" that lower-class people were supposed to harness in contacts with their betters (see Chapter 8).[11] The most extreme case of tone-deafness toward the public transcript involved a young lower-class man from Fleurus near Charleroi. In 1892 he requested to borrow one of the king's uniforms for a carnival procession. Three weeks after his first letter he sent an impatient reminder insisting on the urgency of his request, which again was duly ignored.[12]

Although this young man approached Leopold II as an equal, this was emphatically not the image the king projected. It has often been argued that the success of the modern monarchy hinges on its ability to appear at the same time as extraordinary and commonplace: the king is at once "one of us" and "beyond us."[13] Leopold II was definitely not one of us. All his portraits and pictures show a dour man in uniform or official attire, while the relatable Crown Prince Albert posed in leisurewear or in a collier outfit when visiting coal mines. The image of Leopold II was of a sovereign high above his subjects. Not coincidentally, the king's personal secretary called the money that letter writers received "alms" (*aumônes*).[14] This term reflects an older hierarchical vision of the relationship between monarchs and their subjects, which was hard to reconcile with Belgium's increasingly democratic outlook and, of course, its large socialist movement that preached republicanism.

It is impossible to identify the ideological or party affiliation of the letter writers, but there is one palace inventory, of letters addressed to Prince Albert as heir apparent between 1891 and 1909, that offers some clues. It is the only surviving inventory that contains more extended information about the letter writers.[15] A sample from the year 1908, when Albert received a record 1,328 requests, shows that a mere 1.5 percent of the requesters were *not* awarded some kind of help. The large majority, some 1,230, received 5 or 10 Belgian francs (at a time when a Borinage miner earned 4.13 francs a day), the remainder an amount between 15 and 350 francs. The total sum Prince Albert dispensed on this kind of charity in 1908 was 15,994.5 francs—about 94,000 euros in today's money, a substantial sum that highlights the importance of the custom.

There was an almost perfect gender balance among Albert's letter writers, but a large regional disparity obtained. Sixty-six percent of the letters came from Wallonia, about 26 percent from the Brussels *agglomération*, and only 8 percent from the rest of Flanders. This might have been due to the higher illiteracy rates in rural, Flemish-speaking areas, and the widespread belief that French was the only suitable language for addressing the royal family. Proletarians were clearly overrepresented. Ninety-two percent of the 546 persons that I was able to categorize on the basis of information contained within the inventory had a lower-class background. Forty percent of all letters of request to Prince Albert came from one of the four Walloon mining and steel districts of Liège, the Centre, Charleroi, or the Borinage. Of these, 85 to 99 percent were from industrial workers or miners.

This blue-collar overrepresentation might hint at a potential reservoir of royalist sentiments among the socialist rank and file. It is safe to say that the conditions for fulfilling this potential were largely lacking during Leopold II's reign because of his personal unpopularity. Although the king always donated money when calamity struck and mines were hit by firedamp explosions,[16] socialists were underwhelmed by his acts of charity. In the winter of 1885–1886 the Brussels party paper *Le Peuple* groused that Leopold II had gifted "half a loaf of bread, of inferior quality, and 50 cents" to a number of Brussels' poor, which cost him all of 22 Belgian francs. The paper cynically noted that his charity was going to ruin him.[17]

Despite the general dislike of Leopold II, royal charity and the attendant propaganda of bourgeois newspapers touting the king's philanthropy were not necessarily ineffective. Alfred Defuisseaux, the socialist leader of the Borinage, admitted in his *Grand Catechism of the People* (*Grand catéchisme du Peuple*, 1886) that people cried out "Vive le Roi!" instinctively when they saw the king because they were impressed by the pomp and circumstance of the royal entourage.[18] The public staging of the monarchy may not have increased Leopold's personal popularity, but it may have contributed to the banalization of the institution of the monarchy. Workers may have challenged Leopold II, but they did not question the existence of kingship as such. The monarchy was a banal element of reality to them.[19] Strikingly, workers from red strongholds and even socialist militants continued to ask Leopold II to intervene on their behalf in social conflicts or in court cases, despite muscular statements of party cadres that "we must never ask the king for mercy."[20] Shortly after the suppression of the Spring Revolt of 1886, for instance, striking miners in Charleroi petitioned the king to increase their wages.[21] *Vooruit* cynically commented: "It is like confessing your sins to the devil!"[22] Evidently, some workers in the BWP's target audience still saw the king as the ultimate figure of authority.

There was clearly a tension between the often boisterous socialist protests against the unpopular Leopold II and the tacit acquiescence in the monarchy as part of a status quo that was hard to change. This paradox was fittingly expressed in a report by the Brussels police from the year 1879. Belgian workers, it read, displayed a "strongly rooted, unequivocal hostility" toward the king and the royal family, but they were not about to put their feelings into action. "They would not want to see them struck by the hand of regicide, but they would not complain if they disappeared [. . .]: this is the more or less veiled image of public sentiment in the lower classes."[23] This police agent aptly sketched the royal paradox of the socialists: the deep hostility toward Leopold II went hand in glove with an indifference toward causing him actual harm or ending the institution of the monarchy. As the nineteenth century drew to a close and the BWP started its turn toward oppositional patriotism, the original republicanism of the party turned into hollow phraseology and regicide became a complete taboo.[24] The rising star of Crown Prince Albert played an important part in this shift.

## THE ATTRACTION OF ALBERT

Leopold II was largely unbothered by issues of personal popularity, but Crown Prince Albert was not. He and his entourage were acutely aware of his public image. In 1908 Albert's secretary admonished his staff to ignore letters of request written by a certain Father L'Heureux because "he asks for money in the name of different people, but he doesn't let them know whom it comes from."[25] The priest in question dispensed poor relief from the palace without acknowledging its source. The princely gifts were not supposed to be nameless; people were to know that Albert was being kind to them. His wife Elisabeth's "anonymous" charity had a similar aim. In 1908 the newspapers enthused over an incognito visit Elisabeth made to a bedridden working-class mother in Brussels. The princess went there on foot, accompanied by two staff members, carrying meat, wine, bed linen, and diapers for the baby. The woman in question, the papers reported, was overcome by "so much goodness and simplicity." Although the princess left without "her visit having been noticed in the neighborhood," the papers, even the socialist ones, were full of it.[26]

Ever since Albert's marriage to Elisabeth of Bavaria in 1900, his staff actively promoted the couple's private role as loving parents and decent human beings, to complement their public image as heirs to the throne. As part of a larger European shift toward the modernization and personalization of the monarchy, citizens were prompted to see royals, in the words of Linda Colley, "as unique and as typical, as ritually splendid and remorselessly prosaic, as glorious and *gemütlich* both."[27] The last entailed a closer, more personal contact with their subjects.

When the princely couple's first child, the future Leopold III, was born on November 3, 1901, citizens who sent a letter of congratulation received a personal postcard of Albert and Elisabeth holding hands over the baby's cradle. The captions read: "Gathered round the cradle of little Prince Leopold" and "An intimate scene in Prince Albert's palace." Baby Leopold had great PR value. The minister of the interior advised mayors to give municipal teachers and students the day off in honor of the new prince.[28]

Albert's entourage was well aware of the impact of his actions on public opinion. In 1901 Albert personally intervened to have the convicted anarchist Victor Willems released earlier. Victor Godefroid, the prince's secretary, wanted the minister of justice to speed up the process because "the generous intervention of their Royal Highnesses in favor of Willems, in whom public opinion continues to see nothing but a confused man, has been much praised." For the sake of Prince Albert's PR, Leopold II had had to swallow his pride and his utter aversion to the Left. "I must confess, however," Godefroid drily noted, "that the King only signed the partial grace of Willems with *répugnance*."[29]

A central pillar of Albert's carefully crafted image was his neutrality: unlike his uncle Leopold, he rose above the ideological and political divisions of the time. In April 1902 rumors circulated that Albert would head a battalion of grenadiers to suppress the BWP's general strike. The prince's staff was aghast, but it was quickly reassured when *Le Peuple* opined: "This is mere fantasy. The heir to the throne observes an absolute reserve in our political conflicts."[30] Albert realized full well that riding into the general strike would be political suicide, although the king, tone-deaf to the changing times, had instructed him to fulfill his duty as an officer.[31]

Prince Albert and his staff worked tirelessly to thaw the icy relationship between the court and the BWP. His entourage kept him very well informed of what *Le Peuple* wrote about the monarchy.[32] His visit on June 1, 1899, to the stand of Vooruit at the Industry Fair of Ghent was an important moment in the rapprochement. When Albert expressed his appreciation for the work of Anseele, the Ghent party leaders were so proud that the bourgeois press pilloried them for their "complete *embourgeoisement*."[33] Even in the Borinage, with its republican tradition reaching back to the dissident Parti socialiste républicain (see Chapter 7), things were changing. "A good grade for Prince Albert," the local party paper headlined when he donated five thousand Belgian francs for the treatment of TB patients on the occasion of his marriage.[34]

**FIGURE 3** Postcard sent to citizens who congratulated Prince Albert and Princess Elisabeth on the birth of their first son, Leopold, in 1901. Royal Palace Archives, Cabinet Leopold II, Commandements du Roi, G 84/20.

Socialist city councils in the Borinage even gave the municipal schools the day off to celebrate Prince Leopold's birth in 1901.[35]

Especially after the failed general strike of 1902, which caused a short-term boost of radical republicanism within the BWP, Albert aimed his message explicitly at workers and socialists. Barely three months after the turbulent strike, he asked the Ghent socialists to receive him in the premises of Vooruit, "your grand institution." Albert's letter, which was published extensively in *Vooruit* and *Le Peuple*, explicitly referred to his apolitical image: "One day I will be called upon to be king of all the Belgians and I want to know all my people, not by hearsay, but by personal experience."[36] In the radicalized post-strike climate, the Ghent socialists snubbed Albert, but this did not deter the crown prince from continuing his charm offensive, visiting factories and coal mines all over the country. In the summer of 1902 he descended incognito into a coal pit in the Borinage. The provincial governor had drafted a program that reconciled the prince's safety with the requirements of public relations. The prince and his retinue were to arrive at the mine Les Produits in the village of Flénu at four o'clock, "so that, although the workers had not been warned of our arrival, they would be assembled, and the prince would be able to see them." The manager was to be informed several months (!) in advance to ensure that all the machinery was "in a perfect state of security." "Thus organized," the governor wrote, "this visit right to the center of this socialist region would not be dangerous [. . .]. By contrast it would have resonance and would have a good effect."[37] Visits such as this explain press photos of Albert in a miner's outfit, posing among the colliers.

In 1904 Albert even granted a flag subsidy to a socialist-leaning mutual aid society for postmen from La Louvière. The association, La Postale, was politically neutral, but according to the Belgian Postal Service "the dominant view of the region being socialist, it is likely that it is also that of most members." The postal administration advised the prince to comply with the subsidy request. This would offer a counterbalance to socialism, "an antidote in the vicinity of the poison."[38] Although Albert only gave subsidies for the purchase of a flag to associations of which he was the honorary president, he made an exception for La Postale,[39] undoubtedly to curry favor among socialists.

Once Albert acceded to the throne in late December 1909, the last republican vestiges of the BWP program were quietly dropped. The socialist leadership saw to it that the party's actions could not be interpreted as attacks on the popular new king. When Albert's first address to parliament on November

König Albert (Mitte) im schlichten Gewande des Grubenarbeiters. So lernte der König den Betrieb und die schwere Arbeit der Bergleute in den ▫ ▫ Steinkohlengruben von Charleroy aus eigener Anschauung kennen. ▫ ▫

**FIGURE 4** King Albert visiting a mine in Charleroi. *Welt und Haus*, January 8, 1908, pp. 11–13. Royal Palace Archives, Secretariat of Albert and Elisabeth, 78.1549.

8, 1910, was interrupted by some socialist MPs shouting "Long live general suffrage!," Emile Vandervelde immediately reassured the king: "We are not angry at you, but at the government of fraud and plural suffrage."[40]

Especially after rumors began to circulate that Albert was no fan of the Catholic government and that he was maneuvering behind the scenes for social reform, a complete reconciliation of the BWP with the monarchy was almost inevitable. On July 10, 1911, Albert received an enthusiastic welcome in the socialist stronghold of Charleroi. Two days earlier the unpopular Catholic government of Frans Schollaert had fallen. Rumor had it that the king was behind the defenestration. All local BWP representatives took part in the king's "joyous entry" in Charleroi.[41] More than a thousand workers from the deeply red Charleroi suburb of Gilly had even volunteered to draw the royal carriage.[42] The local party paper, *Le Journal de Charleroi*, no longer saw any contradiction between the monarchy and socialism. As long as the people assented to it, Albert was "the legal representative of the will of the nation."[43] Whether socialists liked it or not, the monarchy had become a self-evident part of the status quo, a notion continually reproduced in public life by all sorts of royalist propaganda. Yet, as the following chapters will make clear, this did not necessarily translate into an undisputed acceptance of Belgian nationhood.

## LEOPOLD II'S SOCIAL IMPERIALISM

From monarchy to colony is but a small step. In 1885 King Leopold II succeeded in carving out a huge colony for himself in Central Africa, taking advantage of the rivalries between Great Britain, France, Portugal, and Germany. The king's search for a colony ran counter to the ambitions of the political and economic elites of Belgium at the time. For one, there was the issue of Belgian neutrality, which could become severely compromised by the king's pursuit of lucrative business opportunities in Africa.

Belgium had no official stake in the newly created Congo Free State, except that both shared the same head of state. Initially Leopold's personal fiefdom in the Congo was in dire financial straits, but things changed drastically after 1895. Ivory trade, but especially the collection of wild rubber, turned out to be hugely profitable. Leopold amassed an enormous fortune, which he partly used for grand urbanist projects in Brussels and his favorite seaside resort of Ostend. Following the international outcry about the inhumane and excessively cruel rubber harvesting methods, Leopold reluctantly renounced his colony. In 1908 the Belgian state officially took over the Congo (the so-called *reprise*), but only after the First World War did Belgian investments begin to pour into the country, turning the colony into one of the world's largest primary commodity producers.

The Congo was not just the personal initiative of Leopold II; imperialism was critical to the king's doctrine of governance.[44] In spite of his personal unpopularity, he believed in a populist monarchy as a top-down corrective to parliamentary democracy. In this he followed Bismarck's lead. In a seminal article from 1970, the German historian Hans-Ulrich Wehler argued that Bismarck's imperial projects were meant to legitimize autocratic rule in a period of rapid social change, "delaying emancipation at home by means of expansion abroad."[45] In other words, colonialism stood in the service of the conservative nation at the expense of democracy. Leopold II saw imperialism as an instrument to unify the Belgian nation, bridge the divides of religion, class, and language, and tame the socialist hordes.

In France and Great Britain imperialism undergirded an agenda of nation-building, but whether colonialist policies were actually successful in turning peasants into patriots is a matter of controversy. Opinions range from the maximalist interpretation that colonial propaganda formed willing imperialists and enthusiastic patriots, and the minimalist view that ordinary people were oblivious to it.[46] In the Belgian case it is clear that a state-driven imperialist agenda did not come about quickly. The colonial project was so entangled with Leopold II's personality and his social imperialism that, at least initially, people of all political stripes found fault with it. Catholics abhorred the king's championing of personal conscription, liberals his autocratic leanings, and socialists his blatant anti-socialism. All were concerned about the financial and diplomatic implications of the colonial adventure.

In the early years of the Congo Free State, the only social milieus receptive to Leopold's imperialism were career servicemen and the Catholic high clergy. The colony was conquered, governed, and managed by detached officers and NCOs from the Belgian army and by Catholic missionaries. These groups were small. In 1886 there were fewer than fifty Belgians in the Congo.[47] In 1908, at the moment the Belgian state took over the Congo, 1,713 Belgians resided in the colony, accounting for slightly more than half of the entire white population.[48] Not even the Belgian *haute finance* was particularly involved. Private investment remained limited before the First World War because "essentially, the exploitation of ivory and rubber created a predatory economy relying on guns instead of guineas."[49]

The year 1895 was pivotal in the propagation of imperialism in Belgium. In that year Leopold II contracted a new private loan for his Congo endeavor. Because this potentially jeopardized the repayment of a previous loan to the Belgian state, the Catholic government planned to take over the colony immediately. A brochure war between supporters and opponents of the colony ensued. Although the government had to abandon its plans, the imperialists had been able to present their case to a wider audience for the first time.[50]

In the following years the imperialist lobby grew steadily and organized several large colonial exhibitions. The Brussels World's Fair of 1897 featured live dioramas with 270 Congolese people in three "traditional" villages in Tervuren, on the site of the later Congo museum. Reportedly, 1,200,000 people visited the fairgrounds.[51] In 1905 the seventy-fifth anniversary of Belgium coincided with the twentieth anniversary of the founding of the Congo Free State. During the national jubilee festivities in Brussels, the Congo was presented to the Belgians as their own colony. In ceremonies, the flag of the Free State was artfully assimilated into the Belgian tricolored flag, the brand new Congolese hymn "Vers l'avenir," also called the "hymn of Belgian expansion," was sung alongside the "Brabançonne." One of the six large floats in the historical parade celebrating Belgium since 1830 was dedicated to the conquest of the Congo.[52] At the World's Fairs of Brussels (1910) and Ghent (1913) the general public was further familiarized with the colony.[53]

The colonial propaganda spilled over into the classroom. The elementary schools of Brussels had been repeatedly instructed to celebrate the "imperialist mission" ever since the publication of the renewed, patriotic curriculum of 1896 (see Chapter 6).[54] From the capital's schools the imperialist message trickled down. From 1905 onward the Congo became a compulsory part of the elementary school curriculum all over Belgium.[55] The elementary teachers of the Tournai region in the province of Hainaut were asked the following question for their pedagogical refresher course in 1907: "To what extent and in what way can the teaching of French [but also geography, history, geometry and agriculture] contribute to the success of the expansionist work?" For grades 3 and 4, they had to prepare a talk about "which products from all over the world a working-class household consumes."[56] Clearly, by 1907 the imperialist message had been tailored for a working-class audience.

The undeniable scale and range of colonial propaganda in the early twentieth century does not in itself prove it had an impact on ordinary Belgians. According to the Belgian historian Vincent Viaene, "it would go too far to say that there was a popular imperial culture in Belgium, as has been argued for Britain and France."[57] For one thing, the colonial lobby reached a much smaller audience than its opponents. Around 1900 the collective circulation of the pro-colonial Belgian press, about a dozen separate titles, was around forty thousand. This number is not insignificant, but it is dwarfed by the sales figures of the anti-colonial press, including the progressive liberal journal *La Réforme* (75,000), *Le Peuple* (70,000), and *Vooruit* (20,000). Revealingly, the colonial fervor of the 1905 jubilee was limited to the capital. At celebrations in the provinces, the Congo was markedly absent.[58]

The most immediate result of the propaganda campaign, Viaene claims, was not so much winning over the Belgian populace, but instead creating a quasi-unanimity within the political and economic establishment about the necessity of a Belgian imperialism and the takeover of the Congo. At a time of high social tensions, the imperialist mission united the army, the clergy, the officialdom, the captains of industry, and the *haute bourgeoisie* around the monarchy.[59] Yet, large swathes of the population remained worried about or even hostile to the *reprise*. Foremost among their concerns were the military and financial implications of having a colony. Who would pay for the development of the Congo? What in case of a Congolese revolt? Would Belgian conscripts, who were already the victim of an unfair "blood tax," have to save the day? All these questions plagued the BWP.

## SOCIALISTS VERSUS "CONGO WORSHIPPERS"

When trying to convert workers, the so-called *Congolâtres* ("Congo worshippers") started from a disadvantage because their propaganda was latently if not openly anti-socialist. In an 1898 brochure the Catholic colonial publicist Alphonse de Haulleville called the Congo "the safety valve for the social machine" at a time when "powerful vapors" were threatening "to make everything explode"[60]—a not so veiled reference to revolutionary socialism. The imperialists' plan was to divert unemployed workers toward Africa before they became disgruntled and joined the BWP, but the Congo never functioned as a Belgian population colony.

The Congo was not really central to the BWP's concerns. The party only paid close attention when Leopold II's colonial activities spilled over into Belgian politics. This happened in 1890 when the state extended a loan of 25 million francs to the Congo Free State; in 1895 when Leopold contracted a new private loan; and in 1908 when the actual *reprise* took place. Before 1895 the BWP's position was one of total rejection. The "Congo" was shorthand for everything that was wrong with the kingdom of Belgium. The word "Congo" itself was close to being a swearword. At suffrage rallies workers carried banners with the inscription "Que Cobourg aille au Congo" (the Coburger [i.e., Leopold II] should go to the Congo).[61]

The radical anti-colonialism of the early years was justified on the ideological ground that imperialism was capitalist exploitation, with the humanitarian argument that the treatment of the indigenous population was inhumane, and with the pragmatic concern that the costs of colonization and the danger to Belgium's neutral status were too high. This latter argument in particular was translated into national, sometimes patriotic language. In July 1890, for instance, Jean Volders called the state loan to Leopold "a dangerous operation for the nation's future" and a capitalist conspiracy "to abase the national dignity."[62]

After 1895 the shift toward oppositional patriotism heralded a new attitude vis-à-vis the Congo. The opponents were still a majority, but like all European social-democratic parties,[63] the BWP fragmented in a leftist bloc of principled anti-imperialists; a faction of pragmatic dissenters who objected to the costs of a takeover; a center group that supported Edouard Bernstein's revisionist colonialism in favor of civilization but was against the excesses of the capitalist exploitation methods; and a right wing that supported imperialism in the name of national greatness.[64] First and foremost among the last were Edmond Picard and Léon Hennebicq, whom Emile Vandervelde irreverently christened the champions of a "lilliputian imperialism."[65] They were the front men of the Jeune Barreau, or Young Bar, a society of hypernationalist lawyers.[66] Picard, a member of the *haute bourgeoisie*, had defected to the BWP from the progressive Liberal Party in 1894.[67] Although a socialist senator, he remained an eccentric and stubborn outsider in the party. His exceedingly nationalist, pro-imperialist, and anti-Semitic views marginalized him. He would leave the party in 1908. Picard linked his ethnic ideas about a millennial "Belgian soul," the so-called *âme belge*, to the country's imperial mission in the Congo. Incidentally, he had gotten the inspiration for his theory of the Belgian soul on the long homeward-bound leg of his journey to the Congo in 1896.

On November 28, 1907, Leopold II signed the Act of Cession, handing over his colony to the Belgian parliament. Immediately, the BWP turned the *reprise* into the central issue of the elections of May 1908. The entire campaign was a clear measure of the party's oppositional patriotism: while rejecting the idea of a colony, party leaders embraced Belgian nationhood. The day after the first round of voting *Le Peuple* published the tellingly entitled manifesto "For our class! For our country!" It ended with the battle cry "Stand up, stand up for the liberation of the proletariat and the deliverance of Belgium."[68] Working-class and national interests had completely merged.

The elections turned into a defeat for the Catholic, pro-colonial government. Its majority in the House of Representatives fell from twelve to eight seats, while the BWP gained four. The takeover of the Congo went along anyhow, despite the unanimous negative vote of the socialist House members on October 18, 1908. Their stand was largely symbolic and marked the end of an era. Emile Vandervelde, the unofficial party leader, had skipped the vote because he had become a pragmatic supporter of the *reprise* as the only way to end the excesses of the inhumane Leopoldian system.[69] His brand of reformist colonialism became the majority view of the party's leaders post-1908. This shift, which had been years in the making, was the result of the BWP's gradual embrace of oppositional patriotism; the imperialist propaganda that had flooded the country ever since 1895; and the death of the deeply unpopular Leopold II in 1909.

"The working classes have radically voted against colonization," the Walloon socialist MP Georges Hubin emphatically declared after the national elections of 1908.[70] But had they? The attitude of grassroots socialists was more complex than that. It was most probably determined by a colonial paradox, something akin to their "royal paradox." They rejected Leopold's rapacious exploitation of the Congo, but at the same time accepted the self-evident status of Belgium as a colonial power (see also Chapter 8). The pro-Congo propaganda did not turn workers into unthinking colonialists, but it did normalize the idea of a colony with its attendant ideology of racial superiority, European civilization, and African barbarism. An "eager Belgian imperialism" would only become possible after the First World War. It took the lionization of Albert I as the king-soldier to restore the image of Leopold II and his colony. Only then could "a lively Belgian patriotism" merge with "a true 'colonial spirit' in the Belgian population."[71]

*Chapter 6*

# SCHOOLING THE NATION

In 1880 Antoine Mertens, a twenty-year-old deaf-mute shoemaker from the Walloon textile city of Verviers, near the German border, sent a tribute to the king. It was a handwritten historical drama entitled "Heroic Dedication—The 600 Franchimontois. Unpublished work decided [sic] to His Majesty Léopld II [sic]."[1] In thirty-seven handwritten pages, Mertens retold one of the classic episodes in Belgian national history: the death of six hundred men from the town of Franchimont at the hands of the Burgundian duke Charles the Bold in 1468. The spelling errors, the unorthodox French, the particular use of punctuation and the often naive wording and grammar of the play suggest that it was Mertens' own initiative and that he was not egged on by some patron. This document provides singular insight into the historical notions working-class pupils took away from school. By Mertens' own account his patriotism had been kindled during his school days at the Royal Institute for Deaf-Mutes and the Blind in Liège. Born around 1860, Mertens had attended the institute until August 1873.[2]

According to the provincial governor of Liège, whom the royal palace asked for more information, Mertens' financial situation was "decidedly precarious." He had to support his mother, his sister was a day laborer, and due to his handicap he had less business than his colleagues.[3] From the Verviers poor relief office he received a meager four Belgian francs a month.[4] The palace thanked Mertens by giving him the not inconsiderable sum of fifty francs, three-quarters of the monthly wage of a Borinage miner, but the secretary of the king did not hide his scorn for the literary quality of the piece: "This work denotes in the author some imagination and historical knowledge, but it is far below the mediocre as far as literary merit goes."[5] What concerns me here is Mertens' "historical knowledge." In four acts he outlined the familiar story of the six hundred soldiers from Franchimont who had attacked the camp of Charles the Bold on the night of October 29, 1468, in an attempt to break the latter's siege of the city of Liège. The Franchimontois were vanquished, but their defeat became one of the central historical myths of Belgian nationalism.[6]

Mertens was a devout and patriotic man. In an accompanying letter to the king he expressed the hope "that our motto will always be *L'union fait la force*, God, King and *Patrie*, and that progress marches with religion and Belgian patriotism." He also admitted to have been inspired by his uncle, a veteran of the Belgian Revolution, who had captured a flag of the Dutch army in the Liège suburb of Rocourt "with five bullets in his chest."[7] This colorful description already gives a hint about Mertens' very masculine and martial interpretation of patriotism and the quirky way in which ordinary people borrowed bourgeois nationalist tropes.

Mertens' play offers us a rare look at grassroots notions of history and the way they were transmitted through school and appropriated and adapted in later life. Even though he was very religious and royalist, which makes him an unlikely supporter of socialism, I will analyze his play in depth because of its uniqueness as a source. Before turning to Mertens and the question of how patriotic schooling worked, or did not work, in practice, the first section sketches the contours of the Belgian educational system, its patriotic intent, and the socialists' reaction to it.

## A PEDAGOGY OF PATRIOTISM

The Belgian constitution of 1830 recognized freedom of education. Joined to the principle of municipal autonomy this created a highly decentralized schooling system that left a great deal of room for private, Catholic initiative. In the 1870s, progressive liberals made plans for an improved and inclusive form of mass education, an effort culminating in the liberal Education Act of 1879, which started the School War. The act's aim was to loosen the Catholic grip on education, establish central control over schools, and limit municipal autonomy and private initiative. In short, it was an attempt to turn Belgian schools into "schools of the nation," but it was immediately repealed after the Catholics regained power in 1884. From that moment on, educational policy was again left to private Catholic or local municipal initiative.

As a result, there was a dual system of elementary schooling during the fin de siècle. On the one hand, there were public schools financed by the state and, on the other hand, so-called free schools, most of which were Catholic and funded by the church.[8] The public option was in the hands of the municipalities. Town councils could found their own schools or adopt a free school, which then became public. In practice this meant that in rural areas and in small towns the public, often adopted, school was controlled by Catholics, while in the larger urbanized and industrial centers liberals and later on socialists managed the public system. In 1907, 43 percent of all elementary pupils in Belgium attended a Catholic, free or adopted, school, and 57 percent a municipal school.[9] There was, however, an important regional imbalance. In the Brussels *agglomération* and in the provinces of Liège and Hainaut, the public network was dominant; in all other provinces, the free, Catholic option.[10]

From the late 1870s onward, the municipal school system was expanded in liberal-controlled cities such as Ghent and Brussels in an effort to reach the lowest classes of society. Because the public network reached the majority of working-class children in industrial and urban centers, my analysis concentrates on these municipal, blue-collar schools.

Although Catholics and liberals did not see eye to eye on education, they basically agreed on the need to teach pupils to love their country, certainly after the foundation of the BWP, the Spring Revolt of 1886, and the extension of voting rights in 1893.[11] Unsurprisingly, the most obvious subject to forge "good patriots" was history,[12] but with a maximum of only two hours per week in the four upper grades, it was important to integrate patriotism in all courses. "There is no subject on the curriculum that cannot contribute to national education,"[13] the liberal education journal *The Future* (*De Toekomst*) professed in 1884. Pedagogues devised patriotic programs for subjects as diverse as natural sciences, geography, spelling, drawing, and music.[14]

A medium many educational professionals had high expectations of consisted of so-called maxims. Before the Second World War, Belgian teachers were advised to conclude every lesson with a moral drawn from the course material. Often, those maxims were patriotic in nature:

*L'union fait la force.*
All people of good will love their homeland.
Defending the fatherland is a duty for all.
We must be able to sacrifice our life for our country.[15]

These so-called *éphémérides du jour*, noteworthy sayings of the day, were supposed to adorn the blackboard all day long and had to be discussed by the children.[16] Exemplary pupils received "badges of honor (the glories of Belgium)," small illustrated cards depicting major episodes and heroes from Belgian history.[17]

The public schools of Brussels were ground zero for the patriotic wave that swept over the country in the closing years of the nineteenth century. In 1896 the Brussels liberal alderman of education, Léon Lepage, who held this crucial post from 1895 to his death in 1909, launched a multipronged program to inspire municipal pupils with an all-consuming love of country. With service orders Lepage encouraged the teachers in the Brussels municipal network to instill "a veritable cult" of the nation into their pupils.[18] To this end he organized a competition for a textbook of moral and civic education. The result was the hyperpatriotic *Practical Guide to Moral and Civic Teaching in Elementary Schools* (1896). This manual stipulated, among other things, that students owed respect to the heroes of the nation and had to worship the national flag, "a sacred relic that we must love and defend." Teachers were advised to recount "with passion" the countless "acts of heroism to prevent the flag from being captured by the enemy" and to put more emphasis on the Belgian revolution in their classes.[19]

Several instructors and school principals responded enthusiastically to Lepage's call and sent their superiors blueprints for a comprehensive patriotic education.[20] The director of City School No. 4, which was almost exclusively attended by "working-class children," presented his views at a pedagogical conference in 1898. He proudly reported that he was present during almost all history classes in the fifth and sixth grades and that he often intervened: "When I feel that the notions of patriotism which the history classes necessarily imply have not been taught with sufficient passion and conviction, I myself resummarize the lesson and I try to give it the [patriotic] character which it should never lack."[21] The extensive curriculum reform of the Brussels's elementary city schools in 1909 continued in the same patriotic vein.[22]

Lepage also harnessed the patriotic potential of the monarchy, the flag, the anthem, and the Belgian revolution. In 1896 he organized a series of official ceremonies attended by Crown Prince Albert, at which all city schools were officially handed a national flag and the pupils received a miniature copy.[23] In the same year Lepage started the new tradition of an annual September pilgrimage of schoolchildren to the Place des Martyrs.[24] Some teachers even raised money among their pupils to lay a laurel wreath at the 1830 monument on Martyrs' Square.[25] From 1900 onward there was a special matinee performance for the public schools of the opera *La Muette de Portici*, which had ignited the Belgian revolution. According to the bourgeois press, all children invariably rose to their feet during the aria "Amour sacré de la patrie," singing along at the top of their voices and frenetically waving tricolored flags and ribbons.[26]

Lepage was especially enamored with the patriotic potential of singing and vocal education, which he considered of "enormous influence."[27] In 1896 he mandated the teaching of the "Brabançonne" in all the municipal schools of Brussels.[28] He also commissioned a new, updated version of the national anthem by Regulus Elime, explicitly intended for school use, which railed against the socialist "word-mongers without a country" (*rhéteurs sans patrie*).[29] On Lepage's initiative, a series of *Singing Anthologies for School and Workshop* were published from 1900 onward which contained an inevitable section of "patriotic songs."[30] Similar songbooks had been in use in public schools all over the country ever since music became a mandatory elementary course in 1878.[31]

A final medium educational professionals revered as a way to mold children's patriotism consisted of school excursions. These had become common in Belgium's elementary schools since 1876.[32] In Brussels, municipal pupils regularly went to the Royal Palace; the Congress Column, which commemorated the writing of the constitution by the National Congress in 1830–1831; city hall; the city archives; the various museums of Brussels; parliament; Martyrs' Square; and the statue of founding father Charles Rogier.[33] An 1897 circular letter enjoined teachers to "use these visits to develop in them [i.e., the pupils] love of their country and love of their city," linking the local to the national.[34] Excursions to the many world exhibitions organized in Belgium during the fin de siècle and the end-of-year trips by train to every corner of the country had the same purpose.[35] Poor pupils could participate in these excursions as liberal and socialist city councils subsidized them.[36]

It is clear that public schooling, especially in Brussels, had a patriotic, sometimes even anti-socialist intent. In theory the BWP promoted national indifference in the schools. The battle against chauvinism was one of the classic resolutions approved by socialist student and teacher associations, usually accompanied by a call to teachers "to develop in the child, not patriotic feelings, but the nobler and greater sentiments of humankind and of universal brotherhood."[37] In practice, however, the BWP settled for banal nationalism. At no point did the party take practical steps to change the existing educational norms and practices that reproduced the self-evident belief in the existence of separate nations.

Socialist city councilors and aldermen were mainly concerned with very tangible school problems: soup delivery, heating, teachers' wages, the appointment of principals, and so on.[38] The content of the classes was of no interest to them as long as it was not blatantly clerical or anti-socialist.[39] The policy concerning school manuals of the Association for Socialist Municipal Councilors is illustrative in this respect. In 1898 the organization compiled a list of recommended manuals and in 1900 of prize books to be awarded to pupils at the end of the school year.[40] Both lists contained titles that reproduced national prejudice, projected the Belgian tradition of freedom back into the distant past, praised Belgian industrial ingenuity, and championed imperialist policies.[41] Only books with a confessional bias were excluded from the lists. In practice, the BWP even outsourced its schoolbook policy, recommending its municipal councilors turn to the liberal Ligue de l'Enseignement (Education League) when selecting school manuals and prize books.[42]

Significantly, wherever socialists became responsible for municipal schools, they did little to counter the nationalist subtext of education. In the Borinage, red city councils simply went along with the existing patriotic practices in schools, merely choosing to overlay them with a veneer of internationalism. In Cuesmes, where a homogeneous socialist council had been elected in 1895, the children of the public schools got the day off on May 1, but also on the national holiday of July 21 and on November 15, the day of Leopold II's patron saint. Because decisions about school holidays were the exclusive realm of the municipal administration, socialists could have simply abolished these days off, but they did not.[43] In the Borinage they even seized on school events to profile themselves as bona fide patriots. In Frameries, where the BWP held an absolute majority, a new public girls' school was inaugurated on August 2, 1908. The entire town council and all the pupils of the municipal schools marched in a parade. The day's climax was a rendition by the local socialist Fanfare ouvrière l'Avenir (Workers' Fanfare Band "The Future") of the overture of the nation's birth opera *The Mute Girl of Portici*.⁴⁴ In August 1912 the school pageant of Pâturages, which the local BWP paper fully owned as "our parade and [. . .] our pupils," was headed by two large Belgian flags and the Belgian coat of arms.⁴⁵ Remarkably, the deep disappointment of the lost parliamentary elections of June 1912 had not given rise to any manifestations of national indifference in the end-of-year ceremonies of the Borinage's municipal schools.

The Ghent socialists did not counter the proliferation of national stereotypes via the schools either, not even after 1909, when they entered the municipal administration and became responsible for public education. The socialist school leagues, which united parents, pupils, graduates, and teachers, still mounted the same traditional apotheosis in the school parades they had been co-organizing since 1907: an It's a Small World–like rendering of global diversity with children dressed up in a dizzying array of nationalities: as Americans, Austrians, Brazilians, Canadians, Chinese, Congolese, Danes, Dutchmen, Englishmen, Frenchmen, Germans, Italians, Japanese, Norwegians, Persians, Russians, Scotsmen, Spaniards, Swedes, and Switzers. The stereotypical depiction of Dutchmen with clogs and Persians with their namesake rugs was a clear expression of banal nationalism, reinforcing the notion of a world logically divided into "natural" homelands.⁴⁶ The rank-and-file's sense of their own nationality, however, was not unilaterally or unambiguously determined by school propaganda, as the next section demonstrates.

## TEACHING PATRIOTISM IN PRACTICE

Scholars investigating Belgian history have often assumed too straightforward a relationship between pedagogical norms, classroom practices, and the internalization of book knowledge.⁴⁷ Yet, there was often no direct line from pedagogue, to teacher, to pupil.

To begin with, before the introduction of compulsory education in 1914 not all Belgian children attended school. In 1897, 80.5 percent of all school-aged children went to an elementary school. Thirteen years later, this had risen to 92.5 percent.⁴⁸ These raw numbers mask a less rosy reality. For one, they reflect the situation on December 31 of each year and mask drop-out and absentee rates. Peasant and working-class children were more likely to attend school during winter time, while staying home in spring and summer.⁴⁹ In 1905 only 22 percent of all children attended elementary school for the full duration of six years from ages six to twelve.⁵⁰ Overcrowded classrooms hampered teaching: in 1882 there were on average fifty-eight elementary pupils per classroom, as compared to fifty-three in England, forty-three in France, and forty in the Netherlands.⁵¹ These averages hid huge outliers in working-class schools. In Hornu in the Borinage there were an average of eighty to a hundred children in first grade classrooms in 1907. One parent complained: "My child has been attending school for three years and hasn't learned anything or almost anything."⁵²

The effectiveness of elementary schooling was questionable, to say the least, especially in the domain of history, the subject par excellence to form patriots. Very revealing is the testimony of Jozef De Graeve, a seventeen-year-old office worker at the People's Press, the cooperative printing firm of the Ghent socialists, who would become a senator in 1932. In 1908 he gave a glimpse of the sterile history education in Ghent's municipal schools:

> Karel stands in front of the classroom . . . to recite his history lesson [. . .]: Philip the Good governed from . . . to . . . His accession to the throne, etc. etc. His wars against the Belgian communes, (a desperate list of facts and dates ensues!) His institutions . . . (Here the disastrous reciter gets confused).⁵³

And pupils did indeed get confused. In Brussels, many were left behind because French was the sole language of education in the municipal elementary schools, although a majority of working-class children spoke Flemish exclusively at the start of their school career.⁵⁴ The result was nothing less than dramatic: 68 percent of elementary graduates were unable to read or write properly in 1898.⁵⁵ What these children retained from the history course did not meet pedagogues' expectations. Alexis Sluys, a well-known Brussels pedagogue and director of the municipal Teachers' Training College, complained in 1897 that "the history of Belgium is simply not known by a majority of the students." He had taken a disconcerting sample in some schools. To the question "Who is the king of Belgium?" he had received "this mind-boggling answer" in City School No. 7: "Napoleon, Sir!" After repeatedly insisting on receiving a better answer, finally a pupil said in a mix of Flemish and French: "De Koning is Leopold deux, roi des Belges, Mijnheer! [The King is Leopold II, King of the Belgians, Sir!]." Betraying his bourgeois bias, Sluys went on to say: "In the defense of the teachers of City School No. 7 it must be noted that it is frequented by a population that is inferior from all points of view." When he asked the pupils about the Belgian Revolution, the answers were "extremely weak." They knew neither the causes nor the major facts of the revolution. Sluys attributed this to inadequate teaching methods. He was particularly doubtful about the efficacy of school excursions into the city. It was not enough simply to point out paintings of major historical events in the museums or to visit Martyrs' Square and city hall. Those trips could be of great importance, "if they are well executed" he added meaningfully.[56] School excursions were a source of concern to pedagogues and principals because teachers often used them to fill time and did not prepare them properly.[57]

Education professionals were anxious about the incorrect knowledge pupils retained from classes and excursions. Their skepticism, however, is not a direct measure of the success, or lack thereof, of the schools' patriotic agenda. People do not need proper historical facts to feel a sense of national belonging. At a socialist rally in Liège in June 1887, for instance, a local militant named Piedboeuf glowingly spoke of "Charles V, who said that the Belgians were the best soldiers of Gaul." He clearly confused the Spanish Habsburg emperor Charles V with Julius Caesar who had written in *De bello Gallico* that the Belgae were the bravest of all the Gauls.[58] Piedboeuf's statement, recorded by a police officer, gives us a look at the historical consciousness of ordinary people, but sources such as these are rare. The play of Antoine Mertens that started this chapter is one such rarity.

Written in 1880 in a school exercise book of thirty-seven pages, Mertens' variation on the classic patriotic theme of the six hundred Franchimontois shows the impact of schooling, and the reach and limits of the patriotic pedagogy. Mertens had probably borrowed liberally from school manuals and popular history books, because his text brimmed with historical details and names that could hardly be considered ready knowledge for a common cobbler. The text also switched haphazardly between elevated and pedestrian style registers, indicating Mertens' shifts between book knowledge and folklore.

Mertens had explicitly written his play for the benefit of the royal couple, Leopold II and his queen consort Maria Henrietta of Austria. Unsurprisingly then, he appealed to several tenets of bourgeois patriotism: the reverence for the national flag and anthem, the veneration of liberty, the eternal battle against foreign despots, the devotion to localism, and respect for the ancient Belgians of Gaul. Remarkably absent were the cult of the constitution and, for a religious man like Mertens, the Catholic faith as the foundation of the Belgian nation.

Mertens' play was heavy on exposition, with only a limited number of speaking characters. The most important ones were the choir of six hundred Franchimontois and their leaders, the national heroes Vincent van Bueren (ca. 1440–1505) and Gossuin de Straille (ca. 1440–1468). They swore a solemn oath upon "our flag," crying out "L'union fait la force" while the "Brabançonne" played at the end of the first act.[59] As self-styled "children of Liberty," the Franchimontois uttered phrases such as "Yes, we will all die for *la patrie*, for our rights, our freedom" in their fight against "a foreign people."[60]

Mertens' play breathed not only patriotism, but also regional and local pride. One of the four acts took place in Mertens' home town of Verviers, at the central square around the so-called *perron*, a stone column crowned with an imperial globe and a cross.[61] Like in all cities that historically fell under the Prince-Bishopric of Liège, the *perron* is *the* symbol of urban autonomy. The colors of Franchimont (green and silver), Verviers (green and white), and Liège (blue and white) were prominently displayed in the scenery and on props, coats of arms, cockades, and ribbons. Mertens' sense of regionalism was focused exclusively on the Liège area and not on Wallonia. The words "Walloon" or "Wallonia" do not appear in the play. Only in his accompanying letter to the king did he refer to "les pays Wallons" (the Walloon regions).[62] Evidently Mertens' play predates the Walloon movement's popularization of the Walloon vocabulary.

It is no coincidence that Mertens did not take the better-known Battle of the Spurs (1302) or the Battle of Worringen (1288) as his subject. Both were historic feats celebrated by Belgian nationalists, but the former was associated with the county of Flanders and the latter with the duchy of Brabant. Mertens' choice for the six hundred Franchimontois reflects his penchant for patriotic exploits with local roots. At the end of the nineteenth century nationalists and regionalists all over Europe increasingly interwove nation, region, and city in an effort to counterbalance the threatening anonymity of mass politics. According to the British historian Robert Colls, region and city became the lens through which the vague, anonymous notion of the nation was seen in a new, more comprehensive and populist light.[63]

Even more striking than the cult of freedom and local pride were Mertens' countless references to the brave ancient Belgians and "our fathers Ambiorix and the Eburones."[64] The text brimmed with phrases in the vein of "we will defend our rights like Ambiorix."[65] The patriotic topos of the Belgians as the bravest of all Gauls was probably one of the most popular folk myths transmitted through the schools because it was less abstract than, say, devotion to the constitution, which was lacking in Mertens' play. Falstaff, a contributor to the socialist paper *L'Avenir du Borinage*, reminisced in 1908 how thirty years earlier he had been drilled at a local public school: "The Ancient Belgians were proud and hospitable, they made beer and soap."[66] This commonplace spoke to the popular imagination thanks to the many prints, engravings, chromos, and wall charts that vividly depicted Belgium's Roman past and that were in use in schools. We probably see a direct influence of these images on Mertens' representation of the six hundred Franchimontois. The Roman fasces that invariably adorned the prints of the conquest of Belgium by Caesar had made such an impression on Mertens that he depicted the Franchimontois as Romans with "the Caesarian ax."[67]

Up to this point, Mertens' play conforms to the norms of bourgeois nationalism, particularly because it also expressed a strong respect for law and order. Mertens described a public meeting of the Franchimontois where "the national guard, the police, the gendarmes maintain order."[68] The pious Mertens probably did not project his fear of socialist agitation back in time, but rather his reaction to the School War between Catholics and liberals that was in full swing in 1880. In a later letter to the king dated January 1, 1881, Mertens mentioned "the dangers to which Belgium is at all times exposed by the division of the parties," an oblique reference to the School War.[69]

The presence of police forces in the play hints on the one hand at Mertens' respect for order and bourgeois decorum, but on the other hand it also points to the potentially rebellious nature of the masses. Mertens' text itself is an example of how top-down discourses were adapted by ordinary people and became potentially subversive in the process. The enormous blood thirst expressed in the play is a fitting illustration of this point. Mertens went beyond the bourgeois nationalist trope of Liberty's call sounding through "the blood of the Eburones."[70] His heroes mused extensively about shedding their own blood, "the blood spilled by [Liberty's] children,"[71] and eagerly plotted the gory death of the nation's enemies. With unconcealed gusto, Mertens described the attack of the Franchimontois on Charles the Bold's encampment as a bloodbath, even though his heroes were completely annihilated. To van Bueren's battle cry "Cut the throats of these miserable victims without mercy," the Franchimontois "rushed into a carnage" "like mad lions, massacring everyone who resisted them." "Pieces of dead bodies" flew around and "a bloody mud" sucked the warriors down. The play's strange combination of order and violent chaos was succinctly expressed in the pre-battle oath the six hundred Franchimontois took: "Let us all have the *civic virtue* [*vertu civique*] of the fire that inspired our forefathers in the [coming] *carnage*."[72]

The play climaxed when the Goddess of Liberty, the only female character, appeared, but even she had "male pride in her eyes."[73] Wrapped in the colors of Franchimont and Verviers and seated on her throne, she was flanked on either side by a Belgian flag. Above her hung a picture of the royal family surrounded by the civic guard, "the Senate and the people." This reassuring image of law and order, including the conservative Senate instead of the more democratic House, was disturbed by Mertens' insistence that the scene also contain "a severed head of a dead person" at the goddess's feet. This apotheosis was the perfect summary of Mertens' patriotism: localism, freedom, royalism, and respect for authority went hand in glove with potential chaos, violence, and male combativity.

Were Antoine Mertens' ideas about Belgium and the Belgian past, which were most probably shaped by his education at the Royal Institute for Deaf-Mutes and the Blind in Liège, representative of the lower classes, and more specifically of the BWP's rank and file? Although Mertens did not attend a regular public school and was probably no socialist, his writings allow us to draw two more general conclusions about popular patriotism and elementary schooling.

First, Mertens' emphasis on male action and violence was a bottom-up expression of nationalism that conflicted with the more cerebral elite celebration of the nation.[74] Mertens probably did not realize how frightening the unhinged crowds in his play appeared to the bourgeoisie. Unwittingly, he gave the masses an almost revolutionary agency of their own. Mertens' case shows the potentially subversive, disruptive, or violent character of bourgeois nationalist discourses when they were appropriated by ordinary people. In a law-abiding milieu like Mertens', this potential remained unfulfilled, but in a socialist, anti-establishment setting it could become politicized. The governing classes were well aware of this, which is why they tried to downplay the revolutionary roots of Belgian nationalism, by for instance moving the celebration of Independence Day to the royalist date of July 21, the day of the swearing in of Leopold I in 1831.

Secondly, if Mertens' patriotism was the result of his schooling, does that prove the success of a patriotic pedagogy? Several scholars have pointed out that memorizing chauvinistic textbooks or hearing teachers sing the nation's praises did not necessarily turn pupils into convinced patriots. The effect of schooling depends on a complex of supporting and competitive social influences inside and outside the classroom, both in the short and the long run.[75] Patriotic educational practices can only be successful over time if they are able to attach themselves to the rhythms of daily life.[76] The Ghent case clearly demonstrates this. As in Brussels, the Ghent municipal schools sought to inculcate patriotism, but their propaganda did not necessarily leave a lasting impression. Patrick, a contributor to *Vooruit* in the years 1888–1895, remembered how as a child he had been proud of the Belgian constitution:

> "Free Belgium, we learned at school, has a constitution and institutions that are the envy of all other countries." And with our rucksack on our back we went home, happy and proud as a peacock, in the firm belief that French,

English, German, Zulu and Chinese schoolchildren were grudgingly envious of us because they did not have such a glorious constitution like us. Little did we know what a constitution was, but who cared.

Patrick's childhood experience clearly illustrates the enthusiasm children could derive from inspiring teachers, memorable school trips, and rousing history lessons, but it also demonstrates their limits. Once Patrick became ensconced in the Ghent socialist milieu with its tradition of radical internationalism and distrust of Belgium, he had "lost every desire [...] to hum the Brabançonne."[77]

Jules De Bleye and Jozef De Graeve had similar experiences. De Bleye, nicknamed Jan the Madman (Jan de Zot), had been a member of the First International and became known as a social painter. In the mid-1850s he had attended a municipal school in Ghent. In a melancholic lookback in 1891 he reminisced: "Whatever lengths they went to drill us, whatever effort they took to sculpt our young minds patriotically, it all came to nothing." He remembered how as a ten-year-old he sang at the prize ceremony of the municipal schools:

> He who does not love his country,
> He who does not love his country,
> Is unworthy of life! [...]
>
> We sang our part (the bass) at the top of our voices and with all the conviction a ten-year-old can muster. There was no other way; we were filled to the brim with true unadulterated patriotism. We had learned that Belgium was our homeland, that is, the native soil where our cradle stood, [and] that we should be ready to sacrifice our earthly possessions and our blood to our beloved homeland.

Now, in 1891 at age forty-five, he called Belgian patriotism "charlatanism" and supported the radical internationalism of "a new humanity."[78]

De Bleye's experience also demonstrates that top-down discourses contained ambiguities, gaps, and inconsistencies that created room for diverging grassroots appropriations. For instance, the Belgian agenda of Ghent's public schools did not always produce the desired effect because it relied heavily on notions of Flemish ethnicity. "Our heart," De Bleye recalled, "trembled with blissful emotion when the school principal himself taught us in the course of history that in the odd 1300s the burghers of Bruges beat to death everyone at the city gate who was unable to pronounce 'Schild en Vrind' with a pure Flemish accent." De Bleye referred to the historical Matins of Bruges (*Brugse metten*). On May 18, 1302, at the time of the matins prayers, the city's militia massacred the local French garrison. To separate the supporters of the count of Flanders from the French king's men, every suspicious person was asked to pronounce the Flemish shibboleth *Des gilden vriend*, "a friend of the [city's] guilds," later corrupted to *Schild en Vrind*, Shield and Friend. French-speakers were unable to do this correctly and were summarily executed. By the end of the nineteenth century this episode had become a central myth of the Flemish movement.

To be sure, an intensely felt regional or ethnic loyalty need not preclude a strong Belgian patriotism. Like many other feats of the medieval county of Flanders, the Matins of Bruges were also an integral part of the Belgian patriotic narrative. They constituted proof of a proto-Belgian quest for independence from France. In Antoine Mertens' play we have seen that region and nation mutually reinforced each other, but De Bleye's case is different. For one thing, while Mertens' regional pride was limited to Liège and did not extend to Wallonia, De Bleye's Flemish inspiration went beyond the ancient county of Flanders. To De Bleye, "Flemish" referred to the modern concept of all Flemish-speakers in northern Belgium.[79]

De Bleye recalled how his teachers had urged him and his fellow students "to read books to arouse our patriotic feelings. We devoured the works of Conscience, who speaks of the dear home country." Hendrik Conscience was the most popular writer of nineteenth-century Belgium (see also Chapter 9).[80] His historic novels, which were a testament to the fusion of Belgian patriotism and Flemish ethnicity, were eagerly read in literate Flemish-speaking working-class circles. The very first purchase that the library of the Fraternal Weavers, the direct predecessor of Vooruit's library, made in 1860 was the collected works of Conscience.[81] At school De Bleye "breathlessly" read Conscience's novels *The Lion of Flanders* (published in 1838, about the 1302 Battle of the Spurs) and *The Peasants' War* (published in 1853, about a Vendée-like peasant rising in the Southern Netherlands in 1798 against the French republic). De Bleye got so carried away by Conscience's novels that, in De Bleye's words,

> we were proud to have beaten up the twelve-year-old boy of Barbara the Walloon (the boy spoke Walloon), after first having set fire to his cap in the stove because he had dared to stare at us! We were constantly taught: all things Walloon are devious and where Walloons sh . . . no grass can grow for seventeen years. Racial hatred was drilled into us.

The motto "all things Walloon are devious" (*wat Walsch is, valsch is*) is a medieval saying that became a battle cry of the Flemish movement in the nineteenth century against French-speakers. By singling out a French-speaking boy for his Flemish wrath, De Bleye had acted upon the Flemish-Walloon ethnic images contained within his school manuals and within Conscience's novels, rather than on their Belgian patriotic content. Strikingly, at age forty-five, De Bleye no longer believed in Belgian patriotism and had renounced "racial" animosity between Flemings and Walloons, but he was still proud of his Flemish heritage and his native tongue.[82]

De Bleye's experience shows how schools, like all nation-building institutions, offered a vocabulary that defined the boundaries of what was sayable about the nation, but ordinary people could combine these words in a syntax of their own. Instead of using the language of Belgian patriotism to merge Belgian nationhood and Flemish ethnicity, De Bleye renounced the former and accepted the latter. The use of a patriotic school-taught vocabulary in an internationalist and working-class syntax also explains the conversion topos in socialist life stories like De Bleye's. "If as individuals got older, their 'experience' of the world did not accord with the language [...] of their elementary education," Stephen Heathorn has contended, "then they had to 'overcome' their primary instruction." Hence the conversion experiences of many workers who came to socialism in later years and rejected the patriotism they had learned at school.[83] Or as De Bleye explained his change of heart: "The delusions of youth are gone. Gradually we came to reality and to a different opinion, yes a completely different opinion."[84]

The already-mentioned Jozef De Graeve, a seventeen-year-old office clerk at the socialist People's Press in Ghent, described a similar "awakening" as De Bleye in 1908. He too recalled how his elementary school teacher had loaded his history classes with patriotic insights such as: "Belgium is one of the richest countries in the world. For its trade and industry, it is ranked ... etc."—and questions like: "Piet! Name me one of the freedoms that the Constitution guarantees to the Belgians."[85] Like De Bleye, De Graeve had lost faith in Belgium over time, but not in Flanders. His belief in Flemish ethnicity was evident in his glowing descriptions of "the sturdy Fleming, traditionally lauded for his diligence."[86] The ambiguous regionalist-nationalist agenda of Ghent's public schools may have nurtured De Graeve's Flemishness. After all, his teacher had also showered them with patriotic nuggets such as: "The Flemings are a diligent and sturdy people! Flanders is one of the most fertile areas of the earth."[87] De Graeve did not blend the Belgian and Flemish vocabularies of his elementary education in a patriotic syntax. He appropriated them differently because the Belgian vocabulary, in contrast to the Flemish one, was no longer structurally maintained and reproduced once he left school and became socialized in the Ghent socialist milieu, with its distrust of Belgium and its tradition of radical internationalism. In sum, top-down discourses needed to be sustained outside of the narrow context of nationalizing institutions, in daily life, to have a lasting impact on ordinary people. And that is exactly where Part II of this book takes us.

**PART II**

# EVERYDAY NATIONALISM

*Performing the Nation in Daily Life*

*Chapter 7*

# ENCOUNTERS WITH THE BELGIAN FLAG AND THE NATIONAL ANTHEM

It was with a mixture of pride and apprehension that Ms. Boitte wrote to her mayor in the fall of 1907. As the headmistress of the municipal girls' school of Cuesmes in the Borinage, she was dutifully following ministerial instructions to fly the national flag at the school's entrance. But, she added, she had had to hang it high enough to make sure "that the kids could not reach it."[1] School principals in Brussels also complained about their pupils' lack of respect for the icons of the nation.[2] The children climbed onto national monuments and even defaced them. Obviously, this insolence was at odds with the message of deference teachers and other brokers of nationalism tried to impress on them. These acts of disrespect reveal the breaches in the nationalists' discourse.

In the national indifference literature such breaches and gaps are interpreted as a deficit of national loyalty. I would argue, however, that not every divergent reaction to trickle-down nationalism necessarily implies rejection, disregard, or opportunistic manipulation of the nation. The gaps can also be instances of what Alf Lüdtke, one of the founders of the German school of *Alltagsgeschichte* (the history of everyday life), has called *Eigen-Sinn* and they may be compatible with working-class expressions of nationalism.

Lüdtke defines *Eigen-Sinn*—a concept similar to James C. Scott's "weapons of the weak"—as "willfulness, spontaneous self-will, a kind of self-affirmation, an act of (re)appropriating alienated social relations."[3] *Eigen-Sinn* involved suspicion of what bourgeois respectability prescribed, and even apprehension about the expectations of workers' organizations. In practice it was manifested in resistance to socialization attempts from above, a subversive appropriation of imposed values, symbolic inversions of existing power relations, and evasive or ironical dealings with outsiders, authority figures, and people with a higher social rank.

Is it possible that what contemporary observers in East Central Europe diagnosed as national indifference on the part of unwilling villagers may have been more infused by *Eigen-Sinn*? Tara Zahra gives the example of frustrated Soviet officials on a mission of national inventory-making in the border area between Poland and Russia in 1925. These census-takers were often exasperated by the responses they received to the questions "What is your nationality?" and "Are you Polish or Ukrainian?" The locals insisted that they were mere farmers, that they belonged to the "Catholic nationality" or that they were simply *tutejzsie*, or "people from here."[4] Zahra interprets these grassroots reactions to official interference as proof of national indifference, but they can also be understood as expressions of *Eigen-Sinn* that in and of themselves reflect little about national identification. Belgian workers exhibited a similar suspicion when strangers asked them politically inflected questions. During a visit to the Borinage in 1885, the Dutch journalist and later co-founder of the Dutch Social-Democratic Labor Party Henri Hubert van Kol asked a local miner whether he had ever seen "a socialist worker." The man answered that he was not sure, but he had indeed met someone "with a brown face wearing a red fez. Could that have been a socialist?"[5] Is it possible that this man was so naïve? At the moment he met Van Kol the Borinage had been the stage of socialist activity for at least six years. Probably he was pulling Van Kol's leg, refusing to share even the most obvious information with a stranger. The Borinage miners were notoriously suspicious of outsiders.[6]

Within the conflicting frameworks of national indifference and *Eigen-Sinn* it is hard to determine what certain acts of disrespect, like Ms. Boitte's pupils' pulling down the national flag, meant in terms of national loyalty. This is the central question underlying Part II of this book. The resonance approach of Part I is biased in the sense that it explicitly directs scholars' attention to the bells and whistles of nationalism.[7] In so doing it misses many mundane practices that perform, or do not perform, the nation in everyday life. That is why Part II turns to ordinary workers in their daily routines. It is the bottom-up view complementing the trickle-down perspective of Part I.

To access the red grassroots, the following chapters use a variety of sources, including police and court interviews of socialist workers, published and unpublished letters to the party press, songs, poems, working-class autobiographies, life stories and reminiscences,[8] and the so-called propaganda pence or proletarian tweets.

## A DESPICABLE BOURGEOIS AND CLERICAL SYMBOL

The roots of the Belgian flag and the national anthem "La Brabançonne" (the Brabantine) lie in the September Days of 1830. On August 26, 1830, Ms. Marie Abts became the Belgian Betsy Ross. By order of the oppositional journalists Lucien Jottrand and Edouard Ducpétiaux she stitched together the very first Belgian flag. Choosing the colors of the former duchy of Brabant—black, yellow, and red—Jottrand and Ducpétiaux stressed the local roots of the rising. Originally the bars of the Belgian flag ran horizontally, but a decree of the provisional government of January 23, 1831, rearranged them vertically in order to differentiate it from the horizontally aligned Dutch flag. The national anthem, "La Brabançonne," had revolutionary roots as well. It was written by the French poet and actor Hippolyte Louis Alexandre Dechet, alias Jenneval, and was sung for the first time in the café L'Aigle d'or (The golden eagle) in Brussels on September 28, 1830, by the Belgian tenor François Van Campenhout. By the end of the nineteenth century both national symbols had been largely stripped of their revolutionary appeal by the same elites that had neutered the cult of the September Days (see Chapter 3). In their bowdlerized, bourgeois versions the flag and the anthem seemed ill fit for the socialist movement.

At the time of the BWP's founding in 1885, socialist attitudes toward the national anthem and flag were in flux. On the one hand, internationalist doctrines prescribed a certain distrust of the symbols epitomizing the division of humankind, a suspicion fueled by the bourgeois repression of workers. On the other hand, brandishing the Belgian tricolor and appropriating the national hymn fitted the double-edged, revolutionary-reformist strategy of the national party leaders.[9] In their attempts to extract reform from the government and from parliament, they threatened revolution while at the same time presenting themselves as the only and true defenders of the nation. This explains why national party rallies sometimes featured tricolored flags with a black mourning badge.[10] The funeral metaphor was meant to express the sadness of the entire nation about the lack of democratic reforms. The "two or three Belgian flags, [. . .] with a mourning veil," however, were usually no match for the dozens of red flags and other revolutionary symbols in the parades.[11]

In the early years of the party, appealing to the official national emblems still fit the older strategies of collective protest based on close ties with local elites, especially in Brussels, where the socialist movement was rooted in the highly skilled artisanal sector and had potential middle-class support. With this in mind, the founding congress of the BWP in August 1885 left its member groups free to choose the color of their banner, "red, blue, black, or *tricolored*."[12] Initially some BWP affiliates in Brussels and even in the party's Walloon industrial bastions had no qualms about displaying the Belgian flag or singing the national anthem.[13]

Things were changing, however. In the late 1880s the decisive transition occurred from the old local, haphazard, and elite-centered repertoires of contention to modern nationally organized and working-class-driven collective protest.[14] In all labor organizations where workers began to organize themselves and chose the socialist path, the Belgian flag and anthem were ousted. By 1898 Emile Vandervelde and Jules Destrée could claim in their book *Le socialisme en Belgique* that "the Marseillaise, in concerts, has replaced the Brabançonne; the red flag has replaced the tricolored flag."[15]

An important catalyst in this shift was the labor revolt that swept through the country in March–April 1886. Riots spread all over the industrial districts of Wallonia and the army killed twenty-four people. The security police reported that workers were so dismayed by the state's violence that they started to denounce the black-yellow-red of the national flag as bourgeois and clerical colors.[16] Paranoia gripped the authorities. Public displays of "seditious" emblems such as the red flag and the "Marseillaise" were outlawed and workers were urged to march behind the truly patriotic symbols of the national flag and the "Brabançonne." To little avail. At a socialist suffrage rally in Liège in September 1886, when informed that the mayor would rather have them use the national flag, there were shouts of "We don't want it."[17] In Ghent, the national anthem could no longer be performed without full-throated protest. On April 20, 1886, in the immediate aftermath of the Spring Revolt, all hell broke loose at a popular pantomime that closed with a parade of different national flags. When the Belgian flag appeared "deafening shouts and whistles rose [. . .] When the director of the theater asked if the pantomime did not please, there were calls that it had nothing to do with the play, but with the

Brabançonne and the Belgian flag, after which the shouting and whistling recommenced."[18]

The case of the Parti socialiste républicain (PSR), which seceded from the BWP between 1887 and 1889, offers an intriguing look at grassroots attitudes in the industrial province of Hainaut. Dissatisfied with the BWP's refusal to call a revolutionary general strike, the PSR broke away in 1887. Headed by Alfred Defuisseaux and his brother, the progressive liberal MP Léon Defuisseaux, two scions of a rich family of lawyers from Mons, the PSR had backing in all industrial regions of the province of Hainaut. The dissidence seriously hurt the BWP, which lost a third of its affiliates. The Borinage and Charleroi were no longer represented in the BWP.

Nicknamed "the Blanqui of Wallonia,"[19] Alfred embraced an anti-German, anti-Flemish, and Gallophile Belgian nationalism inspired by the French revolutionary Auguste Blanqui. Revolutionary Blanquism had been one of the driving forces behind the Commune. Its ideology was based on five pillars: atheism, communism, a conspiratorial penchant for small militant groups, revolution, and patriotism.[20] The PSR mimicked these traits, including the last.

Alfred and the so-called Defuissarts infused their brochures, speeches, and public appearances with a heady dose of Belgian nationalism. Invoking the French republican tradition they claimed that "PATRIOT AND DEMOCRAT are one and the same thing; they were synonyms in 1792."[21] In the cold war of the late 1880s between France and Germany, they were radically opposed to the "Teutonic vermin,"[22] suspecting the Belgian establishment and especially Leopold II of having a hidden German agenda. Their Germanophobia extended to the Flemish movement, which to their mind was intriguing to have Belgium annexed to "the Great Germanic Fatherland."[23] This, the Defuissarts insisted, would not succeed because Belgium belonged to "the old Latin race" and its "elder sister" was France.[24]

During the PSR's short existence there were frequent grassroots incidents involving the national flag. These kerfuffles highlight the increasingly negative feelings the national symbols engendered, but at the same time they illuminate how the workers involved shared a reflexive emotional attachment to Belgianness. In other words, *Eigen-Sinn* or national indifference could coexist with banal nationalism.

On January 31, 1887, on the day of the yearly military draft, a small riot broke out in Mons, the provincial capital adjoining the Borinage region. A band of prospective conscripts from the mining town of Cuesmes marched into town behind a red flag chanting socialist slogans. They came across a group of Catholic draftees from the countryside who were singing patriotic songs and waving the national flag. After a short skirmish the miners captured the Belgian flag, tore it up, and burned it the next Sunday.[25] Although the PSR press minimized the incident as an attack on "the *bourgeois* rag," not on the *national* symbol,[26] the Mons episode put the authorities on edge. In the following year several industrial towns in Hainaut ruled by Catholic or liberal mayors prohibited PSR demonstrations with the red flag and instead suggested the use of the national tricolor. The mayor of Carnières, near Charleroi, notified the local socialists that "the higher authorities consider it [the red flag] to be a revolutionary emblem, moreover it is not Belgian."[27] The PSR supporters were not to be dissuaded. In the Borinage town of Wasmes they circumvented the ban by deploying the French flag.[28] In Morlanwez near La Louvière a PSR parade marched through town without banners, but as soon as it had crossed the municipal border, a red flag was unfurled, and duly refurled upon return. The president of the local socialist section, Alexis Ledoux, explicitly intended this as an act of defiance. In an (unpublished) rhapsodic letter full of spelling and grammatical mistakes to the PSR paper *La République belge*, he taunted his mayor: "The socialists are more cunning than you think mister mayor."[29] This example of *Eigen-Sinn* was surpassed by Jean Callewaert, a member of the PSR and the president of the Belgian Knights of Labor (see Chapter 1).

On May 7, 1888, Callewaert, a semi-literate self-educated man, sent a letter to the PSR paper *La République belge*. As leader of the workers' league of Forchies-la-Manche, near Charleroi, he had been planning the inauguration ceremony of the association's red flag, but the mayor had banned any public display of it. In a rambling, unpunctuated letter in unorthodox French, Callewaert defied the ban in a humoristic and provocative way. Because the mayor had insisted that they use the national flag, Callewaert had a Belgian black-yellow-red flag tailor-made: "the last part of the flag [was] wider than the others [...] our flag was [...] furled around the pole: flying nothing but the red part." On the day of the demonstration, however, the police confiscated this creative "red" Belgian flag. Undeterred, the demonstrators asked if a "real" tricolored flag was permitted and after the police's affirmative answer they came up with ... a French flag.[30]

It is striking that in none of these cases was the Belgian flag rejected as a *national* symbol, but merely as a *bourgeois* or *clerical* emblem. In Carnières, the local socialists called it "the flag of the clerical masters that give them [i.e., the Catholics] all their privileges."[31] Ledoux, for his part, complained "that we do not want to take a flag that we have no place under that it is only of the privileged."[32] Callewaert too emphasized that the tricolor was "the flag of Belgian *Sencitarisme* [sic]," i.e., of bourgeois census voters. He seemed to harbor radically internationalist objections to the flag: "We know perfectly well that the borders have been established by human Stupidity." His internationalism, though, was unorthodoxly intertwined with anti-German, Francophile, and Belgian patriotic sentiments. For one, he claimed to have used the French flag "to protest against the machinations of our masters who would like to turn *our Belgium* with all its children over to the house of hohenzoler [sic] [...] while we are determined that if Belgium should disappear: be French and belong and reunite to a neighbor nation and friend who has shed her blood for our independence!!!"[33] Callewaert's appropriation of *our* Belgium and *our* independence, his ethnic understanding of the Belgian nation as an extended family, and his emphasis on bloodshed can all be interpreted as working-class expressions of nationalism.

Before, during, and after the PSR's dissidence, rank-and-file members in Hainaut expressed a self-evident sense of Belgianness despite their struggles with the Belgian flag and the national anthem. In published and unpublished letters to the party press they railed against "the exploiters of *our beloved Belgium*."[34] The most revealing letter was sent by a certain Thomas Dumonceau to Alfred Defuisseaux' nephew Georges on February 12, 1888. In the phonetic and unpunctuated style of a semi-literate, Dumonceau accused the Catholic government of tampering with the Belgian coins and replacing the national motto *L'union fait la force* with a German text. According to Dumonceau, the authorities were afraid that "the people would understand [the motto] and put it to use." To prevent this and to "prove to the Belgian people [*peuple belge*] that it was German," the government "had written it [the motto] in German on all our coins and money." But, Dumonceau vowed, "we have too much red blood in our veins to be German [...] no never will the Prussians govern us."[35] Dumonceau clearly moved under the spell of the PSR's pro-French and anti-German prejudice, but what had really happened? A royal decree of 1886 had introduced Flemish-language money, putting an end to the exclusive use of French on Belgian coins. Dumonceau had apparently gotten hold of a Flemish coin for the very first time in his life and had mistaken it for German. His apparent unfamiliarity with Flemish, the mother tongue of 60 percent of his compatriots, shows his implicit view of Belgium as an exclusively French-speaking country.

The PSR tapped into a popular tradition of "Francophilia and [...] anti-Germanism" that had existed in the province of Hainaut ever since the defeat of Napoleon in 1815. Some scholars have identified these strains as the only "two political constants" in local folk songs.[36] So it comes as no surprise that the rank and file reacted favorably to the PSR's pro-French and anti-German slogans, chanting or cheering them at meetings. On one such occasion, an undated PSR rally in the town of Tubize, south of Brussels, the audience responded with a roaring "ovation" when Georges Defuisseaux proclaimed: "The Teutons are at our door and if one day we should become Prussian, the Germanic despotism will be even more terrible, because the Germans know that we are descended from the Gauls. They will remember that Caesar once said, the Belgians are the bravest of all Gauls!"[37] In October 1888 the gendarmerie charged a PSR rally in Morlanwez near La Louvière to seize the French flag behind which fifteen hundred protesters were marching. The scene ended in complete mayhem "with cries of: Long live France! Down with the Germans!"[38] A month later, in La Louvière, fourteen hundred PSR supporters saluted the French flag,[39] while Georges Defuisseaux's exhortation "the Walloon workers need to give their lives to defend this flag" was met with "lively applause." A report by the French police, who anxiously surveilled the Belgian socialists on either side of the Franco-Belgian border,[40] noted that "repeated cries of Vive la France! Vive la République! were heard."[41] When Defuisseaux exclaimed "France counts on the Belgians," some people in the audience even shouted back "On the *Walloons!*"[42] The latter cry was quite exceptional at this moment in time. Emphasizing and instrumentalizing Walloon ethnicity would only become a more permanent feature of socialist politics after the turn of the century and the introduction of proportional representation (see Chapter 2 and the next section).

The PSR episode clearly highlights how ethnic and national identifications are dependent on context. At the international level, the late 1880s was a time of flaming Franco-Prussian tensions, exacerbated by the Boulanger affair in France. At the national level, there was growing anxiety among the elite that socialist agitation was a foreign machination to undermine the country's independence and neutrality. The resulting anti-socialist repression radicalized the workers' movement and contributed to the PSR's seceding from the BWP. Within this climate the PSR's critique of the "Flemish" reluctance within the BWP to call a general strike catalyzed Francophile, pro-Belgian, Germanophobe, and anti-Flemish prejudices. In some instances, as evidenced by the shouting in La Louvière, these feelings radicalized into an increasingly Walloon sense of Belgian nationhood. However, once the Boulanger revolution had petered out, Franco-German tensions had de-escalated, and the PSR was reintegrated in the BWP, the social category of Walloonness again lost its salience.

The success of the PSR's patriotic propaganda was dependent on context, but a careful reading of grassroots writings also reveals its limits. Some patriotic symbols and practices were too tied up with the bourgeois and Catholic status quo to be meaningfully appropriated by the PSR's rank and file. The national flag and anthem, but also the cry *Vive la Belgique*, are a case in point. Alfred Defuisseaux concluded several of his articles with a triple shout-out which always included a *Vive la Belgique*: "Long live Belgium! Long live amnesty [for convicted strikers]! Long live general suffrage!"[43] Such rhetorical triads did have an impact on the rank and file. Thomas Dumonceau ended his letter with a similar list: "vive la liberté, legalite [sic, l'égalité] et la Republique [sic]."[44] François Carpent, a further unidentifiable grassroots PSR supporter, did the same in an unpublished reader's letter to *La République Belge*: "Long live the black strike, Long live General Suffrage. Long live the republic."[45] Both pointedly omitted *Vive la Belgique*. Obviously the patriotic campaign of the PSR connected to grassroots notions of Belgianness, but the rank and file determined to a certain extent the confines within which such top-down propaganda could be successful. Ordinary PSR supporters believed in the existence of a Belgian national identity, but not in all tenets of the nationalist creed. Trying to get them to accept the national flag and anthem or to cry out "Long Live Belgium," nationalist topoi deeply associated with the powers that be, was a bridge too far. Ultimately, the PSR case shows that grassroots expressions of national indifference and/or *Eigen-Sinn* could merge with banal nationalism into a working-class sense of nationhood.

## CONQUERING THE FLAG AND THE ANTHEM

As oppositional patriotism became dominant in the BWP after 1895, party cadres began to appropriate the national flag and anthem as labor symbols. They not only made a distinction between a benevolent socialist patriotism and a pernicious bourgeois chauvinism, but also between the good original national symbols of 1830 and the "ridiculous parody" the bourgeoisie had made of them. Like the Belgian revolution, the icons of the nation had been stolen from the proletariat.⁴⁶

The rank and file were slower in coming to terms with the national emblems. The most striking example was provided by a heavily mediatized incident in Charleroi, where a Belgian flag was put to flames. On November 21, 1898, the assize court of Hainaut sentenced two grassroots supporters of the BWP, Emile Degrève and Jean-Baptiste Wayemberg, to six months in prison for "contesting at the root the mandatory force of the laws founding our nationality, affirming that the revolutionary destruction of these laws and of this nationality is near and desirable," as the official indictment read.⁴⁷ On May 23, 1898, Degrève and Wayemberg had burned a Belgian flag in front of the Temple de la Science, the red headquarters of Charleroi. The incident had occurred during a parade, organized by the socialists of Gilly, a Charleroi suburb, while they were celebrating the BWP's victory in the parliamentary elections of the preceding day. The anti-socialist press immediately took umbrage at the affair. While Ghent and other Flemish-speaking BWP branches kept out of the controversy, several French-speaking party papers were quick to minimize what had happened. They duly invoked the doctrine of oppositional patriotism. The national party paper *Le Peuple* wrote: "As internationalist socialists we love our country with a passionate and sincere love, but without using the word 'patrie' to justify the inequality and injustice of the present regime."⁴⁸

According to the conservative liberal *Gazette de Charleroi*, the socialist leadership had watched the entire scene from the balcony of the Temple de la Science and had applauded "this hideous spectacle." All the while the fanfare band had played the "Marseillaise" and the onlookers had performed "an infernal dance."⁴⁹ The socialist *Journal de Charleroi* denied emphatically that any party leaders had engaged in such behavior: "needless to say, we would strongly condemn such an act." What had been assailed, the *Journal* claimed, was not the symbol of national unity, but "the flag of a particular party," an icon of bourgeois and clerical tyranny. To prove this beyond doubt, the *Journal de Charleroi* argued that the tricolor in question had been stolen from the Catholic Cercle Saint Rémy of Gilly and that only the yellow bar, representing the Catholic party, had been burned. The *Journal* emphatically stated: "The piece of yellow rag was set on fire, but it certainly did not represent the national flag."⁵⁰ This was a decidedly odd explanation. Not only is it near impossible to set fire to the middle yellow band of a Belgian flag without also burning the outer black and red bars, the secretary of the Cercle Saint Rémy immediately informed *Le Journal de Charleroi* that no tricolor had been stolen from his society.[51]

Unsurprisingly, the flag incident began to interfere with the electoral campaign for the second round of the parliamentary elections of May 29 and the provincial elections of June 5. The party leadership was seriously bothered by the accusations, fearing voters would believe "that the socialists of Charleroi had insulted the Fatherland and burned the national flag."[52] In an open letter to the press, Léon George, the head of the Gilly socialists, protested vehemently and claimed that agents provocateurs had staged the incident.[53]

Through the beginning of June, *Le Journal de Charleroi* devoted several articles to the flag-burning, each time emphasizing the socialists' respect for the national symbols and even claiming that they loved the tricolor more than the liberals and Catholics.[54] At the end of November 1898, at the time of the assize trial, there was a renewed upsurge of articles in *Le Journal de Charleroi* rehashing the same arguments about the home country and the national flag.[55] After the conviction of Degrève and Wayemberg, the BWP leadership returned to the issue just once. At the national party congress of May 21–22, 1899, Léon Troclet, the leader of the Liège branch of the Socialist Young Guard, proposed sending a "token of sympathy" to the convicted. Emile Vandervelde, while admitting that their sentence was excessive, stressed that all flags deserved respect: "We love our red flag, he said, but we do not want to despise the other flags. In any case, we cannot express our solidarity with this roguery." The party congress agreed with Vandervelde and did not send a letter of support.[56]

The "roguery" in question had attracted an inordinate amount of judicial scrutiny. Following through on the rumor that several socialist dignitaries had cheered the burning, the public prosecutor of Charleroi had been bent on making heads roll.[57] On June 5, 1898, he had urged the police chief of Charleroi to pursue the investigation "with increased urgency."[58] The lengths the judiciary went to were disproportionate to the case. Within a week eighty witnesses, a majority of whom were miners and socialists, were identified and questioned. Contrary to their hope of indicting the leadership, the investigators eventually came up with two small fry. Degrève was a twenty-four-year-old "indigent" miner and the (literal) standard-bearer of the socialist association Libre Pensée from Gilly.[59] "A very exalted socialist militant,"[60] his fifty-nine-year-old partner in crime, Wayemberg, was an illiterate "shopkeeper." He belonged to the "inferior classes," but was "in a well-off position," owning his own house.[61]

With the police pulling out all the stops, a shroud of *omertà* and *Eigen-Sinn* immediately descended over the case, inspiring a massive bout of "amnesia."[62] Early on in the investigation police officer Emile Mélotte noted that of the eighty witnesses the police had interviewed only three had provided useful information.[63] One of them was Zéphir Demoulin, a piano seller, who had watched the flag-burning from the second floor of his house. He had seen someone fold up a newspaper in front of the Temple de la Science, dip it in a beer glass filled with petroleum, and set it on fire. According to Demoulin a second person had held a tattered, but still recognizable tricolor to the flame while a third had actually lit it.[64]

Although Demoulin had been too far removed from the scene to recognize the culprits, Degrève had already come into the investigators' crosshairs by June 1. He had been seen lugging a Belgian flag en route to Charleroi, but on the way back to Gilly he had just been carrying a bare flagpole. Under interrogation Degrève denied everything.[65] No witness directly incriminated him. In early July the police chief of Gilly admitted that the investigation was "extremely difficult": "All the workers know full well that it was Emile Degrève who set fire to the national flag. But they dare not speak; because their lives would be in danger if they did."[66] Most witnesses could recount what had happened, but claimed not to know what type of flag had been burned, nor to be able to give a description of the perpetrators.[67]

Barely five witnesses out of eighty felt the need to condemn what had happened. Adolphe Vandewalle, a seventy-one-year-old barkeep, testified: "While the flag was burning, I told someone, Petit Roux [little Carrot Top—obviously the nickname of a small, red-haired person] who was part of the gang, that it was despicable [*indigne*] to burn the flag, that people did not do that in France, he replied taking me by the shoulder: we are not in France here."[68] To Carrot Top the reverence due to the French *tricolore* clearly did not extend to the Belgian flag.

François Bertrand, a billboard poster, and Emile Stortewagen, a shopkeeper, both of whom lived across from the *locus delicti*, admitted to having seen a flag burn. They confessed: "that offended *even* us," but claimed not to have recognized anyone because a throng of people was dancing around the flag. The addition of "even" (*même*) to their statement shows that their taking offense was what they considered to be politically correct when interrogated by the police.[69]

Two local party cadres were the most explicit in their indignation about the flag-burning. The twenty-four-year-old Théophile Kest, day laborer and manager of Gilly's red cooperative, insisted that they had purposely carried along a Belgian flag in their celebratory parade to demonstrate that they were as patriotic as the Catholic journal *Le Pays wallon*, which had called them nation-less.[70] Léon George, a thirty-nine-year-old shopkeeper who headed the Gilly socialist branch, declared to have stood only seven meters from the scene. Apart from the rising smoke he had not seen anything because a packed mob was blocking his view. He was adamant, nonetheless, that only a yellow band had been torched: "it was said in the crowd that the flag of the Pope was being burned."[71] Denying anything anti-Belgian had transpired, George explicitly condemned anyone who would set fire to the Belgian tricolor: "Although I am a socialist, I am far from approving such an act given the fact that I had hung out a national flag at my home to celebrate the result of the elections."[72]

None of the other seventy-five witnesses felt compelled to add to their testimony that they were scandalized by the flag-burning. Even the accused Degrève and Wayemberg did not try to play the patriot to escape conviction. It seems, therefore, that the efforts of the socialist press and the party cadres to profile themselves as good, flag-loving patriots throughout this entire episode did not resonate at the grassroots level.

In early July, there was a breakthrough in the investigation. After more than a month, the police succeeded in unraveling the full facts of the case. Edouard Hermans, barkeep and barber, testified that Degrève had come to him on May 28, five days after the incident, for his weekly shave and haircut. Oddly, Degrève had wanted his mustache shaved off. According to Hermans, Degrève thought this necessary "in order not to be recognized, because I burned the flag," but Degrève replied that Hermans was misquoting him. All he had said was, "in order not to be recognized, in case they say that I burned the flag."[73] On July 13, one of Degrève's friends, Jules Vanderhaeghen, a twenty-two-year-old smith from Gilly, confessed that it was J. B. Wayemberg who had put fire to the flag.[74] Wayemberg would keep denying any involvement throughout the entire investigation.[75]

Piecing together all the information, the police eventually reconstructed the fateful chain of events. Shortly before the victory parade Degrève had come across a calendar from the Catholic journal *Le Pays wallon* which depicted a tattered red flag on a broken pole with the inscription "What the Communards wanted, we want as well," and a banner reading "Strikes impoverish." Across stood a beaming national tricolor bearing the motto *Dieu et Patrie*

(God and Country) with a pennant that read "Work ennobles." Below the flags the blossoming flowers of "Work"–"Prosperity" and the dead branches of "Strike"–"Misery" were juxtaposed. Smoking chimneys, busy factories, and a happy family scene were contrasted with striking workers, dead industries, and a family being evicted from its home.

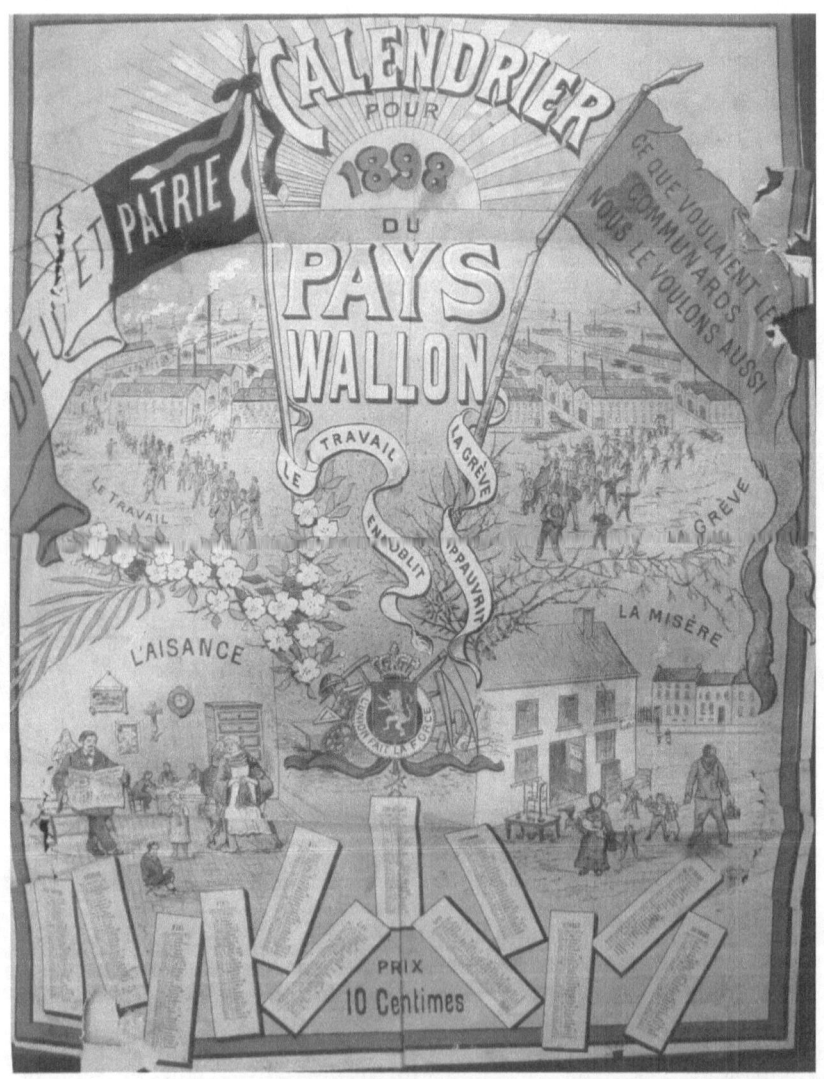

**FIGURE 5** Calendar of the Catholic journal *Le Pays wallon*, 1898. National Archives of Mons, Cours d'assises du Hainaut 1898/18 no. 166.

Degrève had been so agitated by this calendar that he took it to the victory parade along with a Belgian flag, in the words of Vanderhaeghen, "to make fun of the paper 'Le pays wallon.'" During the march from Gilly to Charleroi several people vented their rage on the flag. On arrival at the Temple de la Science it was in tatters. At that moment Wayemberg came outside with a glass of petroleum in which he dipped an issue of *Le Pays wallon*. He lit it and held the flag to the flame.[76]

The entire episode showed that the party cadres were outrunning the rank and file in accepting the tricolor and embracing oppositional patriotism. How differently both groups reacted was perfectly clear when the provenance of the burned flag was established. Fuming about *Le Pays wallon*'s calendar, Degrève had gone looking for a national flag, but where could a right-minded socialist lay his hands on one? Early on in the investigation the rumor that it had been stolen from the Catholic Cercle de Saint Rémy had been disproven. Where did it come from then? The answer was simple: from the Gilly socialists' headquarters. The concierge of the local Maison du Peuple had handed Degrève "the national flag that was kept in-house."[77] Théophile Kest's and Leon George's claim that they had flown the national flag to celebrate the electoral victory, which initially had looked like pandering to the police, suddenly seemed not so far-fetched. Why else would a Maison du Peuple own a Belgian flag?

The flag-burning of Charleroi fits the pattern we have already encountered in Hainaut ten years earlier. The dozens of socialist workers interviewed by the police did not rise to the expectations of bourgeois Belgian nationalism: they failed to be indignant about what had happened, in contrast to the party cadres, who paid tribute to what James C. Scott calls the "public transcript" of indignation (see Chapter 8).[78] Keeley Stauter-Halsted observed a similar gap in pre–World War I Galicia between the peasantry's fiercer "plebeian vision of the nation" and the more sedate patriotic language of educated smallholders who were invested in cross-class alliances for the sake of political reform.[79] Yet the charivari-like mayhem that culminated in the tearing up, setting fire to, and dancing around the Belgian flag, did not necessarily reflect the participants' or bystanders' rejection of Belgian nationhood. The argument that only the yellow, "Catholic" bar of the flag had been targeted need not have been a mere rationalization. When all was said and done, the incident was driven first and foremost by anticlerical sentiment directed against the Catholic journal *Le Pays wallon*.

After the turn of the century, the national flag and anthem gradually evoked less extreme reactions from the rank and file. Some militants complained about the omnipresence of bourgeois symbols during the national jubilee of 1905,[80] but there were no burnings or jeers. Revealingly, in towns with a governing socialist majority, tricolors and the "Brabançonne" remained part and parcel of the yearly city school parades. The grassroots no longer seemed to mind. This was particularly striking in the province of Hainaut where, by 1910, working-class audiences were turning a blind eye to school children carrying tricolored flags, cockades, and ribbons. They even cheered them on.[81] Their new-found deference to the Belgian symbols had a decidedly Walloon quality. In the Borinage village of Pâturages, for instance, the annual school parade of 1913 was the scene of a remarkable celebration of socialism, militarism, Belgian patriotism, and Walloon ethnicity. A crowd of ten thousand watched the parade, headed by the socialist fanfare band, mayor, and aldermen, march onto the town's market square. The municipal school pupils were dressed up as Japanese, Turks, Italians, Chinese, Spaniards, Dutchmen, and Austrians. "Suddenly," *L'Avenir du Borinage* reported, "the applause doubles. Here comes the Walloon flag [. . .]. It advances majestically and proud, between the drummer and the clarion, leading the 'young' fighters of 1830." The socialist paper praised the brave attitude of "our young soldiers," who walked in formation, dressed up as veterans of the Belgian Revolution with guns shouldered, in blue blouses and tricolored sashes. "The crowd is moved. All eyes are wet with tears." In a climactic performance the young soldiers staged military exercises. "The drum beats, the bugle sounds, "Hail to the Flag" [the militaristic song *Salut au drapeau*] is played, and the Gallic rooster [i.e., the Walloon flag], proud and majestic, is lowered: the crowd rises in applause."[82] The positive reception of this parade reflects the rank and file's susceptibility to the increasingly Walloon propaganda of the Hainaut socialists. Tellingly, the very first celebration of the Walloon national holiday on September 28, 1913, was massively attended in the industrial towns of Frameries and Dour in the Borinage and Charleroi, Marcinelle, Gilly, Châtelineau, Couillet, Jumet, and Roux in the Pays Noir. In *Vooruit* an observer noted that attendance was "almost general" "wherever the celebrations were dedicated to the commemoration of the Revolution of September 1830."[83] Is it any wonder then that by 1913 Walloonness had become a selling point? *L'Avenir du Borinage* featured ads for the "Real Walloon Bitter," displaying the Walloon rooster and the Walloon motto *Wallon toujours*. The foregrounding of Walloon ethnicity was a response, as we have seen in Chapter 2, to perceived changes in the electoral landscape. In Hainaut this shift latched onto older grassroots patterns, and more specifically on the pro-French, anti-Flamingant, and anti-German interpretation of Belgian identity that had existed at least since the PSR dissidence.

In the Flemish-speaking stronghold of the BWP, Ghent, there were also fewer serious incidents with flag and anthem after the turn of the century. Yet, critical voices kept surfacing, rejecting the tricolor and the "Brabançonne" not only as *bourgeois* and *clerical* symbols, but also as tokens of *Belgianness* (see

**FIGURE 6** Ad from *L'Avenir du Borinage*, November 16–17, 1913, p. 3.

the jubilee festivities of 1905 in Chapter 3). This anti-Belgian discourse had been around since the founding of the party. In August 1886 some Catholic newspapers had criticized the BWP for demonstrating with the red flag. *Vooruit* had retorted that the "papists" were the first "to deny the so-called national flag" by flying "the sordid papal flag." "And what's more, what does the Belgian tricolor mean to the Flemings? Is that the flag of our forefathers? No, not at all." If it had not been for the 1830 Revolution that "separated us from our brethren, the Northern Netherlands, that infamous national flag would have been history."[84] This diatribe against Belgianness was extraordinary because at that exact moment the Brussels socialists went to great lengths to convince the democratic bourgeoisie that the red flag was not an anti-national symbol and that they were indeed of original Belgian stock.

**FIGURE 7** The Belgian tricolor in the Christian labor movement, 1. *De Domper*, August 16, 1891.

During the whole fin de siècle, both liberal and Catholic Flamingants, as well as the Christian labor movement, severely criticized the Ghent socialists for disrespecting Belgium's national symbols. The Catholic, anti-socialist worker's movement used allegorical prints to hammer home this message. In 1891 the front page of their paper, *De Domper* (*The Dupe*), depicted a respectable Catholic worker. Waving a Belgian flag inscribed with the motto "Religion, family, property," he vanquished the many-headed monster of socialism.

In 1903 the Catholic workers' journal *Volksmaandblad* (*The People's Monthly*) showed an angry mob of socialists, brandishing clubs, knives, pistols, red flags, and Phrygian caps, while calm Christian workers manned the ramparts against them. On the Catholic stronghold, a Belgian flag with the inscription "Thus far and no further!" flew. In the background was a Flemish lion flag.

**FIGURE 8** The Belgian tricolor in the Christian labor movement, 2. *Volksmaandblad: Orgaan van de anti-socialistische werkliedenbond van Gent*, November 1903.

It is no coincidence that the Belgian tricolor was larger and more prominently displayed than the Flemish lion. The positioning of both flags symbolized the subordination of their Flemish to their Belgian loyalty.

The Ghent socialists did not take this bait and instead insisted on the reactionary and anti-Flemish nature of the flag and the anthem. In the run-up to 1905, Steven Prenau, alias Boersen, monopolized *Vooruit*'s coverage of the national jubilee festivities together with the paper's editor-in-chief Aimé Bogaerts. Boersen spurned the national flag and the 1830 Revolution in unusually graphic language. Diplomats had amalgamated "the different ethnic tribes [*volksstammen*] that flourished on Belgium's soil" in a country bounded by "whimsical and random lines on a map" and symbolized by a black-yellow-red flag:

> O national tricolor! How to explain the colors of your unraveling cloth? Red: the blood the people have spilled for freedom; yellow: the gold of affluence and opulence reaped from the spilt blood; black: the Catholic religion [. . .] O national filthy rag, without soul, without meaning to the worker, go to shreds in the storm of international politics and fly into nothingness to the four corners of the earth.[85]

To analyze if and to what extent this anti-Belgian current reflected grassroots sentiments, the next two chapters turn toward Ghent and a unique source: the proletarian tweets.

*Chapter 8*

# PROLETARIAN TWEETS

In October 1894 a group of female textile workers had had enough of the sexual innuendo they were repeatedly subjected to by Catholic priests:

> Do you dare to publish a catechism with questions and answers from confession? 0.10. With questions asked by fat, unmarried priests of girls, 0.10. Pray tell, why do women not confess to nuns and men to priests, 0.10. To God it would not make any difference, 0.10. Or is God also opposed to women's rights, like you *Volkske* [diminutive term for the Catholic anti-socialist newspaper *Het Volk*, *The People*], 0.10. We, seamstresses, find confession filthy, disgusting, immoral, 0.10.[1]

Historians do not often get this close to ordinary workers. It is quite exhilarating to hear them speak this directly. These unfiltered voices have been preserved in a unique working-class source: the propaganda pence.

The propaganda pence were an annotated subscription list for the benefit of the BWP. Every financial gift to the party was accompanied by a short written message and subsequently published in a dedicated section of the party press. "Not only does this section give one the opportunity to tell a joke, say hello to a friend, talk to an acquaintance, denounce an abuse, decry an oppressor, open one's heart," the Ghent party paper *Vooruit* wrote in 1898, "one can also formulate elevated thoughts and proverbs in the propaganda pence, exercise oneself in thinking and writing about socialism and everything that concerns working people."[2] Because workers gave voice to whatever was on their mind and used the propaganda pence to communicate with each other, we can usefully compare them to today's tweets.

A complete tweet took the following form: "For the progress of socialism, J. Albr., 0.10."[3] First came the statement, then the author's initials, full name, or nickname, and possibly his or her occupation and place of residence, and finally the sum donated, in this case 0.10 Belgian francs or 10 centimes.

We can generally distinguish between three types of messages. Forty percent of all tweets merely mentioned the name of the donor: "Bruno, 0.05"; the organization or group behind the gift: "From the vendors of the journal *Vooruit*, 1.90"; or the circumstances of the collection: "Collected at Frans Herri's wedding in Vooruit ['s hall of events], 1.67."[4] Thirty percent of the tweets were socialist(-sounding) reflections, such as "Capitalism resembles an animal, whose open mouth is constantly ready to devour other people's goods, 0.10."[5] The remaining third were idiosyncratically personal statements or comments on daily life, such as "I will not beat my wife, 0.10."[6]

Sometimes people told humorous (ultra) short stories, by paying for consecutive tweets: "How will you ever get a wife, 0.10; you pass yourself off as a pastry cook who earns 35 francs a week and still you have no luck with women, 0.10; what's wrong with you, boy, 0.05."[7] Some workers even struck up conversations and replied to each other's messages in consecutive editions of the paper. Someone from the town of Mechelen would ask: "Cousins Alp. Sch. and Fr. Pr., how is your health, your cousin Fr. L., 0.10."[8] A week later the answer would come from Ghent: "Cousin Fr. L. all is well, Alp. Sch., 0.10; Cousin Fr. L., it couldn't be better, Fr. Pr., 0.10."[9]

For the whole fin de siècle hundreds of thousands of these "proletarian tweets" have been preserved. In this chapter I use a sample of 27,529 tweets published in *Vooruit* between February 1886 and December 1900, from at least a thousand different working-class individuals. Roughly estimated, this accounts for 10 to 15 percent of all tweets published in *Vooruit* during this period.[10]

## A UNIQUE SOURCE

At the end of the nineteenth century newspaper publishing was democratized, in part because production costs declined with mechanization. Although printing a paper came within the reach of organizations run by workers, it remained an expensive endeavor and the working-class press was hard put to make ends meet. In the Belgian case, socialist papers were financed in part through the successful consumer cooperatives of the BWP.

Additional funding came from a particular form of subscription lists: the propaganda pence.

Across Europe a host of different social and ideological groups used annotated subscription lists to collect money for specific, practical goals. In December 1898 the French anti-Semitic and nationalist paper *La Libre Parole* started a subscription list to support the widow of Hubert-Joseph Henry, Alfred Dreyfus' main opponent. Eighteen lists were published, containing the names of the donors, the amount given, and a short anti-Semitic statement. The "Monument Henry," as it was called by its supporters, is an exception in that it has attracted the attention of historians.[11] On the whole, research on sources such as this is thin on the ground.[12]

In the Belgian socialist movement the practice of subscription lists was instituted in 1875. For the first time a separate section called "propaganda pence" appeared in the Antwerp paper *De Werker* (*The Worker*), the official organ of the Belgian branch of the First International. The phenomenon spread to Ghent and Brussels, and over the Belgian border to the Dutch cities of Vlissingen and Amsterdam.[13] From February 1896 onward the Belgian antisocialist Catholic labor movement imitated the practice in its Ghent paper *Het Volk* (The People).

With the founding of the newspaper *Vooruit* in 1884, the Ghent socialists started to publish ad hoc subscription lists for special occasions, such as the parliamentary elections in Germany or large strikes in Belgium and abroad. From February 1886 onward *Vooruit* featured a separate propaganda pence section, published at least twice a week, each time filling an eighth to a quarter of the total copy. The Ghent propaganda pence quickly became the most successful of all such initiatives, yielding substantial sums. In 1894 it gathered 6,018.25 Belgian francs, four times the yearly wage of a Ghent cotton spinner, enough to pay one to two full-time editors.[14]

The Ghent socialists actively publicized their propaganda pence fund by publishing the proceeds half-yearly and naming and shaming neighborhoods and towns that "had not fulfilled their duty."[15] As *Vooruit* was the main Flemish-language socialist paper for Belgium and the north of France, the tweets had very diverse origins. Most obviously hailed from Ghent (18,738 in our sample of 27,529). The rest mainly came from Belgium's two westernmost Flemish-speaking provinces: East and West Flanders (6,063), including the towns of Bruges (980) and Menen/Menin (698); further to the east the Brussels *agglomération* (554), Leuven (611), and Mechelen (426); and finally the northwest of France, from the French border town of Tourcoing up to the city of Lille (1,312).

The success of the propaganda pence fund was a token of the tight socialist pillar community that was taking shape in Ghent. Appeals in *Vooruit*, pamphlets at rallies, and posters across town incessantly reminded workers of their duty to contribute: "Do you, workers, love socialism, yourself, your future, your children? If so, donate weekly [...] to continue the battle."[16] This enthusiasm clearly separated the Ghent socialists from their comrades in other Belgian cities. The latter's *Organisationspatriotismus*, or organizational devotion, was less developed and their propaganda pence were accordingly less popular or even nonexistent. In 1898 Edouard Anseele complained in an open letter to the Brussels party paper *Le Peuple* that in Ghent "the weekly payment for the propaganda pence has become a habit; while in Brussels this is not the case." He wanted his fellow socialists in the capital "to talk and sing for the propaganda pence" "every Sunday when you are among comrades," after every meeting and rally, after "every family party, marriage, baptism, etc."[17] Anseele's appeal apparently fell on deaf ears, because the propaganda pence section in *Le Peuple* was much shorter. As a historical source, the Brussels pence were less interesting because they contained more collective tweets that merely provided the names of the donors and the amount given. In other BWP federations the local press was often too weak and unstructured to support a long-lasting and successful propaganda pence fund.

Over the years the Ghent propaganda pence lost some of their luster. In 1898 they raked in more than 7,000 Belgian francs,[18] but two years later this had fallen to 3,000 francs.[19] As the social-democratic movement in Ghent grew and became more institutionalized and bureaucratic, supporters were solicited so often for their money, time, and energy that they became more selective with their donations. At the same time the *Vooruit* editorial board professionalized.[20] It tried to get a firmer grip on the excessive volume of the propaganda pence section by dissuading individual, unruly tweets and promoting collective, anodyne gifts. For these reasons, my sample runs from February 1886, when the very first separate propaganda pence section was published in *Vooruit*, to December 1900, after which date this source became less voluminous and more controlled by party cadres.

Workers could get their tweets published in Vooruit's newspaper in three ways. In the early years, they dictated or wrote down their statement on a piece of paper or a subscription list at the paper's headquarters or in one of the party premises and red cafés across town. Later, with the growing success of the scheme, the party sent collectors to pick up donations and messages at rallies, in cafés, or even in workers' homes when bread and coal from the cooperative was home-delivered. Finally, it was possible to mail a statement to the paper, enclosing stamps instead of money.

Identifying the authors of the tweets beyond their (self-reported) name or initials is only possible in exceptional cases. Yet we may safely assume that a large portion were ordinary workers rather than party cadres, as they did not heed the official guidelines on contributions, especially about gossip and libel (see below). At the same time the tweeters did not belong to the completely destitute classes either as they were militant and comfortable enough to donate money to the party, albeit in small amounts between 5 and 20 centimes. This reflected the overall composition of the Ghent socialist movement. The rank and file were situated somewhere in between the labor aristocracy and the lumpenproletariat, in a large stratum of low to average skilled and accordingly remunerated factory workers, mainly in the textile industry, but also in metallurgy and the dockyards.[21]

Like other forms of *écritures ordinaires*, the many instances of "ordinary writings" people engage in in daily life,[22] the proletarian tweets have characteristics of both oral and written communication and of both individual and collective activity. The messages, though written, were often in dialect and sometimes employed phonetic signs unfamiliar in standard Flemish-Dutch. Illiterates could and did join in through what is called "mediated literacy."[23] Journal hawkers, acquaintances, and even officially appointed "propaganda pence writers" were at hand to help them.[24] Tweeting was an eminently social activity. On Sundays and after meetings people came together to write collectively. This is evidenced in such statements as "I am a socialist and I will remain one, 0.10. *Me too*, 0.10" and "I don't care, 0.10. Just put something on paper, 0.10," the latter obviously said by someone without inspiration.[25] In socialist gathering places singing, dancing, gaming, and dining often accompanied the collection of tweets.

Writing or dictating the statements was a social affair, and so too was reading them. A *Vooruit* journalist wrote in 1898: "We all know what joy, what satisfaction it brings when one reads or has someone read one's words, one's thoughts, yes, even one's jokes and cracks in the propaganda pence."[26] Because the messages were read out aloud in socialist public places, it is safe to assume that the contributions of illiterates were taken down fairly accurately and not manipulated by the transcriber.

Although the propaganda pence were out in the open, they also had characteristics of what James C. Scott has called "hidden transcripts." According to Scott, the less powerful in society adopt a strategic discourse when addressing their superiors. This so-called public transcript is "the open interaction between subordinates and those who dominate."[27] We cannot take a public transcript at face value because "every subordinate group creates, out of its ordeal, a 'hidden transcript' that represents a critique of power spoken behind the back of the dominant."[28] For such a hidden transcript to surface, two conditions must be met: "first, [...] it is voiced in a sequestered social site where the control, surveillance, and repression of the dominant are least able to reach, and, second, [...] this sequestered social milieu is composed entirely of close confidants who share similar experiences of domination."[29] The propaganda pence fulfill both conditions. Factory owners, bourgeois adversaries, despised foremen, and other dominant groups could read the proletarian tweets, but because of the anonymity the propaganda pence offered, they had no means to control or punish the authors. Neither, for that matter, could BWP officials easily interfere. Senior party echelons were sometimes annoyed by the "deplorable" quality of the messages. As early as 1878 the highest executive council of the Ghent socialists complained that the propaganda pence section in *De Werker* was an "idiotic hodgepodge" of libel, gossip, and "mostly insignificant words."[30] The editorial board of *Vooruit* tried to streamline the tweets by insisting that statements be short and edifying.[31] Outright censorship, however, was minimal, evidenced by coarse remarks that occasioned no intervention: for example, "Jozef fucked [*verneukt*] Marie, 0.10."[32] Because every tweet was linked to a concrete financial contribution that had to be publically accounted for, all statements made it into the paper, either in original form or redacted. The latter, indicated by the phrase "personal statement not published,"[33] were highly unusual. In our entire sample of 27,529, they accounted for just 150 instances, or barely 0.5 percent of all published tweets. Moreover, the (very attentive) readers were quick to denounce the rare censorship, and *Vooruit*'s editors did not stop them: "I protest against the shortening or suppressing of statements, 0.10."[34] Overall the party hardly ever enforced the guidelines with respect to propriety in order not to put off donors. Ultimately, the tweets were explicitly published outside the responsibility of the editorial board. Seen in this light, the pence were a site of *Eigen-Sinn*, occasionally directed against the civilizing attempts of the socialist movement itself.

As a hidden transcript, the proletarian tweets had three major functions. First, they socialized and disciplined those writing and reading the tweets into a cohesive group. Workers behaving improperly were called to account. Strikebreakers and police informers were warned: "There is a scab who calls himself a socialist, 0.10. He'd better not do it again, 0.10."[35] A second important function was taunting opponents. The archenemy of grassroots socialists in Ghent was not so much the bourgeoisie as fellow workers who had "fallen" for the Catholic labor organizations. The "anti-socialists," as they explicitly called themselves, copied the organizational blueprint of the BWP, from unions, cooperative societies, and the press down to the propaganda pence. The intense competition made the relations between both groups very tense. A typical taunt in the propaganda pence read:

> There is no lower form of life than dunces, 0.05. They always talk about the working man and are paid as secret police informers to work against the working people, 0.05. It's strange, they are only concerned about workers' fate where the socialists are strongest, what a joke, 0.05. The dunces' clique does indeed have good intentions concerning working men . . . to hoodwink them, 0.05.[36]

"Dunce," *domper*, or literally "smotherer," someone who smothers/obscures the ideals of the Enlightenment, was the tweeters' preferred slur for the Catholic anti-socialist workers' movement. The anti-socialists ultimately adopted this term of abuse as an honorary title. They even called their own paper *De Domper* (The Dupe).

Especially in sexual matters, socialist workers accused their adversaries of hypocrisy, debauchery, and moral degeneration: "Because the tall foreman from the Lys [factory] received a good beating, 0.10. Because he will no longer try to catch mice behind the cupboard [i.e., grope women], 0.10."[37] A recurring charge against priests was pedophilia: "It [a socialist meeting] was more dignified, papists, 0.10. Than in your caverns, 0.10. Where young girls play 'grow the tree' [a popular children's game that signals a sexual connotation in this context] with the parish priest, 0.10. To whom it may concern, 0.10."[38] Tweets often contained veiled threats like this.

A third major characteristic of the propaganda pence's hidden transcript was its symbolic inversion of power relations. The subordinate could nominally turn the tables on the dominant, a central function of *Eigen-Sinn*. On occasion they did this literally by inverting the names of their opponents. The Catholic paper *News of the Day* (*Nieuws van den Dag*) became *News of the Night*

(*Nieuws van den Nacht*); *The Free Worker* (*De Vrije Werker*), *The Forced Worker* (*De Gedwongen Werker*); the liberal workers' organization Love of Freedom (*De Vrijheidsliefde*), Love of Blacklegs (*Kruipersliefde*). Belittling diminutives were also frequently used. The Catholic workers' movement's paper *The People* (*Het Volk*) was thus targeted: "The Little People [*Het Volkje*] should become larger because it is no longer large enough to wrap up its readers' sandwiches, 0.10."[39]

As the propaganda pence provided anonymity, socialist workers could voice opinions about their "betters" that would have cost them dearly in other circumstances. They addressed their superiors with a gleeful lack of respect, for instance insulting the liberal mayor of Ghent: "The tyrant Lippens will choke in his own filth, 0.65."[40] Workers could criticize social abuses without inhibition, whether minor: "they should scrub the toilets better at Karel De Hemptinne's [factory], 0.30"; or major: "The bosses are acquitted; the dockers are convicted. No, there is no class justice, P.D.V., 0.15."[41] As the last statement shows, sarcasm and irony were powerful tools for reestablishing self-esteem. When Edouard Anseele, the leader of the Ghent socialists, was accused in 1886 by the Catholic paper the *Ghent Townsman* (*De Gentenaar*) of being a slumlord, someone replied in the propaganda pence: "Message to the 'Liar' [i.e., *De Gentenaar*]. Anseele has again bought some houses: I saw him leave the *bazar* [department store] with them, 0.20."[42]

These salient quotes in themselves provide an indication of the themes and social categories prevalent in the propaganda pence, but this rich source allows us to go beyond this intuitive assessment. Thanks to our large sample, we can draw up an identification matrix of the different social categories that were available to Ghent workers in their everyday lives and situate nationhood and ethnicity within this matrix.

### "RED IS OUR FAVORITE COLOR": TWEETS AND IDENTIFICATION[43]

Seventy percent of the propaganda pence messages in my sample, 19,461 tweets to be precise, contained a reference to at least one social category, with many referring to several at once. When someone wrote, "Fellow party members from Church Street, let's not be sidetracked by the dunces' baloney, our deeds will prove who we are, 0.10,"[44] he or she identified with his/her neighborhood and party, while drawing on anti-Catholic sentiments and calling for organizational patriotism. After labeling every tweet in this way, I ended up with the classification of social categories shown in Table 1.[45] If we only take the tweets from Ghent into account, 18,738 in all, 13,031 of them contained a reference to at least one social category (see Table 2).

The most prominent social category in the propaganda pence was *Organisationspatriotismus*, or organizational pride, mentioned in about 45 percent of all tweets. These messages often included calls for unity and organization: "Fellow party members, do your best to make progress, 0.15"; tokens of pride in the high attendance at party rallies: "Never have I witnessed so many people at our meetings, 0.10"; praise for their own organizations: "I visited [the local party headquarters] Vooruit for the first time and I will never leave again, 0.41"; or declarations of devotion to the local leadership: "I want my only son to be like Anseele, a mother, H.L., 0.05."[46] It is not surprising that organizational pride was the most frequently referred to category as the propaganda pence was in itself an expression of *Organisationspatriotismus*.

About a quarter of all tweets referred to class and or socialism. Variations on the literal phrase "we socialists" or "we workers" repeatedly appeared, but these loyalties were also less explicitly expressed in messages glorifying "labor" or "our social struggle" and propagating the "rescue" or "awakening" of the people.[47] These donors identified themselves or their allies as "fellow party members," "companions," "friends of the people," "brothers," "workers," or "laborers."[48] The color red, the red flag, and the "Marseillaise" were often mentioned.[49]

Many workers called themselves victims of persecution and oppression, "factory slaves," "starvelings," or oppressed people living a "dog's life."[50] Some reappropriated the disparaging labels their opponents stuck to them such as "scum" (*krapoel*) and "canaille." This is hardly surprising as one of the most popular battle songs of the Ghent socialists was "Canaille," with its chorus: "You are canaille, they reproached us! Hail to you, O name, which contains so much greatness."[51]

Although they described themselves as "socialists," the tweeters were clearly of the reformist, not the revolutionary type. Over the years, most references to revolution, 215 tweets in total, were ritualized invocations. They mentioned the sale of pins commemorating the Jacobins or performances of the "Marseillaise," the "Communard's Orphan," "Bloody Snowflakes," and other such songs.[52] The last two were written by the Ghent socialist composer Ed Smol. They commemorated the Paris Commune and expressed a formalized form of revolutionary enthusiasm at best, being schmaltzy tearjerkers rather than spirited battle songs. The "Communard's Orphan," for instance, told the story of a girl whose father died as a Communard and who consigned her red doll to his grave "while she sobbed with sad moans."[53]

**TABLE 1** Absolute and relative references to specific social categories in the entire sample of proletarian tweets

| Social category | Absolute number of tweets referring to this category | Percentage of tweets referring to this category[1] |
|---|---|---|
| *Organisationspatriotismus* | 8,484 | 43.58% |
| Working class/socialism | 5,242 | 26.93% |
| Occupational group | 4,069 | 20.90% |
| Street/neighborhood | 2,704 | 13.89% |
| Anti-Catholic sentiments | 2,222 | 11.41% |
| Gender | 1,556 | 7.99% |
| Town | 1,394 | 7.16% |
| Anti-establishment sentiments | 1,314 | 6.75% |
| Internationalism | 470 | 2.41% |
| Anti-militarism | 313 | 1.61% |
| Nation/language/ethnicity | 305 | 1.57% |
| Revolutionary sentiments | 285 | 1.46% |
| Anti-liberal sentiments | 229 | 1.18% |
| Republicanism | 138 | 0.71% |
| Anti-anarchism | 118 | 0.61% |
| Anti-middle-class sentiments | 39 | 0.20% |
| Anti-colonialism | 37 | 0.20% |
| Anti-rural sentiments | 19 | 0.10% |
| Anti-Flemish movement | 10 | 0.05% |

1. Relative to the total number of tweets in which at least one category is mentioned.

**TABLE 2** Absolute and relative references to specific social categories in proletarian tweets from Ghent

| Social category | Absolute number of tweets referring to this category | Percentage of tweets referring to this category[1] |
|---|---|---|
| *Organisationspatriotismus* | 5,859 | 44.96% |
| Working class/socialism | 3,420 | 26.25% |
| Occupational group | 2,904 | 22.29% |
| Street/neighborhood | 2,463 | 18.90% |
| Anti-Catholic sentiments | 1,207 | 9.26% |
| Gender | 1,175 | 9.02% |
| Town | 655 | 5.03% |
| Anti-establishment sentiments | 601 | 4.61% |
| Internationalism | 336 | 2.58% |
| Anti-militarism | 243 | 1.86% |
| Nation/language/ethnicity | 200 | 1.53% |
| Revolutionary sentiments | 136 | 1.04% |
| Anti-liberal sentiments | 109 | 0.84% |
| Republicanism | 85 | 0.65% |
| Anti-anarchism | 68 | 0.52% |
| Anti-middle-class sentiments | 27 | 0.21% |
| Anti-colonialism | 11 | 0.08% |
| Anti-rural sentiments | 7 | 0.05% |
| Anti-Flemish movement | 5 | 0.04% |

1. Relative to the total number of tweets in which at least one category is mentioned.

In 1886, the propaganda pence did contain some unabashedly revolutionary statements, such as: "My last dimes are for gunpowder, D.D.V., 0.10—And mine for a stick of dynamite, 0.15."[54] These were, of course, reactions to the bloody repression of the Spring Revolt of 1886. In the suffrage campaign of 1891–1893, too, violence was sometimes threatened, as in the following tweet from Bruges: "General suffrage or death is our motto from now on, 0.10."[55] Overall, however, there were only 92 tweets that explicitly called for violence and revolution. The majority of these dated from the period 1886–1893, after which they tended to disappear. The victory of plural suffrage in 1893 seems to have made the rank and file more moderate, if it was revolutionary to begin with. The latter is in doubt. Even before 1893 calls for revolution were more sedate than one would expect at first glance. An 1888 tweet from Ghent appears to be boldly revolutionary: "[I donate money] to speed up the day of salvation, *by whatever means*, 0.15," but it was followed by a more nuanced one: "*Preferably, however, as calmly as possible*, if only it comes quickly, 0.10."[56] We see the same ambivalence in an 1890 tweet in French from the northern French city of Roubaix: "Vive la Révolution et l'Evolution, Druant, 0.10."[57] Paradoxically this militant simultaneously celebrated the violent overthrow of capitalism and "évolution," the gradual transformation of society. This was a superb illustration of the party's ambiguous strategy of revolutionary reformism.[58]

In the entire sample, there are only ten outright expressions of support for anarchism, as opposed to 118 explicit denunciations of it. As the social-democratic movement in Ghent cast a broader net of reformist organizations over the city's masses, workers turned against anarchism and revolutionary ideas. As early as 1887, a tweeter from Ghent remarked: "I think it is good that every party member prepare for battle, but continuously ranting and raving about the revolution is utter madness, 0.15."[59] In 1887 the Ghent BWP was challenged by a short-lived anarchist dissidence around August Lootens's magazine *The Uprising (De Opstand)*.[60] This explains such tweets as, "They ask for revolutionaries in the Uprising, not to fight the exploiters and other oppressors, but to fight the workers who want to elevate themselves from their misery, 0.10."[61] Anarchists rejected the "bourgeois" methods of the Ghent social-democratic cooperative movement, but they in turn were accused of siding with the proletariat's enemies in order to divide the working class: "The two dozen revolutionaries (?) have increased the dunces' clique with some extra papists, 0.05."[62] This tweeter mimicked the sarcastic question or exclamation marks journalists of *Vooruit* and the Antwerp party paper *De Werker* used when referring to their opponents.[63]

All in all, the grassroots seemed to be in accord with the reformist course of the party cadres. This was evident in a broadly shared discourse of rights and duties. On their way to the great national suffrage rally in Brussels in August 1890, for example, a group of Ghent workers tweeted, "We fulfill our duties and demand our rights, w. 1.07."[64] Many tweets mentioned classic reformist demands such as universal suffrage and advocated political action to gain higher wages and better working conditions.[65]

Remarkably, only three tweets in the entire sample lauded Karl Marx.[66] This pales in comparison to the 226 explicit tributes to Edouard Anseele and the 43 to his brother-in-arms Edmond Van Beveren. These numbers bear witness both to the Ghent socialists' exceptional organizational pride and to the theoretical poverty of their brand of socialism. The conceptual deficit was also reflected in the very low frequency of the terms "capital," "proletariat," "Marxism," "class," and their cognates. Symptomatically, the founding members of a socialist union in the Ghent suburb of Ledeberg described their program in 1886 as "Freedom, bread and education are our motto, 2.50."[67] Intuitive and emotional descriptions of the socialist program abounded: "Socialism is based on love and justice, 0.10"; "All injustice must disappear, 0.10"; "Only through love and unity will improvement come, 1.54."[68] There was indeed a strong moral subtext in the tweets of "progress," "emancipation," "fraternity," "freedom," "reason," "equality," and "justice."[69]

Nearly as frequent as references to the working class/socialism were those to one's occupation. In this group there is a large overrepresentation of employees of Vooruit's many cooperative enterprises. In 1898 Vooruit employed 327 people, which made it a middle-sized company in local terms—in comparison, the largest cotton mill of Ghent engaged 1,800 workers in 1890 and the sixth largest 350.[70] About 60 percent of the tweets that referred to occupation were written by Vooruit personnel. They contributed messages in the following vein: "By the janitor of the Vooruit premises on the Garenplaats, 0.25" or "A carpenter of Vooruit, 0.20."[71] Three-fourths were service workers: office clerks, sales people in the Vooruit department store, news vendors, printers and delivery personnel of coal and bread; the other fourth were manual laborers, including bakers, woodworkers, and carpenters.

Does the overrepresentation of Vooruit personnel skew our sample toward anodyne, officially sanctioned party opinions? Did these employees echo their employer's voice rather than express their own? There is ample evidence that argues against such a view and reaffirms the propaganda pence as a site of *Eigen-Sinn*. First of all, because of the social pressure on Vooruit's employees to contribute openly to the propaganda pence, we can safely assume that tweets not containing a self-identification as party personnel, meaning 90 percent of our sample of 19,461, came from outside this narrow occupational group. Second, the roughly two thousand tweets from self-identified Vooruit employees came from a relatively small group of individuals. Most of these tweets were weekly recurring messages that merely mentioned the writers' occupation. The "Garenplaats janitor," for instance, occurs thirty-two times in the sample with the exact same tweet. Clearly, structural donations to the propaganda pence were a socially accepted expectation for party-paid employees. In this sense their tweets were (forced) expressions of *Organisationspatriotismus*. If we take this repetition into account, about a fifth of all individual tweeters whose occupation we know were employed by Vooruit. This is still an overrepresentation, but not such a massive one. Ultimately, about 80 percent of the individuals whose occupation we know were not employed by Vooruit. They came from a wide array of industrial occupations, including textile workers, metalworkers, builders, and dockworkers.[72]

The last group of frequent categories were gender, town, neighborhood, and negative identifications against Catholics and the establishment. The propaganda pence are one of the few social sites that offer more insight into socialist women. The tweets of these women reveal their struggles with the party's machismo and with the corresponding gender roles: "We ask the men, when the women have to attend meetings, to stay with the children for an hour, 0.25; The men should have a better understanding of their duty, 0.20."[73] Some male party members were indeed hesitant about the active, public role of women. On the occasion of the BWP's national suffrage rally in Brussels in August 1890, a man from Ghent tweeted without any irony: "If I was master, no women would go to Brussels, E.V.D., 0.10." His wife concurred: "Women cannot go to Brussels, V.D.'s wife, 0.10."[74] But most female tweeters rejected this attitude: "Are we, women, less capable than men, 0.20—We who hold the key to the upbringing of the future generation, 0.20."[75] Another woman asked, "Many have read Bebel's work Woman and Socialism, and they approve of what's in it, but do they act like it, D., 0.10."[76] Gender references pertained not only to women. Nearly half were about the construction of masculinity. Calls for resilience and social struggle often had a subtext of martial masculinity, as shown by this 1886 tweet from Kortrijk: "True men, we only need true men in our midst, C.H.O., 0.10."[77]

References to one's hometown and one's street/neighborhood were in a sense communicating vessels. Messages from Ghent rarely referred to the former, in only 4.61 percent of the cases, but they frequently mentioned the latter, in 18.9 percent of the cases. Because the average tweet came from Ghent and the city was the self-evident frame of reference, there was no need to highlight one's urban origins. By contrast, Ghent tweeters found it important to emphasize their neighborhood, as in: "Those from the St. Peter's neighborhood will not sleep, 0.10."[78] Such references often expressed organizational patriotism. This is hardly surprising since the tight sociability in Ghent's boroughs was intimately linked to the rise of small local societies that were at the root of the socialist movement.[79] As a rule, tweets from outside Ghent marked the hometown aspect more frequently than messages collected within the city.

The two most important Others against whom workers identified themselves were the establishment and Catholics, mentioned in, respectively, 1,314 and 2,222 tweets. Anti-establishment tweets, such as "To be a factory supervisor you have to be a slave driver, 0.10,"[80] targeted a generic enemy that was not further specified in ideological or political terms. This category included among others the bourgeoisie, the authorities, official functionaries, the police, the gendarmerie and civic guard, the judiciary, employers, foremen, slumlords, etc.

The main nemesis of the socialist rank and file were Catholics. A small minority of tweeters explicitly used the terms "nonbelieving" (*vrijzinnig*) or "free-thinking" (*vrijdenkend*) to describe themselves.[81] This shows that grassroots anti-Catholicism did not so much imply a rejection of faith itself but rather an anticlerical dislike of the church and its ministers. The figure of Christ was widely admired. For some militants he was a proto-socialist: "Christ acted very differently, but he was a republican and a socialist, while [the Ghent bishop] Lambrecht is the opposite, 0.10."[82] By contrast, the rank and file's anticlericalism was unambiguous and fierce. In 645 tweets, the church and the clergy were excoriated as "the cursed and oppressive sect," "the black vermin," "the filthy cabal of priests," the "clique of black sloths," "the black executioners," "the fat, lazy, loafing louts they call priests," and "the black child molesters," with black referring to the color of their cloth.[83] Repeatedly complaints were voiced about clerical child abuse and sexual harassment: "Parents keep your children out of the confessional box, remember the questions the priests asked you when you were young and you will know why, 0.20."[84]

This extremely negative attitude extended to the Catholic party and the Christian labor movement. In 424 tweets Catholic party members were called "black scum," "asses," the "filthy race of papists," and "papist dunces."[85] The Catholic anti-socialist workers' movement received the brunt of the tweeters' wrath. No less than 880 tweets contained insults: for example, "What is a dunce? A low-life and cowardly person who sells himself for a few pennies to the enemies of his fellow sufferers and thus volunteers his neck for the slave's chains. He is a foul coward and a sell-out, 0.20."[86] The most innocuous term of abuse was "wage undercutters and scabs."[87] More common and inflammatory labels were "bitches," "creeps," "the filthy dunces' flock," "filthy vermin," "shit shovelers," and "sewer rats."[88]

There was more grassroots invective directed at the clergy, the Catholic party, and anti-socialist workers than at any other of the socialists' competitors. In contrast to the 2,222 anti-Catholic statements, liberals were skewered in only 229 tweets, Flamingants in barely 10. An 1887 tweet from the western border town of Menen/Menin summarized it well: "I'd rather have the liberals than the papists, 0.10."[89] In a word, Catholics were the most significant ideological Other against whom the socialist rank and file identified themselves.

Strikingly, a number of categories and values that were central to the official socialist doctrine barely registered in the propaganda pence. As mentioned, revolutionary sentiments did not occur very frequently, but neither did internationalism, anti-militarism, republicanism, and anti-imperialism. The bulk of all mentions of internationalism in the sample, 360 out of 470 tweets, were implicit references. They included homages to May 1, the French Revolution and the Commune,[90] the sale of Jacobin pins, and performances of the "Marseillaise" and other internationalist songs. Explicit appeals to internationalism were a minority and they exhibit an ambiguity we have already encountered. During the whole fin de siècle, the theory of radical cosmopolitanism was popular among the Ghent leadership, but in practice they could not escape the pull of banal nationalism.[91] The same goes for the propaganda pence. The sample contains 57 radically cosmopolitan messages, such as "Every thought of nationality is nonsense, 0.10,"[92] but the majority of internationalist statements (80 tweets) did not call into question the notion of separate nations. They were very concrete expressions of fraternization, often with German socialists.[93] In the next chapter we will look more closely into this form of national "inter-nationalism."[94]

Anti-militarism was only marginally present in the propaganda pence, mainly as generic references to the activities of the Draftee Circles (*Lotelingskringen*) and the Socialist Young Guard or to anti-militaristic songs such as "The Draftee Song" (*Het lotelingslied*) and "No More Draft, No More Blood Law" (*Geen loting, geen bloedwet meer*). Explicit references to pacifism and denunciations of the army in and of itself were rare.[95] Most tweeters' criticism did not go beyond the bad living conditions in the barracks and the injustice of the lottery system: "As a draftee I curse the blood law, id., 0.15."[96] The occurrence of anti-militarism was highly seasonal, concentrated around the February draw and in September, when the new recruits entered the barracks. These observations dovetail with the conclusion of Chapter 4 that anti-militarism was a ritual performed twice a year, without everyday relevance except for the few convinced cadres of the Socialist Young Guard.

Republicanism was barely mentioned in the propaganda pence. In line with the findings of Chapter 5, the tweeters' wrath was directed against the person of Leopold II, nicknamed Carton, Pol, or Popol, rather than the monarchy as an institution. During the Spring Revolt of 1886, for instance, the king was irreverently addressed as "Pol, old chap, you'd better leave before it is too late, 0.10; Pol, you are soiling your pants, aren't you, 0.10; Pol, you'd better grease up your legs to get running, 0.10."[97] Often, animosity toward Leopold II was linked to his colony, as in this 1887 tweet from Ghent: "If Carton doesn't like it here, he can go to the Congo, 0.10."[98] The Congo was mentioned only thirty-seven times and often served as a warning to the socialists' opponents: they'd better behave or they would end up there. A seaman from Ostend wrote in 1891, "From a sea slave who would like to send the whole pack of exploiters to the Congo, 0.21."[99] In line with the analysis of Chapter 5, none of these tweets were anti-imperialist in the sense that they rejected the notion of a colony. There is even some evidence of a banal form of colonialism in the propaganda pence. One of the cafés party members frequented and where collections were held for the propaganda pence was called the Congo.[100]

Finally, 305 tweets referred in some way to nation, language, or ethnicity. In about 15 percent of these cases they exemplified a self-evident acceptance of the existence of other nationalities, as in this 1893 tweet from Ghent: "Youngsters make yourself heard like our friends from Holland, 0.05."[101] In more than a third of the cases, there was an identification with Flanders. From Bruges came this tweet during the 1892 suffrage campaign: "Papists, if you have any Flemish blood flowing through your veins, you will not reject the discussion [about a constitutional review], otherwise you are cowards and frauds, 0.10."[102] In 10 percent of the cases, reference was made to Wallonia, as in this French tweet from Brussels: "A Walloon, friend of the Flemings, Rasse, 0.25."[103] Belgian identifications were about as frequent; for instance, "With general suffrage, all Belgians will awake, 0.10."[104] There is a final set of fifty-eight messages that referred negatively to the national symbols of Belgium. In 1889, for example, someone from the Brussels suburb of Sint-Pieters-Jette/Jette-Saint-Pierre sarcastically denounced the fiction of legal equality as enshrined in the Belgian constitution: "All Belgians are equal when they sleep, 0.10."[105]

What do all these numbers mean? The high frequency of positive categories such as the working class and organizational pride and of negative ones such as Catholicism and the establishment, likely reflects their everyday relevance. These loyalties were continuously activated and made explicit by daily contacts with hierarchical superiors, priests, and Catholic anti-socialist workers on and off the shop floor.

Conversely, some social categories did not appear frequently in the propaganda pence. Does this mean they had limited appeal or rather that these categories were too self-evident to be mentioned explicitly? The answer differs with the context. The relatively few references to revolution or to the violent overthrow of the capitalist regime do not reflect a form of banalization. After all, the propaganda pence contain at least as many forceful rejections of anarchism and revolution. *Organisationspatriotismus* channeled the negative and potentially violent energy of the rank and file toward the expansion of their own organizations, in a case of what has been termed "negative integration." In anticipation of the collapse of capitalism and the bourgeois order, workers had to lay the organizational groundwork for a takeover of power, an attitude Dieter Groh has characterized as "revolutionary attentism."[106] Anarchism and insurrectionary enthusiasm were at odds with organizational patriotism and the peculiar revolutionary reformism of Belgian socialism.[107] This grassroots reformism spilled over into a more accommodating attitude vis-à-vis the monarchy, the colony, and the army and explains the infrequent occurrence of republican, anti-imperialist, and anti-militarist messages in the propaganda pence.

Just like revolutionary sentiments, hometown loyalty was underrepresented in the propaganda pence, but unlike the former the latter was not peripheral. Jacob Van Artevelde, who led Ghent's rebellion against the French king in the fourteenth century and gave his name to the city's most widely used epithet, the *Arteveldestad* (the city of Artevelde), is only mentioned three times in the entire sample. Yet, given the importance of urban pride as one of the defining characteristics of Ghent socialism,[108] it is hard to assume that the rank and file would have been agnostic about Van Artevelde. Rather, it is more likely that the propaganda pence were so idiosyncratically local that there was hardly any need to express hometown identity explicitly. The distinctive Ghent context also explains the minimal occurrence of animosity toward (the overwhelmingly anti-socialist) farmers and peasants from the surrounding countryside. Within the very urban environment in which Ghent workers lived, there was hardly any opportunity or reason to use the countryside as a foil. While the socialist rank and file were constantly confronted with the urban, anti-socialist Catholic workers' movement, there was no daily conflict with peasants.

These reflections on revolution, the monarchy, the military, the Congo, hometown loyalty, and the countryside bring us to the crucial question: Does the relative absence of language, ethnicity, and nation imply national indifference or a banal form of nationalism that does not speak its name, but is present in the background nonetheless? This question is central to the next chapter.

Chapter 9

# LANGUAGE, THE FLEMISH MOVEMENT, AND THE NATION

"My farewell to the party members in general and my friends on Bijlokevest [Street] in particular; chased from Germany to Belgium and from Belgium to Paris we can only hope to meet friends everywhere, *socialists have no fatherland*, the German, 0.50."[1] In July 1892 this man—we can infer his gender from the original Dutch grammar—announced his imminent departure from Ghent. He had fled his country of origin, Germany, and now had to leave his adopted hometown as well. The radically internationalist motto at the end of his farewell note—*socialists have no fatherland*—did not stop him from instinctively and unreflectively identifying himself as German. The majority of internationalist messages in the propaganda pence did not question the notion of national identity. They reflected an "inter-nationalism" that took the existence of separate nations and distinct ethnolinguistic identities for granted.[2] To get a firmer grasp on such issues, this chapter examines grassroots attitudes toward language, the Flemish movement, "internationalism," the Belgian nation, and Flemish ethnicity.

## GRASSROOTS LANGUAGE USE AND CONTACT

Language equality between French and Flemish was a plank of the official BWP program, but in practice French dominated in the national party institutions. This posed few problems because most Flemish party leaders were functionally bilingual and in the Flemish party branches Flemish was used exclusively.[3] Brussels and Wallonia were another matter altogether.

At the beginning of the twentieth century, the majority of workers in the Brussels *agglomération* and specifically in downtown Brussels and the industrialized western municipalities of Molenbeek, Anderlecht, Koekelberg, and Jette were monolingually Flemish. The capital's party cadres, by contrast, consisted of highly skilled French-speaking craftsmen such as gilders, marble workers, and typographers. They neglected to organize the Flemish-speaking proletariat.[4] Symptomatically, it was not until December 1903 that Brussels had its first Flemish-speaking party organ, the weekly *Gazet van Brussel*. Its success was limited. In 1905 sales peaked at 4,500 copies, but dwindled to 2,080 in 1912, the journal's final year of publication.[5] The *Gazet* was obviously no match for the approximately eighty thousand daily circulation of *Le Peuple* and twenty-five thousand of *Vooruit*.[6]

In Wallonia there were tens of thousands of Flemish-speaking migrant workers, both temporary and permanent. Around the year 1900 they amounted to about forty-five thousand in the province of Liège and sixty thousand in Hainaut.[7] Local concentrations in Walloon industrial centers could be very high. The outlier was Châtelineau, near Charleroi, where 26.97 percent of the population were Flemish-speaking migrants.[8] The local BWP branches neglected to organize these Flemish-speakers and were opposed to granting them language rights. They regarded the Flemish language as a clerical and unenlightened dialect of strikebreakers.[9] Anseele, however, consistently defended the linguistic rights of these migrants. He wanted "both races in Belgium to know both languages."[10] In parliament he called the diffusion of bilingualism in Wallonia "inevitable."[11] This would be a permanent source of conflict with his Walloon colleagues.[12]

In the Flemish-speaking provinces there were few working-class Walloon migrants, but bilingualism was a permanent feature of public life due to the presence of middle-class migrants from the south of the country and, more importantly, indigenous upper- and middle-class French-speakers. In Ghent 7.9 percent of the population spoke French mostly or exclusively according to the official language census of 1910. The American scholar Aristide Zolberg even estimated that a third of Ghent adult males were multilingual.[13] This number seems inflated, certainly for the socialist rank and file.

Hard data on lower-class language use in nineteenth-century Belgium are hard to come by. The official decennial language censuses were biased. They tended to overreport the use of French in the Flemish-speaking provinces. And they were not broken down by social class.[14] The propaganda pence offer us a more comprehensive view on language use and language contact at the grassroots level. Being almost monolingually Flemish, they show a banal, uncontested acceptance of Flemish as the self-evident language of working-class communication. In a sample of over 27,000, there were only 175 French tweets. The overall majority of the latter came from French or Walloon visitors to Ghent; only a negligible number were from workers living in the city itself.

Although the literature emphasizes that public life in Ghent was "strongly gallicized" (*verfranst* or *francisé*),[15] workers lived most of their lives in a monolingually Flemish environment. There is no evidence in our sample of frequent dealings with French speakers. Those contacts did probably occur—when being called in by the boss, when sent on an errand to higher-end shops or city hall—but they were too sporadic or insignificant to leave traces in the propaganda pence. For one, there were hardly any French-speaking workers or foremen in Ghent's factories and working-class neighborhoods. This dovetails with the city's relatively low labor immigration rate due to the slow growth of its textile industry.[16] Because Ghent workers rarely had dealings in and with French, there were few situations in which the social category of language could become a more explicit marker of identity. This lack of language friction made Flemish monolingualism seem self-evident, which—paradoxically—formed the basis for a banal acceptance of vernacular rights.

When Ghent workers were employed in a linguistically mixed environment, language could become a more meaningful social category. This was particularly evident in the main exception on shopfloor monolingualism in Ghent: the state-owned railway arsenal in the suburb of Gentbrugge where Walloon supervisors were employed. The propaganda pence contained clear traces of language friction: "Flemish workers from the arsenal want Flemish bosses, 0.35"; "A Flemish workman wants Flemish bosses in the arsenal, 0.10"; "Because a Walloon foreman from the Arsenal should behave better toward the Flemings, 0.10."[17] Here we clearly see how a sense of language discrimination stimulated ethnic identification in terms of Walloons and Flemings. The Ledeberg branch of the Ghent BWP was probably influenced by the workforce of the arsenal because it explicitly fashioned itself as pro–language rights.[18]

Overall, the Ghent rank and file had a very poor knowledge of French. When French-speaking party members visited Ghent, even simple rallying cries such as "Vivent les mineurs!," "Vivent nos frères wallons!," and "Bienvenue!" had to be learned by heart.[19] During a lockout in 1907, Camiel Lootens, the secretary of the socialist painters' union of Ghent, tried to organize work for his members in Wallonia. He conceded that language was the biggest obstacle: "Almost none knew French. There were some who spoke some soldiers' French, but the majority spoke none at all."[20] The highly sporadic French in the propaganda pence attracted notice precisely because the use of French was rare and, predictably, met with literal incomprehension. In 1900 a Ghent worker complained, "I did not understand a French message, J. De Coninck, o.20."[21]

The rank-and-file's poor knowledge of French was due to the shortcomings of the elementary school system and to the almost complete absence of opportunities to learn and practice French in daily life. Working-class children did not attend the city's schools regularly enough to get an adequate foundation in French (see also Chapter 6). Nor were language teaching methods geared toward practical skills. In 1909 the already mentioned Ghent militant Jozef De Graeve wanted to improve his nephew's French. To his surprise the boy could translate "lion" and "bear," "but when he had to tell me the French term for the chair he was sitting on, he had no idea. The same was true for many other things he sees around him on a daily basis." According to De Graeve, elementary school teachers disregarded working-class children's cultural deprivation and were too focused on abstract theory.[22]

Despite—or possibly due to—their monolingual Flemish environment, Ghent workers had a strong desire to learn French. For the many breadwinners who migrated temporarily or permanently to Wallonia and France it was a simple matter of livelihood.[23] In the summer of 1900, for instance, a lockout forced six hundred Ghent woodworkers out of a job. Some headed south. "If they all had known French," *Vooruit* wrote, "none would have stayed in Ghent."[24] School principals repeatedly reported that the interest in the course of French in both elementary and adult education was very high. In April 1886, for instance, one of them wrote (in French) to the city alderman of education: "The majority of students in adult schools want to learn French. Unfortunately this language is not part of the official curriculum."[25] In early 1909, an elementary school teacher at a Ghent city school asked twenty graduating working-class pupils what courses they would be interested in taking in adult education. This was the result:

Dutch 3/20
French 20/20
Math 20/20
Geography 2/20
History 1/20
Science 8/20
Constitutional law 3/20.[26]

Strikingly, the least popular courses were those central to the nationalization project of Belgian nationalist elites: history, geography, and civics (here referred to as "constitutional law"). The Flamingant pedagogy was equally discarded: a better mastery of Dutch/Flemish was low on these pupils' agenda. Math and French, by contrast, were high on their wish list. The grassroots thirst for French is also evidenced in the propaganda pence. Someone from Bruges posted in 1889: "I regret not speaking French, 0.05."[27] Ghent party members repeatedly asked for language courses: "Some young people who would like to follow a French course in Vooruit, 0.20."[28] Yet, working-class knowledge of French did not seem to improve substantially over the course of the fin de siècle.

## THE FLEMISH MOVEMENT AND ITS LANGUAGE PROGRAM

The monolinguality of Ghent workers' daily life and the concomitant lack of major language tensions help explain why the Ghent socialists were not in the vanguard of the language struggle, unlike their Czech-speaking colleagues and their comrades from Antwerp. In Bohemia and Moravia there was extensive grassroots language contact. This was a potential source of friction that could be politicized into a strong sense of linguistic solidarity.[29] The Antwerp socialists were more closely attuned to the Flemish movement because the booming port city had a larger pool of language-sensitive white-collar workers and attracted more French-speaking labor migrants.[30] Consequently, the socialist rank and file of Antwerp were more intensely exposed to French and potential language tension. In Ghent, by contrast, this type of exposure was mostly lacking. There was simply too little bottom-up pressure on the party to be more prominently engaged in the language struggle. In this sense, I disagree with the American historian Carl Strikwerda's conclusion that the Ghent party top was "out of touch" with its rank and file because of the cadres' neglect of the Flemish movement's language program.[31]

The mutual misunderstanding between socialism and Flamingantism was driven by the Flemish movement's reluctance to support the BWP's democratization thrust. Most petty bourgeois Flamingants had lost the appetite to accommodate workers, especially after the rise of the BWP and the 1886 Spring Revolt. In response to the Flamingants' singular focus on language and their disregard for universal suffrage and social rights,[32] the Ghent socialist leadership completely subordinated the language issue to the social question: once the proletariat received its full rights, the language problem would solve itself. In the meantime, Flamingants were nothing less than "sickly fanatics," "charlatans," "cheats and intriguers."[33]

The anti-Flamingant fervor of party cadres was not shared by the rank and file. Our sample of propaganda pence contains barely ten instances of workers taking aim at the Flemish movement, with seven coming from Ghent. A representative tweet from June 1896 reads: "We sang the Flemish lions to sleep, coach 2452, 1.05."[34] While traveling by train to the nearby city of Aalst, a group of Ghent socialists had apparently met some supporters of the Flemish movement in coach 2452. By singing loudly they had silenced the so-called Flemish lions. The small number and the rather meek nature of the anti-Flamingant tweets stand in stark contrast to the many hundreds and far more vicious swipes at the clergy and the anti-socialist, Catholic workers' movement (see Chapter 8). The rank and file's silence on Flamingants reflects the limited contact both groups had in daily life. The popular initiatives of the liberal Willemsfonds (founded in 1851) and the Catholic Davidsfonds (founded in 1875), the two main Flamingant organizations at the time, were focused on cultural outreach mainly through public libraries.[35] By the 1880s these organizations no longer aimed at the working classes.

There was hardly any explicit support or rejection of the Flemish movement's language concerns in the propaganda pence. To my mind, this absence does not reflect the rank and file's indifference toward or dismissal of the vernacular. Rather, it demonstrates a grassroots acceptance of Flemish language rights as self-evident, not in dispute and hence not in need of explicit mention. Aside from the uncontested monolingualism of Ghent workers' daily life (as argued in the preceding section), there are some banal clues in the propaganda pence that support this reading. At a time when the relations between the Ghent party cadres and Flamingants deteriorated, there were two socialist cafés in Ghent whose names reflected at least some vernacular sensibility: "the estaminet 'The Mother Tongue'" (*De moedertaal*) and Prosper

Bilkyn's pub In Flanders Flemish (*In Vlaanderen Vlaamsch*).³⁶ The latter was the Flemish movement's rallying cry. It is inconceivable that a socialist café in Ghent would have been named after a Catholic party plank like "The Free School" or "Class cooperation." The fact that socialist workers casually accepted the Flamingant-sounding name of these cafés shows that they had no inherent animosity toward the Flemish movement and its language program. This, however, could change in contexts where the Flamingant agenda became overly associated with Catholic or bourgeois demands.

Up to the middle 1890s, the socialist leadership was not concerned at all about the Flemish movement's potential working-class appeal. *Vooruit*'s anti-Flamingant diatribes were motivated by political disagreement and not (yet) by competition for supporters or voters. This armed peace came to an end at the turn of the nineteenth and twentieth centuries. In 1897–1898 the Flemish movement rediscovered the working people in the wake of the joint Catholic-liberal-socialist drive for the Equality Act, which put Flemish on an equal legal footing with French.³⁷

Gradually, the Flemish movement turned into a viable electoral and syndicalist challenge to the Ghent socialist movement. In 1898, the anti-cooperative and Flamingant Free Citizens' League (*Vrije Burgersbond*) captured 5 percent of the vote in the parliamentary elections. After several years of steady growth, the Ghent socialist movement was suddenly confronted with electoral stagnation. On top of that, unionization numbers began to drop, which made the party leadership very sensitive to any possible competition from the Flamingant side.

In the first decade of the twentieth century the Flemish movement experienced a broader breakthrough in society as its demands dovetailed with tertiary sector growth. Liberal and administrative professions had seen their share of the workforce grow from 2.5 percent in 1846 to 5.8 percent in 1905.³⁸ These vocal groups of white-collar employees were especially sensitive to issues of linguistic discrimination. From 1908 onward, the first interest groups for lower civil servants were formed. These nonsocialist unions focused on the language issue. They fully supported the campaign for the vernacularization of the State University of Ghent. The so-called *vervlaamsching* or *flamandisation* of Ghent University focused on the introduction of Flemish as a language of instruction in addition to or instead of French.³⁹ The local BWP branch could not afford to ostracize this white-collar audience in the increasingly competitive electoral and syndicalist landscape of early twentieth-century Ghent. As a sign of outreach, Jan Lampens, the head of the socialist woodworkers union, ran as the champion of the Flemish-speaking railway personnel and the lower civil servants in the parliamentary campaign of 1908. Lampens was elected as the second MP from Ghent besides Anseele.[40] The competition from Flamingant organizations continued all the same. In 1911–1912, the Flamingant Independent City Workers' Union (*Onafhankelijke Stadswerkliedenbond*) and the Flemish Bloc (*Vlaamsch Blok*), an ad hoc electoral cooperation between Christian Democrats, dissident socialists, and the Independent City Workers' Union, were founded. Their explicit aim was to keep white-collar workers away from socialism. One reader of *Vooruit* graphically described the Flemish Bloc as a provocation, meant "to f . . . with the socialists."[41]

The increased electoral and syndicalist competition of Flamingant associations seemed to have an impact on the rank and file. An indirect clue is the evolving insights vis-à-vis the vernacularization of Ghent University. After two debate nights in May 1905, Anseele remained unconvinced that there was grassroots support for the question. Why would workers care about the language spoken at university in the absence of compulsory elementary education?[42] By 1911 Anseele had changed his mind. The populist cross-party campaign of the so-called three crowing roosters—the liberal MP Louis Franck, the Catholic MP Frans Van Cauwelaert, and the socialist MP Camille Huysmans—had warmed the Ghent rank and file to the vernacularization issue. At various rallies workers reacted sympathetically to the roosters' message.[43] On December 18, 1910, Johan Lefevre, a pro-Flemish teacher in the Ghent city schools and a BWP member since 1904, made a passionate plea for a Flemish-speaking university in Ons Huis (Our House), the socialist headquarters in Vrijdagmarkt Square. He was repeatedly interrupted by "enthusiastic applause" and concluded his speech to "thunderous cheers."[44] By contrast, in February 1911 Constant Heynderickx, a progressive liberal who opposed the vernacularization, could barely make himself heard due to constant objections from the audience in Ons Huis.[45] At the general board meeting of the Ghent federation, convened on March 4, 1911, only six people were opposed to vernacularization, a paltry number given that all thirty thousand card-carrying members could in theory participate in the vote.[46]

The campaign for the vernacularization of Ghent University showed that under the right circumstances language could become a more prominent political issue for grassroots socialists, but the crowing roosters' campaign was an exceptional episode. In the absence of more structural language contact and the attendant possibilities for linguistic friction, it would take a serious, concerted effort to politicize language in the daily life of socialist workers. For different reasons the three Ghent organizations that qualified for such an effort were unwilling or unable to take on this mission: the BWP because of its anti-Flamingant position, the Flemish movement because of its petty-bourgeois sensibilities and its relatively weak infrastructure, and Christian Democrats because of the pervasive anti-Catholic prejudice among the socialist rank and file.

## "INTER-NATIONALISM," THE BELGIAN NATION, AND FLEMISH ETHNICITY

In January 1886 two cigar makers from Ghent vented their still simmering indignation over the acts of a man who had died more than half a century earlier:

> **N**apoleon—the scourge of the Netherlands [*Neêrland's geesel*], killer of men,
>
> **A**nnouncer of poverty, peace breaker,
>
> **P**est to the human race, war monger,
>
> **O**ffal, money thief, word breaker,
>
> **L**awless traitor, crowned racketeer,
>
> **E**vil adulterer,
>
> **O**minous rioter, monster, ready for the gallows,
>
> **N**ow take these letters as your name; two cigar makers, J.D. and Ch.W. o.40.[47]

The reference to Neêrland does not express some sense of Greater-Netherlandic nostalgia, but hints at the Dutch origin of this acrostic which was coined during the Napoleonic era itself.[48] Its lasting relevance more than half a century after Napoleon's death reflects the negative collective memory of the French period in Ghent. The generation of Anseele (1856–1938), born around the middle of the nineteenth century, still had a direct link with the French era through their grandparents. In 1898 Paul De Witte (1848–1929), tailor, pioneer, and later dissident of the Ghent socialist movement, reminisced how his grandfather used to "talk about Napoleon, the invasions of the French and the allied."[49] During the 1859 war between France and Piedmont the old man had said "that he wanted them to get a good beating, because the world would never be at peace as long as France existed. [. . .] Usually, those conversations ended by bringing up the twenty-year French rule, with its dictatorship, extortions and horrors."[50] The image of the French as threatening and bellicose lived on in several of the singalongs of Karel Waeri (1842–1898), the immensely popular socialist folk singer of Ghent.[51]

Obviously, this anti-French prejudice was balanced by widespread admiration for France's revolutionary past, but it does show how easily the rank and file slipped into routines of banal nationalism. The unreflective way in which Ghent workers divided the world into separate nationalities with distinct qualities was particularly evident in their expression of "inter-nationalism."[52] In late 1884, for instance, *Vooruit* opened a "subscription list for the election in Germany" to celebrate the breakthrough of the SPD in the Reichstag elections of October 28.[53] Using "Germany" as a *totum pro parte* for the German working class and for German socialism, workers posted messages such as: "For Germany, 0.50" and "For the Germans, 0.50."[54] At the same time they explicitly referred to themselves as Belgian: "Germany ahead, Belgium will follow, 1.00."[55] This background of "inter-nationalist" solidarity was one of three contexts in which the Ghent rank and file identified with Belgium. The other two were emigration to France and civil rights campaigns. Taken together, these three settings account for only a very limited number of references in our sample: barely fourteen tweets from Ghent expressed such a civic identification with Belgium, compared to sixty-one instances expressing a sense of Flemishness.

The Ghent workers' veneration of German social democracy, described by one Belgian scholar as plain "Germanophilia,"[56] was not matched by an equally breathless adoration of French socialism and its underdeveloped social-democratic branch. After all, it was Ghent militants who jump-started the socialist movement in northern France and organized factory workers between Lille and Roubaix, a region that harbored 270,000 Belgian, mainly Flemish-speaking, migrants in 1886.[57] This cross-border militancy was a source of organizational patriotism among Ghent workers, but also of national, international, and socialist pride, as evidenced in this Flemish tweet from Roubaix: "We, Belgians, work for the French Avenir. Long live the International, Long live the red flag, little D.L., 0.20."[58] L'Avenir (The Future) was the socialist, Ghent-run cooperative of Roubaix. It was known locally as the Société belge socialiste.[59] The French environment and the migration context could also trigger Flemish rather than Belgian loyalties, as in this Flemish tweet from Lille: "Come on, *Flemings* of Lille, let's observe the propaganda pence, E.D., 0.10."[60] Significantly, by 1913 the Ghent socialists tailored their northern-French propaganda separately and explicitly toward *Flemings* and (French-speaking) *Belgians*. A bilingual pamphlet mustering support for the general strike in Belgium was addressed in Flemish "to the *Flemish* population of Roubaix and surroundings. Arise! Female and male comrades [*Gezellinen en Gezellen*] assist the big *Flemish* meeting"; and in French "to the *Belgian* workers of Roubaix and surroundings. Arise! *Citoyennes et citoyens* all assist the meeting."[61]

The third context in which Ghent workers identified as Belgian was that of civil rights. Following the national suffrage march in Brussels on August 15, 1886, a Ghent worker called upon all citizens: "*Belgians*, the time has come to rally, 0.16."[62] Equally often, however, this context of political rights activated ethnic identifications, as this example from the same summer demonstrates: "Long live the Walloons and the Flemings, Long live General Suffrage, 0.86."[63] The fraternization of Flemings and Walloons within the socialist movement was a recurring theme, particularly at the time of solidarity actions with Walloon strikers. In the "Subscription List for the Workers in the Borinage" in the spring of 1885, some Ghent workers wrote: "While you are on strike, you do not have to fear explosions nor cave-ins, but a larger enemy (hunger) looms; therefore, *Walloon brothers*, we think of you, some *Flemings*, 1.25."[64] Strikingly, there was no Belgian patriotic subtext to the use of the term "Walloon brothers." It did not refer to the nationalist image of the Belgians as children of the same motherland, but rather to the "inter-nationalist" principle of class solidarity. One Ghent worker phrased it like this in 1886: "While Flemings and Walloons fraternize, they claim universal suffrage and amnesty for Falleur and Schmidt, 0.25; Walloons and Flemings form one and the same class, the class of the oppressed, 0.25."[65] Tellingly, this person imagined Flemings and Walloons as of the same *class*, but not as of the same *nation*. In 1894 a Ghent worker even put the Flemings and the Walloons on the same foot as the French, in effect representing the three of them as separate nationalities united in "inter-nationalism": "Collected while Walloon, French and Flemish brothers sang the Marseillaise, 0.83."[66]

Belgian nationalist commonplaces like the centuries-old struggle for freedom against foreign rule and the call of the Belgian blood—grassroots themes in the Walloon provinces of Liège and Hainaut—were lacking in the propaganda pence. The most significant absence was the Revolution of 1830, both in its social meaning of a proletarian revolution stolen by the bourgeoisie and in its national sense as the moment of the birth of the independent Belgian nation. Our sample contains only one direct reference to 1830 and it is negative. In February 1888, a Ghent militant called on his fellow workers not to spend their money in company stores, but in the socialist cooperative shops:

"Instead of giving our money to the bourgeoisie, *which has held us in a state of humiliation since 1830* and oppresses us with money, we prefer Vooruit which wants the salvation of all, 0.25."[67] One Ghent worker even snubbed Belgian independence. In the summer of 1887, while Franco-German tensions were rising and the independence of the country seemed at stake, he posted: "The Prussians and the French can decide, we will remain socialists, 0.10."[68] Workers were socialists first and foremost, so it did not matter whether Belgium would survive a war between the two European superpowers. This position would have horrified his Hainaut colleagues (see Chapter 7).

Respect for the symbols of the Belgian Revolution was lacking too. In November 1886, someone from Ghent reported: "To the Brabançonne, the audience in [the] Valentino [music hall] responded with the Marseillaise, 0.20; The police sent for reinforcements, 0.20."[69] The national flag was discarded: "The red flag is for the socialists, the tricolored one for the dunces, 0.30."[70] Belgium's founding document did not inspire respect either: "To me the constitution is a filthy piece of paper, 0.10."[71] To be sure, criticism of Belgium as a capitalists' paradise and denunciations of the Belgian flag, the "Brabançonne," and the constitution, also occurred in French-speaking BWP branches, but there, unlike in Ghent, the negative rhetoric always coexisted with a positive discourse of Belgianness.

Ghent workers did not affectionately appropriate "our Belgium." On the contrary, references to Belgium often dripped with cynicism. When Anseele was sentenced to six months in prison in 1886 for having called Leopold II a "murderer of the people" (*volksmoordenaar*), a Ghent militant complained: "In *our, beautiful free Belgium* there are hundreds who are more deserving to appear in the black justice box than our friend, 0.20."[72] Belgium and its cognates could even hold a negative connotation in and of themselves. During the bloody repression of the 1886 Spring Revolt a worker from Ghent volunteered: "Because the *Belgian* class justice should release the unjustly convicted workers; Long Live Falleur, long live our brave Walloon brothers, 1.13."[73] The addition of the adjective "Belgian" only makes sense if it was explicitly meant to draw attention to the injustice perpetrated by *Belgium*. The reference to "our brave Walloon brothers" was in line with the "inter-nationalist" solidarity described above, not with a patriotic understanding of Belgium.

The negative connotation of the Belgian vocabulary is corroborated by the song catalogue of the Ghent socialists. To Edouard Anseele songs were "the strongest cement that binds the mass of workers, a collective soul that is formed by [singing]."[74] Scholars have emphasized that songs shaped and expressed workers' feelings of social belonging, their political awareness, and their ideological norms. The collective and repetitive character of singing anchored the meaning of lyrics "in the hearts as well as the minds of singers/ listeners, making songs 'models of feeling, conduct, and values' central to the formation of group identity," as one historian put it.[75] Viewed in this light, the survey *Vooruit* conducted among its readers in 1908 to find the most popular workers' songs is very revealing. The resulting song collection was published as the *Hundred Songs for the People* (100 *zangen voor het volk*). In this anthology Belgium appeared mainly in a negative context, for instance in the bluntly titled "Belgium Is Worse Than Turkey."[76] The song "Do You Know That Country?" asked a series of rhetorical questions such as "Do you know the country where the sodomites of the Brothers of Charity and murderers are protected?" Invariably the answer was: "Well, that country is the Land of the Belgians [*Belgenland*]!"[77]

The vast majority of the *Hundred Songs for the People* expressed or appealed to the categories of class, organizational patriotism, occupation, and anticlericalism. If they mentioned nationhood or ethnicity at all, Flanders rather than Belgium was invoked. The opening songs of the collection were two undisputed classics of the Ghent socialist movement: Rik van Offel's "Canaille" and Emiel Moyson's "Working Man's Song" (*Werkmanslied*), both of which appealed to "the Flemish people."[78] Other songs in the collection paid homage to "the proud Flemish character," "the people of the Land of Flanders [*Vlaandrenland*]!" and "the sister cities" of "Flanders."[79] The latter was an allusion to "The Three Sister Cities" (*De drie zustersteden*). This epic poem from 1846 by the Flamingant writer Karel Ledeganck celebrated the imbrication of *heimat* and Flemishness. One passage from the poem was proverbial to the socialist rank and file. They could recite or creatively paraphrase Ledeganck's line that the "trades and guilds wanted what was just, and won what they wanted."[80] This quote carried a strong subtext of Flemish ethnicity for socialist audiences. This was abundantly clear on December 25, 1891, when the Ghent socialists held a so-called "Flemish national day" for general suffrage (*Vlaamsche landdag*).[81] The manifesto the Ghent party leader Edmond Van Beveren published for this event concluded with an emotional appeal to Ledeganck's proverbial words:

> Flemings, whatever party you belong to, let us remember our great past! Our fathers did not stand for slavery, did not put up with privilege.
> They wanted what was right
> And won what they wanted.[82]

Variations on these lines had been circulating in the propaganda pence long before 1891 and would continue to do so long afterward, as the following examples show:

> The Flemings do not tolerate slavery, 0.50.
>
> We always wanted what was right and will fight until we have it, 0.10.
>
> What we want is right, 0.20.
>
> We want what is right and win what we want [...], 2.38.
>
> No, the Ghent people do not want it [i.e., the Blood Law] and will show on August 13 [at an anti-militaristic rally] that they want what is right and win what they want, 0.05.[83]

At the same *landdag* in 1891 Anseele also proposed sending a telegram to the congress of the Dutch socialists, "our Northern Netherlandic brothers [*Noord-Nederlandsche broeders*] [...] to close the link between two countries that should never have been separated." Anseele's motion was met with "thunderous cheers."[84] This is the only example I have found of possible grassroots susceptibility to Pan-Netherlandic nationalism. Obviously, the Belgian revolution was not popular among ordinary workers, but neither is there further evidence for Greater-Netherlandic enthusiasm among the rank and file.

What ordinary workers were certainly not oblivious to was the celebration of the Flemish past. The most remarkable expression in the propaganda pence was the appropriation of the Flemish lion. In 1838 the prolific novelist Hendrik Conscience had launched the popular veneration of the Lion of Flanders with his eponymous historic novel.[85] Conscience told the story of the Battle of the (Golden) Spurs, which had taken place in the Flemish city of Kortrijk on July 11, 1302. It had pitted the troops of the French king against the victorious army of the municipalities of the county of Flanders. The latter were led by count Robrecht van Béthune/van Dampierre, whom Conscience lionized as the Lion of Flanders, and by Jan Breydel and Pieter De Coninck, legendary guild leaders from Bruges. After its "rediscovery" in the late eighteenth century, this battle, its protagonists, and the date of July 11, 1302, were elevated to the status of a national symbol. They were considered to be signs of Belgian liberty and a prefiguration of the Belgian revolution. In the second half of the nineteenth century, the Flemish movement appropriated 1302 as a victory of the Flemish nation and proof of the Flemings' resistance against French dominance. In reality 1302 defies easy explanation in terms of nationality. It was a complex conflict in which several tensions of sovereign versus liege, count versus cities, patriciate versus guilds, Ghent versus Bruges, and large versus small cities, interacted.[86]

Conscience's novels had an inordinate impact on the popular imagination of the past throughout the nineteenth century. He was avidly read by and for socialist audiences (see Chapter 6). In the propaganda pence, Conscience's heroes Jan Breydel and Pieter De Coninck, though part of the official Belgian nationalist pantheon, were appropriated in an exclusively local framework. Alluding to Anseele, someone posted in 1886: "We have our De Coninck, who will be our Breydel, o.10."[87] Two years later, a Ghent worker excoriated a Catholic blue-collar organization from Bruges: "If Jan Breidel could take a look at this guild, he would look down with utter contempt on these cowards."[88] In April 1892 a Ghent worker encouraged his fellow party members from Bruges to attend the annual party congress: "Men from Bruges, at Easter you should all come to Ghent with your red flags as true sons of Breydel, Leon, o.10."[89]

Nine years after the publication of Conscience's novel *The Lion of Flanders*, lyricist Hippoliet van Peene and composer Karel Miry wrote the Flemish lion anthem, taking inspiration lyrically from Nikolaus Becker's "Rheinlied" and musically from Robert Schumann's "Sonntags am Rhein." Through the mid-1890s socialist workers from Ghent appropriated this anthem. In 1886 during a particularly turbulent strike at the Grasfabriek, one of the largest cotton mills in Ghent, a Ghent migrant in Roubaix posted a message of support: "Workers, courage, show them that the Flemish lion, although in chains, still has his fangs, V.G.J., o.25."[90] This was a direct reference to the chorus of the "Flemish Lion" anthem: "They will not have him, they will not tame him, the proud Flemish lion, as long as the lion can claw, as long as he has fangs." Four years later, when the liberal mayor Lippens prohibited a general suffrage rally in Ghent, a local militant reacted: "Our demonstration has been banned by the reactionaries, *but they will not tame us*, o.10."[91]

The "Flemish Lion" was an important rallying song for Ghent socialists through the early 1890s. At their universal suffrage referendum of June 12, 1892 (see Chapter 2), it was heard all day long throughout town: "From eight o'clock in the morning in many neighborhoods we sang the Suffrage March, the Marseillaise, *the Flemish Lion*, in a word, any song that arouses, galvanizes, enthuses."[92] The "Flemish Lion" anthem figured prominently in the *Social-Democratic Songs and Poems*,[93] a best-selling collection the Ghent BWP published in a series of reprints between 1881 and 1889, and which sold five thousand copies in 1888 alone.[94] This songbook contained six so-called marching songs, which were meant to be sung at rallies. Two of them were to the tune of the "Flemish Lion." The first one, "They Will Not Have Him" (*Zij zullen hem niet hebben*), appealed exclusively to working-class sensibilities, though it mimicked the phrasing of its model. The second, "Our Flemish Lion" (*Onze Vlaamsche leeuw*), was an ode to Flanders' past, with stanzas such as: "Hear Breidel and De Coninck/Ghent, Bruges of yore/Are there any proud *Klauwaarts*/any proud sons left?"[95] The *Klauwaarts*, literally the claw-men, was a moniker for the followers of the count of Flanders in the thirteenth century. It was used in the second half of the nineteenth century to denote Flamingants, but Ghent socialists appropriated the term as a sign of labor militancy and a reference to the supposed proletarian nature of the thirteenth-century revolt against the French king.

Clearly, socialist commitment was not yet incompatible with singing the "Flemish Lion," but this would change in the course of the 1890s as anti-socialists laid an increasingly exclusive claim to the Flemish lion. On July 24, 1892, the banner of the anti-socialist Catholic workers' movement was inaugurated during a high mass in Ghent's St. Baaf's cathedral. It was a Flemish lion flag, a reinvention of the medieval heraldic symbol of the county of Flanders, depicting a black lion with red claws and tongue on a yellow background. At the concluding public meeting in Valentino Hall the anti-socialists sang "The red flag will yield to our black lion" to the tune of the "Flemish Lion" anthem.[96] A skirmish with socialists ensued, and the freshly consecrated flag was torn apart and soiled with blood. The next day *Vooruit*'s headline, alluding to the Prussians' defeat of the French, read: "the Sedan of the dunces." The socialist paper smirked: "In short, the indomitable Flemish lion was neatly tamed."[97] One tweet summarized the incident as: "Dunces do not grieve, your banner has been consecrated, but it remained in the battle of Sedan, we socialists will make a new Flemish Lion, with the motto Freedom, Equality and Brotherhood. Neighborhood club St-Lievenstraat, 0.52."[98] This worker reappropriated the Flemish lion in a French revolutionary, socialist context. Strikingly, the many other tweets the episode inspired did not explicitly refer to the Flemish lion, but mainly lashed out at the "dunces"—again proving that it was anti-socialists and not Flamingants who were the preferred foil of grassroots socialists. In the ensuing years the instrumentalization of the Flemish lion by Catholic anti-socialists would increasingly alienate Ghent socialist workers.

To conclude, the propaganda pence do not contain many references to Flemish and Belgian nationhood, but these low frequencies signal different underlying patterns. Whereas the rare allusions to Belgium were negative, those to Flanders were instead positive. Accordingly, the minimal references to Flanders reflect an unpoliticized and banal nationalism, while the relative absence of Belgium suggests its limited appeal as a positive category of identification. Overall, however, it is clear from the low incidence of these categories that nation, ethnicity, and language were not that relevant in workers' daily lives. On the surface this seems to confirm the notion that pre–World War I nationalism was merely a concern of (relatively) privileged middle classes, and that workers' daily lives were unilaterally determined by material needs and a complete indifference toward cultural matters. A deeper reading, however, shows that the social categories of Belgian nationhood and Flemish ethnicity were available to workers and could indeed be activated in certain circumstances. Inescapably, identification is a context-dependent process.

In the end, the Ghent case also exposes the limitations of top-down explanations of nationalism as a mere tool of elite manipulation. The frenetic Belgian patriotic outreach and the Flamingant campaigns of the fin de siècle were hardly successful. Workers did not simply adopt middle-class definitions of the nation, but through their sheer volume top-down nationalist discourses were effective by setting structural limits to what ordinary people could think and do. The trickle-down rhetoric normalized the idea of separate nations and established the dominance of banal nationalism over radical cosmopolitanism. Within those constraints socialist workers had agency to construct their own working-class sense of nationhood from the bottom up, in dialogue with the many, competing identity discourses targeted at them from above. It was difficult to think outside the box of the nation, but they could fill the box to their own liking: with Belgian or Flemish, working-class or bourgeois, republican or royalist, colonialist or anti-imperialist notions.

*Epilogue*

# THE FIRST WORLD WAR

"Is this war?" *Le Peuple* asked incredulously on July 27, 1914. A week later, on August 4, the German army invaded Belgium. The BWP was as surprised by the start of the First World War as its sister parties. The leaders of the Second International had been truly convinced that after a period of ups and downs Europe was on the verge of a long-lasting peace. The international proletariat would see to that. At its last meeting in Brussels on July 29, 1914, the International Socialist Bureau, the Second International's executive council, issued a unanimous motion against war, but as soon as hostilities began "the 25-year old structure of the International underwent its own internal disintegration; rhetorical internationalism was not equal to this test."[1] Each party sought and found a scapegoat abroad to justify its support for the war. The German SPD blamed Russia, the BWP Germany.

On August 4, 1914, Belgium's socialist MPs unanimously approved the war credits in parliament. Emile Vandervelde was immediately appointed as minister of state. In 1916 he became an active member of the Council of Ministers and from 1917 on, he served as minister of provisioning. Vandervelde's accession to the government epitomized the *union sacrée* mentality of the BWP. In the spirit of the "sacred union" the party set aside all political differences with its ideological rivals for the duration of the war. Furthermore, unlike in most other belligerent countries, there was hardly any grassroots protest against war participation. The experience of invasion and occupation sustained a moral consensus among the Belgians, preempting any existential challenge to the war effort, even in the harsh years of 1917–1918.² The physical presence of the "enemy" and the German atrocities enabled the political parties, the church, local administrations, and charity organizations to keep a lid on the social tensions caused by wartime deprivation to a larger degree than was possible in other warring, but non-occupied countries.³ The cleavages of class and religion did not disappear, but they were increasingly expressed through a common language of Belgian war patriotism that tended to bridge the prewar gap between working-class and bourgeois nationalism.

## WAR AND HUNGER

The Belgians had a split war experience. About six million of them remained in German-controlled Belgium. Around six hundred thousand spent almost the entire war as refugees in France, the Netherlands, or Great Britain. A tiny western sliver of the country, 5 percent of the entire Belgian territory behind the river Yser, remained free. It harbored 350,000 Belgians, the majority of them soldiers in frontline units.⁴ Because of the swift occupation of the country, the Belgian military was only able to mobilize about 20 percent of potential recruits, a number far below the 54 percent in Great Britain, 85 percent in France, and 86 percent in Germany. Most Belgian males experienced the war as civilians.⁵

The occupied country was cut in two. On the one hand, there was the *Generalgouvernement*, also known as the *Okkupationsgebiet*, under civilian administration, and, on the other hand, the rear area, or *Etappengebiet*, under exclusive military control. The latter comprised about a third of the Belgian territory in the west and the south and sheltered about 22 percent of the occupied Belgian population. Movement between the *Okkupationsgebiet* and the *Etappengebiet*, but also within each zone, was severely limited. In the words of Sophie De Schaepdrijver, the Belgians became prisoners in their own towns, cut off from reliable information, abandoned to hunger, destitution, and violence.⁶

Because of the British trade embargo against Germany, factories closed and food prices skyrocketed in occupied Belgium.⁷ All of a sudden unemployment hit 69 percent, with local peaks of 80 percent in cities and industrial centers.⁸ With domestic food production dislocated by the war and constant German requisitions, there were immediate shortages. Belgium became largely dependent on food imports from abroad, which had already accounted for 78 percent of the Belgians' daily dietary needs before 1914.⁹ Wartime imports never amounted to more than an average of 950 kilocalories per day per person,[10] far below the daily per capita energy requirement of 2,100 kilocalories. As a result 65 percent of the Belgians were chronically malnourished during the war.[11]

Needless to say, hunger and destitution became the most pressing issues facing ordinary Belgians. On August 14, 1914, the Belgian government in exile made the municipalities responsible for food provisioning. Most local authorities were not up to this task as their poor-relief offices were ancien régime relics focused on paternalistic charity rather than wartime provisioning. Following a pattern established during the fin de siècle, private initiative filled the void left by the state. A small group of wealthy American and Belgian businessmen in Brussels founded the National Relief and Food Committee.[12] To circumvent the British embargo, the committee had to obtain its provisions from international charitable aid. To that end, the American engineer and later president Herbert Hoover, who resided in Great Britain at the time, established the American-controlled Commission for Relief in Belgium in concert with the Belgian committee. Throughout the war Hoover and his commission walked a tightrope between the British demanding that the embargo be upheld and the Germans eyeing the imports as potential requisitions.

Using about four thousand local committees, the National Relief and Food Committee soon began to function as the de facto government of occupied Belgium. In the spirit of the *union sacrée*, the local and provincial branches of the national committee were pluralist, with deputies from all pillars. At the top the BWP was represented by *Le Peuple* director Joseph Wauters, who would become minister of reconstruction after the war. Edouard Anseele for his part was one of the most influential members of the provincial committee of the province of East Flanders.

As war progressed, the National Relief and Food Committee also became responsible for the distribution of unemployment benefits. Using the so-called Ghent system, i.e., the provision of official relief through subsidized pillar organizations, the practical implementation was delegated to the socialist and Christian Democratic unions. This explains why, despite the German crackdown on traditional union activities such as strikes and rallies, unionization numbers multiplied throughout the war. Socialist union membership steeply rose from 125,000 in 1914 to 718,000 in 1920 and from 100,000 to 340,000 for the Christian Democratic unions.[13] The involvement of the BWP in the National Relief and Food Committee and the concomitant recognition of the party as a valued pillar of Belgian society explain the rapid integration of socialism in the postwar system.

## POLITICIZING NATIONHOOD, ETHNICITY, AND LANGUAGE

The war not only refocused all political and social tensions through the prism of hunger and destitution, it also turned Belgian nationalism into the self-evident language of resistance. The king, the national flag, and the national anthem became the unquestioned symbols of Free Belgium, even for the socialist rank and file. This did not mean that all social and political tensions simply disappeared under the veil of Belgian unity, but rather that competing groups expressed these tensions in the same, nationalist vernacular.[14]

In the process, prewar expressions of working-class nationalism came closer to mainstream, bourgeois nationalism. Many French-speaking party cadres, who had already fully converted to oppositional patriotism before the war, drifted toward radical war chauvinism, similar to what happened in the labor movements of Germany and Great Britain.[15] Not coincidentally, the prewar frontmen of socialist Wallingantism became the fiercest supporters of the most radical strand of Belgian nationalism, the so-called *jusqu'au bout-isme*. This literal "to the end-ism" pursued the total military defeat of Germany. Because Wallingant militancy was grounded in an exclusively Gallic, Belgian nationalism, it shifted almost effortlessly to a hyperchauvinism.[16]

Although Belgianness became the common language of socialists, prewar tensions of class, ideology, and ethnicity never disappeared completely. Some socialist war songs did express a sense of internationalist disaffection with the conflict and indignation about the shedding of the "poor people's blood."[17] German labor requisitions, for instance, only affected the working class. The fact that about sixty thousand Belgians had to perform forced labor in Germany disrupted the notion of a joint war experience.[18] Likewise, prewar differences between Flemish- and French-speaking BWP members persisted in some form. Peace initiatives such as the Stockholm conference had more appeal in Flemish-speaking BWP branches.[19] The latter generally did not support the war as unconditionally as their French-speaking counterparts and were subject to the internal dissidence of a younger generation that was in some cases swayed by the so-called *Flamenpolitik*.[20]

With its *Flamenpolitik* the German occupying regime reshaped the social-political context in which the language issue was rooted.[21] By realizing long-held demands of the Flemish movement, the Germans tried to untie the bonds that held Belgium together. In October 1916 the state university of Ghent reopened as an exclusively Flemish-speaking institution and near the end of the war Flemish home rule was instituted. The ultimate aim of the *Flamenpolitik* was to create internal discord. In case of a German victory this would facilitate the division of the country between France and Germany. In case of an inconclusive end to the war it would create a faction in Belgian society amenable to a pro-German compromise peace.

German propaganda also tried to win over the so-called *Frontbeweging*. This Front Movement had been founded in the trenches of the Belgian army in response to the acute linguistic tensions between Flemish-speaking soldiers and French-speaking officers. Due to the swifter occupation of Wallonia, Flemish-speakers were overrepresented in the Yser army by 8.9 percentage points. That is to say, they accounted for 64.3 percent of soldiers compared to their 55.4 percent share in the overall Belgian population. The Front Movement never numbered more than about five thousand supporters out of a total of 221,000 Belgian combatants, but the unease about linguistic discrimination was shared by a wider group of soldiers. Most, however, were convinced that addressing this issue would have to wait until after the war.[22] In occupied Belgium, a minority of about fifteen thousand radical Flamingants, the so-called *activisten*, were swayed by the German charm offensive.[23] They were rebuked by the general public, but the entire Flemish movement would carry the odium of collaboration.[24]

After the war the high tide of Belgian nationalism receded surprisingly quickly and language soon became a political wedge issue. In the 1920s Flemish separatism attracted 5 to 10 percent of the Flemish vote. It seemed as if the *Flamenpolitik* had posthumously succeeded in sowing discord. How was this possible given the ostensibly favorable conditions the war had created for strengthening Belgian nationhood and neutralizing the linguistic divide?

The war had tilted fin de siècle Belgium, first, by politicizing nationhood, language, and ethnicity to an unprecedented extent, second, by inadvertently sparking the rapid and radical democratic reforms of 1918–1919, and third, by conflating deprivation, urbanity, and Belgianness.

Before 1914, nationhood, language, and ethnicity were social categories ordinary Belgians, including socialists, could and did marshal in their political struggles and in their daily lives, but they were generally less important and less politicized than class and religion. The social-political background against which these identifications played out was dominated by consociationalism.

The war, however, promoted language, ethnicity, and nationhood to a more prominent position and made them into consistent everyday concerns. Obviously, the occupation brought the national Other, the German enemy, clearly into focus, lending daily relevance to a sense of Belgianness.[25] Popular expressions of wartime resistance such as clandestine songs celebrated Belgian unity. They firmly placed Flemishness within a Belgian context,[26] following King Albert's emotional appeal to the nation on August 5, 1914: "Caesar said to your ancestors: Of all the people of Gaul, the Belgians are the bravest. Glory to you, army of the Belgian people! [. . .] Remember, Flemings, the Battle of the Golden Spurs, and you, Walloons of Liège, that you are now enjoying the honor of the six hundred Franchimontois."[27] During the war German attempts to politicize language and ethnicity were counterproductive. The *Flamenpolitik* emphasized categories that within the context of the occupation were eminently compatible with Belgian nationhood, more so than they had ever been.[28] The long-term effects, however, proved to be centrifugal once the wartime context with its looming national enemy gave way to the political divisions of postwar reconstruction.

To avert revolution and upheaval, leading figures of the National Relief and Food Committee helped to reshape Belgium's postwar outlook. After the Armistice, circumventing the prewar parliament, they granted a host of socialist demands, including "one man, one vote," the eight-hour work day, progressive income tax, and state subsidies for private mutual aid societies and unions. The BWP emerged as one of the undisputed victors of the war. The first national elections in November 1919 were a triumph for the party. With 36 percent of the nationwide vote, seventy socialist MPs were elected to the House of Representatives. The party nearly doubled its prewar seat total and finally broke through in Flanders, winning twenty-three seats, against nine in Brussels and thirty-eight in Wallonia. The Catholic party lost twenty-six seats, but managed to hold on to its position as largest party, with 38 percent of the vote and seventy-three seats.[29] Although the Flemish nationalist Front Party entered parliament with five seats, the Flemish movement was on the losing side of the war. The language program stalled, tainted by the *activist* collaboration.

With socialism on the rise and in an effort to regain its prewar dominance, the Catholic party and its increasingly powerful Christian Democratic wing came to the defense of the tarnished Flemish movement, and began to intensively instrumentalize language and Flemish ethnicity.[30] This alienated liberals and socialists. The latter became even more suspicious as Flemish nationalists mobilized these same categories in their push for devolution and separatism at the exact moment the BWP was taking control of the levers of the Belgian state.

According to Antoon Vrints, the postwar spread of Flemish nationalist militancy followed a pattern established during the German occupation.[31] Vrints contends that urban residents proved more resistant to the *Flamenpolitik* and to the postwar call of Flemish nationalism than rural dwellers. The prewar Flemish movement had been a decidedly urban phenomenon in terms of recruitment and organization. The post-1918 breakthrough of Flemish nationalism, however, had an important rural dimension.[32] One of the main causes, Vrints argues, was differential levels of deprivation experienced by citizens in the countryside and in cities.

During the war, food procurement was the overriding perspective through which ordinary Belgians perceived reality. As the war progressed, destitution, food shortages, and famine spread. Urban and industrial populations increasingly, though not exclusively, articulated their material want through the language of Belgianness. "All the butter in the country belongs to us, Belgians," a group of Liège miners chanted in 1916 while putting up blockades to prevent dairy exports to Germany.[33] Those withholding food for usurious profits on the black market were often decried as bad Belgians, enemies from within. Because the intensity of war deprivation was stronger in cities than in the countryside, urban dwellers were more likely to associate material well-being and the absence of hardship with an idealized version of fin de siècle Belgium. They equated the Flemish militancy of the collaborationist *activisten* with wartime deprivation. In the countryside, these associations were less pronounced as proximity to food producers made material want less pressing than in towns. Rural dwellers even carried the stigma of war profiteers, traitors, and bad Belgians because of their supposed involvement in the black market. In this way the social disruption of the Great War added to the postwar divisiveness of language and ethnicity.

## THE CONTINGENCY OF ETHNICITY: COMPARING BELGIUM AND IMPERIAL AUSTRIA

Belgian historians have intensely debated the nature of the activist collaboration, particularly whether it was instigated by the Germans or rather by radicalized groups within the Flemish movement itself.[34] Regardless of the answer to that question, there seems to be broad agreement that postwar anti-Belgian Flemish nationalism was an outgrowth of prewar ethnic sensibilities in the Flemish movement.[35] From this perspective, the linear and unavoidable rise of Flemish ethnicity has been the driver of Belgium's so-called nationalities conflict. Jeremy King calls this type of reasoning the "ethnicist fallacy,"[36] i.e., the mistaken tendency to treat ethnicity and nationhood as active generators of social change, rather than as social categories that need explanation in and of themselves. A comparison of Belgium and imperial Austria elucidates King's point.

In both states ethnolinguistic movements thrived before the First World War thanks to the liberal freedoms established at the level of the central government. Pieter Judson's assessment of Austria also applies to Belgium: "it was the very constitutional guarantees made by the imperial Habsburg regime that created space for political activism organized specifically around language use."[37] There was a difference in timing though. The Czech movement in Bohemia and Moravia saw its political demands realized much earlier than the Flemish movement. Symptomatically, Prague got its Czech-speaking university in 1882. The Flemish-speaking counterpart in Ghent was realized only in 1930.

According to Miroslav Hroch, this gap reflects the different phasing of both national movements. In Hroch's scheme, the Czech movement broke through to the masses already in the late nineteenth century.[38] After an initial phase A of scholarly interest and a phase B of surging political activity, it entered its phase C of mass agitation.[39] The Flemish movement only reached this mass phase after the First World War. Hroch's scheme is based on a complex analysis of the broader social-economic context underpinning these diverging trajectories. It hinges specifically on the different timing of the rise of national movements in relation to the industrial revolution and the bourgeois-democratic revolution that ended the Ancien Régime. Ultimately, Hroch uses national identity and ethnicity as the explanans rather than the explanandum of the success or lack thereof of national movements. In his classical work *Social Preconditions of National Revival in Europe* he defined the transition from phase B to C as one of "simple awareness of national identity" to "active national consciousness," implicitly lending permanence to national identity as a structural determinant.[40]

The literature on national indifference offers an at least implicit criticism of Hroch's model. It questions the idea of a massive breakthrough of ethnolinguistic nationalism prior to the First World War and inverts Hroch's chain of causality between, on the one hand, national identities and linguistic difference, and on the other hand, nationalist conflict and reform of the state. In the national indifference framework, the institutional reaction of the central government to linguistic agitation made nationhood and ethnicity more relevant among broader reaches of society, not the other way around. State reform prompted mass nationalism instead of mass nationalism prompting state reform.

The Belgian and Austrian states had a different institutional response to the political demands of their respective language movements. To my mind, this explains the fifty-year gap between the Czech and Flemish movements in realizing their program. During the latter third of the nineteenth century, the central government in imperial Austria co-opted nationalist societies to fulfill public duties, especially in the area of education, anchoring these organizations more deeply within the state apparatus. The constitution of 1867 drawn up by German-Austrian liberals granted language rights to every individual. The original intent was not to provide a constitutional basis for "nations" to enforce their collective rights. Liberals saw the language regime purely as an individual facility for *local* issues to be dealt with in any language and for *important* matters to be handled in German. The constitution's framers wrongly assumed that this arrangement would reduce the potential for nationalist conflict.[41] The liberal School Act of 1869 was an important catalyzer. Henceforth, a municipality-supported elementary school had to be established in every locality where (a five-year average of) forty children lived in a four-kilometer radius or a one-hour walk. An 1884 ruling by the Constitutional Court applied this rule to the establishment of minority-language schools. This was the incentive for nationalists to set up private schools in the hope that they would eventually attract forty children and be subsidized by the government.[42] Contrary to the original intention of the liberal framers, the constitutional guarantees stimulated nationalist strife. In order to keep the resulting language conflict under control, the central government in Cisleithania began to subsidize separate nationalist organizations for education, agriculture, tourism, youth care, and so on. By assigning separate but parallel functions to Czech-speaking and German-speaking organizations in Bohemia and Moravia, the Austrian government hoped to divert nationalist energies toward administrative tasks. The result, however, was that nations became gradually recognized as a legal category in Austrian legislation.[43]

Something similar never happened in prewar Belgium. The term "Flemish people" had no legal basis. Within the context of the hyperliberal Belgian political system and the Catholic resistance to state intervention in schooling, the individual freedom of family heads to choose their children's language of instruction remained sacrosanct. In Austria, by contrast, the collective rights of the nation gradually prevailed. Moreover, the social and institutional anchoring of the Flemish movement never went as far as that of the Czech movement. In Belgium, ideological-confessional pillar organizations rather than nationalist organizations were co-opted by the government to perform state functions within the framework of subsidized freedom.[44] In short, while in Austria the development of an ethnically segregated welfare state fed into the nationalities conflict,[45] consociationalism in Belgium, which was driven by ideological and social-economic dissension, had a moderating impact on ethnolinguistic tensions.

The First World War confirmed this divergence. In Belgium, pillar organizations took over state responsibilities at the local level through the National Relief and Food Committee. There were Flemish nationalist initiatives supported by the Germans, but these were less successful and they inevitably carried the odium of collaboration. The wartime situation in imperial Austria was completely different. From day one the state lost the confidence of its citizens and turned into a military dictatorship.[46] Waging what was in effect "a silent war against its own citizens," it alienated its Slavic populations and treated them "as potential irredentists and pro-Russian fifth-columnists."[47] From 1917 onward the Austrian state was increasingly incapable of providing for its citizens and was forced to hand over a whole range of welfare functions in local communities, starting with youth welfare, to ethnonationalist organizations. "Food shortages, labor conditions, and deteriorating infrastructure," Pieter Judson writes, "all became understood through the lens of nation as nationalist organizations gained key responsibilities for distributing aid. This development did not necessarily nationalize populations, but it did implicate the nation in daily life far more effectively than nationalist activists had ever been able to do in the years before the war."[48] Come 1918 ethnonationalist organizations in the Habsburg empire were in a much stronger position than those in Belgium, although the latter would recover rather quickly in the postwar climate of radical democratization (see the preceding section).

In the end, the Austrian and Belgian cases show that ethnonationalism was a decidedly modern reaction to mass politics rather than an atavistic throwback to the past. Ethnicity was a social category constructed, made relevant, and instrumentalized within the context of industrialization and democratization and the attending social and political changes. Any binary classification of European nationalisms into modern Western civic types versus backward Eastern ethnic types is highly reductionist. The Belgian case defies such easy categorizations. The history of the BWP and its rank and file shows that even explicitly civic and modern mass movements harness ethnicity and nationhood. In broader terms, the Belgian and Austrian experiences highlight the situationality of these categories of collective identification. The crucial role of nationhood and ethnicity in the turbulent history of twentieth-century Europe was not determined by their nineteenth-century roots. Rather, the contingent shifts occasioned by the First World War made them into central concerns of ever larger groups of people and turned them, to use Brubaker's terms, from one social category among several others into absolute markers of groupness.[49] The Great War really gave birth to twentieth-century Europe and its obsession with ethnicity and nationalism.

# NOTES

**PREFACE**

1. "Nation-Building from Below: A Social History of National Identity in Belgium," postdoctoral research project 1.2.254.07.N.00 of the FWO-Research Foundation Flanders.

Sections of this book have previously appeared in a number of articles and chapters (see the Bibliography), but they have been substantially and radically reworked to fit my evolving insights.

**INTRODUCTION: WORKERS INTO BELGIANS, FLEMINGS, AND WALLOONS**

1. *The Independent*, September 11, 2007.
2. Michelet quoted by Jean Stengers, "La Belgique de 1830, une 'nationalité de convention'?," in *Histoire et historiens depuis 1830 en Belgique: Revue de l'Université de Bruxelles*, no. 1–2, ed. Hervé Hasquin (Brussels: ULB, 1981), 7. All translations from French, Dutch, and German are the author's.
3. Leopold I quoted in ibid., 9.
4. Louis-Philippe quoted in Hervé Hasquin, *Historiographie et politique en Belgique* (Brussels/Charleroi: ULB/Institut Jules Destrée, 1996), 33.
5. Els Witte, "1828–1847: De constructie van België," in *Nieuwe geschiedenis van België*, vol. 1, *1830–1905*, ed. Els Witte et al. (Tielt: Lannoo, 2005); Lode Wils, *Van Clovis tot Di Rupo: De lange weg van de naties in de Lage Landen* (Leuven: Garant, 2005 [1992]). The British historian Martyn Conway dates the roots of Belgium's existential problems even later, to the institutional crisis created by the Second World War. Martin Conway, *The Sorrows of Belgium: Liberation and Political Reconstruction, 1944–1947* (Oxford: Oxford University Press, 2012).

6. I use the contemporary late nineteenth-century epithet "Flemish"–"Vlaamsch"–"Flamand" to refer to the language spoken in what today is called the "Dutch-speaking" part of Belgium, i.e., Flanders. Flemish dialects are a variation of standard Dutch. Flemish relates to Dutch as American English does to British English.

7. Lode Wils, "De twee Belgische revoluties," in *Nationalisme in België: Identiteiten in beweging 1780–2000*, ed. Kas Deprez and Louis Vos (Antwerp: Houtekiet, 1999), 49. See also Witte, "1828–1847," 194, 98–207; Wils, *Van Clovis tot Di Rupo*, 46–47; Jean Stengers, *Les racines de la Belgique jusqu'à la Révolution de 1830: Histoire du sentiment national en Belgique des origines à 1918* (Brussels: Racine, 2000), 1:27, 171–72; Els Witte, "Inleiding: Natie en democratie, 1890–1921: De probleemstelling," in *Natie en democratie–Nation et démocratie (1890–1921), Acta van het interuniversitair colloquium, Brussel 8–9 Juni 2006*, ed. Els Witte, et al. (Brussels: Koninklijke Vlaamse Academie van België voor Wetenschappen en Kunsten, 2007), 12–14; Remieg Aerts, "Een andere geschiedenis: Een beschouwing over de scheiding van 1830," in *De erfenis van 1830*, ed. Peter Rietbergen and Tom Verschaffel (Leuven: Acco, 2006).

8. Defined broadly as those who "are usually not actively or consciously engaged in concerted, organized nation-building strategies." Marnix Beyen and Maarten Van Ginderachter, "General Introduction: Writing the Mass into a Mass Phenomenon," in *Nationhood from Below: Europe in the Long Nineteenth Century*, ed. Maarten Van Ginderachter and Marnix Beyen (Basingstoke: Palgrave Macmillan, 2012), 10.

9. Eugen Weber, *Peasants into Frenchmen: The Modernization of Rural France, 1870–1914* (London: Chatto and Windus, 1977); Ernest Gellner, *Nations and Nationalism* (Oxford: Blackwell, 1993 [1983]); Benedict Anderson, *Imagined Communities: Reflections on the Origin and Spread of Nationalism* (London: Verso, 1994 [1983]).

10. Eric Hobsbawm, *Nations and Nationalism since 1780: Programme, Myth, Reality* (Cambridge: Cambridge University Press, 1995 [1990]), 130.

11. Parti ouvrier belge/Belgische Werkliedenpartij.

12. My analysis is based on an in-depth investigation of the socialist movement in Ghent, Brussels, the Pays Noir (Black Country) around Charleroi, the Borinage area to the west of Mons, the Centre region around La Louvière, and to a somewhat lesser extent Liège and Antwerp.

13. Jon E. Fox and Cynthia Miller-Idriss, "Everyday Nationhood," *Ethnicities* 8, no. 4 (2008): 537. See also Eleanor Knott, "Everyday Nationalism," *The State of Nationalism*, 2016, https://stateofnationalism.eu/article/everyday-nationalism/; Michael Skey and Marco Antonsich, eds., *Everyday Nationhood: Theorising Culture, Identity and Belonging after Banal Nationalism* (Basingstoke: Palgrave Macmillan, 2017). For a critical perspective, see Anthony D. Smith, "The Limits of Everyday Nationhood," *Ethnicities* 8, no. 4 (2008).

14. Hendrik Defoort, *Werklieden bemint uw profijt! De Belgische sociaaldemocratie in Europa* (Leuven: LannooCampus, 2006).

15. Marnix Beyen, "Belgium: A Nation That Failed to Become Ethnic," in *Statehood Before and Beyond Ethnicity: Minor States in Northern and Eastern Europe*, ed. Linas Eriksonas and Leos Müller (New York: Lang, 2005), 345–46; Guy Vanschoenbeek, "Socialisten: Gezellen zonder vaderland? De BWP en haar verhouding tot het 'vaderland België,'" *Bijdragen tot de eigentijdse geschiedenis/ Cahiers d'histoire du temps présent*, no. 3 (1997); Patrick Pasture, "Kerk, natie en arbeidersklasse: Een essay over collectieve identificatie, in het bijzonder m.b.t. de (christelijke) arbeidersbeweging in België," *Bijdragen tot de eigentijdse geschiedenis/Cahiers d'histoire du temps présent*, no. 6 (1999).

16. Val R. Lorwin, "Linguistic Pluralism and Political Tension in Modern Belgium," *Canadian Journal of History/Annales Canadiennes d'Histoire* 5, no. 1 (1970): 7. This image remains influential to this day, although my own research has demonstrated the potential divisiveness of issues of ethnicity and language. Maarten Van Ginderachter, *Het rode vaderland: De vergeten geschiedenis van de communautaire spanningen in het Belgische socialisme voor WO I* (Tielt/Ghent: Lannoo/Amsab, 2005); Maarten Van Ginderachter, "Social-Democracy and National Identity: The Ethnic Rift in the Belgian Workers' Party (1885–1914)," *International Review of Social History* 52 (2007): 215–40.

17. Paul Ward, *Red Flag and Union Jack: Englishness, Patriotism, and the British Left, 1881–1924* (Rochester, NY: Royal Historical Society/Boydell Press, 1998), 4; Stephen Yeo, "Socialism, the State and Some Oppositional Englishness," in *Englishness: Politics and Culture 1880–1920*, ed. Robert Colls and Philip Dodd (London: Croom Helm, 1986); Stefan Berger, "British and German Socialists between Class and National Solidarity," in *Nationalism, Labour and Ethnicity 1870–1939*, ed. Stefan Berger and Angel Smith (Manchester: Manchester University Press, 1999), 41. See also Jean Jaurès's "patriotisme socialiste." Milorad M. Drachkovitch, *Les socialismes français et allemand et le problème de la guerre, 1870–1914* (Geneva: Studer, 1953), 69–70.

18. See Stefan Berger and Angel Smith, eds., *Nationalism, Labour and Ethnicity 1870–1939* (Manchester: Manchester University Press, 1999); Stephen F. Jones, *Socialism in Georgian Colors: The European Road to Social Democracy, 1883–1917* (Cambridge, MA: Harvard University Press, 2005); Dieter Groh and Peter Brandt, *Vaterlandslose Gesellen: Sozialdemokratie und Nation 1860–1990* (Munich: Beck, 1992); David Allen Harvey, *Constructing Class and Nationality in Alsace, 1830–1945* (DeKalb: Northern Illinois University Press, 2001); Kerstin S. Jobst, *Zwischen Nationalismus und Internationalismus: Die polnische und ukrainische Sozialdemokratie in Galizien von 1890 bis 1914. Ein Beitrag zur Nationalitätenfrage im Habsburgerreich* (Hamburg: Dölling und Galitz, 1996); Ward, *Red Flag and Union Jack*; Robert Stuart, *Marxism and National Identity: Socialism, Nationalism, and National Socialism during the French Fin de Siècle* (Albany: State University of New York Press, 2006); Sabine

Rutar, *Kultur–Nation–Milieu: Sozialdemokratie in Triest vor dem Ersten Weltkrieg* (Essen: Klartext Verlag, 2004); Pieter Van Duin, *Central European Crossroads: Social Democracy and National Revolution in Bratislava (Pressburg), 1867–1921* (New York: Berghahn Books, 2009).

19. One of the exceptions is Jakub Beneš, *Workers and Nationalism: Czech and German Social Democracy in Habsburg Austria, 1890–1918* (Oxford: Oxford University Press, 2016).

20. Jan Craeybeckx, *Arbeidersbeweging en Vlaamsgezindheid voor de Eerste Wereldoorlog* (Brussels: Koninklijke academie voor wetenschappen letteren en schone kunsten van België, 1978), 48; Hendrik Defoort and Guy Vanschoenbeek, "Socialistische Partij," in *Nieuwe encyclopedie van de Vlaamse beweging*, ed. Reginald De Schryver et al. (Tielt: Lannoo, 1998), 3:2780; Harry Van Velthoven, *De Vlaamse kwestie 1830–1914: Macht en onmacht van de Vlaamsgezinden* (Kortrijk: UGA 1982), 109; Patricia Penn Hilden, *Women, Work, and Politics: Belgium 1830–1914* (Oxford: Clarendon, 1993), 43, 101, 306; Carl Strikwerda, *A House Divided: Catholics, Socialists, and Flemish Nationalists in Nineteenth-Century Belgium* (Lanham, MD: Rowman & Littlefield, 1997), 53.

21. Eric Hobsbawm, "Working-Class Internationalism," in *Internationalism in the Labour Movement, 1830–1940*, ed. Frits Van Holthoon and Marcel Van der Linden (Leiden: E.J. Brill, 1988), 1:9; Eric Hobsbawm, "Afterword: Working Classes and Nations," in *Labor Migration in the Atlantic Economies: The European and North American Working Classes during the Period of Industrialization*, ed. Dirk Hoerder (Westport, CT: Greenwood, 1985), 436.

22. Miroslav Hroch, "From National Movement to the Fully-Formed Nation: The Nation-Building Process in Europe," in *Mapping the Nation*, ed. Gopal Balakrishnan (London: Verso, 1996).

23. Gellner, *Nations and Nationalism*.

24. Anthony D. Smith, *The Ethnic Origins of Nations* (Oxford: Blackwell 1994 [1986]).

25. Rogers Brubaker et al., *Nationalist Politics and Everyday Ethnicity in a Transylvanian Town* (Princeton, NJ: Princeton University Press, 2006), 11.

26. On the relationship of regionalism and nationalism, see Linda Colley, *Britons: Forging the Nation, 1707–1837* (New Haven, CT: Yale University Press, 1992); Jean-François Chanet, *L'École républicaine et les petites patries* (Paris: Aubier, 1996); Anne-Marie Thiesse, *Ils apprenaient la France: L'exaltation des régions dans le discours patriotique* (Paris: Editions de la Maison des sciences de l'homme, 1997); Stéphane Gerson, *The Pride of Place: Local Memories and Political Culture in Nineteenth-Century France* (Ithaca, NY: Cornell University Press, 2003); Celia Applegate, *A Nation of Provincials: The German Idea of Heimat* (Berkeley: University of California Press, 1990); Alon Confino, *The Nation as a Local Metaphor: Württemberg, Imperial Germany, and National Memory, 1871–1918* (Chapel Hill: University of North Carolina Press, 1997). On the construction of nationhood at the local level, see Abigail Green, *Fatherlands*:

*State-Building and Nationhood in Nineteenth-Century Germany* (Cambridge: Cambridge University Press, 2001); Keeley Stauter-Halsted, *The Nation in the Village: The Genesis of Peasant National Identity in Austrian Poland, 1848–1914* (Ithaca, NY: Cornell University Press, 2001); Jeremy King, *Budweisers into Czechs and Germans: A Local History of Bohemian Politics, 1848–1948* (Princeton, NJ: Princeton University Press, 2002); Pieter M. Judson, *Guardians of the Nation: Activists on the Language Frontiers of Imperial Austria* (Cambridge, MA: Harvard University Press, 2006); Tara Zahra, *Kidnapped Souls: National Indifference and the Battle for Children in the Bohemian Lands, 1900–1948* (Ithaca, NY: Cornell University Press, 2008); James E. Bjork, *Neither German nor Pole: Catholicism and National Indifference in a Central European Borderland* (Ann Arbor: University of Michigan Press, 2008); Laurence Cole, *Military Culture and Popular Patriotism in Late Imperial Austria* (Oxford: Oxford University Press, 2014); Iryna Vushko, *The Politics of Cultural Retreat: Imperial Bureaucracy in Austrian Galicia, 1772–1867* (New Haven, CT: Yale University Press, 2015); John C. Swanson, *Tangible Belonging: Negotiating Germanness in Twentieth-Century Hungary* (Pittsburgh: Pittsburgh University Press, 2017).

27. For a more extensive view on this literature, see Maarten Van Ginderachter and Jon Fox, eds., *National Indifference and the History of Nationalism in Modern Europe* (London: Routledge, 2019).

28. Zahra, *Kidnapped Souls*; Bjork, *Neither German nor Pole*; Judson, *Guardians of the Nation*; King, *Budweisers into Czechs and Germans*.

29. Compare Reill's "ambiguous," "pluralist," "fearful" nationalists in the mid-nineteenth-century Adriatic: Dominique Kirchner Reill, *Nationalists Who Feared the Nation: Adriatic Multi-Nationalism in Habsburg Dalmatia, Trieste, and Venice* (Stanford, CA: Stanford University Press, 2012).

30. For a critical view of national indifference, see Laurence Cole, "A proposito di 'Guardians of the nation' di Pieter M. Judson: Laurence Cole, 'Alla ricerca della frontiera linguistica: nazionalismo e identità nazionale nell'Austria imperiale,'" *Quaderni storici* 43, no. 2 (2008); Gerald Stourzh, "The Ethnicizing of Politics and 'National Indifference' in Late Imperial Austria," in *Der Umfang der österreichischen Geschichte: Ausgewählte Studien 1990–2010*, ed. Gerald Stourzh (Vienna: Böhlau, 2011), 302–6; Beneš, *Workers and Nationalism*, 13; David Feest, "Spaces of 'National Indifference' in Biographic Research on Citizens of the Baltic Republics 1918–1940," *Journal of Baltic Studies* 48, no. 1 (2017); Per Bolin and Christina Douglas, "'National Indifference' in the Baltic Territories? A Critical Assessment," *Journal of Baltic Studies* 48, no. 1 (2017); Laurence Cole, "Visions and Revisions of Empire: Reflections on a New History of the Habsburg Monarchy," *Austrian History Yearbook* 49 (2018): 272; Maarten Van Ginderachter and Jon Fox, "Introduction," in Van Ginderachter and Fox, eds., *National Indifference and the History of Nationalism in Modern Europe*.

31. Judson, *Guardians of the Nation*, 120 (my italics). See also Rok Stergar, "National Indifference in the Heyday of Nationalist Mobilization? Ljubljana

Military Veterans and the Language of Command," *Austrian History Yearbook* 43 (April 2012): 48; Roberta Pergher, "Staging the Nation in Fascist Italy's 'New Provinces,'" *Austrian History Yearbook* 43, no. April (2012): 98–115.

32. *Vooruit*, February 14, 1890, pp. 3–4; June 2, 1893, p. 4; May 5, 1899, p. 3.

33. For more information on this source, see Maarten Van Ginderachter, "Jean Prolo, waer bestu bleven? Speuren naar de bronnen van 'gewone mensen' in 19de-eeuwse archieven," in *Terug naar de bron(nen): Taal en taalgebruik in de 19de eeuw in Vlaanderen*, in *Verslagen en mededelingen van de Koninklijke Academie voor Nederlandse Taal- en Letterkunde* 114, no. 1, ed. Wim Vandenbussche (Ghent: KANTL, 2004); Bart De Sutter and Maarten Van Ginderachter, "Working Class Voices from the Late Nineteenth Century: Propaganda Pence in a Socialist Paper in Ghent," *History Workshop Journal* 69, no. 1 (2010); Bart De Sutter, "Over dompers, mouchards en papen: Constructie van identiteit, via humor; Casus: De Gentse socialistische strijdpenning in *Vooruit* (1886–1900)" (Master's thesis, Ghent University, 2008); Bart De Sutter, "Humor 'from below' aan het einde van de 19e eeuw: socialisten en 'strijdpenning' in 'Vooruit,'" *Brood en Rozen*, no. 1 (2010); Bart De Sutter, "De Strijdpenning van Vooruit: humor en identiteit bij de socialistische achterban in Gent (1886–1900)," *Vlaams marxistisch tijdschrift* 45, no. 4 (2012).

34. Christopher M. Clark, "The New Catholicism and the European Culture Wars," in *Culture Wars: Secular–Catholic Conflict in Nineteenth-Century Europe*, ed. Christopher M. Clark and Wolfram Kaiser (Cambridge: Cambridge University Press, 2003), 21–22.

35. On the methodological issues relating to everyday nationalism, see Jon Fox and Maarten Van Ginderachter, eds., "Everyday Nationalism's Evidence Problem," themed section of *Nations and Nationalism* 24, issue 3 (2018).

36. Rogers Brubaker, "Ethnicity without Groups," *Archives Européennes de Sociologie* 43, no. 2 (2002).

37. Some readers might object that I leave out the church as a classic institution of nation-building. In Chapter 1 I delve into the role of the church, but it moves to the background in the remaining chapters. Because the BWP was an explicit agent of secularization that tried to break the hold of the church on the working classes and because the party's grassroots supporters were often intensely anticlerical (though not anti-religious), the church, Catholic society, and the Christian working-class movement mainly figure in my narrative as negative sources of identification.

38. Michael Billig, *Banal Nationalism* (London: Sage, 1995).

## CHAPTER 1: A SOCIALIST PILLAR OF A HYPERLIBERAL STATE

1. Lode Wils, "The Two Belgian Revolutions," in *Nationalism in Belgium: Shifting Identities*, ed. Kas Deprez and Louis Vos (London: Macmillan, 1998).

2. Sébastien Dubois, *L'invention de la Belgique: Genèse d'un état-nation* (Brussels: Racine, 2005).

3. Henk De Smaele, "Politiek als hanengevecht of cerebraal systeem: Ideeën over politieke representatie en de invoering van de evenredige vertegenwoordiging in België (1899)," *Bijdragen en betreffende de geschiedenis der Nederlanden* 114, no. 3 (1999).

4. Henk De Smaele, "Eclectisch en toch nieuw: De uitvinding van het Belgisch parlement in 1830–1831," *Bijdragen en mededelingen betreffende de geschiedenis der Nederlanden* 120, no. 3 (2005): 412.

5. Daniel Ziblatt, *Structuring the State: The Formation of Italy and Germany and the Puzzle of Federalism* (Princeton, NJ: Princeton University Press, 2006).

6. Marnix Beyen, "Belgium: A Nation That Failed to Become Ethnic," in *Statehood Before and Beyond Ethnicity: Minor States in Northern and Eastern Europe*, ed. Linas Eriksonas and Leos Müller (New York: Lang, 2005).

7. Jo Tollebeek, "Enthousiasme en evidentie: De negentiende-eeuwse Belgisch-nationale geschiedschrijving," in *De ijkmeesters: Opstellen over de geschiedschrijving in Nederland en België*, ed. Jo Tollebeek (Amsterdam: Bert Bakker, 1994), 64–67.

8. Jan Art, "Social Control in Belgium: The Catholic Factor," in *Social Control in Europe, 1800–2000*, ed. Clive Emsley, Eric Johnson, and Pieter Spierenburg (Columbus: Ohio State University Press, 2004), 2:112–13; Marnix Beyen and Benoît Majerus, "Weak and Strong Nations in the Low Countries: National Historiography and Its 'Others' in Belgium, Luxembourg, and the Netherlands in the Nineteenth and Twentieth Centuries," in *The Contested Nation: Ethnicity, Class, Religion and Gender in National Histories*, ed. Stefan Berger and Chris Lorenz (Basingstoke: Palgrave Macmillan, 2008), 286–87.

9. Janet Louise Polasky, "Transplanting and Rooting Workers in London and Brussels: A Comparative History," *Journal of Modern History* 73, no. 3 (2001): 542.

10. Guy Vanthemsche, *De paradoxen van de staat: Staat en vrije markt in historisch perspectief* (Brussels: VUB Press, 1998), 71–83.

11. Carl Strikwerda, *A House Divided: Catholics, Socialists, and Flemish Nationalists in Nineteenth-Century Belgium* (Lanham, MD: Rowman & Littlefield, 1997), 29.

12. Marcel Van Audenhove, "L'autonomie communale," in *Het openbaar initiatief van de gemeenten in België 1795–1940/L'initiative publique des communes en Belgique 1795–1940* (Brussels: Crédit communal de Belgique, 1986), 71–72.

13. The Walloon coal basins include the Borinage, the Centre around La Louvière, the Black Country around Charleroi, and the Liège area.

14. Figures from Aristide Zolberg, "The Making of Flemings and Walloons: Belgium: 1830–1914," *Journal of Interdisciplinary History* 5, no. 2 (1974): 194–96.

15. Peter Scholliers, "Industrial Wage Differentials in Nineteenth-Century Belgium," in *Income Distribution in Historical Perspective*, ed. Y. S. Brenner, Hartmut Kaelble, and Mark Thomas (Cambridge: Cambridge University Press, 1991).

16. Jan de Vries, *European Urbanization, 1500–1800* (London: Methuen, 1984), 39, 45.

17. Paul Bairoch and Gary Goertz, "Factors of Urbanisation in the Nineteenth Century Developed Countries: A Descriptive and Econometric Analysis," *Urban Studies* 23, no. 4 (1986): 288.

18. Alexander Coppens, "Tussen beleid en administratieve praktijk: De implementatie van het Belgisch migratiebeleid in negentiende-eeuws Brussel" (PhD diss., VUB, 2016), 62.

19. Ibid., 58–59. During the fin de siècle, the Brussels *agglomération* consisted of fourteen communes: Anderlecht, Brussels, Elsene/Ixelles, Etterbeek, Koekelberg, Laken, Schaarbeek, Sint-Gillis/Saint-Gilles, Sint-Jans-Molenbeek/Molenbeek-Saint-Jean, Sint-Joost-ten-Node/Saint-Josse-ten-Noode, Sint-Lambrechts-Woluwe/Woluwe-Saint-Lambert, Sint-Pieters-Jette/Jette-Saint-Pierre, Ukkel/Uccle, Vorst/Forest. Strikwerda, *A House Divided*, 40.

20. Eric Vanhaute, "Leven, wonen en werken in onzekere tijden: Patronen van bevolking en arbeid in België in de 'lange negentiende eeuw,'" *Bijdragen en mededelingen betreffende de geschiedenis der Nederlanden* 118, no. 2 (2003): 159.

21. Bart Van der Herten, *België onder stoom: Transport en communicatie tijdens de 19e eeuw* (Leuven: Universitaire Pers Leuven, 2004), 292.

22. Jordi Martí-Henneberg, "European Integration and National Models for Railway Networks (1840–2010)," *Journal of Transport Geography* 26, Supplement C (2013): 134.

23. Van der Herten, *België onder stoom*, 301, 418.

24. Thierry Eggerickx, "Les migrations internes en Belgique de 1840 à 1939: Un essai de synthèse," in *Histoire de la population de le Belgique et de ses territoires: Actes de la Chaire Quetelet 2005*, ed. Thierry Eggerickx, Jean-Paul Sanderson, and Patrick Deboosere (Louvain-la-Neuve: Presses Universitaires de Louvain, 2010).

25. Vanhaute, "Leven, wonen en werken in onzekere tijden," 175.

26. Jean Stengers and Eliane Gubin, *Le grand siècle de la nationalité belge: De 1830 à 1918*, vol. 2 of *Histoire du sentiment national en Belgique des origines à 1918* (Brussels: Racine, 2002), 25.

27. Lieve Gevers and Louis Vos, "Kerk en nationalisme in Vlaanderen in de 19de en 20ste eeuw," in *Is God een Turk? Nationalisme en religie* (Leuven: Davidsfonds, 1995).

28. Maarten Van Ginderachter and Minte Kamphuis, "The Transnational Dimensions of the Early Socialist Pillars in Belgium and the Netherlands, c. 1885–1914: An Exploratory Essay," *Belgisch tijdschrift voor filologie en geschiedenis/Revue Belge de philologie et d'histoire* 90, no. 4 (2012): 1321–37.

29. Arend Lijphart, ed., *Conflict and Coexistence in Belgium: The Dynamics of a Culturally Divided Society* (Berkeley: University of California, Institute of International Studies, 1981); Zolberg, "The Making of Flemings and Walloons";

Strikwerda, *A House Divided*; Val R. Lorwin, "Linguistic Pluralism and Political Tension in Modern Belgium," *Canadian Journal of History/Annales Canadiennes d'Histoire* 5, no. 1 (1970).

30. Arend Lijphart, "Introduction: The Belgian Example of Cultural Coexistence in Comparative Perspective," in Lijphart, ed., *Conflict and Coexistence in Belgium*, 8.

31. Jan Art, "Van 'klerikalisme' naar 'katholieke zuil' of van 'régime clérical' naar 'CVP-staat': Een benadering van het Vlaams georganiseerd katholicisme in de nieuwste tijd," *Belgisch tijdschrift voor nieuwste geschiedenis/Revue belge d'histoire contemporaine* 13, no. 1 (1982); Hans Righart, "Katholieke verzuiling in België als historisch probleem: Enkele historiografische kanttekeningen," *Belgisch tijdschrift voor nieuwste geschiedenis/Revue belge d'histoire contemporaine* 25, no. 3–4 (1984): 546; Christopher M. Clark and Wolfram Kaiser, eds., *Culture Wars: Secular–Catholic Conflict in Nineteenth-Century Europe* (Cambridge: Cambridge University Press, 2003).

32. Staf Hellemans, *Strijd om de moderniteit: Sociale bewegingen en verzuiling in Europa sinds 1800* (Leuven: Universitaire Pers Leuven, 1990), 101; Wolfram Kaiser, *Christian Democracy and the Origins of European Union* (Cambridge: Cambridge University Press, 2007), 13; Christopher M. Clark, "The New Catholicism and the European Culture Wars," in Clark and Kaiser, eds., *Culture Wars*.

33. Wolfram Kaiser, "'Clericalism—That Is Our Enemy!': European Anticlericalism and the Culture Wars," in Clark and Kaiser, eds., *Culture Wars*; Emiel Lamberts, ed., *Een kantelend tijdperk: De wending van de Kerk naar het volk in Noord-West-Europa, 1890–1910* (Leuven: University Press, 1992).

34. Patrick Pasture, "Introduction: Between Cross and Class. Christian Labour in Europe," in *Between Cross and Class: Comparative Histories of Christian Labour in Europe 1840–2000*, ed. Jan De Maeyer, Lex Heerma van Voss, and Patrick Pasture (Bern: Lang, 2005), 30.

35. For the Dutch situation, see Piet de Rooy, "'Dat de evenaar noch naar links, noch naar rechts doorzwikke': De confessionelen en de moderne natie," in *Nederlandse politiek in historisch en vergelijkend perspectief*, ed. Uwe Becker (Amsterdam: Het Spinhuis, 1993).

36. Guy Vanschoenbeek, "De wortels van de sociaal-democratie in Vlaanderen: Le 'monde socialiste gantois' en de Gentse socialisten voor de Eerste Wereldoorlog" (PhD diss., Ghent University, 1992), 74.

37. Dieter Groh, *Negative Integration und revolutionärer Attentismus: Die deutsche Sozialdemokratie am Vorabend des Ersten Weltkrieges* (Frankfurt am Main: Ullstein, 1973).

38. Herman Balthazar, "100 jaar dagblad Vooruit," *Amsab-tijdingen* 3, no. 1–2 (1984–1985); Bart De Nil, "Leest, leert, denkt en ontspan u!! De Vlaamse sociaal-democratie en de roman" (Master's thesis, Ghent University, 1997), 79, 87; Guy Vanschoenbeek, "Vooruit," in *Nieuwe encyclopedie van de Vlaamse*

*beweging*, ed. Reginald De Schryver et al. (Tielt: Lannoo, 1998), 3:3563–66; Paul De Witte, *De geschiedenis van Vooruit en de Gentsche socialistische werkersvereeniging sedert 1870* (Ghent: A. Hoste, 1898), 251.

39. Vanschoenbeek, "De wortels van de sociaal-democratie in Vlaanderen," 723.

40. Joël Michel, "Le mouvement ouvrier chez les mineurs d'Europe occidentale (Grande-Bretagne, Belgique, France, Allemagne): Etude comparative des années 1880 à 1914" (PhD diss., Lyon III, 1987).

41. Groh, *Negative Integration und revolutionärer Attentismus*; Guy Vanschoenbeek, "Socialisten: Gezellen zonder vaderland? De BWP en haar verhouding tot het 'vaderland België,'" *Bijdragen tot de eigentijdse geschiedenis/Cahiers d'histoire du temps présent* 3 (1997): 240.

42. Throughout this book I will use the terms anti-socialist, Christian (-Democratic) and Catholic working-class, workers' or labor movement interchangeably to refer to the Christian-inspired workers' movement that arose in response to socialism in Ghent.

43. Cf. Strikwerda, *A House Divided*, 134.

44. Art, "Van 'klerikalisme' naar 'katholieke zuil' of van 'régime clérical' naar 'CVP-staat,'" 5; Righart, "Katholieke verzuiling in België als historisch probleem," 548–50.

45. Vanschoenbeek, "De wortels van de sociaal-democratie in Vlaanderen," 183–84, 240, 287, 326, 371.

46. Machteld De Metsenaere, *Taalmuur: Sociale muur? De negentiendeeeuwse taalverhoudingen te Brussel als resultaat van geodemografische en sociale processen* (Brussels: VUB Press, 1988), 17–22.

47. Louis Bertrand, *Histoire de la démocratie et du socialisme en Belgique depuis 1830* (Brussels: Dechenne-Cornély, 1907), 2:378, 650.

48. Strikwerda, *A House Divided*, 13, 39.

49. Hendrik Defoort, *Werklieden bemint uw profijt! De Belgische sociaaldemocratie in Europa* (Leuven: LannooCampus, 2006), 265.

50. Joël Michel, "La Chevalerie du Travail: Force ou faiblesse du mouvement ouvrier belge," *Belgisch tijdschrift voor nieuwste geschiedenis/Revue belge d'histoire contemporaine* 9, no. 1–2 (1978): 117–20. On the Chevaliers du Travail, see also Léon Watillon, *The Knights of Labor in Belgium* (Los Angeles: Institute of Industrial Relations, University of California, Los Angeles, 1959); Maurice Dommanget, *La Chevalerie du Travail française (1893–1911): Contribution à l'histoire du socialisme et du mouvement ouvrier* (Lausanne: Rencontre, 1967), 37–52.

51. M. Renard "L'âme du pays noir," in C. Lemonnier, R. Marius, G. Decamps, V. Van Hassel, and O. Ghilain, *Le Borinage* (n.p.: 1902), 13.

52. Hector Fauvieau, *Le Borinage: Monographie politique, économique, sociale* (Frameries: Union des imprimeries, 1929), 56.

53. Yves Quairiaux, *L'image du Flamand en Wallonie (1830–1914): Essai d'analyse sociale et politique* (Brussels: Editions Labor, 2006), 126–27.

54. Jens Verdure, "En men zou niet fier zijn Vaderlander te wezen? Sociaal-democratie en nationale identiteit voor WO I: Een casusstudie van Antwerpen en Luik" (Master's thesis, Ghent University, 2007), 21.

55. Harry Van Velthoven, "Onenigheid in de Belgische werkliedenpartij: De Vlaamse kwestie wordt een vrije kwestie (1894–1914)," *Belgisch tijdschrift voor nieuwste geschiedenis/Revue belge d'histoire contemporaine* 5, no. 1–2 (1974): 142.

56. For a more detailed description of Belgium's language history since 0 CE, see Kas Deprez and Louis Vos, "Introduction," in *Nationalism in Belgium: Shifting Identities, 1780–1995*, ed. Kas Deprez and Louis Vos (Basingstoke: Macmillan, 1998). A good summary since 1830 can be found in Herman Van Goethem, *Belgium and the Monarchy: From National Independence to National Disintegration* (Brussels: UPS, 2010).

57. *Statistique de la Belgique: Population, Recensement général (15 octobre 1846)* (Brussels: Ministère de l'intérieur, 1849), xxxvi.

58. A note on geographic nomenclature: in multilingual contexts some scholars refuse to use singular place names, arguing that the very language of the geographic descriptor represents a nationalist claim on that particular place. In the case of the Habsburg Empire, for instance, Zahra and Judson talk about Budejovice/Budweis or Stachau/Stachy. Tara Zahra, *Kidnapped Souls: National Indifference and the Battle for Children in the Bohemian Lands, 1900–1948* (Ithaca, NY: Cornell University Press, 2008); Pieter M. Judson, *Guardians of the Nation: Activists on the Language Frontiers of Imperial Austria* (Cambridge, MA: Harvard University Press, 2006). Although I acknowledge the power of language to lay claim to territory, I have chosen not to follow Zahra's and Judson's example for brevity's sake and because of substantial differences between the Belgian and the imperial Austrian case (see below). Instead I have opted for the English-language translation of place names whenever available, as in Brussels for Brussel/Bruxelles or Ghent for Gent/Gand. When not, I chose the official place names of today, as in Liège for the Walloon town of Liège/Luik, Mechelen for the Flemish town of Mechelen/Malines, or the bilingual descriptor for the municipalities in the Brussels *agglomération* (e.g., Elsene/Ixelles).

59. Harry Van Velthoven and Els Witte, "Taalpolitiek en wetgeving," in De Schryver et al., eds., *Nieuwe encyclopedie van de Vlaamse beweging*, 3:3004.

60. Quairiaux, *L'image du Flamand en Wallonie (1830–1914)*, 126–27.

61. Zolberg, "The Making of Flemings and Walloons," 212.

62. Tim Mathias Schmidt, "Sprachnationale Konflikte, Staatsreformdiskurs und Sozialdemokratie: Ein Vergleich zwischen den böhmischen Ländern und Belgien 1894–1938" (PhD diss., Ludwig-Maximilians-Universität München, 2014), 95–96, 104.

63. Van Velthoven and Witte, "Taalpolitiek en wetgeving," 3000.

64. Machteld De Metsenaere et al., "Brussel," in De Schryver et al., eds., *Nieuwe encyclopedie van de Vlaamse beweging*, 1:624.

65. Ibid., 628.

66. Stengers and Gubin, *Le grand siècle de la nationalité belge*, 56–57.

67. Lode Wils, *Van Clovis tot Happart: De lange weg van de naties in de Lage Landen* (Leuven: Garant, 1992), 163–64.

68. Lieve Gevers, "The Catholic Church and the Flemish Movement," in *Nationalism in Belgium: Shifting Identities, 1780–1995*, ed. Kas Deprez and Louis Vos (Basingstoke: Macmillan, 1998).

69. For more details, see Maarten Van Ginderachter, "Nationalist Versus Regionalist? The Flemish and Walloon Movements in *Belle Époque* Belgium," in *Region and State in Nineteenth-Century Europe: Nation-Building, Regional Identities and Separatism*, ed. Joost Augusteijn and Eric Storm (New York: Palgrave Macmillan, 2012).

70. Chantal Kesteloot, "Waalse beweging," in De Schryver et al., eds., *Nieuwe encyclopedie van de Vlaamse beweging*, 1:3635.

71. Quairiaux, *L'image du Flamand en Wallonie (1830–1914)*, 126–27.

72. Henk De Smaele, *Rechts Vlaanderen: Religie en stemgedrag in negentiende-eeuws België* (Leuven: Universitaire Pers Leuven, 2009).

73. Patricia Penn Hilden, *Women, Work, and Politics: Belgium 1830–1914* (Oxford: Clarendon, 1993), 43; Henk De Smaele, "Omdat we uwe vrienden zijn: Religie en partij-identificatie, 1884–1914" (PhD diss., University of Leuven, 2000), 405.

74. Remieg Aerts, "Een andere geschiedenis: Een beschouwing over de scheiding van 1830," in *De erfenis van 1830*, ed. Peter Rietbergen and Tom Verschaffel (Leuven: Acco, 2006), 23; Lode Wils, "De twee Belgische revoluties," in *Nationalisme in België: Identiteiten in beweging 1780–2000*, ed. Kas Deprez and Louis Vos (Antwerp: Houtekiet, 1999), 49; Els Witte, "1828–1847: De constructie van België," in *Nieuwe geschiedenis van België*, vol. 1, *1830–1905*, ed. Els Witte et al. (Tielt: Lannoo, 2005), 194, 98–207.

75. Tom Verschaffel, *Beeld en geschiedenis: Het Belgische en Vlaamse verleden in de romantische boekillustraties* (Turnhout: Brepols, 1987); Tom Verschaffel, "Het verleden tot weinig herleid: De historische optocht als vorm van de romantische verbeelding," in *Romantiek en historische cultuur*, ed. Jo Tollebeek, Frank Ankersmit, and Wessel Krul (Groningen: Historische uitgeverij, 1996); Tom Verschaffel, "Leren sterven voor het vaderland: Historische drama's in het 19de eeuwse België," *Bijdragen en mededelingen betreffende de geschiedenis der Nederlanden* 113, no. 2 (1998); Witte, "1828–1847: De constructie van België," 194, 98–207; Wils, *Van Clovis tot Di Rupo*, 46–47; Stengers and Gubin, *Le grand siècle de la nationalité belge*, 21; Jean Stengers, *Les racines de la Belgique jusqu'à la Révolution de 1830: Histoire du sentiment national en Belgique des origines à 1918* (Brussels: Racine, 2000), 1:27, 171–72; Jeroen Janssens, *De Belgische natie viert: De Belgische nationale feesten 1830–1914* (Leuven: Universitaire Pers Leuven, 2001), 23–46; Jana Wijnsouw, *National Identity and Nineteenth-Century Franco-Belgian Sculpture* (Abingdon: Routledge, 2018).

76. Jakob Vogel, "Military, Folklore, Eigensinn: Folkloric Militarism in Germany and France, 1871–1914," *Central European History* 33, no. 4 (2000): 488.
77. Commission centrale de statistique, *Exposé de la situation du Royaume de 1876 à 1900*, part 1 (Brussels: Piquart, 1907), 455.
78. Nel de Mûelenaere, "Belgen, zijt gij ten strijde gereed? Militarisering in een neutrale natie, 1890–1914" (PhD diss., Antwerp University, 2016), 162.
79. *Leeuwarder Courant*, July 17, 1901, p. 1.
80. *Annuaire statistique de la Belgique 1901* (Brussels: Ministère de l'intérieur), 218–19.
81. Ernest Gellner, *Nations and Nationalism* (Oxford: Blackwell, 1993 [1983]).
82. John Breuilly, "Introduction," in Ernest Gellner, *Nations and Nationalism* (Oxford: Blackwell, 2006), xxxiv.
83. Cf. Nicholas Stargardt, "Gellner's Nationalism: The Spirit of Modernisation?," in *The Social Philosophy of Ernest Gellner*, ed. John Hall and Ian Jarvie (Brill: Leiden, 1996); Breuilly, "Introduction," xxxv, xliii–xlv.
84. Maurice De Vroede, "De weg naar de algemene leerplicht in België," *Bijdragen en mededelingen betreffende de geschiedenis der Nederlanden* 85 (1970): 156.
85. P. Boekholt, "De onderwijswet van 1801 en het begin van de Staatszorg voor het onderwijs in Nederland," in *Tweehonderd jaar onderwijs en de zorg van de Staat*, ed. P. Boekholt et al. (Assen: Koninklijke Van Gorcum, 2002), 5; Ido De Haan, "Van staatszorg tot vrijheidsrecht: De Schoolstrijd in de Nederlandse politiek en samenleving," in *Tot burgerschap en deugd: Volksopvoeding in de negentiende eeuw*, ed. Nelleke Bakker, Rudolf Dekker, and Angélique Janssen (Verloren: Hilversum, 2006), 81; Jan Lenders, "Van kind tot burger: Lager onderwijs en de vorming tot burgerschap in de negentiende eeuw," in Bakker, Dekker, and Janssen, eds., *Tot burgerschap en deugd*.
86. Jeffrey Tyssens, "De vermaledijde staat? Overheid en onderwijsverstrekking in België," in Boekholt et al., eds., *Tweehonderd jaar onderwijs en de zorg van de Staat*, 61–62.
87. Witte, "1828–1847: De constructie van België," 183–84; Gita Deneckere, "1878–1905," in Witte et al., eds., *Nieuwe geschiedenis van België*, vol. 1, *1830–1905*, 477.
88. Paul Wynants et al., "Conflicten als vormgevers en stoorzenders: Ideologische breuklijnen en twee wereldoorlogen," in *Katholiek onderwijs in België: Identiteiten in evolutie 19de–21ste eeuw*, ed. Jan De Maeyer and Paul Wynants (Antwerp: Halewijn, 2016), 82.
89. Alice H. Amsden, *The Rise of "The Rest": Challenges to the West from Late-Industrializing Economies* (Oxford: Oxford University Press, 2001), 60.
90. Harvey J. Graff, *The Legacies of Literacy: Continuities and Contradictions in Western Culture and Society* (Bloomington: Indiana University Press, 1987), 307.

91. Benjamin Seebohm Rowntree, *Land and Labour: Lessons from Belgium* (London: Macmillan, 1910), 264.

92. David Vincent, *The Rise of Mass Literacy: Reading and Writing in Modern Europe* (Cambridge: Polity, 2000), 10.

93. Cf. Graff, *The Legacies of Literacy*, 307.

94. Scholliers, "Industrial Wage Differentials in Nineteenth-Century Belgium," 104, 112.

95. Schmidt, "Sprachnationale Konflikte, Staatsreformdiskurs und Sozialdemokratie," 225–26; Peter Mathias and Sidney Pollard, *The Industrial Economies: The Development of Economic and Social Policies* (Cambridge: Cambridge University Press, 1989), 553, 61.

96. Eliane Gubin, Jean-Pierre Nandrin, and Pierre Van den Dungen, "1846–1878: Het liberale en burgerlijke België," in Witte et al., eds., *Nieuwe geschiedenis van België*, vol. 1, *1830–1905*, 289–93.

97. Ibid., 334; Christina Reimann, *Schule für Verfassungsbürger? Die Bildungsligen und der Verfassungswandel des späten 19. Jahrhunderts in Belgien, England und Frankreich* (Münster: Waxmann, 2016).

98. Patrick Pasture, "Building the Social Security State: A Comparative History of Belgium, the Netherlands and Germany," in De Maeyer, van Voss, and Pasture, eds., *Between Cross and Class*, 267; Strikwerda, *A House Divided*, 260; Jasmien Van Daele, *Van Gent tot Genève: Louis Varlez, een biografie* (Ghent: Academia Press, 2002).

99. Strikwerda, *A House Divided*, 134, 261.

100. Art, "Social Control in Belgium," 119.

101. Marnix Beyen, "Een wankele basis voor de natie: Verkiezingen en nationalisme in België, 1890–1920," in *Natie en democratie–Nation et démocratie (1890–1921), Acta van het interuniversitair colloquium, Brussel 8–9 Juni 2006*, ed. Els Witte et al. (Brussels: Koninklijke Vlaamse Academie van België voor Wetenschappen en Kunsten, 2007), 27–29.

## CHAPTER 2: VOTING THE NATION

1. J. Destrée, "Leur Patrie," *L'Étoile socialiste* 1, issue 4 (December 27, 1894): 1.

2. Paul Kenis, *Het leven van Edward Anseele* (Ghent: De Vlam, 1949 [1930]), 200, 204; Jean Stengers and Eliane Gubin, *Le grand siècle de la nationalité belge: De 1830 à 1918*, vol. 2 of *Histoire du sentiment national en Belgique des origines à 1918* (Brussels: Racine, 2002), 85–86.

3. Rik Van Cauwelaert, *"Ils nous on pris la Flandre": Waals socialisme en Belgische illusies: Van Jules Destrée tot Elio Di Rupo* (Kalmthout: Pelckmans, 2012), 119.

4. On the Belgian electoral system, see Donald Weber, "La marche des opérations électorales: Bepalingen rond kiesverrichtingen in de Belgische kieswetgeving,

1830–1940," *Belgisch tijdschrift voor filologie en geschiedenis/Revue belge de philologie et d'histoire* 81, no. 2 (2003); Romain Van Eenoo, "Kiesstelsels en verkiezingen, 1830–1914," in *Geschiedenis van de Belgische Kamer van Volksvertegenwoordigers 1830–2002*, ed. E. Gerard et al. (Brussels: Kamer van Volksvertegenwoordigers, 2003).

5. "Le serment des manifestants," *Le Peuple*, August 11, 1890, p. 2.
6. "Voor de stemming," *Vooruit*, June 13, 1892.
7. *100 zangen voor het volk* (Ghent: Het Licht, [1908]), 17.
8. *Vooruit*, June 13, 1892, p. 2.
9. "Voor de stemming," *Vooruit*, June 13, 1892.
10. Weber, "La marche des opérations électorales," 316.
11. *Vooruit*, June 13, 1892, p. 2.
12. *Le Peuple*, June 13, 1892, p. 1.
13. Janet Louise Polasky, "A Revolution for Socialist Reforms: The Belgian General Strike for Universal Suffrage," *Journal of Contemporary History* 27, no. 3 (1992): 450.
14. Ibid., 463–64.
15. Jakub Beneš, *Workers and Nationalism: Czech and German Social Democracy in Habsburg Austria, 1890–1918* (Oxford: Oxford University Press, 2016), 106.
16. Polasky, "A Revolution for Socialist Reforms."
17. Marnix Beyen, "Een wankele basis voor de natie: Verkiezingen en nationalisme in België, 1890–1920," in *Natie en democratie–Nation et démocratie (1890–1921), Acta van het interuniversitair colloquium, Brussel 8–9 Juni 2006*, ed. Els Witte et al. (Brussels: Koninklijke Vlaamse Academie van België voor Wetenschappen en Kunsten, 2007), 25–26, 27, 31.
18. Benedict Anderson, *Imagined Communities: Reflections on the Origin and Spread of Nationalism* (London: Verso, 1994 [1983]), 35.
19. Beyen, "Een wankele basis voor de natie," 23–24.
20. John Breuilly, *Nationalism and the State*, 2nd ed. (Manchester: Manchester University Press, 1993); Stengers and Gubin, *Le grand siècle de la nationalité belge*, 86.
21. Jean Puissant, "'La commune pour le socialisme' de Louis Bertrand," *Brood en Rozen*, no. 2 (2000): 119; Jean Puissant, "'L'oeuvre gouvernementale du POB commence' ou le POB à la conquête d'un substitut du pouvoir d'état (1884–1921)," in *Les élections communales et leur impact sur la politique belge (1890–1970)* (Brussels: Crédit communal, 1993).
22. "A Monceau-sur-Sambre," *Le Journal de Charleroi*, January 22, 1896, p. 2.
23. Leopold II refused to appoint socialist mayors, so they had to serve as acting mayors.
24. *Le Journal de Charleroi*, January 25, 1896, p. 1
25. Beyen, "Een wankele basis voor de natie," 28–29.

26. Kevin Callahan, "'Performing Inter-Nationalism' in Stuttgart in 1907: French and German Socialist Nationalism and the Political Culture of an International Socialist Congress," *International Review of Social History* 45 (2000): 56.

27. "Arm, arm Vlaanderen," *Vooruit*, February 7, 1900, p. 1.

28. "Het licht zal komen uit de stad," *Vooruit*, February 11, 1900, p. 1.

29. A.B. [Aimé Bogaerts], "De socialistische propaganda in Vlaanderen," *Vooruit*, November 13, 1900, p. 1.

30. See Paule Verbruggen, "Deelalternatieven voor traditionele godsdienstbeleving in het Gentse socialisme (1870–1914)" (Master's thesis, Ghent University, 1982); Beneš, *Workers and Nationalism*, 46. On grassroots anticlericalism and anti-Catholicism, see also Chapter 8.

31. Anseele in Ghent, Modest Terwagne in Antwerp, and Prosper Van Langendonck in Leuven.

32. *Le Suffrage universel*, June 3, 1900, p. 1.

33. Minutes of the Central Committee of the Ghent socialists, 1899–1901, November 21, 1900 (AMSAB, 32: 104/1).

34. Harry Van Velthoven, *De Vlaamse kwestie 1830–1914: Macht en onmacht van de Vlaamsgezinden* (Kortrijk: UGA 1982), 214–17.

35. National Party Council of the BWP, June 5, 1912 (AMSAB, 118/35).

36. *Le Peuple*, June 8, 1912, p. 2.

37. *L'Avenir du Borinage*, July 29, 1910, p. 2.

38. Falstaff, "Réflexions d'un Borain: Il y a flamand et flamand," *L'Avenir du Borinage*, June 22, 1907, p. 1.

39. "L'inauguration du Monument commémoratif," *L'Avenir du Borinage*, September 25, 1911, pp. 1–2.

40. "Manifestation wallonne," *L'Avenir du Borinage*, August 10, 1913, p. 1; "Au Borinage: Mons," *Le Peuple*, August 19, 1913, p. 5; "L'etiquette wallonne," *L'Avenir du Borinage*, August 20, 1913, p. 1; "La Défense wallonne," *L'Avenir du Borinage*, August 28, 1913, p. 1; "La Défense wallonne," *L'Avenir du Borinage*, August 30, 1913, p. 1; Jeannine Lothe, "Les débuts du mouvement wallon," in *La Wallonie, Le Pays et les Hommes: Histoire, économies, sociétés*, ed. Hervé Hasquin (Brussels: La Renaissance du Livre, 1976), 2:201.

41. On William I's language policies, see Rik Vosters and Wim Vandenbussche, "Wijzer worden over Willem? Taalgebruik in Vlaanderen ten tijde van het Verenigd Koninkrijk der Nederlanden (1814–1830)," *Internationale Neerlandistiek*, no. 3 (2008); Rik Vosters and Janneke Weijermans, eds., *Taal, cultuurbeleid en natievorming onder Willem I* (Brussels: KVAB, 2011).

42. C. Vautel, "Joyeusetés flamingantes," *L'Avenir du Borinage*, January 13, 1911, p. 1.

43. "La visite royale," *L'Avenir du Borinage*, September 8–9, 1913, pp. 1–2.

44. "Lettre du Borinage: Le roi à Mons," *Le Peuple*, September 5, 1913, p. 5.

## CHAPTER 3: NATIONALIST CELEBRATIONS AND MASS ENTERTAINMENT

1. Els Witte, "1828–1847: De constructie van België," in *Nieuwe geschiedenis van België*, vol. 1, *1830–1905*, ed. Els Witte et al. (Tielt: Lannoo, 2005), 79–80.
2. Jeroen Janssens, *De Belgische natie viert: De Belgische nationale feesten 1830–1914* (Leuven: Universitaire Pers Leuven, 2001), ix.
3. Ibid., 47, 57, 62, 109, 17.
4. J. Volders, "L'oubli de son origine," *Le Peuple*, September 21, 1888, p. 1; *Le Peuple*, September 22, 1888, p. 1; "L'escamotage," *Le Peuple*, September 23, 1888, p. 2; C. De Paepe, "Louis De Potter," *Le Peuple*, September 24, 1888, p. 1.
5. For the classic rendering of this theme, see Maurice Bologne, *L'insurrection prolétarienne de 1830 en Belgique* (Brussels: Eglantine 1929).
6. E.g., the Norman conquest in British socialism. Paul Ward, *Red Flag and Union Jack: Englishness, Patriotism, and the British Left, 1881–1924* (Rochester, NY: Royal Historical Society/Boydell Press, 1998), 7.
7. "La manifestation populaire," *Le Peuple*, September 24, 1888, pp. 1–2.
8. "Les nouvelles du jour," *Le Peuple*, October 6, 1888, p. 1.
9. *Le Peuple*, January 4, 1886, p. 1; March 18, 1886, p. 1.
10. Janet Louise Polasky, "A Revolution for Socialist Reforms: The Belgian General Strike for Universal Suffrage," *Journal of Contemporary History* 27, no. 3 (1992).
11. The Belgian revolution was a common trope at protest rallies in Liège. See, for instance, the socialist leader of Liège, Blanvalet: Gendarmerie surveillance report of a socialist meeting in Liège on September 25, 1886 (National Archives Liège, Sûreté publique de la province de Liège, Première partie, XIV.A.199); and Police surveillance report of a socialist meeting in Liège on June 15, 1886 (City Archives Liège, Archives de police, carton XLIII, 1–531). See also Gendarmerie surveillance report of a socialist meeting in Liège on March 22, 1887 (National Archives Liège, Sûreté publique de la province de Liège, Première partie, XV.A.46); Police surveillance report of a socialist meeting in Liège on April 3, 1887 (City Archives Liège, Archives de police, carton XLIV, 1–160).
12. *Le Peuple*, September 28, 1886, p. 1. See also Vanhelewyck, a militant of the Ligue Ouvrière bruxelloise, which was affiliated with the BWP, at a workers' rally in Brussels (Gendarmerie surveillance report of a socialist meeting in Brussels on October 2, 1886, City Archives of Brussels, Fonds Politie, Pol. 176, Le mouvement ouvrier XII 21).
13. Police surveillance report of a socialist universal suffrage meeting in Liège on September 26, 1886 (National Archives Liège, Sûreté publique de la province de Liège, Première partie, XIV.A.229).
14. "Le Peuple aux révolutionnaires de 1830," *Le Peuple*, September 23, 1896, p. 1.

15. Gendarmerie surveillance report of a socialist demonstration in Brussels on September 24, 1899 (National Archives Anderlecht, Parket-generaal bij het Hof van Beroep te Brussel, 235); "A la place des Martyrs: La manifestation socialiste," *Le Peuple*, September 26, 1899, p. 2.

16. Ch. Max, "Réflexions sur les fêtes," *Le Peuple*, July 25, 1891, p. 1.

17. Jakob Vogel, *Nationen im Gleichschritt: Der Kult der "Nation in Waffen" in Deutschland und Frankreich, 1871–1914* (Göttingen: Vandenhoeck & Ruprecht, 1997), 222, 260.

18. Jean Claes, "Fête nationale," *Le Peuple*, August 10, 1886, p. 2. See also "La première journée," *Le Peuple*, August 23, 1887, p. 1; Ch. Max, "Grandes fêtes nationales," *Le Peuple*, July 14, 1891, p. 1; "Les fêtes nationales," *Le Peuple*, July 23, 1893, p. 2, and July 21, 1894, p. 3; Joe, "La fête des dupes," *Le Peuple*, July 24, 1894, pp. 1–2.

19. Un Liégeois, "Que fête-t-on," *Le Peuple*, August 23, 1887, p. 1.

20. Jakob Vogel, "Militärfeiern in Deutschland und Frankreich als Rituale der Nation (1871–1914)," in *Nation und Emotion: Deutschland und Frankreich im Vergleich 19. und 20. Jahrhundert*, ed. Etienne François, Hannes Siegrist, and Jakob Vogel (Göttingen: Vandenhoeck und Ruprecht, 1995), 207–8.

21. See, for instance, "La première journée," *Le Peuple*, August 23, 1887, p. 1; "Çà et là," *Le Peuple*, August 19, 1886, pp. 1–2.

22. "La première journée," *Le Peuple*, August 23, 1887, p. 1; see also "Le roi à Houdeng," *La Liberté*, June 10, 1888, p. 2.

23. Vogel, *Nationen im Gleichschritt*, 222.

24. "La parade patriotique," *Le Peuple*, September 24, 1896, p. 1; see also G.P., "A Liège: L'anniversaire de dimanche," *Le Peuple*, October 1, 1890, pp. 2–3; G. Defnet, "Les 'fêtes nationales,'" *Le Peuple*, July 20–21, 1891, pp. 1–2.

25. Jacques Prolo, "Les mineurs 'royalistes' à Bruxelles," *Le Peuple*, July 25 1890, pp. 1–2; "Lettre du Borinage: Le roi à Mons," *Le Peuple*, September 5, 1913, p. 5.

26. Vogel, "Militärfeiern in Deutschland und Frankreich als Rituale der Nation (1871–1914)," 209.

27. "Le cortège historique," *Le Peuple*, August 3, 1897, p. 1.

28. "Les fêtes nationales," *Le Peuple*, July 24, 1901, p. 1.

29. "Fêtes nationales," *Le Peuple*, July 23, 1904, p. 1 (my emphasis).

30. Aimé Bogaerts, "Ons zondagspraatje: De onafhankelijkheidsfeesten," *Vooruit*, June 18, 1905, p. 1.

31. *Le Peuple*, May 10, 1905, p. 2.

32. National Party Council of the BWP, June 22, 1904 (AMSAB, 118/18).

33. "Au conseil général," *Le Peuple*, July 14, 1904, p. 1.

34. "A la Chambre," *Le Peuple*, December 24, 1904, p. 1.

35. *Le Peuple*, July 3, 1905, p. 1.

36. Émile Vandervelde, "Le prolétariat et les fêtes nationales," *L'Avenir du Borinage*, August 9, 1905, p. 1; see also C. Huysmans, "De opwekking van den

militaristischen geest op den buiten," *Vooruit*, August 7, 1899, p. 1; "Socialisme et royauté," *L'Avenir de Schaarbeek: Organe hebdomadaire des ligues ouvrières du canton*, August 22, 1909, pp. 1-2.

37. "Note de la rédaction," *L'Avenir du Borinage*, August 5-6, 1905; see also L. Piérard, "La patrie belge," *Le Peuple*, September 12, 1905, p. 1.

38. "De 75e verjaringsfeesten der onafhankelijkheid van België," *Vooruit*, July 27, 1904, p. 1.

39. P., "De omwenteling van 1830," *Vooruit*, July 22, 1905, p. 2; "De 75e verjaringsfeesten der onafhankelijheid van België," *De Werker*, July 27, 1904.

40. See, for instance, S. Boersen, "De omwenteling van 1830," *De Werker*, August 29, 1904; A. Bogaerts, "Vaderlandsliefde! Geldverspilling!," *De Werker*, November 15, 1904.

41. S. Boersen, "Ons 1905," *Vooruit*, December 12 and 29, 1903, p. 1. Also published in *De Werker*, December 12, 1903.

42. A. Bogaerts, "De revolutie van't jaar 30," *Vooruit*, July 4, 1905, p. 1, and July 5-6, 1905, p. 1.

43. Edouard Anseele, *De Omwenteling van 1830: Historische roman* (Ghent: Hage, 1882), i-iii. See Maarten Van Ginderachter, *Het rode vaderland: De vergeten geschiedenis van de communautaire spanningen in het Belgische socialisme voor WO I* (Tielt/Ghent: Lannoo/Amsab, 2005), 71-75.

44. F. Hardyns, "Vaderlandsliefde en socialisme I en II," *Vooruit*, August 2 and 3, 1904, p. 1. Also published in *De Werker*, August 2, 1904.

45. "De onafhankelijkheids(?)feesten van België: Verklaring van het Centraal Comiteit der gentsche Werkersvereenigingen," *Vooruit*, May 15, 1905, p. 1.

46. Aimé Bogaerts, "Wij feesten niet," *Vooruit*, June 18, 1905, p. 1. Also published in *De Werker*, June 18, 1905.

47. *Vooruit*, May 15, 1905, p. 1; F.H., "De officieele leugens beginnen," *Vooruit*, May 23, 1905, p. 1; [Aimé Bogaerts], "Ongelooflijk," *Vooruit*, May 24, 1905, p. 3.

48. "De toestand der werkstaking," *Vooruit*, July 8, 1905, p. 1.

49. National Archives Mons, Jemappes Fonds I, XI, 748.

50. "Réclame patriotique," *Le Peuple*, July 26, 1905, p. 2.

51. Serge Jaumain, *Les petits commerçants belges face à la modernité (1880-1914)* (Brussels: Ed. de l'Université de Bruxelles, 1995), 35.

52. Peter Scholliers, "Kledingaankopen en de zin van het leven, of economie en identiteit in België vanaf het laatste kwart van de 19e eeuw," in *Op weg naar de consumptiemaatschappij: Over het verbruik van voeding, kleding en luxegoederen in België en Nederland (19e-20e Eeuw)*, ed. Yves Segers (Amsterdam: Aksant, 2002), 56.

53. *Le Peuple*, January 2, 1887, p. 3; December 24, 1895, p. 4; November 2, 1899, p. 4; August 12, 1905, p. 1; October 27, 1906, p. 1; April 16, 1910, p. 4; July 2, 1910, p. 4.

54. *Le Peuple*, June 9, 1895, p. 3.

55. "Çà et là," *Le Peuple*, July 7, 1886, p. 1. On pageants and historical consciousness, see Janssens, *De Belgische natie viert*, 91–97; Tom Verschaffel, "Aanschouwelijke Middeleeuwen: Historische optochten en vaderlandse drama's in het negentiende-eeuwse België," *Theoretische geschiedenis* 26, no. 2 (1999).

56. See, for instance, the pageant on the occasion of the fiftieth anniversary of the Belgian railroad system: "Het feest der spoorwegen," *Vooruit*, June 24 and 25, 1885, p. 3; and "Binnenland. Brussel: De Spoorwegstoet," *Vooruit*, August 4 and 5, 1885, pp. 1–2. On the pageant on the occasion of the unveiling of the historical statues in the park of the Kleine Zavel/Petit Sablon in Brussels, see "Le cortège historique des 20 et 27 juillet," *Le Peuple*, June 30, 1890, pp. 2–3; Jacques Prolo, "Le cortège historique," *Le Peuple*, July 22, 1890, pp. 1–2; Anne Carre and Hugo Lettens, "De Kleine Zavel: Een polemiek over de zestiende eeuw," in *Mise en scène: Keizer Karel en de verbeelding van de negentiende eeuw*, ed. Robert Hoozee, Jo Tollebeek, and Tom Verschaffel (Ghent: Mercatorfonds, 2000); Janssens, *De Belgische natie viert*, 172–77. On the pageant during the Independence Day celebrations of 1901 in Brussels, see "Les fêtes à Bruxelles," *Le Peuple*, July 23, 1901, pp. 1–2. On the historical pageant during the jubilee festivities of 1905 in Brussels, see *Vooruit*, July 4, 1905, p. 2.

57. Marie Mergeay, "Multiplicatie en popularisatie: Van Karel V tot Keizer Karel," in Hoozee, Tollebeek, and Verschaffel, *Mise en scène*, 88.

58. L.M., "Cocher! à la Renaissance!!," *Le Peuple*, April 10, 1889, p. 2; see also "Petite chronique théâtrale," *Le Peuple*, December 23, 1885, p. 4; *Le Peuple*, February 8, 1886, p. 2; *Le Peuple*, February 14, 1886.

59. "Au cinéma," *Le Peuple*, January 5, 1913, p. 1.

60. V.H., "Uit Saventhem," *De Gazet van Brussel*, August 5, 1905, pp. 2–3.

## CHAPTER 4: AN ANTI-MILITARISTIC STATE IN MILITARISTIC TIMES

1. Nel de Mûelenaere, "Belgen, zijt gij ten strijde gereed? Militarisering in een neutrale natie, 1890–1914" (PhD diss., Antwerp University, 2016), 228–29.

2. Jean Stengers and Eliane Gubin, *Le grand siècle de la nationalité belge: De 1830 à 1918*, vol. 2 of *Histoire du sentiment national en Belgique des origines à 1918* (Brussels: Racine, 2002), 27–29; Luc De Vos, "De militaire diensplicht en haar rol binnen natievorming en democratie, 1890–1921," in *Natie en democratie–Nation et démocratie (1890–1921)*, Acta van het interuniversitair colloquium, Brussel 8–9 Juni 2006, ed. Els Witte et al. (Brussels: Koninklijke Vlaamse Academie van België voor Wetenschappen en Kunsten, 2007); Richard Boijen, "Het leger als smeltkroes van de natie?," *Bijdragen tot de eigentijdse geschiedenis/Cahiers d'histoire du temps présent*, no. 3 (1997).

3. Josephine Hoegaerts, *Masculinity and Nationhood, 1830–1910: Constructions of Identity and Citizenship in Belgium* (Basingstoke: Palgrave Macmillan, 2014); De Mûelenaere, "Belgen, zijt gij ten strijde gereed?"; Bruno Benvindo, *Des hommes en guerre: Les soldats belges entre ténacité et désillusion 1914–1918* (Brussels: Archives générales du royaume, 2005); Nel de Mûelenaere

and Josephine Hoegaerts, eds., "Country and Army in the Making: The Belgian Military in the Long Nineteenth Century," special issue of *Journal of Belgian History* 46, issue 2 (Brussels: 2016); Mario Draper, *The Belgian Army and Society from Independence to the Great War* (Basingstoke: Palgrave Macmillan, 2018).

4. Marie-Thérèse Bitsch, "La Belgique entre la France et l'Allemagne," in *France–Belgique, 1848–1914: Affinités, Ambiguïtés: Actes du colloque des 7, 8, 9 mai 1996*, ed. Marc Quaghebeur and Nicole Savy (Brussels: Labor, 1997); Christophe Bechet, "Traverser la Belgique? De L'Indépendance au Plan Schlieffen (1839–1905)" (PhD diss., Université de Liège, 2012).

5. David Stevenson, "Battlefield or Barrier? Rearmament and Military Planning in Belgium, 1902–1914," *International History Review* 29, no. 3 (2007): 476.

6. De Mûelenaere, "Belgen, zijt gij ten strijde gereed?," 31.

7. Stevenson, "Battlefield or Barrier?," 478.

8. Based on *Annuaire statistique de la Belgique* (Brussels: Monnom, 1887), 85.

9. Alfons De Cock, "De militaire loting," *Volkskunde* 7 (1894).

10. Dave Warnier and Luc De Vos, "De dienstplicht in België historisch bekeken: Een politieke en militaire evolutie (1830–2010)," *Volkskunde* 111, no. 4 (2010): 340.

11. See, for instance, the naturalist author Horace Van Offel's novel *Une armée de pauvres* (Rotterdam: Meindert Boogaerdt Jr., 1905).

12. Arne Dewolf, "'Par dégoût de service': De motieven van deserteurs uit het Belgische leger voor de krijgsraad van Antwerpen (1879–1911)" (Bachelor's thesis, Antwerp University, 2013).

13. De Mûelenaere, "Belgen, zijt gij ten strijde gereed?," 182.

14. Ibid., 183.

15. Eline De Keulenaer, "'Hij doet aanmerken dat hij van goed gedrag en zeden is': Public en hidden transcripts in Oost-Vlaamse armenbrieven 1882–1926" (Master's thesis, Ghent University, 2007).

16. De Mûelenaere, "Belgen, zijt gij ten strijde gereed?," 42.

17. Eric Defoort, "Het Belgische nationalisme vóór de Eerste Wereldoorlog," *Tijdschrift voor geschiedenis* 85, no. 4 (1972); Vincent Viaene, "King Leopold's Imperialism and the Origins of the Belgian Colonial Party, 1860–1905," *Journal of Modern History* 80, no. 4 (2008): 758.

18. Quoted by de Mûelenaere, "Belgen, zijt gij ten strijde gereed?," 115 (my emphasis).

19. Ibid., 148–50.

20. Nel de Mûelenaere, "Van kazernevrees naar kazernelust? Het vrijwilligerssysteem in België," *Leidschrift* 32, no. 2 (2017).

21. Henk De Smaele, *Rechts Vlaanderen: Religie en stemgedrag in negentiende-eeuws België* (Leuven: Universitaire Pers Leuven, 2009), 253–54; Stevenson, "Battlefield or Barrier?"

22. Lieutenant Deglimes, *Education morale du soldat, conférence donnée aux officiers du 1er régiment de chasseurs à pied, le 14 janvier 1899* (Marchienne-au-Pont, 1899), 13, 29. Quoted by de Mûelenaere, "Belgen, zijt gij ten strijde gereed?," 149.

23. Capitaine J. Wodon, *Essai sur l'éducation morale militaire considérée dans ses rapports avec la discipline* (Arlon: G. Everling, 1901). Quoted by ibid., 177.

24. C., "Socialisme et l'armée," *L'Indépendance Belge* 68, no. 155 (May 13, 1897). Quoted by ibid., 128.

25. Ibid., 234.

26. A. Antoine, *¾ d'heure à la caserne: Scènes drôlatiques et fantaisistes de la vie militaire* (Mont-sur-Marchienne: Zéphir Demoulin, n.d.), 7. Quoted by ibid., 150.

27. Josephine Hoegaerts, "Manoeuvring Men: Masculinity as Spatially Defined Readability at the Grandes Manoeuvres of the Belgian Army, 1882–1883," *Gender, Place & Culture* 17 (2010).

28. Jakob Vogel, "Military, Folklore, Eigensinn: Folkloric Militarism in Germany and France, 1871–1914," *Central European History* 33, no. 4 (2000).

29. De Mûelenaere, "Belgen, zijt gij ten strijde gereed?," 61, 64. Only after the First World War would the veterans' movement become *incontournable* in Belgian politics. See Antoon Vrints and Martin Schoups, *De overlevenden: De Belgische oud-strijders tijdens het interbellum* (Antwerp: Polis, 2019).

30. De Mûelenaere, "Belgen, zijt gij ten strijde gereed?," 259.

31. "A Bruxelles: Le militarisme envahissant!," *L'Étincelle* 1, issue 1 (October 15, 1913): 4–5.

32. Quoted by de Mûelenaere, "Belgen, zijt gij ten strijde gereed?," 56.

33. J. Volders, "Le militarisme," *Le Peuple*, January 30, 1887, p. 1.

34. Dieter Groh and Peter Brandt, *Vaterlandslose Gesellen: Sozialdemokratie und Nation 1860–1990* (Munich: Beck, 1992), 38.

35. Ibid., 78, 114–15, 27; Marcel Van der Linden, "The National Integration of the European Working Classes, 1871–1914: Exploring the Causal Configuration," *International Review Of Social History* 33, no. 3 (1988): 285.

36. "Oorlog aan den oorlog," *Vooruit*, November 15, 1899, p. 1; "Oorlog," *Vooruit*, November 16, 1899, p. 1; Pick, "Patriotisme!," *Le Peuple*, September 9, 1900, p. 1; J. Lekeu, "Sauce belge," *Le Peuple*, September 13, 1900, p. 1; Guy Vanschoenbeek, "De wortels van de sociaal-democratie in Vlaanderen: Le 'monde socialiste gantois' en de Gentse socialisten voor de Eerste Wereldoorlog" (PhD diss., Ghent University, 1992), 577.

37. Report by the préfecture de police de Paris on the labor unrest of 1886 in Belgium, March 28, 1886 (Archives of the préfecture de police of Paris, Ba 197).

38. Luc Peiren, "Een merkwaardig en ongekend congres van de BWP op 25 en 26 december 1886," *Amsab-tijdingen* 11 (1991); Police report on a BWP congress, December 25–26, 1886 (City Archives Brussels, Fonds Politie, Pol. 176, XII, 27, and 214, I, 1); Report of the Sûreté Publique to Leopold II, February 1,

1887 (Royal Palace Archives, Brussels, Cabinet Leopold II, General part. 2085); Report of the préfecture de police de Paris, December 30, 1886 (Archives of the préfecture de police of Paris, Ba 197).

39. Vanschoenbeek, "De wortels van de sociaal-democratie in Vlaanderen," 635–36; Guy Vanschoenbeek, "Ontstaan, situering en karakterisering van de Socialistische Jonge Wacht, 1886–1914: Bijdrage tot de studie van politieke jongerenbewegingen" (Master's thesis, Ghent University, 1978), 116.

40. Vanschoenbeek, "Ontstaan, situering en karakterisering van de Socialistische Jonge Wacht, 1886–1914," 199.

41. "Le congrès national des Jeunes Gardes," *La Jeunesse socialiste*, August 1903, pp. 2–4.

42. Groh and Brandt, *Vaterlandslose Gesellen*, 78, 127.

43. "XXVIIe congrès du PO," *Le Peuple*, March 25, 1913, pp. 1–2; "Le congrès national du Parti socialiste belge: La question militaire," *L'Avenir du Borinage*, March 26, 1913, p. 2.

44. Note to the minister of war on soldiers who approve of the strikes and are to be surveilled, November 11, 1886 (Royal Army Museum, Fonds 21, Intervention of the armed forces to maintain order: 1834–1912. Investigation into the reliability of conscripts [1891–1907], A 544).

45. Excerpt from a report by Lieutenant General Vandersmissen to the minister of war, May 30, 1887 (Royal Army Museum, Fonds 21, Intervention of the armed forces to maintain order: 1834–1912, 401–3: Note with excerpts from reports about the strikes of 1886, 1887, 1891, and 1893, A 401–3).

46. Excerpts from reports of major strikes that have occurred in the country since 1886, n.d. (Royal Army Museum, Fonds 21, Intervention of the armed forces to maintain order: 1834–1912, 401–3).

47. Note dated May 6, 1893, in Excerpts from reports of major strikes that have occurred in the country since 1886, n.d. (Royal Army Museum, Fonds 21, Intervention of the armed forces to maintain order: 1834–1912, 401–3: Note with excerpts from reports about the strikes of 1886, 1887, 1891 and 1893, A 401–3).

48. *Vooruit*, February 18, 1893, p. 1.

49. Ibid., June 17, 1893, p. 1.

50. Guy Vanschoenbeek and Eric Defoort, "Hippoliet De Boos, of hoe een socialistische held een vergeten dissident wordt," *Amsab-tijdingen* 5, no. 3–4 (1987).

51. Number of recruits belonging to the classes of 1891 to 1894 (Royal Army Museum, Fonds 21, Intervention of the armed forces to maintain order: 1834–1912, Investigation into the reliability of recruits [1891–1907], A 539–40, 543).

52. *Le Peuple*, November 26, 1895, pp. 1–2; Vanschoenbeek, "Ontstaan, situering en karakterisering van de Socialistische Jonge Wacht, 1886–1914," 205.

53. Gita Deneckere, "Oorlog en vrede," in *Nieuwe geschiedenis van België*, vol. 1, *1830–1905*, ed. Els Witte et al. (Lannoo: Tielt, 2005), 641; Luc De Vos, *Het effectief van de Belgische krijgsmacht en de militiewetgeving, 1830–1914*, Centrum

Voor Militaire Geschiedenis, Bijdragen 20 (Brussels: Koninklijk Legermuseum, 1985), 258; Guy Vanschoenbeek, "Leger en socialisme voor de Eerste Wereldoorlog," *Belgisch tijdschrift voor militaire geschiedenis* 23, no. 3 (1979): 238.

54. Note to the minister of war on soldiers who approve of the strikes and are to be surveilled, November 11, 1886 (Royal Army Museum, Fonds 21, Intervention of the armed forces to maintain order: 1834–1912, Investigation into the reliability of conscripts [1891–1907], A 544).

55. Martine Vermandere, "Door gelijke drang bewogen? De socialistische partij en haar jeugdbeweging, 1886–1944," *Bijdragen tot de eigentijdse geschiedenis/Cahiers d'histoire du temps présent*, no. 8 (2011): 226.

56. Vanschoenbeek, "Leger en socialisme voor de Eerste Wereldoorlog."

57. De Vos, *Het effectief van de Belgische krijgsmacht en de militiewetgeving, 1830–1914*, 258–59.

58. Vanschoenbeek, "Leger en socialisme voor de Eerste Wereldoorlog," 239.

59. Insubordination cases numbered 724 out of a total of 4,511 cases for eleven sample years: 1886, 1887, 1889, 1892, 1893, 1895, 1898, 1901, 1902, 1904, and 1911. Jasper Smets, "'Dienen in vrede': Socialistische subversie in het Belgische leger" (Bachelor's thesis, Antwerp University, 2013), 16.

60. Ibid., 16–17, 21ff.

61. Vanschoenbeek, "Ontstaan, situering en karakterisering van de Socialistische Jonge Wacht, 1886–1914," 160.

62. Dewolf, "'Par dégoût de service.'"

63. Smets, "'Dienen in Vrede,'" 25.

64. Vanschoenbeek, "Ontstaan, situering en karakterisering van de Socialistische Jonge Wacht, 1886–1914," 205–6.

65. Ibid., 101–3, 108, 16.

66. POB, Féd. Brux., Rapports . . . exercice 1912–1913, p. 49. Quoted by ibid., 107.

67. Claude Renard, "Un aspect du socialisme avant 1914: Les attitudes politiques et idéologiques du Parti ouvrier belge dans les débats sur la défense nationale (1885–1913)" (Master's thesis, ULB, 1973), 210ff.; Frank Uytterhaegen and Guy Vanschoenbeek, "Nawoord," in Jozef Volckaert, *En dat alles voor een paar tirannen: Herinneringen van een socialistische arbeider, met aantekeningen en een naschrift van Frank Uyttterhaegen en Guy Vanschoenbeek* (Leuven: Kritak, 1983), 109; Vanschoenbeek, "De wortels van de sociaal-democratie in Vlaanderen," 649.

68. "La Hestre," *La Jeunesse c'est l'avenir*, November 1913, p. 9. Quoted by Vanschoenbeek, "Ontstaan, situering en karakterisering van de Socialistische Jonge Wacht, 1886–1914," 135.

69. *La Jeunesse c'est l'avenir*, October 1912, p. 13. Quoted by ibid., 136.

70. Ibid.

71. R. [Hendrik De Man], "Klassebewustzijn," *De Zaaier*, issue 4 (October 1903): 172.

72. Demiurgos, "Wat is socialisme?," *De Zaaier*, issue 4 (October 1903): 178–81.

73. Ferdinand Mercier, "Où allons-nous?," *La Jeunesse c'est l'avenir*, vol. 7, issue 2 (February 1912): 5.

74. Florian Wautelet, "Où allons-nous?," *La Jeunesse c'est l'avenir*, vol. 7, issue 4 (April 1912): 8.

75. Emile Hénin, "Où allons-nous?," *La Jeunesse c'est l'avenir*, vol. 7, issue 3 (March 1912): 5. See also "A propos d'une article," *La Jeunesse c'est l'avenir*, vol. 7, issue 3 (March 1912): 5.

76. Anne-Françoise Perin, *Théâtre ouvrier en Wallonie (1900–1940): Bilan d'une recherche* (Brussels: Cahiers JEB, 1979), 39.

77. Vanschoenbeek, "Ontstaan, situering en karakterisering van de Socialistische Jonge Wacht, 1886–1914," 101–3, 108.

78. B.Y., "La grande fête militaire," *Le journal de Charleroi*, August 17, 1896, p. 1.

79. "La fête militaire," *Le Journal de Charleroi*, August 21, 1896, p. 1.

80. *Le Journal de Charleroi*, May 9 and 10, 1897, p. 1. See also B.Y., "Les anciens militaires," *Le Journal de Charleroi*, April 20, 1897, p. 3; "La fête des Ex-sous-officiers," *Le Journal de Charleroi*, May 27, 1898, p. 2.

81. "Kamer," *Vooruit*, November 30, 1900, p. 2.

82. See in particular the Ghent socialists' rejection of the 1905 jubilee celebrations, discussed in Chapter 3.

83. Lode Wils, *Het ontstaan van de Meetingpartij te Antwerpen en haar invloed op de Belgische politiek* (Antwerp: Nederlandsche Boekhandel, 1963); Lode Wils, "Meetingpartij," *Nieuwe encyclopedie van de Vlaamse beweging*, ed. Reginald De Schryver et al. (Tielt: Lannoo, 1998), 2:2026–28.

84. F.G., "Militarisme," *De Werker*, February 9, 1896 (my emphasis).

85. Laurence Cole, *Military Culture and Popular Patriotism in Late Imperial Austria* (Oxford: Oxford University Press, 2014), 19.

## CHAPTER 5: THE ROYAL AND COLONIAL PARADOX

1. A. M. Clarke to Leopold II, March 6, 1903 (Royal Palace Archives, Cabinet Leopold II, Commandments of the King, G series, 102/344).

2. As the majority of historical research into the Belgian monarchy has been of a political and institutional nature, the study of its broader societal impact has been limited. See, for example, Laurence Van Ypersele, *Le Roi Albert: Histoire d'un mythe* (Ottignies: Quorum, 1995).

3. Based on the following inventories of letters: *Indicateur particulier 1863–1898* (Royal Palace Archives, Reading Room); *Demandes de secours, gratifications, souscriptions (correspondance entrée) 1902–1923 (registre G102)* (Royal Palace Archives, Cabinet Albert I, 10); *Indicateur générale 1923–1978* (Royal Palace Archives, Reading Room); *Indicateurs 227–228 Service de la Reine 1921–1939* (Royal Palace Archives, Secretariat of Queen Elisabeth, 227–28); *Registres*

*des lettres entrées (demandes d'emplois, de secours, de distinctions honorifiques, ...) 1894–1909* (Royal Palace Archives, Commandements Prince Albert, 1–10, 11).

4. For more information on these sources, see Maarten Van Ginderachter, "Public Transcripts of Royalism: Pauper Letters to the Belgian Royal Family (1880–1940)," in *Mystifying the Monarch: Studies on Discourse, Power and History*, ed. Gita Deneckere and Jeroen Deploige (Amsterdam: Amsterdam University Press, 2006); Maarten Van Ginderachter, "'If Your Majesty Would Only Send Me a Little Money to Help Buy an Elephant': Letters to the Belgian Royal Family (1880–1940)," in *Ordinary Writings, Personal Narratives*, ed. Martyn Lyons (Bern: Peter Lang, 2007), 69–83.

5. Van Ginderachter, "'If Your Majesty Would Only Send Me a Little Money to Help Buy an Elephant.'"

6. Daniel Fabre, "Introduction: Seize terrains d'écriture," in *Par écrit: Ethnologie des écritures quotidiennes*, ed. Daniel Fabre (Paris: Editions de la Maison des sciences de l'homme, 1997), 10; Martyn Lyons, *The Writing Culture of Ordinary People in Europe, c. 1860–1920* (Cambridge: Cambridge University Press, 2013).

7. Frank Prochaska, *Royal Bounty: The Making of a Welfare Monarchy* (New Haven, CT: Yale University Press, 1995), 8.

8. Van Ginderachter, "'If Your Majesty Would Only Send Me a Little Money to Help Buy an Elephant.'"

9. Laurence Van Ypersele, "L'image du roi dans la caricature politique en Belgique de 1884 à 1914," *Belgisch tijdschrift voor nieuwste geschiedenis/Revue belge d'histoire contemporaine* 26, no. 1–2 (1996): esp. 146–47.

10. Justinien Van Drooghenbroeck (a self-employed gilder from Brussels) to the king (in French), January 9, 1903 (Royal Palace Archives, Cabinet Leopold II, Commandements du roi, G102/121); Florentin Gilon (a married painter from Chênée, Wallonia, who studied at the Académie des Beaux Arts de Liège) to the king (in French), June 16, 1899 (Royal Palace Archives, Cabinet Leopold II, Commandements du roi, G98/58). See also Joseph Gérard (a married mechanics worker from Mons, Wallonia) to the king (in French, letter written by a middle-class supporter on his behalf), July 27, 1899 (Archives Royal Palace, Cabinet Leopold II, Commandements du roi, G99/07); Marcel Grégoire (a music teacher from Tongeren, Flanders) to the king (in French), December 3, 1888 (Archives Royal Palace, Cabinet Leopold II, Commandements du roi, G81/05).

11. James C. Scott, *Domination and the Arts of Resistance: Hidden Transcripts* (New Haven, CT: Yale University Press, 1990), 94.

12. Edouard Tamenne (from Fleurus) to the king (in French), February 22, 1892 (Royal Palace Archives, Cabinet Leopold II, Commandements du roi, G87/07).

13. Linda Colley, *Britons: Forging the Nation, 1707–1837* (New Haven, CT: Yale University Press, 1992), 232.

14. Edmond de Carton de Wiart to E. Delvoie, October 31, 1907 (Royal Palace Archives, Cabinet Leopold II, Commandements du roi, G102/713).

15. *Registres des lettres entrées (demandes d'emplois, de secours, de distinctions honorifiques, . . . ) 1894–1909* (Royal Palace Archives, Commandements Prince Albert, 1–10, 11).

16. Royal Palace Archives, Cabinet Leopold II, Commandments of the King, G Secours, gratifications et inscriptions 80/46; *Le Peuple*, December 15, 1885, p. 1; *Le Peuple*, January 4, 1886, p. 1; *Le Hainaut: Journal Quotidien*, November 23, 1888; *Petit Journal de Mons et du Hainaut*, November 23, 1888.

17. *Le Peuple*, January 4, 1886, p. 1.

18. Alfred Defuisseaux, *Le Grand catéchisme du Peuple* (Brussels: Le Peuple, 1886), 4.

19. Cf. Michael Billig, *Banal Nationalism* (London: Sage, 1995).

20. Henri Roger during a meeting of the executive bureau of the Borinage federation, October 19, 1892 (General National Archives, Brussels, 751/2).

21. Royal Palace Archives, Cabinet Leopold II, Commandments du roi, M. Varia 18/24.

22. "Werkstakingen," *Vooruit*, April 21, 1886, p. 3.

23. Report by the Brussels police on the attitude of the working classes, August 1, 1879 (City Archives Brussels, Fonds Politie, Pol. 194, XIX).

24. Philippe Raxhon, *La mémoire de la Révolution française: Entre Liège et Wallonie* (Brussels: Labor, 1996), 44. See also Gita Deneckere, "Sire, het volk mort: Collectieve actie in de sociale geschiedenis van de Belgische staat, 1831–1940" (PhD diss., Ghent University, 1994), 99.

25. Commandements Prince Albert, Index 1onr. 14416, entry of April 1, 1908 (Royal Palace Archives).

26. *Le Peuple*, February 11, 1908, p. 1.

27. Colley, *Britons*, 232.

28. Circular letter from the Ministry of Interior and Public Education to the provincial governors on the occasion of the birth of Prince Leopold, November 9, 1901 (National Archives Mons, Cuesmes, X.1178).

29. Note by Prince Albert's secretary, July 17, 1901 (my emphasis) (Royal Palace Archives, Commandements Prince Albert, 41, 4861).

30. "Le Prince Albert," *Le Peuple*, April 18, 1902 (Royal Palace Archives, Commandements Prince Albert, 43, unnumbered, between 6833 and 8036).

31. Deneckere, "Sire, het volk mort," 106.

32. See the scrapbook with clippings about the monarchy from *Le Peuple* (1905–1913) (Royal Palace Archives, Private secretariats Albert and Elisabeth, 332).

33. Quoted by J. Lekeu, "Visite princière," *Le Peuple*, June 8, 1899, p. 1.

34. "Un bon point au prince Albert," *Le Suffrage universel*, September 30, 1900, p. 1.

35. Circular letter from the Ministry of Interior and Public Education to

provincial governors on the occasion of the birth of Prince Leopold, November 9, 1901 (National Archives Mons, Cuesmes, X.1178).

36. "Een prinselijk bezoek," *Vooruit*, July 18, 1902, p. 1; "Vooruit et le prince Albert," *Le Peuple*, July 19, 1902, p. 1.

37. The governor of Hainaut to the aide de camp of Prince Albert, July 12, 1902 (Royal Palace Archives, Commandements Prince Albert, 16, 7314). See also the visit of the princely couple on November 16, 1903, to L'Agrappe mine in Frameries ("Dernière heure, Le Prince Albert à Frameries," *Le Suffrage universel*, November 1, 1903, p. 2).

38. The Postal Administration to the secretary of Prince Albert, July 5, 1904 (Royal Palace Archives, Commandements Prince Albert, 14, 8676).

39. The secretary of Prince Albert to the Postal Administration, July 11, 1904 (Royal Palace Archives, Commandements Prince Albert, 14, 8676).

40. Belgian Chamber of Representatives, Session of November 8, 1910.

41. The so-called *Joyeuses entrées* or *Blijde Intredes* were a nineteenth-century reinvention of royal visits celebrating the indissoluble bond between sovereign and people ever since the Burgundian dukes.

42. Emile Housiaux, "Le socialisme et le roi," *Le Peuple*, July 14, 1911.

43. Marcellus, "Monarchie et socialisme," *Le Journal de Charleroi*, July 12, 1911, p. 1.

44. Vincent Viaene, "King Leopold's Imperialism and the Origins of the Belgian Colonial Party, 1860–1905," *Journal of Modern History* 80, no. 4 (2008).

45. Hans-Ulrich Wehler, "Bismarck's Imperialism 1862–1890," *Past & Present* 48 (August 1970): 154.

46. For the maximalist interpretation, see Catherine Hall and Sonya O. Rose, eds., *At Home with the Empire: Metropolitan Culture and the Imperial World* (Cambridge: Cambridge University Press, 2006); Colley, *Britons*; David Cannadine, *Ornamentalism: How the British Saw Their Empire* (Oxford: Oxford University Press, 2001); Pascal Blanchard and Sandrine Lemaire, *Culture coloniale: La France conquise par son empire, 1871–1931* (Paris: Autrement, 2003); Alice L. Conklin, *A Mission to Civilize: The Republican Idea of Empire in France and West Africa, 1895–1930* (Stanford, CA: Stanford University Press, 1997). For the minimalist, see Bernard Porter, *The Absent-Minded Imperialists: Empire, Society and Culture in Britain* (Oxford: Oxford University Press, 2004); Andrew S. Thompson, *The Empire Strikes Back? The Impact of Imperialism on Britain from the Mid-Nineteenth Century* (Harlow: Longman, 2005).

47. Matthew G. Stanard, *Selling the Congo: A History of European Pro-Empire Propaganda and the Making of Belgian Imperialism* (Lincoln: University of Nebraska Press, 2011), 18.

48. Vincent Viaene, "Reprise–Remise: De Congolese identiteitscrisis van België rond 1908," in *Congo in België: Koloniale cultuur in de metropool*, ed. Vincent Viaene, David Van Reybrouck, and Bambi Ceuppens (Leuven: Universitaire Pers Leuven, 2009), 44.

49. Viaene, "King Leopold's Imperialism and the Origins of the Belgian Colonial Party, 1860–1905," 759.
50. Ibid., 764.
51. Stanard, *Selling the Congo*, 38.
52. Tom Verschaffel, "Congo in de Belgische zelfrepresentatie," in Viaene, Van Reybrouck, and Ceuppens, eds., *Congo in België*, 69.
53. Stanard, *Selling the Congo*, 54, 97.
54. Ville de Bruxelles, *Guide pour l'enseignement pratique de la morale et du civisme à l'école primaire* (Brussels: Imprimerie Baertsoen, 1896), 19.
55. Stanard, *Selling the Congo*, 135, 50.
56. Jules Noël, "Le Congo et l'école," *L'Avenir du Borinage*, April 7, 1907, p. 1.
57. Viaene, "King Leopold's Imperialism and the Origins of the Belgian Colonial Party, 1860–1905," 763–64.
58. Ibid., 764, 769.
59. Ibid., 789.
60. Quoted by ibid., 777.
61. Police surveillance report of a socialist universal suffrage meeting in Liège on September 26, 1886 (National Archives Liège, Sûreté publique de la province de Liège, Première partie, XIV.A.229).
62. J. Volders, "Le grand couplet de l'accord patriotique," *Le Peuple*, July 27, 1890, p. 1; see also J. Volders, "Un mariage forcé," *Le Peuple*, April 24, 1890, p. 1.
63. Preben Kaarsholm, "The South African War and the Response of the International Socialist Community to Imperialism between 1896 and 1908," in *Internationalism in the Labour Movement, 1830–1940*, ed. Frits Van Holthoon and Marcel Van der Linden (Leiden: E.J. Brill, 1988), 1:57–58; Fritjof Tichelman, "Socialist 'Internationalism' and the Colonial World: Practical Colonial Policies of Social Democracy in Western Europe before 1940 with Particular Reference to the Dutch SDAP," in Van Holthoon and Van der Linden, eds., *Internationalism in the Labour Movement, 1830–1940*, 1:87–108.
64. Guy Vanthemsche, "De Belgische socialisten en Congo 1895–1960," *Brood en Rozen*, no. 2 (1999): 33–34.
65. Émile Vandervelde, "Confiteor," *Le Peuple*, January 13, 1902, p. 1.
66. Eric Defoort, "Het Belgische nationalisme vóór de Eerste Wereldoorlog," *Tijdschrift voor geschiedenis* 85, no. 4 (1972).
67. On Picard, see Bart Coppein, *Dromen van een nieuwe samenleving: Intellectuele biografie van Edmond Picard* (Brussels: Larcier, 2011).
68. "Pour notre classe! Pour notre Pays," *Le Peuple*, May 25, 1908, p. 1.
69. Vanthemsche, "De Belgische socialisten en Congo 1895–1960," 34–35; Janet Louise Polasky, *The Democratic Socialism of Emile Vandervelde: Between Reform and Revolution* (Oxford: Berg, 1995), 54–82.
70. Quoted by Vanthemsche, "De Belgische socialisten en Congo 1895–1960," 33.

71. Guy Vanthemsche, "The Historiography of Belgian Colonialism in the Congo," in *Europe and the World in European Historiography*, ed. Csaba Lévai (Pisa: Edizioni Plus, 2006), 92–93.

## CHAPTER 6: SCHOOLING THE NATION

1. Antoine Mertens, "Dévouement-Héroique de 600 Franchimontois: Oeuvre inédit décidée [sic] à sa Majesté Léopld II [sic] Comédie-historique-dramatique en six actes et en 4 tableaux" (Royal Palace Archives, Brussels, Cabinet Leopold II, Commandments of the King, G Secours, gratifications et inscriptions 64/25). All subsequent sources relating the Mertens case have the same archival reference.

2. Antoine Mertens to Leopold II, June 8, 1880.

3. The provincial governor of Liège to the secretary of the king, June 22, 1880, and Antoine Mertens to Leopold II, January 1, 1881.

4. Antoine Mertens to Leopold II, January 6, 1881.

5. The secretary of the king to the provincial governor of Liège, June 11, 1880.

6. Sophie Rottiers, "De eer van de zeshonderd Franchimontezen," in *De grote mythen uit de geschiedenis van België, Vlaanderen en Wallonië*, ed. Anne Morelli (Berchem: EPO, 1996).

7. Antoine Mertens to Leopold II, June 28, 1880.

8. Private, Catholic schools also received state subsidies after 1895 within the framework of *liberté subsidiée*. Paul Wynants, Byls Henk, and Arthe Van Laer, "Het juridisch en institutioneel kader: Van de vrijheid van onderwijs tot de huidige debatten," in *Katholiek onderwijs in België: Identiteiten in evolutie 19de–21ste eeuw*, ed. Jan De Maeyer and Paul Wynants (Antwerp: Halewijn, 2016).

9. Benjamin Seebohm Rowntree, *Land and Labour: Lessons from Belgium* (London: Macmillan, 1910), 272.

10. Paul Wynants et al., "Conflicten als vormgevers en stoorzenders: Ideologische breuklijnen en twee wereldoorlogen," in De Maeyer and Wynants, eds., *Katholiek onderwijs in België*, 82.

11. Kristof Dams, "De constructie van de burger in het pedagogisch debat in België, 1879–1914" (Master's thesis, Ghent University, 1995), 112–13, 133–38.

12. *De Toekomst*, 1881, p. 433, quoted by ibid., 55.

13. *De Toekomst*, 1884, p. 224, quoted by ibid.

14. Ibid., 133; "Petite chronique: Les travaux de conférence," *L'Étincelle* 2, no. 7 (July 15, 1914): 3; Register of summaries of the monthly conferences of Brussels Municipal School No. 19 (June 26, 1909, through May 11, 1914), December 9, 1909 (City Archives Brussels, I.P.II, 38, Dossier 2); Ville de Bruxelles, *L'enseignement du chant dans les écoles primaires*, 1909 (City Archives Brussels, I.P.II, 28).

15. Ville de Bruxelles, *Guide pour l'enseignement pratique de la morale et du civisme à l'école primaire* (1896), p. 19. See also Jean-Jacques Hoebanx,

"L'histoire de Belgique dans quelques manuels scolaires," in *Histoire et historiens depuis 1830 en Belgique. Revue de l'Université de Bruxelles*, nos. 1–2, ed. Hervé Hasquin (Brussels: ULB, 1981), 68.

16. Note by Séverin, principal of Municipal School No. 3 or 13, to the Brussels alderman of education, entitled "Développement du sentiment patriotique," February 26, 1896; Minutes of the principals' conference of May 17, 1898 (City Archives Brussels, I.P.II, 19).

17. Minutes of the principals' conference, reunions of 1878 to 1883, March 7, 1878 (City Archives Brussels, I.P.II, 1).

18. Service orders from the alderman of education to the teaching staff, January 7, 1895, and May 1, 1897, quoted in report by the Commission de révision du programme de l'enseignement primaire of the Brussels municipal schools, 1908–1909 (City Archives Brussels, I.P.II, 3).

19. Ville de Bruxelles, *Guide pour l'enseignement pratique de la morale et du civisme à l'école primaire* (1896), 18–19; Minutes of the Conférence des Chefs d'école, October 1, 1896 (City Archives Brussels, I.P.II, 19).

20. See note by Séverin, principal of Municipal School No. 3 or 13, to the Brussels alderman of education, entitled "Développement du sentiment patriotique," February 26, 1896; four undated reports from the period 1896–1907 on civic education by Senhelle, J. Moulan, Pappaert, and Delhaye, four elementary teachers from the Brussels municipal schools (City Archives Brussels, I.P.II, 19).

21. Minutes of the Conférence des Chefs d'école, May 13, 1898 (City Archives Brussels, I.P.II, 19).

22. Report of the Commission de révision du programme de l'enseignement primaire of the Brussels municipal schools, 1908–1909 (City Archives Brussels, I.P.II, 3).

23. E. Picard, "Trop tard! trop tard!," *Le Peuple*, May 8, 1896, p. 1; and dossier about a visit of Prince Albert and Princess Elisabeth to the Brussels municipal schools 4 and 17 on November 28, 1904, 1902–1904 (Royal Palace Archives, Brussels, Commandments of Prince Albert, 16, 6612).

24. Jeroen Janssens, *De Belgische natie viert: De Belgische nationale feesten 1830–1914* (Leuven: Universitaire Pers Leuven, 2001), 192.

25. Register of summaries of the monthly conferences of Brussels Municipal School No. 19 (June 26, 1909, through May 11, 1914), December 9, 1909 (City Archives Brussels, I.P.II, 38, Dossier 2).

26. Janssens, *De Belgische natie viert*, 195.

27. Circular letter from the Brussels alderman of education to the municipal schools, July 7, 1898 (City Archives Brussels, I.P.II, 28); Service order 51, January 16, 1900 (City Archives Brussels, I.P.II, 28).

28. "Brabançonne et Brabançonnes," *Le Peuple*, August 22, 1896, p. 1.

29. "Brrrrabançonne," *Le Peuple*, July 19, 1896, p. 1.

30. Circular letter from the Brussels alderman of education to the municipal

schools, July 7, 1898 (City Archives Brussels, I.P.II, 28); Service order 51, January 16, 1900 (City Archives Brussels, I.P.II, 28).

31. Josephine Hoegaerts, *Masculinity and Nationhood, 1830–1910: Constructions of Identity and Citizenship in Belgium* (Basingstoke: Palgrave Macmillan, 2014), 101.

32. Ibid., 69.

33. H. Huygh, principal of Municipal School No. 17, to the alderman of education, April 9, 1898 (City Archives Brussels, I.P.II, 38, Dossier 1); Proposal of the History Section of the Commission de révision du programme de l'enseignement primaire of the Brussels municipal schools, 1908–1909 (proofs) (City Archives Brussels, I.P.II, 3).

34. Quoted by Janssens, *De Belgische natie viert*, 194.

35. World's fairs were held in Antwerp in 1885, Brussels in 1888, Antwerp in 1894, Brussels in 1897, Liège in 1905, Brussels in 1910, and Ghent in 1913.

36. Conférence des chefs d'écoles: Procès verbaux des réunions de 1878 à 1883, May 2, 1878, and June 5, 1879 (City Archives Brussels, I.P.II, 1); Note of the Administration communale de Bruxelles, Direction de l'instruction publique et des beaux arts, to the secretariat of Prince Albert, November 19, 1904 (Royal Palace Archives, Commandements Prince Albert, 16, 6612); Registre des comptes-rendus des conférences mensuelles of Brussels Municipal School No. 19 (June 26, 1909, through May 11, 1914), May 21, 1910 (City Archives Brussels, I.P.II, 38, Dossier 2).

37. "Le congrès international des étudiants socialistes à Bruxelles," *Le Peuple*, December 23, 1891, p. 1; see also "Vaderlandsliefde," *Vooruit*, August 12, 1895, p. 1; S. Boersen, "Blaaskaak," *Vooruit*, January 29, 1896, p. 1; G. Gérard, "Le patriotisme," *Le Suffrage universel*, December 16, 1900, p. 1; "Le Congo et l'école," *L'Avenir du Borinage*, April 7, 1907, p. 1; "A Bruxelles: Le militarisme envahissant!," *L'Étincelle* 1, no. 1 (October 15, 1913): 4–5; "Petite chronique: Préparation militaire," *L'Étincelle* 2, no. 2 (February 15, 1914): 3.

38. See the Questions and Answers section of *Le Mouvement Communal*, the magazine for socialist municipal councilors, 1905–1908.

39. See "Un Ardennais, Inspecteurs et livres classiques," *Le Journal de Charleroi*, March 19, 1896, p. 1; "Fédération des conseillers communaux," *Le Journal de Charleroi*, April 14, 1896, p. 1; "Livres scolaires," *Le Peuple*, July 9, 1900, p. 1; Emile Vinck, "Socialisme communal: Livres scolaires," *Le Peuple*, August 3, 1901, p. 1; Falstaff, "Borinage-revue," *L'Avenir du Borinage*, August 15, 1908, p. 2; "Discussion du projet de loi Schollaert," *L'Avenir du Borinage*, June 8, 1911, p. 2.

40. "Livres classiques recommandés par le comité du congrès [des conseillers communaux socialistes] de Noël 1898," *Bulletin Communal des conseillers communaux socialistes*, in *L'Avenir social*, vol. 4 (Brussels, 1899), 318–20, 360; "Livres scolaires," in ibid., vol. 5 (1900), 439–42; Fiat lux, "Livres scolaires," in ibid., 500–503; "Livres pour distribution de prix," in ibid., 365–80.

41. For instance, *Secondes lectures récréatives et instructrices* by Slosse and Sonnet, *La 3e Expédition belge au Pays noir* by Jerôme Becker, *L'inquisition en Belgique* by Duverger, five books by the patriotic historian Théodore Juste, and *Le chemin de fer* by L. Hymans.

42. "Conseillers communaux!," *Le Mouvement Communal*, issue 4 (April 1907): 104. On the Ligue de l'Enseignement, see *Histoire de la Ligue de l'Enseignement 1864–1989* (Brussels: Ligue de l'Enseignement et de l'Education permanente, 1990).

43. Règlement et programme types des écoles primaires communales (Extrait du *Moniteur Belge* du 26 mai 1897, n° 146) (Brussels: Imprimerie-lithographie JB Stevens, 1897), 12; Letter from Fernand Delbastaille, the socialist alderman of education of Cuesmes, November 10, 1910; Minutes of the Cuesmes municipal council, July 21, 1908; Instruction of the Cuesmes municipal council to the municipal schools, July 17, 1912, and November 12, 1913 (National Archives Mons, Cuesmes, X.1178).

44. "Chronique régionale: Frameries," *L'Avenir du Borinage*, July 18, 1908, p. 2.

45. A. Delattre, "Fêtes scolaires à Pâturages," *L'Avenir du Borinage*, August 14, 1912, p. 1.

46. F. Hardyns, "Twee stoeten," *Vooruit*, July 25, 1912, p. 1; "De schooloptocht," *Vooruit*, July 22, 1913, p. 6.

47. See, for instance, Marc Depaepe, *Orde in vooruitgang: Alledaags handelen in de Belgische lagere school (1880–1970)* (Leuven: Universitaire Pers Leuven, 1999), 43; Karl Catteeuw, "Als de muren konden spreken . . . : Schoolwandplaten en de geschiedenis van het Belgisch lager onderwijs" (PhD diss., KU Leuven, 2005); Tine Hens, Kaat Wils, and Saartje Vanden Borre, *Oorlog in tijden van vrede: De Eerste Wereldoorlog in de klas 1918–1940* (Kalmthout: Pelckmans, 2015); Matthias Meirlaen, *Revoluties in de klas: Secundair geschiedenisonderwijs in de Zuidelijke Nederlanden, 1750–1850* (Leuven: Universitaire Pers Leuven, 2014); Jean Stengers and Eliane Gubin, *Le grand siècle de la nationalité belge: De 1830 à 1918*, vol. 2 of *Histoire du sentiment national en Belgique des origines à 1918* (Brussels: Racine, 2002), 22–24; Hoegaerts, *Masculinity and Nationhood, 1830–1910*, 74.

48. Marc Depaepe et al., "L'enseignement primaire," in *Histoire de l'enseignement en Belgique*, ed. Dominique Grootaers (Brussels: CRISP, 1998), 113.

49. Marc Depaepe, "Kwantitatieve analyse van de Belgische lagere school (1830–1911)," *Belgisch tijdschrift voor nieuwste geschiedenis/Revue belge d'histoire contemporaine* 10, no. 1–2 (1979): 48–49.

50. Seebohm Rowntree, *Land and Labour*, 268.

51. Depaepe, "Kwantitatieve analyse van de Belgische lagere school (1830–1911)," 47.

52. As quoted by A. Dugauquier, "L'enseignement à Hornu," *L'Avenir du Borinage*, March 24, 1907, p. 1.

53. J. De Graeve, "School," *De Volksschool* 1, no. 8 (October 11, 1908): 2–3.

54. Machteld De Metsenaere, *Taalmuur: Sociale muur? De negentiende-eeuwse taalverhoudingen te Brussel als resultaat van geodemografische en sociale processen* (Brussels: VUB Press, 1988), 26; Harry Van Velthoven, *De Vlaamse kwestie 1830–1914: Macht en onmacht van de Vlaamsgezinden* (Kortrijk: UGA, 1982), 288; Harry Van Velthoven, "Taal en onderwijspolitiek te Brussel, 1878–1914," *Taal en sociale integratie* 4 (1981): 278–83.

55. Van Velthoven, "Taal en onderwijspolitiek te Brussel, 1878–1914," 269, 339.

56. Report by Alexis Sluys, October 18, 1897 (City Archives Brussels, I.P.II, 19).

57. Register of summaries of the monthly conferences of Brussels Municipal School No. 19 (June 26, 1909, through May 11, 1914), May 21, 1910 (City Archives Brussels, I.P.II, 35).

58. Police surveillance report of a socialist rally in Liège on June 2, 1887 (City Archives Liège, Archives de police, carton XLIV, 1–160). Quoted by Jens Verdure, "En men zou niet fier zijn Vaderlander te wezen? Sociaal-democratie en nationale identiteit voor WO I: Een casusstudie van Antwerpen en Luik" (Master's thesis, University of Ghent, 2007), 55.

59. Mertens, "Dévouement-Héroique," 8.

60. Ibid., 16, 31.

61. Ibid., 9.

62. Antoine Mertens to Leopold II, June 28, 1880.

63. Robert Colls, "Architecture and Regional Identity," in *Sources of Regionalism in the Nineteenth Century: Architecture, Art and Literature*, ed. Linda Van Santvoort, Jan De Maeyer, and Tom Verschaffel (Leuven: Universitaire Pers Leuven, 2008), 22–23.

64. Mertens, "Dévouement-Héroique," 26.

65. Ibid., 20.

66. Falstaff, "Borinage-revue," *L'Avenir du Borinage*, August 15, 1908, p. 2.

67. Mertens, "Dévouement-Héroique," 10.

68. Ibid., 9.

69. Antoine Mertens to Leopold II, January 1, 1881.

70. Mertens, "Dévouement-Héroique," 20. See also ibid., 13, 36.

71. Ibid., 30. See also ibid., 16, 20.

72. Ibid., 24, 26 (my emphasis), 28–29.

73. Ibid., 33–34.

74. Cf. Antoon Vrints, *Het theater van de straat: Publiek geweld in Antwerpen tijdens de eerste helft van de twintigste eeuw* (Amsterdam: Amsterdam University Press, 2011).

75. Marc Depaepe, "Introduction," in *Manuels et chansons scolaires au Congo Belge*, ed. Marc Depaepe, Jan Briffaerts, and Pierre Kita Kyankenge Masandi (Louvain: Presses Universitaires de Louvain, 2003), 16; Jonathan E. Rose, *The Intellectual Life of the British Working Classes* (New Haven, CT: Yale University Press, 2002 [2001]).

76. Alf Lüdtke, "Einleitung," in *Eigen-Sinn: Fabrikalltag, Arbeitererfahrungen und Politik vom Kaiserreich bis in den Faschismus* (Hamburg: Ergebnisse, 1993), 15; David Allen Harvey, *Constructing Class and Nationality in Alsace, 1830–1945* (DeKalb: Northern Illinois University Press, 2001), 8.

77. Patrick, "Het artikel 310," *Vooruit*, November 29, 1889, p. 1.

78. Jan De Zot, "Tap in, tap uit," *Vooruit*, August 3, 1891, p. 1.

79. Maarten Van Ginderachter, *Het rode vaderland: De vergeten geschiedenis van de communautaire spanningen in het Belgische socialisme voor WO I* (Tielt/Ghent: Lannoo/Amsab, 2005), 69.

80. On the significance of Hendrik Conscience, see Marnix Beyen, "Literatuur als vlag: Hendrik Conscience en de choreografie van de massa," *Verslagen en mededelingen van de Koninklijke Academie voor Nederlandse Taal- en Letterkunde* 123, no. 2–3 (2013).

81. Katrien Arnaut, "De ontwikkeling van de socialistische bibliotheken te Gent tussen 1830 en 1890," *Amsab-tijdingen* 3, no. 1–2 (1984): 47.

82. Jan De Zot, "Tap in, tap uit," *Vooruit*, March 10, 1890, p. 1.

83. Stephen Heathorn, *For Home, Country, and Race: Constructing Gender, Class, and Englishness in the Elementary School, 1884–1914* (Toronto: University of Toronto Press, 2000), 20.

84. Jan De Zot, "Tap in, tap uit," *Vooruit*, August 3, 1891, p. 1.

85. De Graeve, "School," 2–3.

86. J. De Graeve, "Zieltogend Vlaanderen," *Vooruit*, April 20, 1909, p. 2.

87. De Graeve, "School," 2–3.

### CHAPTER 7: ENCOUNTERS WITH THE BELGIAN FLAG AND THE NATIONAL ANTHEM

1. Ms. Boitte to the municipal secretary, October 10, 1907, in dossier about the mandate for municipal schools to have a national flag (National Archives Mons, Cuesmes, X.1178).

2. Conférence des chefs d'écoles: Procès verbaux des réunions de 1878 à 1883, May 2, 1878 (City Archives Brussels, I.P.II, 1).

3. Alf Lüdtke, "Glossary of Selected Terms and Abbreviations," in *The History of Everyday Life: Reconstructing Historical Experiences and Ways of Life* (Princeton, NJ: Princeton University Press, 1995); James C. Scott, *Weapons of the Weak: Everyday Forms of Peasant Resistance* (New Haven, CT: Yale University Press, 1985).

4. Tara Zahra, "Imagined Non-Communities: National Indifference as a Category of Analysis," *Slavic Review* 69 (2010): 102.

5. Quoted by Hendrik Defoort, "De derde arm: Socialisme en coöperatie in Europa voor 1914" (PhD diss., Ghent University, 2002), 246.

6. Jean Puissant, *L'évolution du mouvement ouvrier socialiste dans le Borinage* (Brussels: Palais des Académies, 1982), 77.

7. Jon E. Fox and Cynthia Miller-Idriss, "Everyday Nationhood," *Ethnicities* 8, no. 4 (2008).

8. Working-class autobiographies, life stories, and reminiscences are rather sparse for Belgium compared to France, Britain, and Germany. Sven Steffens, "La vie d'un maçon au 19e siècle: 'Rik De Metselaer' (1852)," *Les Cahiers de la Fonderie*, no. 19 (December 1995): 12.

9. Janet Louise Polasky, "A Revolution for Socialist Reforms: The Belgian General Strike for Universal Suffrage," *Journal of Contemporary History* 27, no. 3 (1992): 463–64.

10. "La manifestation," *Le Peuple*, August 11, 1890, pp. 1–2; "La manifestation de 10 août," *La Bataille*, August 17, 1890, p. 3; Gita Deneckere, "Sire, het volk mort: Collectieve actie in de sociale geschiedenis van de Belgische staat, 1831–1940" (PhD diss., Ghent University, 1994), 361, 742.

11. *Le Peuple*, August 17, 1886, pp. 1–2.

12. *Vooruit*, August 21, 1885, p. 1 (my emphasis).

13. See for instance "La Ligue ouvrière St Gilloise," *Le Peuple*, February 23, 1886, p. 2; Police surveillance report of a socialist meeting in Carnières, July 5, 1886, and in Charleroi-Nord, August 1, 1886 (National Archives Anderlecht, Cour d'appel de Bruxelles-Parquet-général, 225).

14. Charles Tilly, *Regimes and Repertoires* (Chicago: University of Chicago Press, 2006); Deneckere, "Sire, het volk mort," xv–xviii, 623–24.

15. Jules Destrée and Émile Vandervelde, *Le socialisme en Belgique* (Paris: Giard et Brière, 1898), 46.

16. Patricia Penn Hilden, *Women, Work, and Politics: Belgium 1830–1914* (Oxford: Clarendon, 1993), 163.

17. Report by the French commissaire spécial of Jeumont, September 27, 1886 (Departmental Archives of the Nord in Lille, Série M, 162/5).

18. *Vooruit*, April 20, 1886, p. 3.

19. L. Pépin, "Gustave Hervé et l'Hervéisme," *L'Avenir du Borinage*, December 8, 1912, p. 1.

20. Jacques Kergoat, "France," in *The Formation of Labour Movements, 1870–1914: An International Perspective*, ed. Marcel van der Linden and Jürgen Rojahn (Leiden: E.J. Brill, 1990), 1:169.

21. Achille Juste, "Chronique d'après la lutte: Chatelineau," *La République belge*, October 30, 1887, p. 3 (original emphasis).

22. X. Sérau, "La Belgique vendue," *La République belge*, January 8, 1888, p. 1.

23. Léon Defuisseaux, "Leopold II accusé de haute trahison," *La République belge*, January 15, 1887, p. 1.

24. Herbert de Gravonne, "Aux Belges," *La République belge*, March 11, 1888, pp. 1–2.

25. *En avant pour le SU*, February 6, 1887, p. 2; *Le Combat*, March 13,

1887, p. 3; Report by the French commissaire spécial of Feignies, January 31 and February 1, 1887 (Departmental Archives of the Nord in Lille, Série M, 162/7).

26. Charles Durand, *Le Combat*, March 13, 1887, p. 3 (my emphasis).

27. The mayor of Carnières to the local Ligue ouvrière, February 22, 1888 (Archives of the Université Libre de Bruxelles, Fonds Defuisseaux, 310A)

28. *La République belge*, September 2, 1888, p. 3.

29. A. Ledoux to *La République belge*, [May 1888] (Archives of the Université Libre de Bruxelles, Fonds Defuisseaux, 310A).

30. Jean Callewaert to *La République belge*, May 7, 1888 (Archives of the Université Libre de Bruxelles, Fonds Defuisseaux, 310A).

31. "Mouvement socialiste Républicain," *La République belge*, March 11, 1888, p. 3

32. A. Ledoux to *La République belge*, [May 1888] (Archives of the Université Libre de Bruxelles, Fonds Defuisseaux, 310A).

33. Jean Callewaert to *La République belge*, May 7, 1888 (Archives of the Université Libre de Bruxelles, Fonds Defuisseaux, 310A).

34. [A self-identified "worker" from Verviers], "Tribune populaire," *En avant pour le SU*, June 6, 1886, p. 3 (my emphasis). See also [Nicolas Colson, a worker from Jumet near Charleroi, who had emigrated to the United States], "Correspondance d'Amérique," *La Liberté*, May 6, 1888, p. 1; Isidore Godfrin [a small self-employed shoemaker from Dour in the Borinage], "La mine aux mineurs ou à l'Etat," *La Bataille*, January 12, 1890, p. 2; François Carpent to *La République belge*, n.d. [1888] (Archives of the Université Libre de Bruxelles, Fonds Defuisseaux, 310A); E. D. [a miner], "Frameries," *La Liberté*, March 11, 1888, p. 2; a certain Pierre in a short, unpublished postcard to *La République belge*, March 7, 1888 (Archives of the Université Libre de Bruxelles, Fonds Defuisseaux, 310F).

35. Letter from Thomas Dumonceau to Georges Defuisseaux, February 12, 1888 (Archives of the Université Libre de Bruxelles, Fonds Defuisseaux, 312C).

36. Roger Pinon, "Contribution à l'étude de la chanson politique et sociale dans la province de Hainaut aux XIXe et XXe siècles," in *Recueil d'études d'histoire hainuyère offertes à Maurice A. Arnould*, ed. Jean-Marie Cauchies and Jean-Marie Duvosquel (Mons: Hannonia, 1983), 2:528.

37. Handwritten report of a PSR meeting in Tubize, n.d. (Archives of the Université Libre de Bruxelles, Fonds Defuisseaux, 311A).

38. "Insulte au drapeau français," *La République belge*, October 21, 1888, p. 3.

39. "Meeting monstre de protestation à La Louvière," *La République belge*, November 25, 1888, p. 3; Champal, "Le meeting de La Louvière," *La Liberté*, November 25, 1888, p. 3.

40. Jean Puissant, *Sous la loupe de la police française, le bassin industriel du Centre (1885–1893)* (Haine-Saint-Pierre: Cercle d'histoire et de folklore Henri Guillemin, 1988).

41. Police Report by the commissaire spécial of Feignies, November 19, 1888 (Departmental Archives of the Nord in Lille, Série M.630/8).

42. "Meeting monstre de protestation à La Louvière," p. 3 (my emphasis).

43. *En avant pour le SU*, November 28, 1886, p. 1; see also A. Defuisseaux, "La manifestation du 15 août," *En avant pour le SU*, August 8, 1886, p. 1; A. Defuisseaux," Malheur aux vaincus," *Le Combat*, September 11, 1887, p. 1.

44. Letter from Thomas Dumonceau to Georges Defuisseaux, February 12, 1888 (Archives of the Université Libre de Bruxelles, Fonds Defuisseaux, 312C).

45. François Carpent to *La République belge*, n.d. [1888] (Archives of the Université Libre de Bruxelles, Fonds Defuisseaux, 310A).

46. "1830," *L'Avenir du Borinage*, September 26–27, 1904, p. 3.

47. Bill of indictment, July 28, 1898. All subsequent references to the judicial process derive from the National Archives of Mons, Cours d'assises du Hainaut 1898/18, no. 166.

48. "Une histoire de drapeaux," *Le Peuple*, May 25, 1898, pp. 1–2; see also "Les drapeaux brûlés," *Le Peuple*, August 14, 1898, p. 1; "Une affaire de drapeau," *Le Suffrage universel*, May 29, 1898, p. 3.

49. "Un scandale inouï," *La Gazette de Charleroi*, May 24, 1898, p. 2.

50. "Un scandale inouï," *Le Journal de Charleroi*, May 25, 1898, p. 2.

51. Omer Boulanger, "Encore le drapeau," *Le Journal de Charleroi*, June 5, 1898, p. 2.

52. "Comment on écrit l'histoire," *Le Journal de Charleroi*, May 27, 1898, p. 2.

53. "Agents provocateurs," *Le Journal de Charleroi*, May 28, 1898, p. 2.

54. In *Le Journal de Charleroi*, see "Commentaires incohérents," May 27, 1898, p. 2; "Un perfidie qui rate," May 20, 1898, p. 2; "L'histoire du drapeau St Rémy," May 29, 1898, p. 2; "Les confrères loyaux," May 30, 1898, p. 2; "Le drapeau national brûlé," May 31, 1898, p. 3; Omer Boulanger, "Encore le drapeau," June 5, 1898, p. 2.

55. In *Le Journal de Charleroi*, see "Le procès du drapeau," November 20, 1898, p. 1; "L'affaire du drapeau," November 22, 1898, p. 1; "L'affaire du drapeau," November 23, 1898, p. 1; Philippe Dufrasne, "Drapeau brûlé?!," November 20, 1898, p. 1.

56. *Compte-rendu du 15me congrès annuel tenu à Leuven les 21 et lundi 22 mai 1899* (Brussels, 1899).

57. Official witness report by Léon George, June 28, 1898, 3 pages.

58. The public prosecutor of Charleroi to the chief of police of Charleroi, June 5, 1898.

59. Statistique criminelle, Feuille de renseignements, July 13, 1898.

60. Official witness report by Augustin Bellière, adjunct police commissioner of Gilly, July 15, 1898.

61. Statistique criminelle, Feuille de renseignements, July 14, 1898.

62. Procès-verbal by Emile Henrion, chief of police of Gilly, July 12, 1898.

63. Procès-verbal by Emile Mélotte, adjunct police commissioner of the Quartier Nord A, about his attempts to identify the culprits, May 27, 1898, 2 pages.

64. Official witness report by Zéphir Demoulin, June 21, 1898.
65. Procès-verbal by Augustin Bellière, adjunct police commissioner of Gilly, June 1, 1898.
66. Official witness report by Emile Henrion, police commissioner of Gilly, July 12, 1898; see also police commissioner of Gilly to the public prosecutor, June 7, 1898.
67. Procès-verbal by Émile Mélotte, adjunct police commissioner of the Quartier Nord A, May 31, 1898; official witness report by Achille Chagiaut, police officer in Charleroi, June 28, 1898; official witness report by Joseph Lambot, June 21, 1898.
68. Procès-verbal by Mélotte.
69. Procès-verbal by Emile Strille, adjunct police commissioner of the Quartier Centre, May 28, 1898.
70. Official witness report by Théophile Kest, July 19, 1898.
71. Official witness report by Léon George, June 28, 1898.
72. Procès-verbal by Joseph Leroy, deputy constable of Gilly, June 3, 1898, and testimony by Léon George, June 28, 1898.
73. Official witness report by Edouard Hermans, July 12, 1898.
74. Procès-verbal by the police of Gilly, July 13, 1898.
75. Official witness report by J.B. Wayemberg, July 15, 1898; Bill of indictment, July 28, 1898.
76. Official witness report by Jules Vanderhaeghen, July 15, 1898.
77. Official witness report by Jules Vanderhaeghen and Emile Degrève, July 15, 1898.
78. James C. Scott, *Domination and the Arts of Resistance: Hidden Transcripts* (New Haven, CT: Yale University Press, 1990).
79. Keeley Stauter-Halsted, *The Nation in the Village: The Genesis of Peasant National Identity in Austrian Poland, 1848–1914* (Ithaca, NY: Cornell University Press, 2001), 243–45.
80. Reader's letter from a French-speaking militant from Elsene/Ixelles, *Le Peuple*, June 26, 1905, p. 2.
81. Luc, "Chronique régionale. Dour: Les distributions des prix," *L'Avenir du Borinage*, August 12, 1909, p. 2; A. Delattre, "Fêtes scolaires à Pâturages," *L'Avenir du Borinage*, August 14, 1912, p. 1.
82. "Les fêtes scolaires au Borinage: A Pâturages," *L'Avenir du Borinage*, August 14, 1913, p. 1.
83. "Roux: De fête wallonne," *Vooruit*, October 2, 1913, p. 7.
84. V., "De roode vlag," *Vooruit*, August 25, 1886, p. 1.
85. S. Boersen, "Ons 1905," *Vooruit*, December 12 and 29, 1903, p. 1.

## CHAPTER 8: PROLETARIAN TWEETS

1. *Vooruit*, October 19, 1894, p. 4.
2. Ibid., October 22, 1898, p. 1.
3. Ibid., August 1, 1892, p. 4.

4. Ibid., February 15, 1886, p. 4; August 26, 1898, p. 4.
5. Ibid., June 20, 1890, p. 4.
6. Ibid., August 26, 1898, p. 4.
7. Ibid.
8. Ibid., December 7, 1887, p. 4.
9. Ibid., December 14, 1887, p. 4.

10. In the academic year 2005–2006 I supervised a random sample by thirty students as part of the second year undergraduate course on "Historical Practice" at Ghent University. Each student was assigned half a year of the (then not yet digitized) newspaper *Vooruit* in the period February 1886–December 1900. I would like to thank the following students (in order of assigned semester): Michèle Verstraete, Bregt Vermeulen, Vaast Vanoverschelde, Myriam Vandenheuvel, Jeroen Vandenbussche, Sara Vandekerckhove, Siggi Van Geyte, Gerd Van de Kauter, Wout Van Caimere, Ralph Urmel, Bert Segier, Peter Schildermans, Stijn Rooms, Wouter Pollet, Wim Nuyens, Fréderic Lehembre, Hans Haustraete, Bart De Sutter, Hanneleen De Seranno, Bas De Roo, Tim De Craene, Ewoud De Clercq, Jolien De Baets, Cedric D'Haese, Ann-Sophie Claeys, An-Marie Buyse, Matthias Boeykens, Gijs Anseeuw, Hannes Algoed, and Eline Adam.

For each month, the students were asked to enter into the database the full propaganda pence section published on the fifteenth of that month or the earliest day after that. If they did not reach a minimum of six hundred entries of individual tweets, they had to expand their sample with the next complete propaganda pence section after the fifteenth of that month. Some students—as students are wont to—did not comply with this last request and added additional propaganda pence sections at the beginning or the end of the month. This did not distort the sample because there was no system to the sequence or type of tweets *Vooruit* published on any particular day or in any particular week.

All tweets were brought together in one large database by Bart De Sutter, who wrote a master's thesis on the subject under my supervision: De Sutter, "Over dompers, mouchards en papen: Constructie van identiteit, via humor; Casus: De Gentse socialistische strijdpenning in *Vooruit* (1886–1900)" (Ghent University, 2008). Subsequently I went through the entire database, checked every single tweet individually, corrected them where necessary, and assigned labels to them. I also added 1,744 tweets that had been missed by the students, although they belonged in the sample.

11. Danielle Delmaire, "Antisémitisme des catholiques au vingtième siècle: De la revendication au refus," in *Catholicism, Politics and Society in Twentieth-Century France*, ed. Kay Chadwick (Liverpool: Liverpool University Press, 2000), 27.

12. Propaganda pence or similar practices are summarily mentioned in some publications on the Belgian, Dutch, and Italian socialist movements: Holde Lhoest-Offerman, *Recueil de documents relatifs à la propagande des mouvements socialistes au XIXe siècle à Bruxelles* (Brussels: Archives générales du royaume,

1967), 34; Bart De Wilde, "Seks op en naast de werkvloer: De seksualiteitsbeleving van arbeiders en de houding van de vakbeweging," in *Begeerte heeft ons aangeraakt: Socialisten, sekse en seksualiteit* (Ghent: Provinciebestuur van Oost-Vlaanderen, 1999), 158; Dennis Bos, *Waarachtige volksvrienden: De vroege socialistische beweging in Amsterdam 1848–1894* (Amsterdam: Bert Bakker, 2001), 404; Maurizio Ridolfi, "'L'industria della propaganda' e il partito: Stampa e editoria nel socialismo italiano prefascista," *Studi storici* 33, no. 1 (1992).

13. Bert Altena, "Een broeinest der anarchie: Arbeiders, arbeidersbeweging en maatschappelijke ontwikkeling: Vlissingen 1875–1929 (1940)" (PhD diss., Amsterdam University, 1989), 14; Bos, *Waarachtige volksvrienden*, 404.

14. *Vooruit*, December 5, 1894, p. 1.

15. Ibid.

16. Ibid., November 4, 1898, p. 1.

17. Lettre ouverte d'Anseele, *Le Peuple*, August 9, 1898, p. 1.

18. *Vooruit*, December 30, 1898, p. 1.

19. Minutes of the Central Committee of the Ghent socialists, 1899–1901, January 23, 1901 (AMSAB, 32: 105.2).

20. See Stefan Joosten, "De krant Vooruit voor Wereldoorlog I" (Master's thesis, VUB, 2003), 36–37.

21. Guy Vanschoenbeek, "'Arbeid adelt': De arbeidersaristocratie als verklaring voor het reformisme in de arbeidersbeweging," *Belgisch tijdschrift voor filologie en geschiedenis/Revue belge de philologie et d'histoire* 76, no. 4 (1998): 1052–59.

22. Daniel Fabre, "Introduction," in *Ecritures ordinaires*, ed. Daniel Fabre and Jean-Pierre Albert (Paris: Bibliothèque publique d'information P.O.L., 1993), 11; Martyn Lyons, *The Writing Culture of Ordinary People in Europe, c. 1860–1920* (Cambridge: Cambridge University Press, 2013).

23. Martyn Lyons, "Ordinary Writings or How the 'Illiterate' Speak to Historians," in *Ordinary Writings, Personal Narratives*, ed. Martyn Lyons (Bern: Peter Lang, 2007), 23ff.

24. *Vooruit*, November 15, 1889, p. 4.

25. Ibid., November 26, 1887, p. 4 (my emphasis); June 16, 1888, p. 4.

26. Ibid., October 22, 1898, p. 1.

27. James C. Scott, *Domination and the Arts of Resistance: Hidden Transcripts* (New Haven, CT: Yale University Press, 1990), 18–19.

28. Ibid., xii.

29. Ibid., 120.

30. *De Werker*, November 3, 1878, p. 2.

31. *Vooruit*, October 22, 1898, p. 1; November 5, 1898, pp. 1–2; January 8, 1906, pp. 2–3.

32. Ibid., February 8, 1896, p. 4.

33. Ibid., December 14, 1888, p. 4.

34. Ibid., June 20, 1890, p. 4.

35. Ibid., August 16, 1895, p. 4.
36. Ibid., August 6, 1887, p. 4.
37. Ibid., July 18, 1890, p. 4.
38. Ibid., December 14, 1888, p. 4.
39. Ibid., January 18, 1895, p. 4.
40. Ibid., October 17, 1890, p. 4.
41. Ibid., December 20, 1889, p. 3; August 3, 1900, p. 3.
42. Ibid., May 15 and 16, 1886, p. 4.
43. Ibid., January 18, 1889, p. 4.
44. Ibid., December 3, 1887, p. 4.
45. The sum of the absolute numbers in Tables 1 and 2 exceeds the total number of tweets in the entire sample because most tweets referred to more than one social category.
46. *Vooruit*, February 15, 1886, p. 4; April 15, 1886, p. 4; February 18, 1888, p. 4; June 19 and 20, 1886, p. 3.
47. Ibid., February 3, 1899, p. 4; July 15, 1892, p. 4; May 20, 1892, p. 4; July 14, 1888, p. 4; December 17, 1899, p. 3; September 3, 1887, p. 4.
48. Ibid., December 29, 1900, p. 4; March 15, 1896, p. 4; October 18, 1898, p. 3; May 4, 1900, p. 3; May 20, 1892, p. 4; April 16, 1894, p. 4.
49. Ibid., October 2, 1893, p. 4; July 30, 1899, p. 3; January 2, 1893, p. 4.
50. Ibid., April 21, 1888, p. 4; July 18, 1890, p. 4; January 15 and 17, 1887, p. 4.
51. *100 zangen voor het volk* (Ghent: Het Licht, [1908]), 3.
52. "From a Jacobin pin, 0.25," *Vooruit*, April 19, 1889, p. 4.
53. *100 zangen voor het volk*, 87.
54. *Vooruit*, July 17, 1886, p. 4.
55. Ibid., August 1, 1892, p. 4.
56. Ibid., September 15, 1888, p. 3 (my emphasis).
57. Ibid., July 18, 1890, p. 4.
58. Janet Louise Polasky, "A Revolution for Socialist Reforms: The Belgian General Strike for Universal Suffrage," *Journal of Contemporary History* 27, no. 3 (1992).
59. *Vooruit*, August 6, 1887, p. 4.
60. Hendrik Defoort, *Werklieden bemint uw profijt! De Belgische sociaaldemocratie in Europa* (Leuven: LannooCampus, 2006), 256–57.
61. *Vooruit*, September 4, 1887, p. 4.
62. Ibid., October 1, 1887, p. 4.
63. De Loting, *De Werker*, February 15, 1885; and *Vooruit*, January 19, 1887, p. 2.
64. *Vooruit*, August 15, 1890, p. 3.
65. Ibid., December 16, 1892, p. 3; October 3, 1892, p. 4.
66. Seventy-two tweets, however, referred to the "Marx circle," the Ghent socialist choir.

67. *Vooruit*, February 15, 1886, p. 4.
68. Ibid., February 18, 1888, p. 4; November 21, 1890, p. 4; December 1, 1893, p. 4.
69. Ibid., October 3, 1892, p. 4; August 14, 1891, p. 4; January 13, 1890, pp. 3–4; December 14, 1888, p. 4; December 21, 1888, p. 4; June 12 and 13, 1886, p. 4; April 1, 1899, p. 4.
70. Guy Vanschoenbeek, "De wortels van de sociaal-democratie in Vlaanderen: Le 'monde socialiste gantois' en de Gentse socialisten voor de Eerste Wereldoorlog" (PhD diss., Ghent University, 1992), 412, and appendix 6, p. 13.
71. *Vooruit*, November 25, 1897, p. 4; June 2, 1893, p. 4.
72. The following are from *Vooruit*: "Because as a flax worker I have to endure so much at work, 0.10," October 13, 1888, p. 3; "The foundry workers from the Metal Workers Union make great propaganda, bravo, men, 0.20," November 16, 1888, p. 4; "The bricklayers did not drink a pint of beer, and gave to the propaganda pence [instead], 0.50," May 6, 1887, p. 4; "A dock worker who will not forsake the red banner despite all the lies and dirt [from anti-socialists], 0.16," September 18, 1891, p. 4.
73. *Vooruit*, November 16, 1886, p. 4.
74. Ibid., August 15, 1890, p. 3.
75. Ibid., November 21, 1890, p. 4.
76. Ibid., November 4, 1892, p. 3.
77. Ibid., May 15 and 16, 1886, p. 4.
78. Ibid., February 15, 1886, p. 4.
79. Hendrik Defoort, "De derde arm: Socialisme en coöperatie in Europa voor 1914" (PhD diss., Ghent University, 2002), 236; Louis Varlez, "La Fédération ouvrière gantoise," *Musée social*, no. 1 (1899): 2.
80. *Vooruit*, July 19, 1889, p. 4.
81. Ibid., May 15, 1891, p. 4; November 17, 1893, p. 4.
82. Ibid., November 16, 1888, p. 4.
83. Ibid., September 1, 1888, p. 3; July 3, 1899, p. 4; July 14, 1888, p. 3; February 13, 1892, p. 4; October 16, 1886, p. 4.
84. Ibid., September 24, 1887, p. 4.
85. Ibid., April 15, 1886, p. 4; January 12, 1892, p. 4; August 18, 1888, p. 4; December 3, 1887, p. 4.
86. Ibid., July 30, 1887, p. 3.
87. Ibid., October 29, 1887, p. 4.
88. Ibid., June 12 and 13, 1886, p. 4; March 17, 1888, p. 4; September 24, 1887, p. 4; October 1, 1887, p. 4; October 15, 1896, p. 4.
89. Ibid., August 27, 1887, p. 4.
90. "Long live the Commune, 0.10," *Vooruit*, July 17, 1891, p. 4.
91. Maarten Van Ginderachter, *Het rode vaderland: De vergeten geschiedenis van de communautaire spanningen in het Belgische socialisme voor WO I* (Tielt/Ghent: Lannoo/Amsab, 2005), 365–68.

92. *Vooruit*, August 8, 1890, p. 4.
93. "Long live the German brothers, 0.50," *Vooruit*, March 5, 1887, p. 4.
94. Kevin Callahan, "'Performing Inter-Nationalism' in Stuttgart in 1907: French and German Socialist Nationalism and the Political Culture of an International Socialist Congress," *International Review of Social History* 45 (2000).
95. "Long live peace, 0.20," *Vooruit*, March 1, 1889, p. 4.
96. *Vooruit*, November 26, 1887, p. 4.
97. Ibid., April 12, 1886, p. 3.
98. Ibid., September 20, 1887, p. 4.
99. Ibid., January 16, 1891, p. 4.
100. "Collected in the Congo, after singing the song the First of May, by P.F.," *Vooruit*, June 13, 1892, p. 4; "Friends from the Congo, stay true to your word and come to the meeting Sunday July 27 at 4 in the afternoon at Verschuere's; the whole Congo has to be there: bravo to the bartender for keeping everything so tidy. 2.20," *Vooruit*, July 18, 1890, p. 4.
101. *Vooruit*, December 21, 1893, p. 4.
102. Ibid., June 14, 1892, p. 4.
103. Ibid., February 1, 1889, p. 4.
104. "Uit Menen," *Vooruit*, January 12, 1892, p. 4.
105. *Vooruit*, March 15, 1889, p. 4.
106. Dieter Groh, *Negative Integration und revolutionärer Attentismus: Die deutsche Sozialdemokratie am Vorabend des Ersten Weltkrieges* (Frankfurt am Main: Ullstein, 1973).
107. Polasky, "A Revolution for Socialist Reforms."
108. Van Ginderachter, *Het rode vaderland*; Vanschoenbeek, "De wortels van de sociaal-democratie in Vlaanderen"; Defoort, *Werklieden bemint uw profijt!*

## CHAPTER 9: LANGUAGE, THE FLEMISH MOVEMENT, AND THE NATION

1. *Vooruit*, July 1, 1892, p. 4 (my emphasis).
2. Kevin Callahan, "'Performing Inter-Nationalism' in Stuttgart in 1907: French and German Socialist Nationalism and the Political Culture of an International Socialist Congress," *International Review of Social History* 45 (2000).
3. On language relations within the BWP institutions, see Maarten Van Ginderachter, *Het rode vaderland: De vergeten geschiedenis van de communautaire spanningen in het Belgische socialisme voor WO I* (Tielt/Ghent: Lannoo/Amsab, 2005), 330–37.
4. Machteld De Metsenaere, *Taalmuur: Sociale muur? De negentiende-eeuwse taalverhoudingen te Brussel als resultaat van geodemografische en sociale processen* (Brussels: VUB Press, 1988), 25–26, 138–40.
5. POB, Fédération bruxelloise, *Rapports des secrétaires, Exercices 1912–1913* (Brussels, 1914), 78–79.
6. Statistics from Louis Bertrand, *Histoire de la démocratie et du socialisme en Belgique depuis 1830* (Brussels: Dechenne-Cornély, 1907), 2:378, 650; and

Bart De Nil, "Leest, leert, denkt en ontspan u!! De Vlaamse sociaal-democratie en de roman" (Master's thesis, Ghent University, 1997), 79, 87.

7. Gaston Durnez, "Taalminderheden: Vlamingen in Wallonië," in *Nieuwe encyclopedie van de Vlaamse beweging*, ed. Reginald De Schryver et al. (Tielt: Lannoo, 1998), 3:2974.

8. Yves Quairiaux, "Les 'Flaminds' avant 1914 en Wallonie: Du dénigrement à l'assimilation," in *L'image de l'autre dans l'Europe du Nord-Ouest à travers l'histoire: Actes du colloque Villeneuve d'Asq, 24–26 nov. 1994*, ed. Jean-Pierre Jessenne and Martine Aubry (Lille: 1996), 241.

9. Yves Quairiaux, "Le stéréotype du Flamand en Wallonie: Explications économiques et sociales (1880–1940)," in *Stéréotypes nationaux et préjugés raciaux aux XIXe et XXe siècles: Sources et méthodes pour une approche historique*, ed. Jean Pirotte (Louvain-La-Neuve: Collège Erasme Bureau du Recueil/ Editions Nauwelaerts, 1982), 150; Joël Michel, "Corporatisme et internationalisme chez les mineurs européens avant 1914," in *Internationalism in the Labour Movement 1830–1940*, ed. Frits Van Holthoon and Marcel Van der Linden (Leiden: E.J. Brill, 1988), 2:442; Frank Caestecker, "Vakbonden en etnische minderheden, een ambigue verhouding: Immigratie in de Belgische mijnbekkens 1900–1940," *Brood en Rozen*, no. 1 (1997): 53–54; Yves Quairiaux, "Présence flamande dans le Centre," in *Mémoires d'une région: Le Centre (1830–1914)* (Morlanwez: Musée royal de Mariemont, 1984), 201; Quairiaux, "Les 'Flaminds' avant 1914 en Wallonie," 251; Carl Strikwerda, *A House Divided: Catholics, Socialists, and Flemish Nationalists in Nineteenth-Century Belgium* (Lanham, MD: Rowman & Littlefield, 1997), 62, 201–2; Harry Van Velthoven and Els Witte, *Taal en politiek: De Belgische casus in een historisch perspectief* (Brussels: VUB Press, 1998), 34. Cf. John J. Kulczycki, *The Foreign Worker and the German Labor Movement: Xenophobia and Solidarity in the Coal Fields of the Ruhr, 1871–1914* (Oxford: Berg 1994).

10. *Vooruit*, May 31, 1905, p. 1.

11. *Annales parlementaires Chambre des représentants*, 1897–1898, March 11, 1898, pp. 834–35.

12. Van Ginderachter, *Het rode vaderland*, 330ff.

13. Aristide Zolberg, "The Making of Flemings and Walloons: Belgium 1830–1914," *Journal of Interdisciplinary History* 5, no. 2 (1974): 221.

14. Mark Deweerdt, "Taalgrens," in De Schryver et al., eds., *Nieuwe encyclopedie van de Vlaamse beweging*, 3:2949–62; De Metsenaere, *Taalmuur*; Kaat Louckx, "The Nation-State in Its State-istics (Belgium, 1846–1947)," *Nations and Nationalism* 23, no. 3 (2017): 511.

15. Gita Deneckere, "Gent," in De Schryver et al., eds., *Nieuwe encyclopedie van de Vlaamse beweging*, 2:1254.

16. Guy Vanschoenbeek, "De wortels van de sociaal-democratie in Vlaanderen: Le 'monde socialiste gantois' en de Gentse socialisten voor de Eerste Wereldoorlog" (PhD diss., Ghent University, 1992), 74.

17. *Vooruit*, November 22, 1889, p. 3; December 15, 1889, p. 3; April 28, 1899, p. 3; see in particular the propaganda pence of April and May 1899.

18. Maarten Van Ginderachter, "Vaderland in de Belgische Werkliedenpartij (1885–1914): Sociaal-democratie en nationale identiteit from below; Een casusstudie van Gent, Brussel en de Borinage" (PhD diss., Ghent University, 2005), 588.

19. "Long live the miners!," "Long live our Walloon brothers!," "Welcome!" De Borains te Gent, *Vooruit*, May 15, 1894, p. 3.

20. Camiel Lootens, *De geschiedenis van de Gentschen schildersbond: 1876–1926* (Ghent: Volksdrukkerij, 1926), 40.

21. *Vooruit*, July 13, 1900, p. 3.

22. J. De Graeve, "Eene vriendschappelijke opmerking," *De Volksschool* 1, issue 11 (April 1909): 3.

23. "Het Nederlandsch congres," *Vooruit*, August 25, 1891, p. 1.

24. "De Lockout der houtbewerkers en onze flaminganten," *Vooruit*, June 27, 1900, p. 1.

25. Van Swieten, principal of Municipal School No. 11 to the alderman of education of Ghent, April 16, 1886 (City Archives Ghent, U 398); see also L. Labaud, member of the board of the Municipal Evening School of the Nieuw Begijnhofstraat, to the alderman of education of Ghent, September 1895, and P. Van Hauwaert, principal of the Municipal School of the Begijnhofplaats, to the alderman of education of Ghent, June 11, 1895 (City Archives Ghent, U 417).

26. C., "Nog over adultenonderwijs," *De Volksschool* 3, issue 1 (June 1910).

27. *Vooruit*, January 18, 1889, p. 4.

28. Ibid., December 20, 1889, p. 3. See also ibid., December 20, 1895, p. 4.

29. Hans Mommsen, "Das Problem der internationalen Integration in der böhmischen Arbeiterbewegung," in *Arbeiterbewegung und Nationale Frage: Ausgewählte Aufsätze*, ed. Hans Mommsen (Göttingen: Vandenhoeck und Ruprecht, 1979), 170; Jakub Beneš, *Workers and Nationalism: Czech and German Social Democracy in Habsburg Austria, 1890–1918* (Oxford: Oxford University Press, 2016), 56, 60.

30. Harry Van Velthoven, "Onenigheid in de Belgische werkliedenpartij: De Vlaamse kwestie wordt een vrije kwestie (1894–1914)," *Belgisch tijdschrift voor nieuwste geschiedenis/Revue belge d'histoire contemporaine* 5, no. 1–2 (1974): 142.

31. Strikwerda, *A House Divided*, 314.

32. Maarten Van Ginderachter, "Social-Democracy and National Identity: The Ethnic Rift in the Belgian Workers' Party (1885–1914)," *International Review of Social History* 52, no. 2 (2007): 214–40.

33. The following are from *Vooruit*: "Om te sluiten," September 11, 1899, p. 1; "Weg met de charlatans," November 18, 1889, p. 1; "Ernstig werk voor de flaminganten," November 8, 1889, p. 1; "Brusschelsche Briefwisseling," March 26, 1889, p. 3.

34. *Vooruit*, June 18, 1896, p. 4.
35. Deneckere, "Gent," 1260.
36. On the Mother Tongue, see *Vooruit*, June 19 and 20, 1886, p. 3; see also *Vooruit*, August 13, 20, 27, 1887, p. 1; October 1, 1887, p. 4; November 16, 1888, p. 4. On the In Flanders Flemish café, see *Vooruit*, August 24, 1894, p. 4; see also *Vooruit*, December 11–12, 1886, p. 4; May 14, 1894, p. 3; February 1, 1895, p. 4; May 31, 1895, p. 4; May 17, 1896, p. 3; June 13, 1897, p. 4; August 26, 1898. See also Vanschoenbeek, "De wortels van de sociaal-democratie in Vlaanderen," appendix p. 128.
37. Gita Deneckere, *1900: België op het breukvlak van twee eeuwen* (Tielt: Lannoo, 2006), 192ff.
38. Zolberg, "The Making of Flemings and Walloons," 204.
39. Harry Van Velthoven, *De Vlaamse kwestie 1830–1914: Macht en onmacht van de Vlaamsgezinden* (Kortrijk: UGA 1982), 186–89.
40. Van Ginderachter, *Het rode vaderland*, 288–89.
41. "om de socialisten te kl . . . ." Gentil Comhaire, "Briefwisseling," *Vooruit*, September 28, 1911, p. 5.
42. Van Ginderachter, *Het rode vaderland*, 265–67.
43. Minutes of the Central Committee of the Ghent socialists, January 11, 1911, and January 29, 1911 (AMSAB, 32: 107/1); J.D.G., "Rond de vervlaamsching der Gentsche hoogeschool," *Vooruit*, January 14, 1911, p. 5; *Vooruit*, February 10 and 12, 1911, p. 1; "Grootsche meeting voor de Vlaamsche hoogeschool," *Vooruit*, February 21 and 22, 1911, p. 5; Albéric Deswarte, "Flamandisons l'université de Gand: Réponse à Emile Vandervelde," *Le Peuple*, March 8, 1911; "De Ontvangst op het stadhuis + Vlaanderen's kunstdag," *Vooruit*, July 18 and 19, 1911, p. 5.
44. "De Vlaamsche hoogschool: Voordracht gehouden in ons Huis op zondag 18 december 1910 door gezel Joh. Lefevre," *Vooruit*, December 22 and 23, 1910, p. 1.
45. Vanschoenbeek, "De wortels van de sociaal-democratie in Vlaanderen," 337.
46. The figure on party membership is from ibid., 723. "Algemeene bestuursvergadering van den 4 March: De vervlaamsching der Gentsche hoogeschool gestemd," *Vooruit*, March 7, 1911, p. 6; March 8, 1911, p. 5
47. *Vooruit*, January 27, 1886, p. 4 (my emphasis).
48. Danny Beckers, *Het despotisme der mathesis: Opkomst van de propaedeutische functie van de wiskunde in Nederland, 1750–1850* (Hilversum: Verloren, 2003), 104.
49. Paul De Witte, *De geschiedenis van Vooruit en de Gentsche socialistische werkersvereeniging sedert 1870* (Ghent: A. Hoste, 1898), 561.
50. Ibid., 62.
51. "'De expositie van Parijs,' 'De kl . . . ,' 23 juni 1876, 'Boulanger,'" in

*Verzameling der volledige kluchtige en politieke liederen van Karel Waeri* (Ghent: Geschiedkundige heruitgeverij, 2001 [1899]), 4–8, 400–406, 116–19.

52. Callahan, 'Performing Inter-Nationalism' in Stuttgart in 1907."
53. *Vooruit*, November 4, 1884, p. 4.
54. Ibid., November 4, 1884, p. 4; November 6, 1884, p. 4.
55. Ibid., November 6, 1884, p. 4; "German socialists, persevere in your struggle, the Belgians will follow you, R.D.E.A., 2 fr.," *Vooruit*, November 7, 1884, p. 3.
56. Vanschoenbeek, "De wortels van de sociaal-democratie in Vlaanderen," 190.
57. Eric Vanhaute, "Leven, wonen en werken in onzekere tijden: Patronen van bevolking en arbeid in België in de 'lange negentiende eeuw,'" *Bijdragen en mededelingen betreffende de geschiedenis der Nederlanden* 118, no. 2 (2003): 159.
58. *Vooruit*, November 21, 1890, p. 4.
59. Hendrik Defoort, *Werklieden bemint uw profijt! De Belgische sociaaldemocratie in Europa* (Leuven: LannooCampus, 2006), 291–92.
60. *Vooruit*, August 15, 1890, p. 4 (my emphasis).
61. Pamphlet, *Grand meeting en flamand et en français*, February 21, 1913 (my emphasis) (Departmental Archives of the Nord in Lille, Série M.630/20).
62. *Vooruit*, June 11, 1886, p. 4 (my emphasis).
63. Ibid., August 23, 1886, p. 4.
64. Ibid., March 24, 1885, p. 4.
65. Ibid., November 13–14, 1886, p. 4. Falleur and Schmidt were Walloon labor leaders who had been convicted for inciting the 1886 Spring riots in Wallonia.
66. Ibid., December 7, 1894, p. 4.
67. Ibid., February 18, 1888, p. 4 (my emphasis).
68. Ibid., August 27, 1887, p. 4.
69. Ibid., November 27–28, 1886, p. 4. See also ibid., October 26, 1888, p. 4.
70. Ibid., November 17, 1899, p. 3. See also ibid., April, 1887, p. 4; ibid., February 26, 1887, p. 4.
71. Ibid., October 16, 1886, p. 4.
72. Ibid., May 15–16, 1886, p. 4 (my emphasis).
73. Ibid., August 17, 1886, p. 4 (my emphasis); see also ibid., March 23, 1885, p. 4.
74. Quoted by Frank Uytterhaegen and Guy Vanschoenbeek, "Nawoord," in Jozef Volckaert, *En dat alles voor een paar tirannen: Herinneringen van een socialistische arbeider, met aantekeningen en een naschrift van Frank Uytterhaegen en Guy Vanschoenbeek* (Leuven: Kritak, 1983), 112.
75. Raymond C. Sun, "'Hammer Blows': Work, the Workplace, and the Culture of Masculinity among Catholic Workers in the Weimar Republic," *Central European History* 37, no. 2 (2004): 249.

76. X., "België is slechter als Turkije," in *100 zangen voor het volk* (Ghent: Het Licht, [1908]), 33.
77. X., "Kent gij dat land?," in ibid., 95–96.
78. Emile Moyson, "Werkmanslied," in ibid., 5; Hendrik Van Offel, "Het Kanalje," in ibid., 3–4.
79. X., "De roode vaan," in ibid., 51; X., "De arme dichter," in ibid., 99–100; Emiel Moyson, "Het stemrecht voor elkeen," in ibid., 19–20.
80. "Neringen en Gilden [. . .] wilden wat was regt, en wonnen wat zy wilden."
81. "De Vlaamsche Landdag te Gent," *Vooruit*, December 26, 1891, p. 1.
82. E.V.B., *Vlamingen! Algemeen stemrecht: Strijdblad uitgegeven ter gelegenheid van den Vlaamschen Landdag op 25 december 1891 bijeengeroepen te Gent* (pamphlet), 1891, p. 1.
83. *Vooruit*, March 17, 1888, p. 4; April 21, 1888, p. 4; February 18, 1888, p. 4; February 3, 1893, p. 4; July 16, 1897, p. 4.
84. Ibid., December 26, 1891, p. 2.
85. Marnix Beyen, "Literatuur als vlag: Hendrik Conscience en de choreografie van de massa," *Verslagen en mededelingen van de Koninklijke Academie voor Nederlandse Taal- en Letterkunde* 123, no. 2–3 (2013); Tom Verschaffel, "De Brabançonne en de Vlaamse Leeuw," in *Nationale hymnen: Het Wilhelmus en zijn buren*, ed. Louis Peter Grijp (Nijmegen: SUN, 1998).
86. Jo Tollebeek and Tom Verschaffel, "Guldensporenslag," in De Schryver et al., eds., *Nieuwe encyclopedie van de Vlaamse beweging*, 2:1382–86.
87. *Vooruit*, October 26, 1886, p. 4.
88. Ibid., May 12, 1888, p. 3.
89. Ibid., April 5, 1889, p. 3.
90. Ibid., January 30 and 31, 1886, p. 4.
91. Ibid., November 21, 1890, p. 4 (my emphasis).
92. "Voor de stemming," *Vooruit*, June 13, 1892.
93. *Sociaal-demokratische liederen en gedichten: Uitgave der Belgische socialistische arbeiderspartij (Afdeeling Gent)* (Ghent, 1881).
94. Hendrik Vandecaveye, "Het Gentse proletariërslied, 1860–1914: Historische situering van een sociaal-kulturele verschijningsvorm van de arbeidersbeweging" (Master's thesis, Ghent University, 1978), 81.
95. "Onze Vlaamsche leeuw," in *Sociaal-demokratische liederen en gedichten*, 45–46 (my emphasis).
96. "Geslagen en tevreden," *Vooruit*, July 25, 1892, p. 1.
97. "Het Sedan der dompers," *Vooruit*, July 25, 1892, p. 1.
98. *Vooruit*, July 29, 1892, p. 4.

**EPILOGUE: THE FIRST WORLD WAR**

1. Georges Haupt, *Socialism and the Great War: The Collapse of the Second International* (Oxford: Clarendon, 1972), 2.

2. Antoon Vrints, "Eenheid in verdeeldheid: Tegenstellingen in België tijdens de 1ste WO," *Belgisch tijdschrift voor nieuwste geschiedenis/Revue belge d'histoire contemporaine* 44, no. 2–3 (2014): 30–31.

3. Bruno Benvindo and Benoît Majerus, "Belgien zwischen 1914 und 1918: Ein Labor für den totalen Krieg," in *Durchhalten! Krieg und Gesellschaft im Vergleich 1914–1918*, ed. Arnd Bauerkämper and Elise Julien (Göttingen: Vandenhoeck Ruprecht, 2010), 141. On the German atrocities, see John Horne and Alan Kramer, *German Atrocities, 1914: A History of Denial* (New Haven, CT: Yale University Press, 2001).

4. Benvindo and Majerus, "Belgien zwischen 1914 und 1918," 127; Vrints, "Eenheid in Verdeeldheid," 13.

5. Bruno Benvindo, *Des hommes en guerre: Les soldats belges entre ténacité et désillusion, 1914–1918* (Brussels: Archives générales du royaume, 2005), 34.

6. Sophie De Schaepdrijver, *La Belgique et la Première Guerre mondiale* (Brussels: Archives & Musée de la Littérature, 2004), 116.

7. My account of wartime deprivation is mainly based on Giselle Nath, *Brood willen we hebben! Honger, sociale politiek en protest tijdens de Eerste Wereldoorlog in België* (Antwerp: Manteau, 2013).

8. Mandy Nauwelaerts, "De socialistische syndikale beweging na de Eerste Wereldoorlog (1919–1921)," *Belgisch tijdschrift voor nieuwste geschiedenis/Revue belge d'histoire contemporaine* 4, no. 3–4 (1973): 345.

9. Branden Little, "Commission for Relief in Belgium (CRB)," in *1914–1918-Online: International Encyclopedia of the First World War*, ed. Ute Daniel et al. (Berlin: Freie Universität Berlin, 2014), https://encyclopedia.1914-1918-online.net/home/.

10. Peter Scholliers and F. Daelemans, "Standards of Living and Standards of Health in Wartime Belgium," in *The Upheaval of War: Family, Work and Welfare in Europe, 1914–1918*, ed. Jay Winter and R. Wall (Cambridge: Cambridge University Press, 1988), 145.

11. J. Demoor and A. Slosse, "L'alimentation des Belges pendant la guerre et les conséquences," *Bulletin de l'Académie royale de Médecine de Belgique* 30 (1920): 506. Referenced by Nath, *Brood willen we hebben!*

12. Comité National de Secours et d'Alimentation/Nationaal Hulp- en Voedingskomiteit.

13. Geert Van Goethem and Wouter Steenhaut, *Wording en strijd van het socialistisch vakverbond van Antwerpen* (Antwerp: AMSAB, 1994), 55; Leo Picard, "Tussen de twee wereldoorlogen," in *Geschiedenis van de socialistische arbeidersbeweging in België*, ed. Jan Dhondt (Antwerp: Ontwikkeling, 1960–1968), 494.

14. Vrints, "Eenheid in verdeeldheid."

15. Marcel Liebman, *Les socialistes belges 1914–1918: Le P.O.B. face à la guerre* (Brussels: Vie ouvrière, 1986), 13; Dieter Groh and Peter Brandt, *Vaterlandslose Gesellen: Sozialdemokratie und Nation 1860–1990* (Munich: Beck, 1992), 85; Paul Ward, *Red Flag and Union Jack: Englishness, Patriotism, and the*

*British Left, 1881–1924* (Rochester, NY: Royal Historical Society/Boydell Press, 1998), 141, 61.

16. Maarten Van Ginderachter, "Democratisering en nationale integratie in de Belgische Werkliedenpartij (1890–1920)," in *Natie en democratie–Nation et démocratie (1890–1921), Acta van het interuniversitair colloquium, Brussel 8–9 Juni 2006*, edited by Els Witte et al. (Brussels: Koninklijke Vlaamse Academie van België voor Wetenschappen en Kunsten, 2007).

17. Barbara Deruytter, "The Layering of Belgian National Identities during the First World War," in *Nations, Identities and the First World War: Shifting Loyalties to the Fatherland*, ed. Nico Wouters and Laurence Van Ypersele (London: Bloomsbury, 2018). See also ongoing research by Barbara Deruytter at Ghent University.

18. Benvindo and Majerus, "Belgien zwischen 1914 und 1918," 140.

19. The Stockholm conference of 1917 was an unsuccessful attempt to resuscitate the Second Socialist International on the basis of a program of permanent world peace.

20. Mieke Sertyn, "Het socialistisch aktivisme tijdens de Eerste Wereldoorlog," *Belgisch tijdschrift voor nieuwste geschiedenis/Revue belge d'histoire contemporaine* 7, no. 1–2 (1976); Daniël Vanacker, *Het activistisch avontuur* (Ghent: Stichting Mens en Kultuur, 1991); Maarten Van Ginderachter, *Het rode vaderland: De vergeten geschiedenis van de communautaire spanningen in het Belgische socialisme voor WO I* (Tielt/Ghent: Lannoo/Amsab, 2005), 359–64; Mieke Claeys-Van Haegendoren, *25 jaar Belgisch socialisme: Evolutie van de verhouding van de Belgische Werkliedenpartij tot de parlementaire democratie in België van 1914 tot 1940* (Antwerp: Standaard, 1967), 66, 72, 101–2.

21. See in particular Sophie De Schaepdrijver, "Occupation, Propaganda, and the Idea of Belgium," in *European Culture in the Great War*, ed. Aviel Roshwald and Richard Stites (Cambridge: Cambridge University Press, 1999).

22. Benvindo, *Des hommes en guerre*, 63–72; Antoon Vrints and Martin Schoups, *De overlevenden: De Belgische oud-strijders tijdens het interbellum* (Antwerp: Polis, 2019).

23. Benvindo and Majerus, "Belgien zwischen 1914 und 1918," 136.

24. De Schaepdrijver, *La Belgique et la Première Guerre mondiale*.

25. Frank Caestecker and Antoon Vrints, "The National Mobilisation of German Immigrants and Their Descendants in Belgium, 1870–1920," in *Germans as Minorities during the First World War: A Global Comparative Perspective*, ed. Panikos Panayi (Burlington, VT: Ashgate, 2014).

26. Deruytter, "The Layering of Belgian National Identities during the First World War."

27. "A l'Armée de la Nation-Aan het leger van de Natie," *Moniteur Belge/Belgisch Staatsblad*, August 7, 1914.

28. De Schaepdrijver, "Occupation, Propaganda, and the Idea of Belgium," 291.

29. Michel Dumoulin et al., *Nieuwe geschiedenis van België*, vol. 2, *1905–1950* (Tielt: Lannoo, 2006), 920.

30. Patrick Pasture, "The Temptations of Nationalism: Regionalist Orientations in the Belgian Christian Labour Movement," in *Working-Class Internationalism and the Appeal of National Identity: Historical Debates and Current Perspectives*, ed. Patrick Pasture and Johan Verberckmoes (Oxford: Berg, 1998); Lode Wils, "De historische verstrengeling tussen de christelijke arbeidersbeweging en de Vlaamse beweging," *Vlaanderen, België, Groot-Nederland: Mythe en geschiedenis; Historische opstellen, gebundeld en aangeboden aan de schrijver bij het bereiken van zijn emeritaat als hoogleraar aan de K.U. Leuven* (Leuven: Davidsfonds, 1994).

31. Antoon Vrints, "'All the Butter in the Country Belongs to Us, Belgians': Well-Being and Lower-Class National Identification in Belgium during the First World War," in *Nationhood from Below: Europe in the Long Nineteenth Century*, ed. Maarten Van Ginderachter and Marnix Beyen (Basingstoke: Palgrave Macmillan, 2012).

32. Bruno De Wever, *Greep naar de macht: Vlaams-nationalisme en nieuwe orde; Het VNV 1933–1945* (Tielt: Lannoo, 1994), 220–21.

33. Vrints, "'All the Butter in the Country Belongs to Us, Belgians,'" 238.

34. See in particular Lode Wils, *Flamenpolitik en aktivisme: Vlaanderen tegenover België in de Eerste Wereldoorlog* (Leuven: Davidsfonds, 1974); Lode Wils, "Het aandeel van de 'Flamenpolitik' in de Vlaamse natievorming," *Belgisch tijdschrift voor nieuwste geschiedenis/Revue belge d'histoire contemporaine* 44, no. 2–3 (2015); Vanacker, *Het activistisch avontuur*; Lode Wils, *Onverfranst, onverduitst? Flamenpolitik, activisme, frontbeweging* (Kapellen: Pelckmans, 2014).

35. Wils, "Het aandeel van de 'Flamenpolitik' in de Vlaamse natievorming," 218; Harry Van Velthoven, *Scheurmakers en carrièristen: De opstand van christendemocraten en katholieke flaminganten, 1890–1914* (Kapellen: Uitgeverij Pelckmans, 2014).

36. Jeremy King, "The Nationalization of East Central Europe: Ethnicism, Ethnicity, and Beyond," in *Staging the Past: The Politics of Commemoration in Habsburg Central Europe, 1848 to the Present*, ed. Maria Bucur and Nancy M. Wingfield (West Lafayette, Indiana: Purdue University Press, 2001).

37. Pieter M. Judson, *Guardians of the Nation: Activists on the Language Frontiers of Imperial Austria* (Cambridge, MA: Harvard University Press, 2006), 9.

38. Miroslav Hroch, *Social Preconditions of National Revival in Europe: A Comparative Analysis of the Social Composition of Patriotic Groups among the Smaller European Nations* (Cambridge: Cambridge University Press, 2000 [1985]).

39. Miroslav Hroch, "From National Movement to the Fully-Formed Nation: The Nation-Building Process in Europe," in *Mapping the Nation*, ed. Gopal Balakrishnan (London: Verso, 1996), 81.

40. Hroch, *Social Preconditions of National Revival in Europe*, 11.

41. Judson, *Guardians of the Nation*, 12–13.
42. Ibid., 24–25.
43. Ibid., 168.
44. Maarten Van Ginderachter and Minte Kamphuis, "The Transnational Dimensions of the Early Socialist Pillars in Belgium and the Netherlands, c. 1885–1914: An Exploratory Essay," *Belgisch tijdschrift voor filologie en geschiedenis/Revue Belge de philologie et d'histoire* 90, no. 4 (2012): 113–29.
45. Tara Zahra, *Kidnapped Souls: National Indifference and the Battle for Children in the Bohemian Lands, 1900–1948* (Ithaca, NY: Cornell University Press, 2008), 67.
46. See John Deák, *Forging a Multinational State: State Making in Imperial Austria from the Enlightenment to the First World War* (Stanford, CA: Stanford University Press, 2015), 262ff.
47. John W. Boyer, "Silent War and Bitter Peace: The Revolution of 1918 in Austria," *Austrian History Yearbook* 34 (January 2003): 11; Jakub Beneš, *Workers and Nationalism: Czech and German Social Democracy in Habsburg Austria, 1890–1918* (Oxford: Oxford University Press, 2016), 219.
48. Judson, *Guardians of the Nation*, 227–28.
49. Rogers Brubaker et al., *Nationalist Politics and Everyday Ethnicity in a Transylvanian Town* (Princeton, NJ: Princeton University Press, 2006), 11.

# BIBLIOGRAPHY

**ARCHIVAL SOURCES**

AMSAB. Institute for Social History, Ghent. 9.1: Karel Hannick; 17: SM Het licht Gent; 32: BSP-federatie Gent-Eeklo; 47: Socialistische vrijdenkersbond Gent; 52: Avanti; 60: Fonds Edward Anseele; 118: Minutes of the National Party Council and Bureau of the BWP; 176: Charles Dineur; 191: Bond voor het Algemeen Stemrecht; 202: Massart Théophile; 204: Fédération des mutualités socialistes du Centre; 487: César De Paepe.

Archives of the préfecture de police of Paris. Fonds Ba: documents provenant principalement du 1er Bureau du Cabinet Ba 197. Le socialisme en Belgique 1873-1891. Ba 911-912, Ba 1474, Ba 1510.

Archives of the Université Libre de Bruxelles. Fonds Defuisseaux.

City Archives Antwerp. MA 541/5, 6, 7, 2993, Rapporten over werkstakingen.

City Archives Brussels. Fonds Politie, Pol. 176-178, 193-195, 209, 211, 214, 215; Fonds Instruction publique, I.P. and I.P. II; Fonds Bienfaisance publique.

City Archives Ghent. Reeks R: Politie; Reeks U: Onderwijs.

City Archives Liège. Sûreté publique de la province de Liège, carton (manifestations) XLII-LXIX.

Departmental Archives of the Nord in Lille. Série M: autorités, élections, police politique, police de la sûreté, police administrative, etc. M151, M154, M162, M169, M619, M630.

General National Archives, Brussels. Ministerie van Justitie, Administration de la sûreté publique 137-143; Ministerie van Justitie, Bestuur van de Wetgeving, 2, 3, 12; MF 751/1-2, Archives du Parti socialiste Mons; MF 775, Danhier, Alfred; MF 781, Delattre, Achille; MF 1004/1-11, Archives de la fédération des métallurgistes du Borinage (1913-1960); MF 1329, Institut Belge de science Politique, Papiers Paul Conreur (1883-1947); MF 1392, Institut Belge de science Politique, Archives de Mr Walter Thibaut; MF 1405, En avant pour le SU; MF 1427, La Liberté; MF 1510, Broqueville, Charles de; MF 2134 192, manuscript: Commissariat de police en chef, Ville de Liège, Service de la sûreté, Dossier mouvement socialiste et anarchiste à Liège de 1878 à 1888, 1888.

Institut Emile Vandervelde, Brussels. Archives Emile Vandervelde, Abs, Robert, Catalogue I et III, Lettres, documents, manuscrits, etc., 1969, 1972

National Archives Anderlecht. Provinciaal bestuur van Brabant. Kabinet van de gouverneur (1846–1944). I. Affaires politiques en II. Fêtes et cérémonies publiques; Hof van Beroep Brussel, Dossiers des appels en matière correctionnelle, 1885–1891 in Parket-generaal bij het Hof van Beroep te Brussel 210–48.

National Archives Beveren-Waas. Archief Provincie Oost-Vlaanderen, Openbare orde en veiligheid, Onlusten.

National Archives Liège. Sûreté publique de la province de Liège, Première partie, XIV.A.36–229, XV.A.46–47, 81.

National Archives Mons. Commune de Jemappes Fonds I et II; Commune de Wasmes; Commune de Cuesmes; Cours d'assises du Hainaut, 1898/18 no. 166.

Royal Army Museum, Brussels. Fonds 21, Intervention of the armed forces to maintain order: 1834–1912.

Royal Palace Archives, Brussels. Cabinet Leopold II, General part 1181, 1188, 1285, 2039, 2040, 2055–57, 2058, 2070–84, 2085, 2086, 2122, 2123, 2124; Cabinet Leopold II, Commandments of the King, G Secours, gratifications et inscriptions 64/25, Dossier Antoine Mertens; Cabinet Albert I, Archives of the cabinet of King Albert (1909–1914 and 1919–1934), 1–27, 278–279, 398; Cabinet Albert I, Secretariat "Commandements du roi" (1909–1923), G/102 Demandes de secours, gratifications, souscriptions; Secretariat of Queen Elisabeth (1900–1965), 227–28, and Secours I; Private secretariats Albert and Elisabeth; 332; Secretariat "Commandements Prince Albert" (1900–1909), 1–43; Secretariat of Prince Albert and Princess Elisabeth, 68–72, 78–79.

**PRESS**

*De Afrosser*. Antwerp, 1912–1913.
*De Arbeid*. Antwerp, 1902 and 1906.
*De Bouwnijverheid*. Antwerp, 1892.
*De Bouwwerker*. Antwerp, 1908–1913.
*De Diamantbewerker*. Antwerp, 1895–1901 and 1904–1907.
*De Dokker*. Antwerp, 1902–1903.
*De Dokwerker*. Antwerp, 1907–1908.
*De Dokwerkersgazet van Antwerpen*. Antwerp, 1894.
*De Gazet van Brussels. Weekblad voor het arrondissement*. Brussels, 1903–1912.
*De Jonge Wacht*. Antwerp, 1891.
*De Klopper*. Antwerp, 1902.

*De Metaalbewerker.* Antwerp, 1906–1907.
*De Moyson's bode.* Antwerp, 1906, 1909, 1913.
*De Schijvenschuurder.* Antwerp, 1898, 1908, 1910.
*De Sociaal-Demokraat.* Antwerp, 1909.
*De Strijd.* Antwerp, 1906.
*De Transportarbeider.* Antwerp, 1914.
*De Wacht.* Antwerp, 1892–1897.
*De Werker.* Antwerp, 1895–1914.
*En avant pour le Suffrage universel.* Borinage, 1886–1887.
*Kosmos.* Antwerp, 1895, 1901–1902.
*L'Avant-garde. Organe du Parti ouvrier belge. Journal hebdomadaire.* Brussels, 1887.
*L'Avenir du Borinage et de l'Arrondissement de Mons. Organe quotidien officiel de la Fédération socialiste boraine.* Borinage, 1904–1914.
*L'Avenir social. Revue du Parti ouvrier belge.* Brussels, 1896–1907.
*L'Étincelle. Bulletin mensuel de la Centrale du personnel enseignant socialiste de Belgique.* Brussels, 1913–1914.
*L'Étoile socialiste. Revue populaire hebdomadaire du socialisme International/ Revue hebdomadaire du socialisme International.* Brussels, 1894–1898.
*La Bataille. Organe de la démocratie socialiste républicaine.* Borinage, 1895.
*La Bataille. Organe hebdomadaire du Parti socialiste belge/du Parti socialiste républicain/Organe socialiste républicain.* Borinage, 1889–1891.
*La Jeunesse c'est l'avenir. Organe de propagande et d'éducation de la Fédération wallonne des Jeunes Gardes socialistes belges (des provinces du Hainaut et de Namur).* 1908–1913.
*La Jeunesse socialiste. Organe de propagande et d'éducation de la Fédération Nationale des Jeunes Gardes socialistes.* 1903–1904.
*La Liberté. Organe de la démocratie ouvrière du Hainaut/de la démocratie ouvrière.* Borinage, 1888–1889.
*La Maison de Verre. Organe officieux de l'administration communale de Quaregnon.* 1909.
*La République belge. Organe hebdomadaire du Parti socialiste républicain.* Borinage, 1887–1888.
*La République. Organe hebdomadaire du Parti républicain belge.* Borinage, 1889.
*La République. Organe quotidien de la démocratie socialiste belge.* Borinage, 1895.
*Le Combat. Organe socialiste républicain.* Borinage, 1887.
*Le Cri du Peuple. Organe socialiste.* Borinage, 1891.
*Le Droit du Peuple. Organe hebdomadaire socialiste.* Borinage, 1891.
*Le Journal de Charleroi.* 1896–1897.
*Le Mouvement Communal. Bulletin de la Fédération des conseillers communaux*

du Parti Ouvrier/Revue mensuelle de la Fédération des conseillers communaux du Parti Ouvrier. Brussels, 1905–1908, 1912.

Le Peuple. Organe quotidien de la démocratie socialiste. Brussels, 1885–1914.

Le Suffrage universel. Organe socialiste quotidien/Organe hebdomadaire socialiste borain/Organe socialiste républicain/Organe officiel de la Fédération socialiste. Borinage, 1891–1903.

Ontwapening. Antwerp, 1901.

Onze Strijd. Antwerp, 1903, 1906–1907.

Vooruit. Ghent, 1884–1914.

### LITERATURE

100 zangen voor het volk. Ghent: Het Licht, [1908].

Aerts, Remieg. "Een andere geschiedenis: Een beschouwing over de scheiding van 1830." In *De erfenis van 1830*, edited by Peter Rietbergen and Tom Verschaffel, 15–33. Leuven: Acco, 2006.

Altena, Bert. "Een broeinest der anarchie: Arbeiders, arbeidersbeweging en maatschappelijke ontwikkeling: Vlissingen 1875–1929 (1940)." PhD diss., Amsterdam University, 1989.

Amsden, Alice H. *The Rise of "The Rest": Challenges to the West from Late-Industrializing Economies.* Oxford: Oxford University Press, 2001.

Anderson, Benedict. *Imagined Communities: Reflections on the Origin and Spread of Nationalism.* London: Verso, 1994 [1983].

Anseele, Edouard. *De omwenteling van 1830: Historische roman.* Ghent: Hage, 1882.

Applegate, Celia. *A Nation of Provincials: The German Idea of Heimat.* Berkeley: University of California Press, 1990.

Arnaut, Katrien. "De ontwikkeling van de socialistische bibliotheken te Gent tussen 1830 en 1890." *Amsab-tijdingen* 3, no. 1–2 (1984): 45–56.

Art, Jan. "Social Control in Belgium: The Catholic Factor." In *Social Control in Europe, 1800–2000*, vol. 2, edited by Clive Emsley, Eric Johnson, and Pieter Spierenburg, 112–24. Columbus: Ohio State University Press, 2004.

———. "Van 'klerikalisme' naar 'katholieke zuil' of van 'régime clérical' naar 'CVP-staat': Een benadering van het Vlaams georganiseerd katholicisme in de nieuwste tijd." *Belgisch tijdschrift voor nieuwste geschiedenis/Revue belge d'histoire contemporaine* 13, no. 1 (1982): 1–21.

Avanti. *Een terugblik: Proeve eener geschiedenis der Gentsche arbeidersbeweging gedurende de 19de eeuw, met naschrift door E. Anseele.* Ghent: Volksdrukkerij, 1908.

Bairoch, Paul, and Gary Goertz. "Factors of Urbanisation in the Nineteenth Century Developed Countries: A Descriptive and Econometric Analysis." *Urban Studies* 23, no. 4 (1986): 285–305.

Balthazar, Herman. "De Gentse werkersverenigingen in 1887." *Handelingen der Maatschappij voor Geschiedenis en Oudheidkunde te Gent* 18 (1964): 59–99.

———. "100 jaar dagblad Vooruit." *Amsab-tijdingen* 3, no. 1–2 (1984–1985): 9–21.
Bechet, Christophe. "Traverser la Belgique? De L'Indépendance au Plan Schlieffen (1839–1905)." PhD diss., Université de Liège, 2012.
Beckers, Danny. *Het despotisme der mathesis: Opkomst van de propaedeutische functie van de wiskunde in Nederland, 1750–1850*. Hilversum: Verloren, 2003.
Beneš, Jakub. *Workers and Nationalism: Czech and German Social Democracy in Habsburg Austria, 1890–1918*. Oxford: Oxford University Press, 2016.
Benvindo, Bruno. *Des hommes en guerre: Les soldats belges entre ténacité et désillusion, 1914–1918*. Brussels: Archives générales du royaume, 2005.
Benvindo, Bruno, and Benoît Majerus. "Belgien zwischen 1914 und 1918: Ein Labor Für den totalen Krieg." In *Durchhalten! Krieg und Gesellschaft im Vergleich 1914–1918*, edited by Arnd Bauerkämper and Elise Julien, 127–48. Göttingen: Vandenhoeck Ruprecht, 2010.
Berger, Stefan. "British and German Socialists between Class and National Solidarity." In *Nationalism, Labour and Ethnicity 1870–1939*, edited by Stefan Berger and Angel Smith, 31–63. Manchester: Manchester University Press, 1999.
Berger, Stefan, and Angel Smith, eds. *Nationalism, Labour and Ethnicity 1870–1939*. Manchester: Manchester University Press, 1999.
Bertrand, Louis. *Histoire de la démocratie et du socialisme en Belgique depuis 1830*, vol. 2. Brussels: Dechenne-Cornély, 1907.
Beyen, Marnix. "Belgium: A Nation That Failed to Become Ethnic." In *Statehood Before and Beyond Ethnicity: Minor States in Northern and Eastern Europe*, edited by Linas Eriksonas and Leos Müller, 341–52. New York: Lang, 2005.
———. "Een wankele basis voor de natie: Verkiezingen en nationalisme in België, 1890–1920." In Witte et al., *Natie en democratie–Nation et démocratie (1890–1921)*, 21–31.
———. "Literatuur als vlag: Hendrik Conscience en de choreografie van de massa." *Verslagen en mededelingen van de Koninklijke Academie voor Nederlandse Taal- en Letterkunde* 123, no. 2–3 (2013): 121–38.
Beyen, Marnix, and Benoît Majerus. "Weak and Strong Nations in the Low Countries: National Historiography and Its 'Others' in Belgium, Luxembourg, and the Netherlands in the Nineteenth and Twentieth Centuries." In *The Contested Nation: Ethnicity, Class, Religion and Gender in National Histories*, edited by Stefan Berger and Chris Lorenz, 283–310. Basingstoke: Palgrave Macmillan, 2008.
Beyen, Marnix, and Maarten Van Ginderachter. "General Introduction: Writing the Mass into a Mass Phenomenon." In *Nationhood from Below: Europe in the Long Nineteenth Century*, edited by Maarten Van Ginderachter and Marnix Beyen, 3–22. Basingstoke: Palgrave Macmillan, 2012.

Billig, Michael. *Banal Nationalism*. London: Sage, 1995.
Bitsch, Marie-Thérèse. "La Belgique entre la France et l'Allemagne." In *France-Belgique, 1848–1914: Affinités, Ambiguïtés: Actes du colloque des 7, 8, 9 mai 1996*, edited by Marc Quaghebeur and Nicole Savy, 143–50. Brussels: Labor, 1997.
Bjork, James E. *Neither German nor Pole: Catholicism and National Indifference in a Central European Borderland*. Ann Arbor: University of Michigan Press, 2008.
Blanchard, Pascal, and Sandrine Lemaire. *Culture coloniale: La France conquise par son empire, 1871–1931*. Paris: Autrement, 2003.
Boekholt, P. "De onderwijswet van 1801 en het begin van de Staatszorg voor het onderwijs in Nederland." In *Tweehonderd jaar onderwijs en de zorg van de Staat*, edited by P. Boekholt, H. Van Crombrugge, N. L. Dodde and Jeffrey Tyssens, 3–10. Assen: Koninklijke Van Gorcum, 2002.
Bogaerts, Aimé. *Socialistische liederen, eerste bundel: Inleiding*. Ghent: Samenwerkende Volksdrukkerij, 1906.
Boijen, Richard. "Het leger als smeltkroes van de natie?." *Bijdragen tot de eigentijdse geschiedenis/Cahiers d'histoire du temps présent*, no. 3 (1997): 55–70.
Bolin, Per, and Christina Douglas. "'National Indifference' in the Baltic Territories? A Critical Assessment." *Journal of Baltic Studies* 48, no. 1 (2017): 13–22.
Bologne, Maurice. *L'insurrection prolétarienne de 1830 en Belgique*. Brussels: Eglantine 1929.
Bos, Dennis. *Waarachtige volksvrienden: De vroege socialistische beweging in Amsterdam 1848–1894*. Amsterdam: Bert Bakker, 2001.
Boyer, John W. "Silent War and Bitter Peace: The Revolution of 1918 in Austria." *Austrian History Yearbook* 34 (January 2003): 1–56.
Breuilly, John. "Introduction." In Ernest Gellner, *Nations and Nationalism*, xiii–liii. Oxford: Blackwell, 2006.
———. *Nationalism and the State*. 2nd ed. Manchester: Manchester University Press, 1993.
Brubaker, Rogers. "Ethnicity without Groups." *Archives Européennes de Sociologie* 43, no. 2 (2002): 163–89.
Brubaker, Rogers, Margit Feischmidt, Jon Fox, and Liana Grancea. *Nationalist Politics and Everyday Ethnicity in a Transylvanian Town*. Princeton, NJ: Princeton University Press, 2006.
Caestecker, Frank. "Vakbonden en etnische minderheden, een ambigue verhouding: Immigratie in de Belgische mijnbekkens 1900–1940." *Brood en Rozen*, no. 1 (1997): 51–63.
Caestecker, Frank, and Antoon Vrints. "The National Mobilisation of German Immigrants and Their Descendants in Belgium, 1870–1920." In *Germans as Minorities during the First World War: A Global Comparative Perspective*, edited by Panikos Panayi, 123–46. Burlington, VT: Ashgate, 2014.

Callahan, Kevin. "'Performing Inter-Nationalism' in Stuttgart in 1907: French and German Socialist Nationalism and the Political Culture of an International Socialist Congress." *International Review of Social History* 45 (2000): 51–87.

Cannadine, David. *Ornamentalism: How the British Saw Their Empire.* Oxford: Oxford University Press, 2001.

Carre, Anne, and Hugo Lettens. "De Kleine Zavel: Een polemiek over de zestiende eeuw." In *Mise en scène: Keizer Karel en de verbeelding van de negentiende eeuw*, edited by Robert Hoozee, Jo Tollebeek, and Tom Verschaffel, 59–63. Ghent: Mercatorfonds, 2000.

Catteeuw, Karl. "Als de muren konden spreken . . . : Schoolwandplaten en de geschiedenis van het Belgisch lager onderwijs." PhD diss., KU Leuven, 2005.

*Cent ans de chansons sociales, 1885–1985.* Brussels: PAC, 1985.

Chanet, Jean-François. *L'École républicaine et les petites patries.* Paris: Aubier, 1996.

Claeys-Van Haegendoren, Mieke. *25 jaar Belgisch socialisme: Evolutie van de verhouding van de Belgische Werkliedenpartij tot de parlementaire democratie in België van 1914 tot 1940.* Antwerp: Standaard, 1967.

Clark, Christopher M. "The New Catholicism and the European Culture Wars." In *Culture Wars: Secular–Catholic Conflict in Nineteenth-Century Europe*, edited by Christopher M. Clark and Wolfram Kaiser, 11–46. Cambridge: Cambridge University Press, 2003.

Clark, Christopher M., and Wolfram Kaiser, eds. *Culture Wars: Secular–Catholic Conflict in Nineteenth-Century Europe.* Cambridge: Cambridge University Press, 2003.

Cole, Laurence. "A proposito di 'Guardians of the Nation: Activists on the Frontiers of Imperial Austria' di Pieter M. Judson: Laurence Cole, 'Alla ricerca della frontiera linguistica: nazionalismo e identità nazionale nell'Austria imperiale.'" *Quaderni storici* 43, no. 2 (2008): 501–12.

———. *Military Culture and Popular Patriotism in Late Imperial Austria.* Oxford: Oxford University Press, 2014.

———. "Visions and Revisions of Empire: Reflections on a New History of the Habsburg Monarchy." *Austrian History Yearbook* 49 (2018): 261–80.

Colley, Linda. *Britons: Forging the Nation, 1707–1837.* New Haven, CT: Yale University Press, 1992.

Colls, Robert. "Architecture and Regional Identity." In *Sources of Regionalism in the Nineteenth Century: Architecture, Art and Literature*, edited by Linda Van Santvoort, Jan De Maeyer, and Tom Verschaffel, 17–31. Leuven: Universitaire Pers Leuven, 2008.

Confino, Alon. *The Nation as a Local Metaphor: Württemberg, Imperial Germany, and National Memory, 1871–1918.* Chapel Hill: University of North Carolina Press, 1997.

Conklin, Alice L. *A Mission to Civilize: The Republican Idea of Empire in France and West Africa, 1895–1930.* Stanford, CA: Stanford University Press, 1997.

Conway, Martin. *The Sorrows of Belgium: Liberation and Political Reconstruction, 1944–1947*. Oxford: Oxford University Press, 2012.
Coppein, Bart. *Dromen van een nieuwe samenleving: Intellectuele biografie van Edmond Picard*. Brussels: Larcier, 2011.
Coppens, Alexander. "Tussen beleid en administratieve praktijk: De implementatie van het Belgisch migratiebeleid in negentiende-eeuws Brussel." PhD diss., VUB, 2016.
Craeybeckx, Jan. *Arbeidersbeweging en Vlaamsgezindheid voor de Eerste Wereldoorlog*. Brussels: Koninklijke academie voor wetenschappen letteren en schone kunsten van België, 1978.
Dams, Kristof. "De constructie van de burger in het pedagogisch debat in België, 1879–1914." Master's thesis, Ghent University, 1995.
De Cock, Alfons. "De militaire loting." *Volkskunde* 7 (1894): 173–85.
De Haan, Ido. "Van staatszorg tot vrijheidsrecht: De Schoolstrijd in de Nederlandse politiek en samenleving." In *Tot burgerschap en deugd: Volksopvoeding in de negentiende eeuw*, edited by Nelleke Bakker, Rudolf Dekker, and Angélique Janssen, 81–103. Verloren: Hilversum, 2006.
De Keulenaer, Eline. "'Hij doet aanmerken dat hij van goed gedrag en zeden is': Public en hidden transcripts in Oost-Vlaamse armenbrieven 1882–1926." Master's thesis, Ghent University, 2007.
De Metsenaere, Machteld. *Taalmuur: Sociale muur? De negentiende-eeuwse taalverhoudingen te Brussel als resultaat van geodemografische en sociale processen*. Brussels: VUB Press, 1988.
De Metsenaere, Machteld, Els Deslé, Anja Detant, Ann Mares, Sabine Parmentier, and Luc Sieben. "Brussel." In De Schryver et al., *Nieuwe encyclopedie van de Vlaamse beweging*, 1:622–52.
De Mûelenaere, Nel. "Belgen, zijt gij ten strijde gereed? Militarisering in een neutrale natie, 1890–1914." PhD diss., Antwerp University, 2016.
——. "Van kazernevrees naar kazernelust? Het vrijwilligerssysteem in België." *Leidschrift* 32, no. 2 (2017): 75–93.
De Mûelenaere, Nel, and Josephine Hoegaerts, eds. "Country and Army in the Making: The Belgian Military in the Long Nineteenth Century." Special issue of *Journal of Belgian History* 46, Issue 2. Brussels, 2016.
De Nil, Bart. "Leest, leert, denkt en ontspan U!! De Vlaamse sociaal-democratie en de roman." Master's thesis, Ghent University, 1997.
De Rooy, Piet. "'Dat de evenaar noch naar links, noch naar rechts doorzwikke': De confessionelen en de moderne natie." In *Nederlandse politiek in historisch en vergelijkend perspectief*, edited by Uwe Becker, 69–93. Amsterdam: Het Spinhuis, 1993.
De Schaepdrijver, Sophie. *La Belgique et la Première Guerre mondiale*. Brussels: Archives & Musée de la Littérature, 2004.
——. "Occupation, Propaganda, and the Idea of Belgium." In *European Culture in the Great War*, edited by Aviel Roshwald and Richard Stites, 267–95. Cambridge: Cambridge University Press, 1999.

De Schryver, Reginald, Bruno De Wever, Gaston Durnez, Lieve Gevers, Pieter Van Hees, and Machteld De Metsenaere, eds. *Nieuwe encyclopedie van de Vlaamse beweging*, 3 vols. Tielt: Lannoo, 1998.

De Smaele, Henk. "Eclectisch en toch nieuw: De uitvinding van het Belgisch parlement in 1830–1831." *Bijdragen en mededelingen betreffende de geschiedenis der Nederlanden* 120, no. 3 (2005): 408–16.

———. "Omdat we uwe vrienden zijn: Religie en partij-identificatie, 1884–1914." PhD diss. University of Leuven, 2000.

———. "Politiek als hanengevecht of cerebraal systeem: Ideeën over politieke representatie en de invoering van de evenredige vertegenwoordiging in België (1899)." *Bijdragen en mededelingen betreffende de geschiedenis der Nederlanden* 114, no. 3 (1999): 328–57.

———. *Rechts Vlaanderen. Religie en stemgedrag in negentiende-eeuws België*. Leuven: Universitaire Pers Leuven, 2009.

De Sutter, Bart. "De Strijdpenning van Vooruit: Humor en identiteit bij de socialistische achterban in Gent (1886–1900)." *Vlaams marxistisch tijdschrift* 45, no. 4 (2012): 88–101.

———. "Humor 'from below' aan het einde van de 19e eeuw: Socialisten en 'strijdpenning' in 'Vooruit.'" *Brood en Rozen*, no. 1 (2010): 31–47.

———. "Over dompers, mouchards en papen: Constructie van identiteit, via humor; Casus: De Gentse socialistische strijdpenning in *Vooruit* (1886–1900)." Master's thesis, Ghent University, 2008.

De Sutter, Bart, and Maarten Van Ginderachter. "Working Class Voices from the Late Nineteenth Century: Propaganda Pence in a Socialist Paper in Ghent." *History Workshop Journal* 69, no. 1 (2010): 133–45.

De Vos, Luc. "De militaire diensplicht en haar rol binnen natievorming en democratie, 1890–1921." In Witte et al., *Natie en democratie–Nation et démocratie (1890–1921)*.

———. *Het effectief van de Belgische krijgsmacht en de militiewetgeving, 1830–1914*. Centrum Voor Militaire Geschiedenis, Bijdragen 20. Brussels: Koninklijk Legermuseum, 1985.

De Vries, Jan. *European Urbanization, 1500–1800*. London: Methuen, 1984.

De Vroede, Maurice. "De weg naar de algemene leerplicht in België." *Bijdragen en mededelingen betreffende de geschiedenis der Nederlanden* 85 (1970): 141–66.

De Weerdt, Denise. *Het verslagboek van de Gentse sectie van de Vlaamse socialistische partij in de jaren 1877–1878: Bijdrage tot de geschiedenis van de arbeidersbeweging*. Brussels: Paleis der Academiën, 1957.

De Wever, Bruno. *Greep naar de macht: Vlaams-nationalisme en nieuwe orde; Het VNV 1933–1945*. Tielt: Lannoo, 1994.

De Wilde, Bart. "Seks op en naast de werkvloer: De seksualiteitsbeleving van arbeiders en de houding van de vakbeweging." In *Begeerte heeft ons aangeraakt: Socialisten, sekse en seksualiteit*, 143–78. Ghent: Provinciebestuur van Oost-Vlaanderen, 1999.

De Witte, Paul. *Alles is omgekeerd: Hoe de werklieden vroeger leefden 1848–1918. Geannoteerd en van een nawoord voorzien door Helmut Gaus en Guy Vanschoenbeek*. Leuven: Kritak, 1986 [1924].

———. *De geschiedenis van Vooruit en de Gentsche socialistische werkersvereeniging sedert 1870*. Ghent: A. Hoste, 1898.

Deák, John. *Forging a Multinational State: State Making in Imperial Austria from the Enlightenment to the First World War*. Stanford, CA: Stanford University Press, 2015.

Defoort, Eric. "Het Belgische nationalisme vóór de Eerste Wereldoorlog." *Tijdschrift voor geschiedenis* 85, no. 4 (1972): 524–42.

Defoort, Hendrik. "De derde arm: Socialisme en coöperatie in Europa voor 1914." PhD diss., Ghent University, 2002.

———. *Werklieden bemint uw profijt! De Belgische sociaaldemocratie in Europa*. Leuven: LannooCampus, 2006.

Defoort, Hendrik, and Guy Vanschoenbeek. "Socialistische Partij." In De Schryver et al., *Nieuwe encyclopedie van de Vlaamse beweging*, 3:2777–89.

Delmaire, Danielle. "Antisémitisme des catholiques au vingtième siècle: De la revendication au refus." In *Catholicism, Politics and Society in Twentieth-Century France*, edited by Kay Chadwick, 26–46. Liverpool: Liverpool University Press, 2000.

Demoen, Erik, *Liederen der industriële revolutie: een exploratie doorheen de wereld van het volkslied en het populaire lied in de 19de eeuw*. 3 vols. Ghent: Ver. voor Industriële Archeol., 1987.

Deneckere, Gita. "1878–1905." In *Nieuwe geschiedenis van België*, vol. 1, 1830–1905, edited by Els Witte, Jean-Pierre Nandrin, Eliane Gubin, and Gita Deneckere, 443–664. Tielt: Lannoo, 2005.

———. *1900: België op het breukvlak van twee eeuwen*. Tielt: Lannoo, 2006.

———. "Gent." In De Schryver et al., *Nieuwe encyclopedie van de Vlaamse beweging*, 2:254–69.

———. "Oorlog en vrede." In *Nieuwe geschiedenis van België*, vol. 1, 1830–1905, edited by Els Witte, Eliane Gubin, Jean-Pierre Nandrin, and Gita Deneckere, 640–49. Lannoo: Tielt, 2005.

———. "Sire, het volk mort: Collectieve actie in de sociale geschiedenis van de Belgische Staat, 1831–1940." PhD diss., Ghent University, 1994.

Depaepe, Marc. "Introduction." In *Manuels et chansons scolaires au Congo Belge*, edited by Marc Depaepe, Jan Briffaerts, and Pierre Kita Kyankenge Masandi, 7–29. Louvain: Presses Universitaires de Louvain, 2003.

———. "Kwantitatieve analyse van de Belgische lagere school (1830–1911)." *Belgisch tijdschrift voor nieuwste geschiedenis/Revue belge d'histoire contemporaine* 10, no. 1–2 (1979): 21–81.

———. *Orde in vooruitgang: Alledaags handelen in de Belgische lagere school (1880–1970)*. Studia Paedagogica. New Series 25. Leuven: Universitaire Pers Leuven, 1999.

Depaepe, Marc, Luc Minten, Frank Simon, and Maurice De Vroede. "L'enseignement primaire." In *Histoire de l'enseignement en Belgique*, edited by Dominique Grootaers, 111–91. Brussels: CRISP, 1998.

Deprez, Kas, and Louis Vos. "Introduction." In *Nationalism in Belgium: Shifting Identities, 1780–1995*, edited by Kas Deprez and Louis Vos. Basingstoke: Macmillan, 1998.

Deruytter, Barbara. "The Layering of Belgian National Identities during the First World War." In *Nations, Identities and the First World War: Shifting Loyalties to the Fatherland*, edited by Nico Wouters and Laurence Van Ypersele, 155–174 London: Bloomsbury, 2018.

Destrée, Jules, and Émile Vandervelde. *Le socialisme en Belgique*. Bibliothèque socialiste internationale 4. Paris: Giard et Brière, 1898.

Deweerdt, Mark. "Taalgrens." In De Schryver et al., *Nieuwe encyclopedie van de Vlaamse beweging*, 3:2949–62.

Dewolf, Arne. "'Par dégoût de service': De motieven van deserteurs uit het Belgische leger voor de krijgsraad van Antwerpen (1879–1911)." Bachelor's thesis, Antwerp University, 2013.

Dommanget, Maurice. *La Chevalerie du travail française (1893–1911): Contribution à l'histoire du socialisme et du mouvement ouvrier*. Lausanne: Rencontre, 1967.

Drachkovitch, Milorad M. *Les socialismes français et allemand et le problème de la guerre, 1870–1914*. Geneva: Studer, 1953.

Draper, Mario. *The Belgian Army and Society from Independence to the Great War*. Basingstoke: Palgrave Macmillan, 2018.

Dubois, Sébastien. *L'invention de la Belgique: Genèse d'un état-nation*. Brussels: Racine, 2005.

Dumoulin, Michel, Emmanuel Gerard, Mark Van den Wijngaert, and Vincent Dujardin. *Nieuwe geschiedenis van België*, vol. 2, 1905–1950. Tielt: Lannoo, 2006.

Durnez, Gaston. "Taalminderheden: Vlamingen in Wallonië." In De Schryver et al., *Nieuwe encyclopedie van de Vlaamse beweging*, 3:2974–94.

Eggerickx, Thierry. "Les migrations internes en Belgique de 1840 à 1939: Un essai de synthèse." In *Histoire de la population de la Belgique et de ses territoires: Actes de la Chaire Quetelet 2005*, edited by Thierry Eggerickx, Jean-Paul Sanderson and Patrick Deboosere, 293–336. Louvain-la-Neuve: Presses Universitaires de Louvain, 2010.

Fabre, Daniel. "Introduction." In *Ecritures ordinaires*, edited by Daniel Fabre and Jean-Pierre Albert, 1–30. Paris: Bibliothèque publique d'information P.O.L., 1993.

———. "Introduction: Seize terrains d'écriture." In *Par écrit: Ethnologie des écritures quotidiennes*, edited by Daniel Fabre, 1–56. Paris: Editions de la Maison des sciences de l'homme, 1997.

Fauvieau, Hector. *Le Borinage: Monographie politique, économique, sociale*. Frameries: Union des imprimeries, 1929.

Feest, David. "Spaces of 'National Indifference' in Biographic Research on Citizens of the Baltic Republics 1918–1940." *Journal of Baltic Studies* 48, no. 1 (2017): 55–66.

Fox, Jon, and Cynthia Miller-Idriss. "Everyday Nationhood." *Ethnicities* 8, no. 4 (2008): 536–63.

Fox, Jon, and Maarten Van Ginderachter, eds. "Everyday Nationalism's Evidence Problem." Themed section of *Nations and Nationalism* 24, issue 3 (2018).

Fredericq, Paul. *Vlaamsch België sedert 1830*, vol. 1. Ghent: Vuylsteke, 1905.

Gellner, Ernest. *Nations and Nationalism*. Oxford: Blackwell, 1993 [1983].

Gerson, Stéphane. *The Pride of Place: Local Memories and Political Culture in Nineteenth-Century France*. Ithaca, NY: Cornell University Press, 2003.

Gevers, Lieve. "The Catholic Church and the Flemish Movement." In *Nationalism in Belgium: Shifting Identities, 1780–1995*, edited by Kas Deprez and Louis Vos, 110–18. Basingstoke: Macmillan, 1998.

Gevers, Lieve, and Louis Vos. "Kerk en nationalisme in Vlaanderen in de 19de en 20ste eeuw." In *Is God een Turk? Nationalisme en religie*, 33–64. Leuven: Davidsfonds, 1995.

Graff, Harvey J. *The Legacies of Literacy: Continuities and Contradictions in Western Culture and Society*. Bloomington: Indiana University Press, 1987.

Green, Abigail. *Fatherlands: State-Building and Nationhood in Nineteenth-Century Germany*. Cambridge: Cambridge University Press, 2001.

Groh, Dieter. *Negative Integration und revolutionärer Attentismus: Die deutsche Sozialdemokratie am Vorabend des Ersten Weltkrieges*. Frankfurt am Main: Ullstein, 1973.

Groh, Dieter, and Peter Brandt. *Vaterlandslose Gesellen: Sozialdemokratie und Nation 1860–1990*. Munich: Beck, 1992.

Gubin, Eliane, Jean-Pierre Nandrin, and Pierre Van den Dungen. "1846–1878: Het liberale en burgerlijke België." In *Nieuwe geschiedenis van België*, vol. 1, 1830–1905, edited by Els Witte, Jean-Pierre Nandrin, Eliane Gubin, and Gita Deneckere, 237–440. Tielt: Lannoo, 2005.

Hall, Catherine, and Sonya O. Rose, eds. *At Home with the Empire: Metropolitan Culture and the Imperial World*. Cambridge: Cambridge University Press, 2006.

Harvey, David Allen. *Constructing Class and Nationality in Alsace, 1830–1945*. DeKalb: Northern Illinois University Press, 2001.

Hasquin, Hervé. *Historiographie et politique en Belgique*. Brussels/Charleroi: ULB/Institut Jules Destrée, 1996.

Haupt, Georges. *Socialism and the Great War: The Collapse of the Second International*. Oxford: Clarendon, 1972.

Heathorn, Stephen. *For Home, Country, and Race: Constructing Gender, Class, and Englishness in the Elementary School, 1884–1914*. Toronto: University of Toronto Press, 2000.

Hellemans, Staf. *Strijd om de moderniteit: Sociale bewegingen en verzuiling in Europa sinds 1800*. Kadoc-Studies 10. Leuven: Universitaire Pers Leuven, 1990.

Hens, Tine, Kaat Wils, and Saartje Vanden Borre. *Oorlog in tijden van vrede: De Eerste Wereldoorlog in de klas 1918–1940*. Kalmthout: Pelckmans, 2015.

Hilden, Patricia Penn. *Women, Work, and Politics: Belgium 1830–1914*. Oxford: Clarendon, 1993.

*Histoire de la Ligue de l'Enseignement 1864–1989*. Brussels: Ligue de l'Enseignement et de l'Education permanente, 1990.

Hobsbawm, Eric. "Afterword: Working Classes and Nations." In *Labor Migration in the Atlantic Economies: The European and North American Working Classes during the Period of Industrialization*, edited by Dirk Hoerder. Westport, CT: Greenwood, 1985.

———. *Nations and Nationalism since 1780: Programme, Myth, Reality*. Cambridge: Cambridge University Press 1995 [1990].

———. "Working-Class Internationalism." In *Internationalism in the Labour Movement, 1830–1940*, vol. 1, edited by Frits Van Holthoon and Marcel Van der Linden, 3–16. Leiden: E.J. Brill, 1988.

Hoebanx, Jean-Jacques. "L'histoire de Belgique dans quelques manuels scolaires." In *Histoire et historiens depuis 1830 en Belgique. Revue de l'Université de Bruxelles*, nos. 1–2, edited by Hervé Hasquin, 61–80. Brussels: ULB, 1981.

Hoegaerts, Josephine. "Manoeuvring Men: Masculinity as Spatially Defined Readability at the Grandes Manoeuvres of the Belgian Army, 1882–1883." *Gender, Place & Culture* 17 (2010): 249–68.

———. *Masculinity and Nationhood, 1830–1910: Constructions of Identity and Citizenship in Belgium*. Basingstoke: Palgrave Macmillan, 2014.

Horne, John, and Alan Kramer. *German Atrocities, 1914: A History of Denial*. New Haven, CT: Yale University Press, 2001.

Hroch, Miroslav. "From National Movement to the Fully-Formed Nation: The Nation-Building Process in Europe." In *Mapping the Nation*, edited by Gopal Balakrishnan, 78–97. London: Verso, 1996.

———. *Social Preconditions of National Revival in Europe: A Comparative Analysis of the Social Composition of Patriotic Groups among the Smaller European Nations*. Cambridge: Cambridge University Press, 2000 [1985].

Janssens, Jeroen. *De Belgische natie viert: De Belgische nationale feesten 1830–1914*. Leuven: Universitaire Pers Leuven, 2001.

Jaumain, Serge. *Les petits commerçants belges face à la modernité (1880–1914)*. Brussels: Ed. de l'Université de Bruxelles, 1995.

Jobst, Kerstin S. *Zwischen Nationalismus und Internationalismus: Die polnische und ukrainische Sozialdemokratie in Galizien von 1890 bis 1914: Ein Beitrag zur Nationalitätenfrage im Habsburgerreich*. Hamburg: Dölling und Galitz, 1996.

Jones, Stephen F. *Socialism in Georgian Colors: The European Road to Social Democracy, 1883–1917*. Cambridge, MA: Harvard University Press, 2005.

Joosten, Stefan. "De krant Vooruit voor Wereldoorlog I." Master's thesis, VUB, 2003.

Judson, Pieter M. *Guardians of the Nation: Activists on the Language Frontiers of Imperial Austria*. Cambridge, MA: Harvard University Press, 2006.

Kaarsholm, Preben. "The South African War and the Response of the International Socialist Community to Imperialism between 1896 and 1908." In *Internationalism in the Labour Movement, 1830–1940*, vol. 1, edited by Frits Van Holthoon and Marcel Van der Linden, 42–67. Leiden: E.J. Brill, 1988.

Kaiser, Wolfram. *Christian Democracy and the Origins of European Union*. Cambridge: Cambridge University Press, 2007.

———. "'Clericalism—That Is Our Enemy!': European Anticlericalism and the Culture Wars." In *Culture Wars: Secular–Catholic Conflict in Nineteenth-Century Europe*, edited by Christopher M. Clark and Wolfram Kaiser, 47–76. Cambridge: Cambridge University Press, 2003.

Kenis, Paul. *Het leven van Edward Anseele*. Ghent: De Vlam, 1949 [1930].

Kergoat, J. "France." In *The Formation of Labour Movements, 1870–1914: An International Perspective*, vol. 1, edited by Marcel Van der Linden and Jürgen Rojahn, 163–90. Leiden: E.J. Brill, 1990.

Kesteloot, Chantal. "Waalse beweging." In De Schryver et al., *Nieuwe encyclopedie van de Vlaamse beweging*, 3:3635–51.

King, Jeremy. *Budweisers into Czechs and Germans: A Local History of Bohemian Politics, 1848–1948*. Princeton, NJ: Princeton University Press, 2002.

———. "The Nationalization of East Central Europe: Ethnicism, Ethnicity, and Beyond." In *Staging the Past: The Politics of Commemoration in Habsburg Central Europe, 1848 to the Present*, edited by Maria Bucur and Nancy M. Wingfield, 112–52. West Lafayette, IN: Purdue University Press, 2001.

Knott, Eleanor. "Everyday Nationalism." *The State of Nationalism*, 2016. https://stateofnationalism.eu/article/everyday-nationalism/.

Kulczycki, John J. *The Foreign Worker and the German Labor Movement: Xenophobia and Solidarity in the Coal Fields of the Ruhr, 1871–1914*. Oxford: Berg 1994.

Lamberts, Emiel, ed. *Een kantelend tijdperk: De wending van de Kerk naar het volk in Noord-West-Europa, 1890–1910*. Kadoc-Studies 13. Leuven: University Press, 1992.

Lenders, Jan. "Van kind tot burger: Lager onderwijs en de vorming tot burgerschap in de negentiende eeuw." In *Tot burgerschap en deugd: Volksopvoeding in de negentiende eeuw*, edited by Nelleke Bakker, Rudolf Dekker, and Angélique Janssen, 11–34. Verloren: Hilversum, 2006.

Lhoest-Offerman, Holde. *Recueil de documents relatifs à la propagande des mouvements socialistes au XIXe siècle à Bruxelles*. Brussels: Archives générales du royaume, 1967.

Liebman, Marcel. *Les socialistes belges 1914–1918: Le P.O.B. face à la guerre*. Brussels: Vie ouvrière, 1986.

Lijphart, Arend, ed. *Conflict and Coexistence in Belgium: The Dynamics of a Culturally Divided Society*. Berkeley: University of California, Institute of International Studies, 1981.

———. "Introduction: The Belgian Example of Cultural Coexistence in Comparative Perspective." In *Conflict and Coexistence in Belgium: The Dynamics of a Culturally Divided Society*, edited by Arend Lijphart, 1–13. Berkeley: University of California, Institute of International Studies, 1981.
Little, Branden. "Commission for Relief in Belgium (CRB)." In *1914–1918–Online: International Encyclopedia of the First World War*, edited by Ute Daniel, Peter Gatrell, Oliver Janz, Heather Jones, Jennifer Keene, Alan, Kramer, and Bill Nasson. Berlin: Freie Universität Berlin, 2014. https://encyclopedia.1914-1918-online.net/home/.
Lootens, Camiel. *De geschiedenis van de Gentschen schildersbond: 1876–1926*. Ghent, Volksdrukkerij, 1926.
Lorwin, Val R. "Linguistic Pluralism and Political Tension in Modern Belgium." *Canadian Journal of History/Annales Canadiennes d'Histoire* 5, no. 1 (1970).
Lothe, J. "Les débuts du mouvement wallon." In *La Wallonie, le Pays et les Hommes: Histoire, économies, sociétés*, vol. 2, edited by Hervé Hasquin, 191–210. Brussels: La Renaissance du Livre, 1976.
Louckx, Kaat. "The Nation-State in Its State-istics (Belgium, 1846–1947)." *Nations and Nationalism* 23, no. 3 (2017): 505–23.
Lüdtke, Alf. "Einleitung." In *Eigen-Sinn, Fabrikalltag, Arbeitererfahrungen und Politik vom Kaiserreich bis in den Faschismus*, 9–22. Hamburg: Ergebnisse, 1993.
———. "Glossary of Selected Terms and Abbreviations." In Alf Lüdtke, *The History of Everyday Life: Reconstructing Historical Experiences and Ways of Life*, 313–15. Princeton, NJ: Princeton University Press, 1995.
Lyons, Martyn. "Ordinary Writings or How the 'Illiterate' Speak to Historians." In *Ordinary Writings, Personal Narratives*, edited by Martyn Lyons. Bern: Peter Lang, 2007.
———. *The Writing Culture of Ordinary People in Europe, c. 1860–1920*. Cambridge: Cambridge University Press, 2013.
Martí-Henneberg, Jordi. "European Integration and National Models for Railway Networks (1840–2010)." *Journal of Transport Geography* 26, Supplement C (2013): 126–38.
Mathias, Peter, and Sidney Pollard. *The Industrial Economies: The Development of Economic and Social Policies*. Cambridge: Cambridge University Press, 1989.
Meirlaen, Matthias. *Revoluties in de klas: Secundair geschiedenisonderwijs in de Zuidelijke Nederlanden, 1750–1850*. Leuven: Universitaire Pers Leuven, 2014.
Mergeay, Marie. "Multiplicatie en popularisatie: Van Karel V tot Keizer Karel." In *Mise en scène: Keizer Karel en de verbeelding van de negentiende eeuw*, edited by Robert Hoozee, Jo Tollebeek, and Tom Verschaffel, 80–93. Ghent: Mercatorfonds, 2000.
Michel, Joël. "Corporatisme et internationalisme chez les mineurs européens avant 1914." In *Internationalism in the Labour Movement 1830–1940*, vol.

2, edited by Frits Van Holthoon and Marcel Van der Linden, 440–59. Leiden: E.J. Brill, 1988.

———. "La Chevalerie du Travail: Force ou faiblesse du mouvement ouvrier belge." *Belgisch tijdschrift voor nieuwste geschiedenis/Revue belge d'histoire contemporaine* 9, no. 1–2 (1978): 117–64.

———. "Le mouvement ouvrier chez les mineurs d'Europe occidentale (Grande-Bretagne, Belgique, France, Allemagne): Etude comparative des années 1880 à 1914." PhD diss., Lyon III, 1987.

Mommsen, Hans. "Das Problem der internationalen Integration in der böhmischen Arbeiterbewegung." In *Arbeiterbewegung und Nationale Frage: Ausgewählte Aufsätze*, edited by Hans Mommsen, 166–79. Göttingen: Vandenhoeck und Ruprecht, 1979.

Nath, Giselle. *Brood willen we hebben! Honger, sociale politiek en protest tijdens de Eerste Wereldoorlog in België*. Antwerp: Manteau, 2013.

Nauwelaerts, Mandy. "De socialistische syndikale beweging na de Eerste Wereldoorlog (1919–1921)." *Belgisch tijdschrift voor nieuwste geschiedenis/Revue belge d'histoire contemporaine* 4, no. 3–4 (1973): 343–76.

*Nederlandsche en Fransche socialistische liederen en gedichten*: Eerste reeks. Ghent: Gentsche Afdeeling der Werklieden-Partij, 1896.

*Nederlandsche en Fransche socialistische liederen en gedichten*: Tweede reeks. Ghent: Gentsche Afdeeling der Werklieden-Partij, 1902.

Pasture, Patrick. "Building the Social Security State: A Comparative History of Belgium, the Netherlands and Germany." In *Between Cross and Class. Comparative Histories of Christian Labour in Europe 1840–2000*, edited by Jan De Maeyer, Lex Heerma van Voss, and Patrick Pasture, 251–84. Bern: Lang, 2005.

———. "Introduction: Between Cross and Class. Christian Labour in Europe." In *Between Cross and Class: Comparative Histories of Christian Labour in Europe 1840–2000*, edited by Jan De Maeyer, Lex Heerma van Voss, and Patrick Pasture, 9–48. Bern: Lang, 2005.

———. "Kerk, natie en arbeidersklasse: Een essay over collectieve identificatie, in het bijzonder m.b.t. de (christelijke) arbeidersbeweging in België." *Bijdragen tot de eigentijdse geschiedenis/Cahiers d'histoire du temps présent*, no. 6 (1999): 7–36.

———. "The Temptations of Nationalism: Regionalist Orientations in the Belgian Christian Labour Movement." In *Working-Class Internationalism and the Appeal of National Identity: Historical Debates and Current Perspectives*, edited by Patrick Pasture and Johan Verberckmoes, 107–49. Oxford: Berg, 1998.

Peiren, Luc. "Een merkwaardig en ongekend congres van de BWP op 25 en 26 december 1886." *Amsab-tijdingen* 11 (1991): 17.

Pergher, Roberta. "Staging the Nation in Fascist Italy's 'New Provinces.'" *Austrian History Yearbook* 43, no. April (2012): 98–115.

Perin, Anne-Françoise. *Théâtre ouvrier en Wallonie (1900–1940): Bilan d'une recherche*. Brussels: Cahiers JEB, 1979.

Picard, Leo. "Tussen de twee wereldoorlogen." In *Geschiedenis van de socialistische arbeidersbeweging in België*, edited by Jan Dhondt, 483–516. Antwerp: Ontwikkeling, 1960–1968.

Pinon, Roger. "Contribution à l'étude de la chanson politique et sociale dans la province de Hainaut aux XIXe et XXe siècles." In *Recueil d'études d'histoire hainuyère offertes à Maurice A. Arnould*, vol. 2, edited by Jean-Marie Cauchies and Jean-Marie Duvosquel, 527–36. Mons: Hannonia, 1983.

POB, Fédération bruxelloise. *Rapports des secrétaires, Exercices 1912–1913*. Brussels: POB, 1914.

Polasky, Janet Louise. *The Democratic Socialism of Emile Vandervelde: Between Reform and Revolution*. Oxford: Berg, 1995.

———. "A Revolution for Socialist Reforms: The Belgian General Strike for Universal Suffrage." *Journal of Contemporary History* 27, no. 3 (1992): 449–66.

———. "Transplanting and Rooting Workers in London and Brussels: A Comparative History." *Journal of Modern History* 73, no. 3 (2001): 528–60.

Porter, Bernard. *The Absent-Minded Imperialists: Empire, Society and Culture in Britain*. Oxford: Oxford University Press, 2004.

Prochaska, Frank. *Royal Bounty: The Making of a Welfare Monarchy*. New Haven, CT: Yale University Press, 1995.

Puissant, Jean. "'La commune pour le Socialisme' de Louis Bertrand." *Brood en Rozen*, no. 2 (2000): 124–28.

———. *L'évolution du mouvement ouvrier socialiste dans le Borinage*. Brussels: Palais des Académies, 1982.

———. "'L'oeuvre gouvernementale du POB commence' ou le POB à la conquête d'un substitut du pouvoir d'état (1884–1921)." In *Les élections communales et leur impact sur la politique belge (1890–1970)*, 75–105. Brussels: Crédit communal, 1993.

———. *Sous la loupe de la police française, le bassin industriel du Centre (1885–1893)*. Haine-Saint-Pierre: Cercle d'histoire et de folklore Henri Guillemin, 1988.

Quairiaux, Yves. "Les 'Flaminds' avant 1914 en Wallonie: Du dénigrement à l'assimilation." In *L'image de l'autre dans l'Europe du Nord-Ouest à travers l'histoire: Actes du colloque Villeneuve d'Asq, 24–26 nov. 1994*, edited by Jean-Pierre Jessenne and Martine Aubry, 237–53. Lille, 1996.

———. "Le stéréotype du Flamand en Wallonie: Explications économiques et sociales (1880–1940)." In *Stéréotypes nationaux et préjugés raciaux aux XIXe et XXe siècles: Sources et méthodes pour une approche historique*, edited by Jean Pirotte, 138–51. Louvain-La-Neuve: Collège Erasme Bureau du Recueil/ Editions Nauwelaerts, 1982.

———. *L'image du Flamand en Wallonie (1830–1914): Essai d'analyse sociale et politique*. Brussels: Editions Labor, 2006.

———. "Présence flamande dans le Centre." In *Mémoires d'une région: Le Centre (1830–1914)*, 183–229. Morlanwez: Musée royal de Mariemont, 1984.

Raxhon, Philippe. *La mémoire de la Révolution française: Entre Liège et Wallonie*. Brussels: Labor, 1996.

Reill, Dominique Kirchner. *Nationalists Who Feared the Nation: Adriatic Multi-Nationalism in Habsburg Dalmatia, Trieste, and Venice*. Stanford, CA: Stanford University Press, 2012.

Reimann, Christina. *Schule für Verfassungsbürger? Die Bildungsligen und der Verfassungswandel des späten 19. Jahrhunderts in Belgien, England und Frankreich*. Münster: Waxmann, 2016.

Renard, Claude. "Un aspect du socialisme avant 1914: Les attitudes politiques et idéologiques du Parti ouvrier belge dans les débats sur la défense nationale (1885–1913)." Master's thesis, ULB, 1973.

Ridolfi, Maurizio. "'L'industria della propaganda' e il partito: Stampa e editoria nel socialismo italiano prefascista." *Studi storici* 33, no. 1 (1992): 33–80.

Righart, Hans. "Katholieke verzuiling in België als historisch probleem: Enkele historiografische kanttekeningen." *Belgisch tijdschrift voor nieuwste geschiedenis/Revue belge d'histoire contemporaine* 25, no. 3–4 (1984): 541–64.

Rose, Jonathan E. *The Intellectual Life of the British Working Classes*. New Haven, CT: Yale University Press, 2002 [2001].

Rottiers, Sophie. "De eer van de zeshonderd Franchimontezen." In *De grote mythen uit de geschiedenis van België, Vlaanderen en Wallonië*, edited by Anne Morelli, 65–75. Berchem: EPO, 1996.

Rutar, Sabine. *Kultur–Nation–Milieu: Sozialdemokratie in Triest vor dem Ersten Weltkrieg*. Essen: Klartext Verlag, 2004.

Schmidt, Tim Mathias. "Sprachnationale Konflikte, Staatsreformdiskurs und Sozialdemokratie: Ein Vergleich zwischen den böhmischen Ländern und Belgien 1894–1938." PhD diss., Ludwig-Maximilians-Universität München, 2014.

Scholliers, Peter. "Industrial Wage Differentials in Nineteenth-Century Belgium." In *Income Distribution in Historical Perspective*, edited by Y. S. Brenner, Hartmut Kaelble, and Mark Thomas, 96–116. Cambridge: Cambridge University Press, 1991.

———. "Kledingaankopen en de zin van het leven, of economie en identiteit in België vanaf het laatste kwart van de 19e eeuw." In *Op weg naar de consumptiemaatschappij: Over het verbruik van voeding, kleding en luxegoederen in België en Nederland (19e–20e eeuw)*, edited by Yves Segers, 43–65. Amsterdam: Aksant, 2002.

Scholliers, Peter, and F. Daelemans. "Standards of Living and Standards of Health in Wartime Belgium." In *The Upheaval of War: Family, Work and Welfare in Europe, 1914–1918*, edited by Jay Winter and R. Wall, 139–58. Cambridge: Cambridge University Press, 1988.

Scott, James C. *Domination and the Arts of Resistance: Hidden Transcripts*. New Haven, CT: Yale University Press, 1990.

———. *Weapons of the Weak: Everyday Forms of Peasant Resistance*. New Haven, CT: Yale University Press, 1985.

Seebohm Rowntree, Benjamin. *Land and labour: Lessons from Belgium.* London: Macmillan, 1910.
Sertyn, Mieke. "Het socialistisch aktivisme tijdens de Eerste Wereldoorlog." *Belgisch tijdschrift voor nieuwste geschiedenis/Revue belge d'histoire contemporaine* 7, no. 1–2 (1976): 169–96.
Skey, Michael, and Marco Antonsich, eds. *Everyday Nationhood: Theorising Culture, Identity and Belonging after Banal Nationalism.* Basingstoke: Palgrave Macmillan, 2017.
Smets, Jasper. "'Dienen in vrede': Socialistische subversie in het Belgische leger." Bachelor's thesis, Antwerp University, 2013.
Smith, Anthony D. *The Ethnic Origins of Nations.* Oxford: Blackwell 1994 [1986].
———. "The Limits of Everyday Nationhood." *Ethnicities* 8, no. 4 (2008): 563–73.
Stanard, Matthew G. *Selling the Congo: A History of European Pro-Empire Propaganda and the Making of Belgian Imperialism.* Lincoln: University of Nebraska Press, 2011.
Stargardt, Nicholas. "Gellner's Nationalism: The Spirit of Modernisation?." In *The Social Philosophy of Ernest Gellner*, edited by John Hall and Ian Jarvie, 171–89. Leiden: E.J. Brill, 1996.
Stauter-Halsted, Keeley. *The Nation in the Village: The Genesis of Peasant National Identity in Austrian Poland 1848–1914.* Ithaca, NY: Cornell University Press, 2001.
Steffens, Sven. "La vie d'un maçon au 19e siècle: 'Rik De Metselaer' (1852)." *Les Cahiers de la Fonderie* (December 1995): 26–32.
Stengers, Jean. "La Belgique de 1830, une 'nationalité de convention'?" In *Histoire et historiens depuis 1830 en Belgique: Revue de l'Université de Bruxelles*, no. 1–2, edited by Hervé Hasquin, 7–19. Brussels: ULB, 1981.
———. *Les racines de la Belgique jusqu'à la Révolution de 1830: Histoire du sentiment national en Belgique des origines à 1918*, vol. 1. Brussels: Racine, 2000.
Stengers, Jean, and Eliane Gubin. *Le grand siècle de la nationalité Belge: De 1830 à 1918.* Vol. 2 of *Histoire du sentiment national en Belgique des origines à 1918.* Brussels: Racine, 2002.
Stergar, Rok. "National Indifference in the Heyday of Nationalist Mobilization? Ljubljana Military Veterans and the Language of Command." *Austrian History Yearbook* 43 (April 2012): 45–58.
Stevenson, David. "Battlefield or Barrier? Rearmament and Military Planning in Belgium, 1902–1914." *International History Review* 29, no. 3 (2007): 473–507.
Stourzh, Gerald. "The Ethnicizing of Politics and 'National Indifference' in Late Imperial Austria." In *Der Umfang der österreichischen Geschichte: Ausgewählte Studien 1990–2010*, edited by Gerald Stourzh, 283–323. Vienna: Böhlau, 2011.

Strikwerda, Carl. *A House Divided: Catholics, Socialists, and Flemish Nationalists in Nineteenth-Century Belgium.* Lanham, MD: Rowman & Littlefield, 1997.

Stuart, Robert. *Marxism and National Identity: Socialism, Nationalism, and National Socialism during the French Fin de Siècle.* Albany: State University of New York Press, 2006.

Sun, Raymond C. "'Hammer Blows': Work, the Workplace, and the Culture of Masculinity among Catholic Workers in the Weimar Republic." *Central European History* 37, no. 2 (2004): 245–71.

Swanson, John C. *Tangible Belonging: Negotiating Germanness in Twentieth-Century Hungary.* Pittsburgh: Pittsburgh University Press, 2017.

Thiesse, Anne-Marie. *Ils apprenaient la France: L'exaltation des régions dans le discours patriotique.* Paris: Editions de la Maison des sciences de l'homme, 1997.

Thompson, Andrew S. *The Empire Strikes Back? The Impact of Imperialism on Britain from the Mid-Nineteenth Century.* Harlow: Longman, 2005.

Tichelman, Fritjof. "Socialist 'Internationalism' and the Colonial World: Practical Colonial Policies of Social Democracy in Western Europe before 1940 with Particular Reference to the Dutch SDAP." In *Internationalism in the Labour Movement, 1830–1940,* vol. 1, edited by Frits Van Holthoon and Marcel Van der Linden, 87–108. Leiden: E.J. Brill, 1988.

Tilly, Charles. *Regimes and Repertoires.* Chicago: University of Chicago Press, 2006.

Tollebeek, Jo. "Enthousiasme en evidentie: De negentiende eeuwse Belgisch-nationale geschiedschrijving." In *De ijkmeesters: Opstellen over de geschiedschrijving in Nederland en België,* edited by Jo Tollebeek, 57–74. Amsterdam: Bert Bakker, 1994.

Tollebeek, Jo, and Tom Verschaffel. "Guldensporenslag." In De Schryver et al., *Nieuwe encyclopedie van de Vlaamse beweging,* 2:1382–86.

Tyssens, Jeffrey. "De vermaledijde staat? Overheid en onderwijsverstrekking in België." In *Tweehonderd jaar onderwijs en de zorg van de Staat,* edited by P. Boekholt, H. Van Crombrugge, N. L. Dodde, and Jeffrey Tyssens, 60–74. Assen: Koninklijke Van Gorcum, 2002.

Uytterhaegen, Frank, and Guy Vanschoenbeek. "Nawoord." In Jozef Volckaert, *En dat alles voor een paar tirannen: Herinneringen van een socialistische arbeider, met aantekeningen en een naschrift van Frank Uytterhaegen en Guy Vanschoenbeek,* 79–138. Leuven: Kritak, 1983.

Van Audenhove, Marcel. "L'autonomie communale." In *Het openbaar initiatief van de gemeenten in België 1795–1940/L'initiative publique des communes en Belgique 1795–1940,* 69–83. Brussels: Crédit communal de Belgique, 1986.

Van Cauwelaert, Rik. *"Ils nous ont pris la Flandre": Waals socialisme en Belgische illusies: Van Jules Destrée tot Elio Di Rupo.* Kalmthout: Pelckmans, 2012.

Van Daele, Jasmien. *Van Gent tot Genève: Louis Varlez, een biografie*. Ghent: Academia Press, 2002.
Van der Herten, Bart. *België onder stoom: Transport en communicatie tijdens de 19e eeuw*. Studies in Social and Economic History 32. Leuven: Universitaire Pers Leuven, 2004.
Van der Linden, Marcel. "The National Integration of the European Working Classes, 1871–1914: Exploring the Causal Configuration." *International Review Of Social History* 33, no. 3 (1988): 285–311.
Van Duin, Pieter. *Central European Crossroads: Social Democracy and National Revolution in Bratislava (Pressburg), 1867–1921*. New York: Berghahn Books, 2009.
Van Eenoo, Romain. "Kiesstelsels en verkiezingen, 1830–1914." In *Geschiedenis van de Belgische Kamer van Volksvertegenwoordigers 1830–2002*, edited by E. Gerard, Ludo de Witte, Eliane Gubin, and Jean-Pierre Nandrin. Brussels: Kamer van Volksvertegenwoordigers, 2003.
Van Ginderachter, Maarten. "Contesting National Symbols: Belgian Belle Époque Socialism between Rejection and Appropriation." *Social History* 34, no. 1 (2009): 55–73.
———. "Democratisering en nationale integratie in de Belgische Werkliedenpartij (1890–1920)." In Witte et al., *Natie en democratie–Nation et démocratie (1890–1921)*, 85–96.
———. *Het rode vaderland: De vergeten geschiedenis van de communautaire spanningen in het Belgische socialisme voor WO I*. Tielt/Ghent: Lannoo/Amsab, 2005.
———. "How to Gauge Banal Nationalism and National Indifference in the Past: Proletarian Tweets in Belgium's Belle Époque." *Nations and Nationalism* 24, no. 3 (2018): 579–93.
———. "'If Your Majesty Would Only Send Me a Little Money to Help Buy an Elephant': Letters to the Belgian Royal Family (1880–1940)." In *Ordinary Writings, Personal Narratives*, edited by Martyn Lyons, 69–83. Bern: Peter Lang, 2007.
———. "Jean Prolo, waer bestu bleven? Speuren naar de bronnen van 'gewone mensen' in 19de-eeuwse archieven." In *Terug naar de bron(nen): Taal en taalgebruik in de 19de eeuw in Vlaanderen*. In *Verslagen en mededelingen van de Koninklijke Academie voor Nederlandse Taal- en Letterkunde* 114, no. 1, edited by Wim Vandenbussche, 19–31. Ghent: KANTL, 2004.
———. "Nationalist Versus Regionalist? The Flemish and Walloon Movements in *Belle Époque* Belgium." In *Region and State in Nineteenth-Century Europe: Nation-Building, Regional Identities and Separatism*, edited by Joost Augusteijn and Eric Storm, 209–26. Basingstoke: Palgrave Macmillan, 2012.
———. "Public Transcripts of Royalism: Pauper Letters to the Belgian Royal Family (1880–1940)." In *Mystifying the Monarch: Studies on Discourse,*

*Power and History*, edited by Gita Deneckere and Jeroen Deploige, 223–34. Amsterdam: Amsterdam University Press, 2006.

———. "Social-Democracy and National Identity: The Ethnic Rift in the Belgian Workers' Party (1885–1914)." *International Review of Social History* 52, no. 2 (2007): 215–40.

———. "An Urban Civilization: The Case of Municipal Autonomy in Belgian History 1830–1914." In *Nationalism and the Reshaping of Urban Communities in Europe, 1848–1914*, edited by William Whyte and Oliver Zimmer, 110–30. Basingstoke: Palgrave Macmillan, 2011.

———. "Vaderland in de Belgische Werkliedenpartij (1885–1914): Sociaal-democratie en nationale identiteit from below; Een casusstudie van Gent, Brussel en de Borinage." PhD diss., Ghent University, 2005.

Van Ginderachter, Maarten, and Jon Fox. "Introduction." In *National Indifference and the History of Nationalism in Modern Europe*, edited by Maarten Van Ginderachter and Jon Fox, 1–14. London: Routledge, 2019.

———, eds. *National Indifference and the History of Nationalism in Modern Europe*. London: Routledge, 2019.

Van Ginderachter, Maarten, and Minte Kamphuis. "The Transnational Dimensions of the Early Socialist Pillars in Belgium and the Netherlands, c. 1885–1914: An Exploratory Essay." *Belgisch tijdschrift voor filologie en geschiedenis/Revue Belge de philologie et d'histoire* 90, no. 4 (2012): 113–29.

Van Ginderachter, Maarten, and Joep Leerssen. "Denied Ethnicism: On the Walloon Movement in Belgium." *Nations and Nationalism* 18, no. 2 (2012): 230–46.

Van Goethem, Geert, and Wouter Steenhaut. *Wording en strijd van het socialistisch vakverbond van Antwerpen*. Antwerp: AMSAB, 1994.

Van Goethem, Geert, and Michel Vermote. *1885–1985: Honderd jaar socialisme. Een Terugblik*. Ghent: Amsab, 1985.

Van Goethem, Herman. *Belgium and the Monarchy: From National Independence to National Disintegration*. Brussels: UPA, 2010.

Van Velthoven, Harry. *De Vlaamse kwestie 1830–1914: Macht en onmacht van de Vlaamsgezinden*. Kortrijk: UGA, 1982.

———. "Onenigheid in de Belgische werkliedenpartij: De Vlaamse kwestie wordt een vrije kwestie (1894–1914)." *Belgisch tijdschrift voor nieuwste geschiedenis/Revue belge d'histoire contemporaine* 5, no. 1–2 (1974): 123–66.

———. *Scheurmakers en carrièristen: De opstand van christendemocraten en katholieke flaminganten, 1890–1914*. Kapellen: Uitgeverij Pelckmans, 2014.

———. "Taal en onderwijspolitiek Brussel, 1878–1914." *Taal en sociale integratie* 4 (1981): 261–387.

Van Velthoven, Harry, and Els Witte. *Taal en politiek: De Belgische casus in een historisch perspectief*. Brussels: VUB Press, 1998.

———. "Taalpolitiek en wetgeving." In De Schryver et al., *Nieuwe encyclopedie van de Vlaamse beweging*, 3:2994–3043.

Van Ypersele, Laurence. *Le Roi Albert: Histoire d'un mythe.* Ottignies: Quorum, 1995.

———. "L'image du roi dans la caricature politique en Belgique de 1884 à 1914." *Belgisch tijdschrift voor nieuwste geschiedenis/Revue belge d'histoire contemporaine* 26, no. 1–2 (1996): 133–64.

Vanacker, Daniël. *Het activistisch avontuur.* Ghent: Stichting Mens en Kultuur, 1991.

Vandecaveye, Hendrik. "Het Gentse proletariërslied, 1860–1914: Historische situering van een sociaal-kulturele verschijningsvorm van de arbeidersbeweging." Master's thesis, Ghent University, 1978.

Vanhaute, Eric. "Leven, wonen en werken in onzekere tijden: Patronen van bevolking en arbeid in België in de 'lange negentiende eeuw.'" *Bijdragen en mededelingen betreffende de geschiedenis der Nederlanden* 118, no. 2 (2003): 153–78.

Vanschoenbeek, Guy. "'Arbeid adelt': De arbeidersaristocratie als verklaring voor het reformisme in de arbeidersbeweging." *Belgisch tijdschrift voor filologie en geschiedenis/Revue belge de philologie et d'histoire* 76, no. 4 (1998): 1021–61.

———. "De wortels van de sociaal-democratie in Vlaanderen: Le 'monde socialiste gantois' en de Gentse socialisten voor de Eerste Wereldoorlog." PhD diss., Ghent University, 1992.

———. "Leger en socialisme voor de Eerste Wereldoorlog." *Belgisch tijdschrift voor militaire geschiedenis* 23, no. 3 (1979): 219–62.

———. "Ontstaan, situering en karakterisering van de Socialistische Jonge Wacht, 1886–1914: Bijdrage tot de studie van politieke jongerenbewegingen." Master's thesis, Ghent University, 1978.

———. "Socialisten: Gezellen zonder vaderland? De BWP en haar verhouding tot het 'vaderland België.'" *Bijdragen tot de eigentijdse geschiedenis/Cahiers d'histoire du temps présent*, no. 3 (1997): 237–55.

———. "Vooruit." In De Schryver et al., *Nieuwe encyclopedie van de Vlaamse beweging*, 3:3563–66.

Vanschoenbeek, Guy, and Eric Defoort. "Hippoliet De Boos, of hoe een socialistische held een vergeten dissident wordt." *Amsab-tijdingen* 3–4, no. 81–98 (1987): 81–98.

Vanthemsche, Guy. "De Belgische socialisten en Congo 1895–1960." *Brood en Rozen*, no. 2 (1999): 31–65.

———. *De paradoxen van de staat: Staat en vrije markt in historisch perspectief.* Brussels: VUB Press, 1998.

———. "The Historiography of Belgian Colonialism in the Congo." In *Europe and the World in European Historiography*, edited by Csaba Lévai, 89–119. Pisa: Edizioni Plus, 2006.

Varlez, Louis. "La Fédération ouvrière gantoise." *Musée social*, no. 1 (1899).

Verbruggen, Paule. "Deelalternatieven voor traditionele godsdienstbeleving in het Gentse socialisme (1870–1914)." Master's thesis, Ghent University, 1982.

Verdure, Jens. "En men zou niet fier zijn Vaderlander te wezen? Sociaal-democratie en nationale identiteit voor WO I: Een casusstudie van Antwerpen en Luik." Master's thesis, Ghent University, 2007.

Vermandere, Martine. "Door gelijke drang bewogen? De socialistische partij en haar jeugdbeweging, 1886–1944." *Bijdragen tot de eigentijdse geschiedenis/ Cahiers d'histoire du temps présent*, no. 8 (2011): 225–56.

Verschaffel, Tom. "Aanschouwelijke Middeleeuwen: Historische optochten en vaderlandse drama's in het negentiende-eeuwse België." *Theoretische geschiedenis* 26, no. 2 (1999): 129–48.

———. *Beeld en geschiedenis: Het Belgische en Vlaamse verleden in de romantische boekillustraties*. Turnhout: Brepols, 1987.

———. "Congo in de Belgische zelfrepresentatie." In *Congo in België: Koloniale cultuur in de metropool*, edited by Vincent Viaene, David Van Reybrouck, and Bambi Ceuppens, 63–80. Leuven: Leuven University Press, 2009.

———. "De Brabançonne en de Vlaamse Leeuw." In *Nationale hymnen: Het Wilhelmus en zijn buren*, edited by Louis Peter Grijp, 162–83. Nijmegen: SUN, 1998.

———. "Het verleden tot weinig herleid: De historische optocht als vorm van de romantische verbeelding." In *Romantiek en historische cultuur*, edited by Jo Tollebeek, Frank Ankersmit, and Wessel Krul, 297–320. Groningen: Historische uitgeverij, 1996.

———. "Leren sterven voor het vaderland: Historische drama's in het 19de eeuwse België." *Bijdragen en mededelingen betreffende de geschiedenis der Nederlanden* 113, no. 2 (1998): 145–76.

*Verzameling der volledige kluchtige en politieke liederen van Karel Waeri*. Ghent: Geschiedkundige heruitgeverij, 2001 [1899].

Viaene, Vincent. "King Leopold's Imperialism and the Origins of the Belgian Colonial Party, 1860–1905." *Journal of Modern History* 80, no. 4 (2008): 741–90.

———. "Reprise–Remise: De Congolese identiteitscrisis van België rond 1908." In *Congo in België: Koloniale cultuur in de metropool*, edited by Vincent Viaene, David Van Reybrouck, and Bambi Ceuppens, 43–62. Leuven: Universitaire Pers Leuven, 2009.

Vincent, David. *The Rise of Mass Literacy: Reading and Writing in Modern Europe*. Cambridge: Polity, 2000.

Vogel, Jakob. "Militärfeiern in Deutschland und Frankreich als Rituale der Nation (1871–1914)." In *Nation und Emotion: Deutschland und Frankreich im Vergleich 19. und 20. Jahrhundert*, edited by Etienne François, Hannes Siegrist, and Jakob Vogel, 199–214. Göttingen: Vandenhoeck und Ruprecht, 1995.

———. "Military, Folklore, Eigensinn: Folkloric Militarism in Germany and France, 1871–1914." *Central European History* 33, no. 4 (2000): 487–504.

———. *Nationen im Gleichschritt: Der Kult der "Nation in Waffen" in Deutsch-*

*land und Frankreich, 1871–1914*. Göttingen: Vandenhoeck & Ruprecht, 1997.

Vosters, Rik, and Wim Vandenbussche. "Wijzer worden over Willem? Taalgebruik in Vlaanderen ten tijde van het Verenigd Koninkrijk der Nederlanden (1814–1830)." *Internationale Neerlandistiek*, no. 3 (2008): 2–22.

Vosters, Rik, and Janneke Weijermans, eds. *Taal, cultuurbeleid en natievorming onder Willem I*. Brussels: KVAB, 2011.

Vrints, Antoon. "'All the Butter in the Country Belongs to Us, Belgians': Well-Being and Lower-Class National Identification in Belgium during the First World War." In *Nationhood from Below: Europe in the Long Nineteenth Century*, edited by Maarten Van Ginderachter and Marnix Beyen, 230–49. Basingstoke: Palgrave Macmillan, 2012.

———. "Eenheid in verdeeldheid: Tegenstellingen in België tijdens de 1ste WO." *Belgisch tijdschrift voor nieuwste geschiedenis/Revue belge d'histoire contemporaine* 44, no. 2–3 (2014): 10–35.

———. *Het theater van de straat: Publiek geweld in Antwerpen tijdens de eerste helft van de twintigste eeuw*. Amsterdam: Amsterdam University Press, 2011.

Vrints, Antoon, and Martin Schoups. *De overlevenden: De Belgische oud-strijders tijdens het interbellum*. Antwerp: Polis, 2019.

Vushko, Iryna. *The Politics of Cultural Retreat: Imperial Bureaucracy in Austrian Galicia, 1772–1867*. New Haven, CT: Yale University Press, 2015.

Ward, Paul. *Red Flag and Union Jack: Englishness, Patriotism, and the British Left, 1881–1924*. Rochester, NY: Royal Historical Society/Boydell Press, 1998.

Warnier, Dave, and Luc De Vos. "De dienstplicht in België historisch bekeken: Een politieke en militaire evolutie (1830–2010)." *Volkskunde* 111, no. 4 (2010): 339–57.

Watillon, Léon. *The Knights of Labor in Belgium*. Los Angeles: Institute of Industrial Relations, University of California, Los Angeles, 1959.

Weber, Donald. "La marche des opérations électorales: Bepalingen rond kiesverrichtingen in de Belgische kieswetgeving, 1830–1940." *Belgisch tijdschrift voor filologie en geschiedenis/Revue belge de philologie et d'histoire* 81, no. 2 (2003): 311–42.

Weber, Eugen. *Peasants into Frenchmen: The Modernization of Rural France, 1870–1914*. London: Chatto and Windus, 1977.

Wehler, Hans-Ulrich. "Bismarck's Imperialism 1862–1890." *Past & Present* 48 (August 1970): 119–55.

Wijnsouw, Jana. *National Identity and Nineteenth-Century Franco-Belgian Sculpture*. Abingdon: Routledge, 2018.

Wils, Lode. "De historische verstrengeling tussen de christelijke arbeidersbeweging en de Vlaamse beweging." In Lode Wils, *Vlaanderen, België, Groot-Nederland: Mythe en geschiedenis*, 241–57. Leuven: Davidsfonds, 1994.

———. "De twee Belgische revoluties." In *Nationalisme in België: Identiteiten in beweging 1780–2000*, edited by Kas Deprez and Louis Vos, 43–50. Antwerp: Houtekiet, 1999.

———. *Flamenpolitik en aktivisme: Vlaanderen tegenover België in de Eerste Wereldoorlog*. Leuven: Davidsfonds, 1974.

———. "Het aandeel van de 'Flamenpolitik' in de Vlaamse natievorming." *Belgisch tijdschrift voor nieuwste geschiedenis/Revue belge d'histoire contemporaine* 44, no. 2–3 (2015): 216–37.

———. *Het ontstaan van de Meetingpartij te Antwerpen en haar invloed op de Belgische politiek*. Antwerp: Nederlandsche Boekhandel, 1963.

———. "Meetingpartij." In De Schryver et al., *Nieuwe encyclopedie van de Vlaamse beweging*, 2:2026–28.

———. *Onverfranst, onverduitst? Flamenpolitik, activisme, frontbeweging*. Kapellen: Pelckmans, 2014.

———. "The Two Belgian Revolutions." In *Nationalism in Belgium: Shifting Identities*, edited by Kas Deprez and Louis Vos, 33–41. London: Macmillan, 1998.

———. *Van Clovis tot Di Rupo: De lange weg van de naties in de Lage Landen*. Leuven: Garant, 2005 [1992].

———. *Van Clovis tot Happart: De lange weg van de naties in de Lage Landen*. Leuven: Garant, 1992.

Witte, Els. "1828–1847: De constructie van België." In *Nieuwe geschiedenis van België*, vol. 1, 1830–1905, edited by Els Witte, Jean-Pierre Nandrin, Eliane Gubin, and Gita Deneckere, 27–235. Tielt: Lannoo, 2005.

———. "Inleiding: Natie en democratie, 1890–1921: De probleemstelling." In Witte et al., *Natie en democratie–Nation et démocratie (1890–1921)*, 7–18.

Witte, Els, Ginette Kurgan-Van Hentenryk, Emiel Lamberts, Herman Balthazar, Gita Deneckere, Philippe Raxhon, Paul Wynants, Marnix Beyen, and Frans-Jos Verdoodt, eds. *Natie en democratie–Nation et démocratie (1890–1921), Acta van het interuniversitair colloquium, Brussel 8–9 Juni 2006*. Brussels: Koninklijke Vlaamse Academie van België voor Wetenschappen en Kunsten, 2007.

Wynants, Paul, Vincent Dujardin, Henk Byls, and Sarah Van Ruyskensvelde. "Conflicten als vormgevers en stoorzenders: Ideologische breuklijnen en twee wereldoorlogen." In *Katholiek onderwijs in België: Identiteiten in evolutie 19de–21ste eeuw*, edited by Jan De Maeyer and Paul Wynants, 79–105. Antwerp: Halewijn, 2016.

Wynants, Paul, Byls Henk, and Arthe Van Laer. "Het juridisch en institutioneel kader: Van de vrijheid van onderwijs tot de huidige debatten." In *Katholiek onderwijs in België: Identiteiten in evolutie 19de–21ste eeuw*, edited by Jan De Maeyer and Paul Wynants, 34–63. Antwerp: Halewijn, 2016.

Yeo, Stephen. "Socialism, the State and Some Oppositional Englishness." In *Englishness: Politics and Culture 1880–1920*, edited by Robert Colls and Philip Dodd, 308–69. London: Croom Helm, 1986.

Zahra, Tara. "Imagined Non-Communities: National Indifference as a Category of Analysis." *Slavic Review* 69 (2010): 93–119.

———. *Kidnapped Souls: National Indifference and the Battle for Children in the Bohemian Lands, 1900–1948*. Ithaca, NY: Cornell University Press, 2008.

Ziblatt, Daniel. *Structuring the State: The Formation of Italy and Germany and the Puzzle of Federalism*. Princeton, NJ: Princeton University Press, 2006.

Zolberg, Aristide. "The Making of Flemings and Walloons: Belgium: 1830–1914." *Journal of Interdisciplinary History* 5, no. 2 (1974): 179–235.

# INDEX

*Page numbers in italics indicate illustrative material.*

Abts, Marie, 107
Albert I, crown prince and later King of the Belgians, 33, 39, 42, 85, 91, 168; appeal to nation during war, 168; letters of request to, 72–74; public image, 72, 73, 75–80, 90, 93; relationship with workers and socialists, 76–80
anarchism, 18, 66, 76, 134, 135, 136, 142. *See also* revolution
Anderson, Benedict, 4
Anseele, Edouard, 40, 153; on 1905 jubilee participation, 49–50; imprisonment, 156; involvement in ethnic-linguistic issues, 33, 40, 50, 69, 146, 152, 158; involvement in wartime relief efforts, 165; monarchy, 76; in propaganda pence, 132, 133, 137, 159; on propaganda pence, 128
anthem. *See* national flag and anthem
anticlericalism, 13, 16–18, 35, 40, 42, 49, 50, 92, 107–111, 114–15, 119, 121, 125, 134–35, 139–40, 142–43, 146, 151, 153, 157, 159, 180n37, 190n30
anti-French sentiments 153–54
anti-German sentiments, 25, 63, 109, 111–13, 121
anti-militarism, 55–70, 134, 135, 140–41, 142, 158
anti-socialist movement. *See* Christian labor movement
Antwerp, 2, 15, 19, 22, 26, 34, 49, 50, 206n35; anti-militarism in, 57, 66, 69–70; socialism in, 20, 21–22, 127, 137, 149, 176n12, 190n31
army, 55–70; barracks, 56, 59–61, 64–66, 69–70, 141; in First World War, 164, 167; illiteracy in, 27; nationalism in, 58–59; in plays, 67–68; socialism and, 61–70
Association of Belgian Societies for Physical Exercise as a Preparation for Military Service, 61, 63
Auber, Daniel, 43
Austria. *See* Habsburg Austria

banal nationalism, 10, 47, 74, 92, 93, 109, 113, 140–43, 147, 150, 154, 161
Bastien, Arthur, 41
Becker, Nikolaus, 159
Belgian Workers Party. See BWP
Bernstein, Edouard, 84
Bertrand, François, 116
Le Bien Public (newspaper), 51
Bismarck, Otto von, 80
Black Country (Pays noir around Charleroi). See Charleroi
Blanqui, Auguste, 109
blood law/blood tax. See lottery system for military service
Boersen (Steven Prenau), 50, 124
Bohemia, 23, 149, 170–71, 185n58
Bogaerts, Aimé, 49, 50, 124
Borinage, 2, 20–21, 34, 40–42, 50, 65, 74, 76, 78, 88, 92–94, 96, 105, 106, 109–110, 120–22, 155, 176n12, 181n13, 201n20
Brassine, Joseph-Jacques, 64, 65
Breydel, Jan, 130, 159, 160
Brothers of Charity, 7, 157
Brubaker, Rogers, 6, 173
Brussels, 12, 15, 23, 26, 58, 61, 64, 67, 122, 146; agglomération, 15, 20, 73, 89, 127, 146, 182n19, 185n58; and Belgian monarchy, 72–75, 80–82; and 1830 revolution, 43–53, 107–8; First World War in, 163, 165; and geographic nomenclature, 185n58; language in, 20, 22–23, 25, 27, 145–46; elementary education in, 89–92, 94, 105; socialism in, 18, 20, 34–35, 127–28, 137, 138, 142, 145–46, 155, 168; urbanization in, 15–16
BWP (Belgian Workers Party): campaign for universal suffrage, 33–40, 35, 138; and 1830 revolution, 44–52, 156; establishment and growth of, 18–22; ethnicity and language in, 5, 9, 34, 42, 39–42, 145–53, 173; and the First World War, 163, 165–66, 168–69; organization of, 7, 18–21, 125, 126, 128, 131; PSR, 109–13; and reformism, 4, 18, 21, 36–38, 46, 85, 107, 119, 133, 136–37, 142, 154; relationship with monarchy, 38, 66, 71–80, 134, 135, 139–41, 142; scholarship on connection to nationalism, 4–5; view of colonialism, 83–85; view of educational system, 27, 92–93, 98–101; view of military, 61–67, 70; view of national celebrations, 44–52; view of national symbols (flag and anthem), 107–24

Callewaert, Jean, 110–11
Carpent, François, 113
Catholicism and Catholic party: and anticlericalism, 19–20, 111, 114, 117–19, 122, 123, 123–24, 125, 131–32, 140, 160, 184n42; and colonialism, 81, 83–84; connection to Flemish movement, 25–26, 168; Counter-Reformation, 13–14; and 1830 revolution, 12, 14, 49–51; and elementary education, 28, 88–89, 97; and government, 16, 79, 84, 113, 168; and monarchy, 81; and pillarization, 7, 14, 16–20, 30, 60–63, 67–68; and proportional representation, 39–40; and secularism, 16–18; and suffrage, 33, 37–40; view of military, 56, 58, 60–63, 65, 67, 81, 110
Catholic labor movement. See Christian labor movement
census suffrage, 8, 29, 33–34, 36, 111
Centre area (around La Louvière). See La Louvière

INDEX  259

Charleroi, 2, 20–22, 33, 38, 40, 60, 64, 68–69, 73, 74, 79, 79, 109–110, 114–19, 120, 146, 176n12, 181n13
Chevaliers du Travail. *See* Knights of Labor
Chomé, Léon, 57–58, 61
Christian democracy. *See* Christian labor movement
Christian labor movement 7, 19–20, 30, 122, 123, 123–24, 125, 127, 131–32, 140, 142–43, 150, 152–53, 160, 165, 168, 170, 180n37, 184n42
church, 12–14, 16–17, 28, 89, 139, 164, 180n37
civic guard, 56, 64, 97, 139
Clarke, A. M., 71
Cole, Laurence, 70
Colley, Linda, 75
Colls, Robert, 96
colonialism, 9, 30, 38, 58, 71, 80–85, 134, 135, 141, 142, 143, 161. *See also* imperialism
commemorations and festivals, 43–53, 82, 91; BWP appropriation of 1830 revolution, 44–47, 50, 52, 120, 122, 124, 155–56; Independence Day, 9, 41, 42, 44, 47–48, 53, 98, 194n56; and mass consumption, 51–53; national jubilee (1905), 44, 48–52, 82, 120, 122, 124, 194n56, 199n82
Commission for Relief in Belgium, 165
commodification, of nationalism, 51–53
Congo, 9, 30, 58, 71, 80–85, 141, 143, 218n100
Conscience, Hendrik, 100–101, 158–59, 209n80
conscription. *See* military service
consociationalism. *See* pillarization
Conway, Martyn, 175n5

Counter-Reformation, 13–14
*Courrier de Bruxelles* (journal), 50
court, royal. *See* monarchy
culture wars (*Kulturkampf*), 7, 17
Czech nationalism, 6, 23, 149, 170–72

De Bleye, Jules, 99–101
De Coninck, Pieter, 158, 159
De Graeve, Jozef, 94, 99, 101–2, 148
De Schaepdrijver, Sophie, 164
De Smaele, Henk, 25–26
De Witte, Paul, 153
Dechet, Hippolyte Louis Alexandre (alias Jenneval), 107
defensive war, 56, 61, 63
Defuisseaux, Alfred, 74, 109, 111, 113
Defuisseaux, Georges, 111, 112
Defuisseaux, Léon, 109
Deglimes, Lieutenant, 59
Degrève, Emile, 114–19
Demoulin, Zéphir, 116, 196n26
Destrée, Jules, 33–34, 108
*De Domper* (newspaper), 122, 123, 131
drama societies, 67–69
Dreyfus, Alfred, 127
Ducpétiaux, Edouard, 107
Dumonceau, Thomas, 111, 113
Dutch Revolt (1566–1648), 11–12

East Central Europe, 6, 23, 106, 149, 170–72
education, 87–102; attendance rates in elementary schools, 93–94; colonial propaganda in elementary, 82; free Catholic vs. public elementary education, 88–89; language in elementary, 94, 100–101, 148, 171–72; literacy rates, 27–29; nationalism in elementary schools, 89–102, at university level, 50, 151–52, 167, 170
Education Act (1879), 16, 88–89

*Eigen-Sinn*, 48, 59, 105–6, 113, 130
Elime, Regulus, 91
Elisabeth of Bavaria, Queen of the Belgians, 75–76, 77
ethnicist fallacy, 170
ethnicity. *See* language and ethnicity
everyday nationalism, 3–4, 8–10, 106, 132, 168, 180n35
excursions, school, 91, 94–95

federal *vs.* unitary states, 13
First World War, 3, 5, 6, 22, 80–81, 85, 163–73
flag. *See* national flag and anthem
*Flamenpolitik*, 166–69
Flemish. *See* language and ethnicity
Flemish lion (as a symbol, anthem or flag), 123–24, 150, 158–60
Flemish movement, 24–26, 149–53, 166–70, 172
folkloric militarism, 60
food shortages and relief during WWI, 164–66, 169
Fox, Jon E., 4
Franck, Louis, 152
France, 3, 11, 13, 14, 23, 24, 25, 27, 28, 29, 40, 41, 47, 48, 56, 60, 62, 70, 80, 81, 82, 93, 100, 109, 112, 116, 127–28, 148, 153–54, 164, 167
Francophilia, 111–12, 121, 153–54
French socialism, 18, 47, 154
French. *See* language and ethnicity
Front Movement, 167
*The Future* (journal), 89

Gauls, 26, 41, 42, 46, 95, 96, 112, 120, 168
*Gazette de Charleroi* (newspaper), 114
*Gazet van Brussel* (newspaper), 146
Gellner, Ernest, 4, 5, 27, 29
gender, 36, 73, 134, 135, 125, 138–39. *See also* masculinity

general strikes for universal suffrage in Belgium, 20, 36, 37, 64, 76, 78, 109, 113, 154
George, Léon, 115, 117, 119
Germanophilia, 140, 154
German socialism, 4, 18, 19, 37, 47–48, 62, 63, 154, 163
Germany, 3, 11, 13, 27–28, 29, 56, 59, 60, 63, 70, 80, 111–12, 127, 145, 156, 160; occupation of Belgium, 163–69
gerrymandering, 39
Ghent, 2, 7; economy and society in, 14–15, 18–19, 26, 82; elementary education in, 89, 93–94, 98–99, 101–2; First World War in, 165, 167, 170; internationalism in, 153–61; language in, 22, 146–53; opposition to 1905 jubilee, 50–51; socialism in, 18–19, 22, 33; socialist antimilitarism in, 62–65, 69; socialist attitudes towards the monarchy in, 76, 78; socialist attitudes towards the national flag and anthem, 10, 49, 108, 121–24; socialist campaign for general suffrage in, 34–36, 39–40. *See also* propaganda pence
Gilly, 79, 114–19, 120
Godefroid, Victor, 76
Great Britain, 12, 19, 21, 28, 29, 51, 93, 164, 165
Greater-Netherlandic nationalism, 50, 153, 158
Groh, Dieter, 19, 142

Habsburg Austria 6, 12, 13, 14, 23, 37, 41, 70, 95, 169–73, 185n58
Hardyns, Ferdinand, 50, 51
Haulleville, Alphonse de, 83
Hemptinne, Charles de, 7, 132
Hénin, Emile, 68–69
Hennebicq, Léon, 30, 84
Henry, Hubert-Joseph, 127

Hermans, Edouard, 117
Heynderickx, Constant, 152
hidden transcripts (James C. Scott), 130–32
Hobsbawm, Eric, 4, 5
Hoover, Herbert, 165
Hroch, Miroslav, 5, 170
Hubin, Georges, 85
Huysmans, Camille, 152

illiteracy, 27–29, 73, 129
imperialism, 9, 30, 38, 80–85, 92, 141, 142, 161. *See also* colonialism
Independence Day (of Belgium), 9, 41–53, 98
industrialization and urbanization, 3, 5, 8, 14–16, 20, 25–26, 27–29, 38, 39, 52, 80, 89, 146, 167, 172
internationalism, 4, 10, 49, 51, 64, 92, 99, 101, 102, 107, 111, 114, 134, 135, 140, 145, 153–61, 163, 166

Jemappes, 41,
Jenneval (Dechet, Hippolyte Louis Alexandre), 107
Jeune Barreau (Young Bar), 58, 84
Joseph II, Holy Roman Emperor, 12, 14, 23
Jottrand, Lucien, 107
*Le Journal de Charleroi* (journal), 69, 79, 114–15
Judson, Pieter, 170, 172, 185n58

Kest, Théophile, 116–17, 119
King, Jeremy, 170
Knights of Labor (Chevaliers du Travail), 21, 110, 184n50
Kol, Henri Hubert van, 106
*Kulturkampf* (culture wars), 7, 17

labor movement, Catholic. *See* Christian labor movement
labor movement, socialist. *See* BWP

labor strikes and revolts, 18, 20, 36–37, 51, 57, 61, 62, 64, 74, 76, 78, 89, 108–9, 113, 117–18, 127, 131, 136, 141, 146, 150, 154, 155, 156, 159, 165. *See also* general strikes for universal suffrage in Belgium
La Louvière, 2, 20–21, 22, 40, 65, 67, 68, 74, 78, 110, 112–13, 176n12, 181n13
Lampens, Jan, 152
language and ethnicity, 1, 3, 5–6, 8, 9, 10, 26, 50, 51, 84, 111, 132, 134, 135, 141, 143, 145–61; bilingualism *vs.* monolingualism, 10, 19, 22–24, 40–41, 145–50, 154, 185n58; connection to national symbols, 121–24; connection to suffrage, 33–42; emergence of Belgian vocabulary, 12; in imperial Austria, 6, 23, 70, 169–73; and Flemish movement, 24–26, 149–53, 166–70, 172; and geographic nomenclature, 185n58; and industrialization (Gellner), 27; and internationalism, 153–61; language acts, 24, 25, 40, 111; language border, 2, 23; in the military, 55, 57, 70, 167; and pillarization, 18, 22–26, 81, 166–69; and PSR pro-French agenda, 109–13; in schools, 94, 99–101, 148, 171–72; and Walloon movement, 25–26, 40–42, 112, 120–21, 166; wartime politicization of, 166–69, 172–73
Ledeganck, Karel, 157
Ledoux, A., 110–11
Lefevre, Johan, 152
Legros, Alphonse, 57–58
Leo XIII, Pope, 17
Leopold I, King of the Belgians, 1, 44, 98
Leopold II, King of the Belgians: accused of German agenda, 109;

colonial efforts, 9, 30, 80–85; hostility toward, 74–75, 92, 141, 156; letters of request to, 71–72, 74, 85–86; public image, 9, 66, 72, 73, 74, 76, 94, 95; signing of personal conscription into law, 55

Leopold III, King of the Belgians, 76, 77, 78

Lepage, Léon, 90–91

letters of request, 71–75, 87–88

liberalism and liberal party: and anticlericalism and secularism, 7, 16–18; in Belgian constitution and institutions, 3, 11–30, 37, 44, 56, 170–71; and colonialism, 81, 82; and education, 88–92; and elections, 36, 38, 39–40; role in Belgian independence, 12; and pillarization, 20, 60–61, 63, 67–68, 97, 150, 168; and socialism, 46–47, 49, 57, 59, 84, 109–10, 114, 115, 123, 132, 134, 135, 140, 151–52, 159

*liberté subsidiée* (subsidized freedom), 30, 165, 172

*La Libre Parole* (newspaper), 127

Liège, 2, 15, 19, 20, 21, 22, 33, 34, 38, 46, 47, 49, 64, 74, 87–88, 89, 95–96, 98, 100, 108, 115, 146, 155, 168, 169, 176n12, 181n13, 185n58, 191n11

Lijphart, Arend, 17

*The Lion of Flanders* (Conscience), 100, 158–59

literacy, 27–29, 73, 100, 110–11, 115, 129–30

*The Little Whip* (Het Zweepken, journal), 7

Lootens, August, 136

Lootens, Camiel, 148

Lorand, Georges, 61

Lorwin, Val R., 4

lottery system for military service, 9, 27, 55–66, 70, 83, 141, 158

Louis-Philippe I, King of France, 3

Lüdtke, Alf, 48, 105

Luxemburg, Rosa, 37

Marseillaise, 42, 46, 64, 108, 114, 133, 140, 155, 156, 159

Marxism, 4, 37, 137, 216n66

masculinity, 88, 138–39. *See also* gender

mass consumption and entertainment, 51–53

Max, Charles, 47

mediated literacy, 129

Mélotte, Emile, 116

Mercier, Ferdinand, 67–68

Mertens, Antoine, 87–88, 95–98, 100

Michelet, Jules, 1

military. *See* army

military service, 9, 18, 27, 38, 55–70, 81, 83, 109, 141

Miller-Idriss, Cynthia, 4

Miry, Karel, 159

*Moeder Vooruit* (Mother Forward), 19

monarchy, 9, 12, 71–85, 91; and colonialism, 80–85; letters of request to, 71–74, 87–88; socialist attitudes toward, 74–80, 141, 142. *See also* BWP, relationship with monarchy

Moravia, 23, 149, 170, 171

Moyson, Emiel, 157

*The Mute Girl of Portici*, 43, 44, 52, 91, 93

Napoleon I, 12, 94, 112, 153

national flag and anthem, 37, 41–42, 47–49, 52, 58, 69, 82, 88, 90–91, 93, 95, 97, 105–24; in Christian labor movement, 122, 123, 123–24, 159–60; BWP view of, 10, 49, 107–13, 110–11, 113–14, 121–24; flag-burning, 114–19; grassroots attitudes toward, 10, 99, 110–11, 114–22, 156, 166

national indifference, 6, 10, 47, 92–93, 105–6, 109, 113, 143, 170–71
nationalism. *See* army, nationalism in; banal nationalism; BWP, ethnicity and language in; colonialism; commemorations and festivals; commodification, of nationalism; education; everyday nationalism; Flemish lion; Flemish movement; Greater-Netherlandic nationalism; imperialism; Independence Day (of Belgium); language and ethnicity; national flag and anthem; national jubilee; oppositional or radical patriotism; propaganda pence, nationalism and internationalism in; regionalism
national jubilee (1905), 48–51, 81–82, 120, 122, 124
National Relief and Food Committee, 165, 168, 172
*La Nation armée* (brochure), 61
nation in arms, 61–62
negative integration, 19, 142
Netherlands, 2, 3, 11–12, 14, 15, 16, 17, 24, 26–29, 43, 44, 50, 52, 88, 94, 106, 107, 122, 127, 153, 158, 164
neutrality (of Belgium in international politics), 56, 63, 80, 83, 112

oppositional or radical patriotism: 4, 8, 34, 38–39, 75, 113–14, 119, 166, colonial application of, 84–85; military application of, 62, 63, 69; rationalization of celebration participation, 48, 49–50; rise of, 38–39
Orangists, 26
ordinary people, 3–4, 6, 7–8, 27, 72, 81–82, 88, 95, 97–98, 101–2, 106, 113, 125, 129, 158, 161, 165, 167, 169; defined, 176n8
ordinary writings, 129

*Organisationspatriotismus* (organizational devotion), 19, 128, 132–35, 137–39, 142, 154, 157

Pan-Netherlandic nationalism. *See* Greater-Netherlandic nationalism
Parti socialiste républicain (PSR), 76, 109–13, 121
patriotism. *See* nationalism; oppositional patriotism
*Le Pays wallon* (journal), 117–19, 118
*The Peasants' War* (Conscience), 100
*Le Peuple* (newspaper): as anti-colonial, 82, 84; on Belgian revolution and commemoration, 44, 45, 46, 48, 49; circulation of, 20, 146; and First World War, 163, 165; on monarchy, 74, 76, 78; and nationalism, 52, 114; propaganda pence section in, 128
Picard, Edmond, 29–30, 84
pillarization, 17–20, 25, 30, 42, 60–61, 68, 128, 165, 172
Poland, 106,
Prenau, Steven (alias Boersen), 50, 124
propaganda pence, 125–61; anti-establishment and anti-Catholic sentiments in, 125, 139–40, 160; classification of social categories in, 10, 132–33, 134, 135; female contributors to, 125, 138; language in, 146–47, 148, 150; nationalism and internationalism in, 140–43, 154–56, 158, 161; occupations of contributors to, 137–38, 217n72; social functions of, 129–32; socialist discourse in, 133, 136–37; as source, 7–8, 125–26, 214n10; as subscription list, 126–29
proportional representation, 5, 9, 39–40, 112

Protestants, 12, 14, 28
Prussia. *See* Germany
PSR. *See* Parti socialiste républicain
public transcript (James C. Scott), 72–73, 119, 130

railroad network (in Belgium), 16, 29
red flag, 34, 41, 42, 46, 63, 108, 110, 115, 117, 122, 123, 133, 154, 156, 159, 160,
*La Réforme* (journal), 82
reformism (in Belgian socialism), 4, 18, 21, 36–38, 46, 85, 107, 119, 133, 136–37, 142, 154
regionalism, connection to nationalism, 6, 24, 96–97, 100, 101, 178n26
religion. *See* Catholicism and Catholic party
republicanism. *See* BWP, relationship with monarchy
*La République belge* (newspaper), 110, 113
revolts and strikes. *See* labor strikes and revolts
revolution: attitude toward 1830, in BWP, 42, 44–50, 52, 72, 88, 90, 91, 94, 114, 120, 122, 124, 155–56, 158; attitude toward, in BWP, 4, 18–19, 21, 36–38, 83, 98, 107–8, 133, 134, *135*, 136, 140, 142–43, 154, 160; events of Belgian, 12–14, 23, 43, 107; in PSR discourse, 109–13. *See also* anarchism; Brussels, and 1830 revolution; BWP, and 1830 revolution; Catholicism and Catholic party, and 1830 revolution; commemorations and festivals, BWP appropriation of 1830 revolution; labor strikes and revolts; *Le Peuple* on Belgian revolution and commemoration; revolutionary attentism
revolutionary attentism, 142

Robat, Joseph, 38
Robrecht van Béthune, Count, 158
Rousseau, Emile, 40–41
Rousseau, Jean-Jacques, 12
Rowntree, Benjamin Seebohm, 28–29
royal court. *See* monarchy
Russia, 36, 62, 63, 106, 163, 172

schools. *See* education
School War (1878–1884), 16–17, 25, 28, 29, 88, 97
Schumann, Robert, 159
Scott, James C., 72, 105, 119, 130
secularization, 14, 16–18, 19, 39
September Days, 44–47, 107
Sluys, Alexis, 94
Smith, Anthony D., 5
Smol, Ed, 133
social democracy (in Belgium), see BWP, and reformism; reformism (in Belgian socialism)
socialism and socialists (in Belgium). See BWP
*Le socialisme en Belgique* (Vandervelde and Destrée), 108
socialist singing, 34, 112, 133, 140, 141, 150, 156–57, 159–60, 166, 168
*Sower* (De Zaaier, journal), 67
SPD (German Social Democratic Party), 4, 19, 47, 62, 63, 154, 163
Spring Revolt (1886), 18, 57, 62, 64, 74, 89, 108, 136, 141, 150, 156
Stauter-Halsted, Keeley, 119
Stortewagen, Emile, 116
strikes and revolts. *See* labor strikes and revolts
Strikwerda, Carl, 149
subscription lists. *See* propaganda pence
substitution system in military service, 27, 55–57, 61, 65, 70
suffrage, 8, 12, 18, 20, 29, 33–42, 46, 65; campaign for universal,

34–37, 35, 79, 83, 108, 113, 136–38, 141, 142, 150, 155, 157, 159; nationalism and, 37–39; role of ethnicity, 39–42
SYG (Socialist Young Guard), 62–63, 65–69, 115, 141

Troclet, Léon, 49, 115
theater, 52, 53, 67–68, 87–88, 95–98, 100, 108

unitary *vs.* federal states, 13–14
United Kingdom of the Netherlands, 12, 14, 24, 50
urbanization and industrialization, 3, 5, 8, 14–16, 20, 25–26, 27–29, 38, 39, 52, 80, 89, 146, 167, 172

Van Artevelde, Jacob, 142–43
Van Beveren, Edmond, 137, 157
Van Campenhout, François, 107
Van Cauwelaert, Frans, 152
Vanderhaeghen, Jules, 117, 119
Vandersmissen, Alfred, 62, 64, 197n45
Vandervelde, Emile, 27, 42, 49–50, 63, 79, 84–85, 108, 115, 163
Vandewalle, Adolphe, 116
Van Offel, Horace, 195n11
Van Offel, Hendrik, 157
Van Peene, Hippoliet, 159
Verviers, 64, 87, 96, 97, 211n34
Viaene, Vincent, 82
Vogel, Jakob, 60
Volders, Jean, 61, 83–84
*Volksmaandblad* (journal), 123, 123–24
*Vooruit* (newspaper): as anti-Catholic, 160; as anti-colonial, 82; on Belgian nationhood, 49–50, 120, 122, 124; circulation of, 19, 22, 146; on Flemish nationhood and Flemish movement, 39, 51, 148, 151, 152; as internationalist, 154; on monarchy, 74, 78; on suffrage, 34–36. *See also* propaganda pence
voting. *See* suffrage
Vrints, Antoon, 169

Waeri, Karel, 154
Wallonia and Walloon movement, 1–3, 20–22, 24–26, 28–29, 33, 38, 40–42, 68, 73, 96, 100, 108, 109, 112, 117–21, 142, 145, 146, 148, 166–68
Wautelet, Florian, 68
Wauters, Joseph, 165
Wayemberg, Jean-Baptiste, 114–19
Weber, Eugen, 4
Wehler, Hans-Ulrich, 80
*De Werker* (newspaper), 22, 50, 70, 127, 130, 137
Willems, Victor, 76
William I, King of the Netherlands, 12, 16, 28, 43–44, 50, 52, 190n41
Wodon, J., 59
women, social and political position of, 28, 29, 36, 63, 75, 97, 125, 131, 138, 155
World's Fairs, 81–82, 206n35
World War I, 3, 5, 6, 22, 80–81, 85, 163–73

Young Bar. *See* Jeune Barreau

Zahra, Tara, 106, 185n58
Ziblatt, Daniel, 13
Zolberg, Aristide, 146

The authorized representative in the EU for product safety and compliance is:
Mare Nostrum Group
B.V Doelen 72
4831 GR Breda
The Netherlands

www.ingramcontent.com/pod-product-compliance
Lightning Source LLC
Chambersburg PA
CBHW031803220426
43662CB00007B/511